W9-AXF-679

The Life of
ROBERT SIDNEY

Frontispiece. **Robert Sidney, Earl of Leicester (1563–1626). Artist unknown, ca. 1588.** *Courtesy of National Portrait Gallery, London.*

The Life of
ROBERT SIDNEY

Earl of Leicester (1563–1626)

MILLICENT V. HAY

Folger Books
Washington: The Folger Shakespeare Library
London and Toronto: Associated University Presses

Associated University Presses
440 Forsgate Drive
Cranbury, NJ 08512

Associated University Presses
25 Sicilian Avenue
London WC1A 2QH, England

Associated University Presses
2133 Royal Windsor Drive
Unit 1
Mississauga, Ontario
Canada L5J 1K5

Library of Congress Cataloging in Publication Data

Hay, Millicent V., 1945–
    The life of Robert Sidney.

    "Folger books."
    Bibliography: p.
    Includes index.
    1. Sidney, Robert.   2. Soldiers—Great Britian—
Biography.   3. Diplomats—Great Britain—Biography.
4. Great Britain—Court and courtiers—Biography.
I. Title.
DA358.S54H39   1984   941.05′5′0924   [B]   82-49311
ISBN 0-918016-70-3

Printed in the United States of America

Contents

Maps

Tables

Abbreviations

1	Youth and Education	15
2	Sidney's Career Begins	32
3	The Sidney Heir: Courtier, Soldier, Diplomat	50
4	Assuming Office: The New Governor of Flushing	72
5	Military Exploits in the Low Countries	97
6	The Administration of Flushing	111
7	Sidney at the Court of Queen Elizabeth I	144
8	Domestic Life and Personal Business	171
9	Poet and Patron	195
10	Sidney at the Court of King James I	210

Bibliography 233

Appendix: Genealogical Table 243

Index 248

Maps

Walcheren Island   76

The Siege of Sluys   98

Sluys   100

The Field of Turnhout   104

The Plan of the Manor House at Otford, 1516   190

Tables

Money and Gifts Dispensed by Philip Sidney   52

Sidney's Yearly Income, 1586   54

Composition of Companies   56

Organization of the English Army   74

Sidney's Presences In and Absences from Flushing, 1589–1603   138

Sidney's Pedigree, 1598   158

Sidney-Smythe Family Connections   224

Genealogical Table   244

Abbreviations

The following list of abbreviations and short forms that appear in the notes following each chapter is provided for the reader's convenience. Full citations may be found in the bibliography.

Additional MS 12066	"Income and Expenses of the First Earl of Leicester, 1622," Additional MS 12066, British Library, London, England
Akrigg	G. P. B. Akrigg, *Jacobean Pageant*
Birch	Thomas Birch, *The Court and Times of James I*
Bourne	H. R. Fox Bourne, *A Memoir of Philip Sidney*
Bradley	Sir Philip Sidney, *The Correspondence of Philip Sidney and Hubert Languet,* ed. William A. Bradley
Brown, *English Politics*	Alexander Brown, *English Politics in Early Virginia History*
Brown, *Genesis*	Alexander Brown, *Genesis of the United States*
Cal. Border Papers	Great Britain, Public Record Office, *Calendar of Border Papers*
Cal. Scot. Papers	Great Britain, Public Record Office, *Calendar of Scottish Papers*
Christ Church Letters	Typescript translations of the Latin letters from Robert Dorsett to Philip Sidney, preserved at the library of Christ Church College, Oxford
Collins	Arthur Collins, ed., *Letters and Memorials of State*
Cruickshank	Charles G. Cruickshank, *Elizabeth's Army*
CSP Dom.	*Great Britain, Public Record Office, Calendar of State Papers, Domestic Series, of the Reigns of Edward VI, Mary, Elizabeth, and James I*
CSP For.	Great Britain, Public Record Office, *Calendar of State Papers, Foreign Series, of the Reign of Elizabeth, 1558–1582*
CSP Venice	Great Britain, Public Record Office, *Calendar of State Papers and Manuscripts Existing in the Archives and Collections of Venice*

Abbreviations

DNB	*Dictionary of National Biography*
Feuillerat	Sir Philip Sidney, *The Complete Works of Sir Philip Sidney*, ed. Albert Feuillerat
Greville	Sir Fulke Greville, *Works of Fulke Greville, Lord Brooke*, vol. 4, *The Life of Philip Sidney*
Herford, *Jonson*	Benjamin Jonson, *Ben Jonson*, 11 vols., ed. C. H. Herford and E. M. Simpson
HMC Buccleuch	Great Britain, Historical Manuscripts Commission, *Report on the MSS of the Duke of Buccleuch and Queensbury*
HMCD	Great Britain, Historical Manuscripts Commission, *Report on the MSS of Lord De L'Isle and Dudley Preserved at Penshurst Place*
HMC Downshire	Great Britain, Historical Manuscripts Commission, *Report on the MSS of the Marquess of Downshire*
HMC Salisbury	Great Britain, Historical Manuscripts Commission, *Calendar of the MSS of the Most Honorable the Marquis of Salisbury, K.G., Preserved at Hatfield House*
KAO De L'Isle	Dudley and De L'Isle MSS, Kent Archives Office, Maidstone, England
L & A CSP For.	Great Britain, Public Record Office, *List and Analysis of the Calendar of State Papers, Foreign Series*
McClure	John Chamberlain, *Letters of John Chamberlain*, ed. N. E. McClure

Acknowledgments

I would like to thank my husband, John L. Hay, whose patience and support made this project possible.

Professors Retha M. Warnicke, Doris C. Powers, and John X. Evans gave their detailed criticism and advice throughout the writing of the manuscript. Professor Warnicke's guidance as a professional historian was especially valuable.

William Sidney, Viscount De L'Isle, kindly consented to my use of the Sidney manuscripts at the Kent Archives Office, and provided a special viewing of Penshurst for me and my party when we were in England.

[1]

Youth and Education

Robert Sidney came into the world at a time when England was populated by titans. Among his contemporaries were William Shakespeare, Ben Jonson, Sir Robert Cecil, Sir Walter Raleigh, and Sir Francis Bacon. He was the fifth of six children, of whom three were destined to excel. His elder brother, Philip, achieved lasting fame as a poet and courtier before his early death, and their sister, Mary, also left her mark in the history of English letters and politics. The three other siblings died before they reached full maturity: Margaret as an infant, Thomas and Ambrosia at the dawn of adulthood. His father's generosity to all the children gave Robert, the middle son, an opportunity to make his impression on the future of his nation and his faith. Provided Elizabeth's new reign, in its sixth year at the time of Robert's birth, survived in stable condition, every sign pointed toward a prosperous career in military or civil service for him.

Born at Penshurst Place, November 19, 1563, Robert was perhaps named in honor of his maternal uncle, Robert Dudley, soon to be dubbed earl of Leicester. Robert's father, Sir Henry Sidney, K.G. (Knight of the Order of the Garter), was the queen's lord deputy in Ireland, the most enlightened she had ever assigned to that post. An intelligent, humane man, Sir Henry wanted his children to take their places as leaders in the complex, shifting government that guided England as it matured into a major Protestant power. So, to the already hefty advantages of birth and position to which Robert was born, Sir Henry added a broad education in the new humanist style, taking care also to polish the boy's considerable innate personal charm.

The Elizabethan Sidneys descended from Nicholas Sydney, son of William Sydney of Kingsham by his third wife Thomasyne, daughter of John Barrington and widow of William Lundesford. Nicholas made a match with Anne, daughter of Sir William Brandon and aunt of Charles Brandon, duke of Suffolk, who was a brother-in-law of Henry VIII. The late C. L. Kingsford, editor of the Dudley and De L'Isle papers, observed that this marriage "really made the fortunes of the later Sidneys."[1] Nicholas' son, William, advanced at the court of Henry VIII, probably with

15

Suffolk's help. Knighted after serving at Flodden in 1513, he was made Chamberlain to the Prince of Wales in 1538. Sir William greatly increased and consolidated the Sidney landholdings between 1514 and 1543, obtaining Robertsbridge Abbey, the site of lucrative iron mining operations, all the abbey's land in Sussex and Kent, the manor of Easton in Hampshire, lands at Michelmarsh (also in Hampshire), and the lands of St. Swithun's Priory at Winchester. His most important acquisition came on April 25, 1552, when Edward VI granted him Penshurst Place,[2] which Sir William made the Sidney family seat. It remains so to this day.

Sir William married Anne Pagenham, daughter of Sir Hugh Pagenham and widow of Thomas Fitzwilliam, the elder brother of William Fitzwilliam, earl of Southampton.[3] In addition to their son, Henry, they had four daughters: Mary, wife of Sir William Dormer of Ascot, Buckinghamshire; Lucy, wife of Sir James Harrington of Exton, Rutland; Anne, wife of Sir William Fitzwilliam; and Frances, wife of Thomas Radcliffe, earl of Sussex.[4]

Henry Sidney, "a man of excellent natural wit, large heart, sweet conversation,"[5] early established his importance in the Tudor courts. As Sir William's only surviving son, he inherited Penshurst, as well as the large land grants Edward had made to his father. Henry spent his boyhood as the prince's constant companion and playfellow. When Edward succeeded to the English crown, he appointed his friend Henry Sidney one of the four principal gentlemen of his privy chamber. In 1550, Sidney was knighted, at the same time as Sir William Cecil. For the occasion, Edward bestowed on him a number of minor offices, including the position of chief cupbearer for life. He remained high in the king's esteem. Four days before Edward died, he granted Sir Henry the manor and borough of Wotton Bassett in Wiltshire.

Sidney's relationship with the king made him an influential figure at Edward's court, and that prominence attracted the attention of John Dudley, earl of Warwick (later duke of Northumberland). On March 29, 1551, Dudley cemented a potentially profitable bond with Sidney by giving him his eldest daughter, Mary, in marriage. In this way, Sidney became involved in his father-in-law's ambitious scheme to place Lady Jane Grey and Guildford Dudley on the throne. Presumably with the object of supporting Northumberland's planned coup d'état, Sidney obtained a license (May 8, 1553) to retain fifty gentlemen and yeomen in addition to his menial servants. He witnessed the will conferring the crown on Lady Jane, and was holding the king in his arms when Edward expired.[6]

Sir Henry quickly grasped the direction that events were taking. Despite his own and his sons' later devotion to the Protestant cause, he abandoned Northumberland and, the day following her accession, swore adherence to Queen Mary. By declaring his loyalty to Mary and to the Catholic faith, he escaped the series of executions and disgraces visited upon the Dudley family in 1553–54, and even managed to maintain a position at court. The following year he accompanied John Russell, earl of

Bedford, to Spain to obtain ratification of the marriage articles between Mary and Philip. Covertly, he seems to have attempted to enlist sympathy in those quarters for his Dudley brothers-in-law. The duchess of Northumberland indicated in her will that she had some reason to be grateful to the duke and duchess of Alva and to Don Diego de Mendoza; presumably the Spanish dignitaries were influenced by Bedford and Sidney, both Protestant sympathizers, to intercede with Mary on behalf of the duchess's sons, Ambrose, Robert, and Henry Dudley.[7] In November of 1554, all the grants made to Sidney and to his father were confirmed, rewarding him for his discreet change of party at a critical *nexus*. On November 30, the king honored Sir Henry by standing godfather to his first-born son, naming the child Philip, while the duchess of Northumberland, still in a precarious political and religious position, was the boy's godmother.

In 1556, Sir Henry accompanied his brother-in-law, Thomas Radcliffe, earl of Sussex, the new lord deputy of Ireland, to Dublin. In the ensuing year and a half, he saw combat action and gained enough experience to take on the responsibilities of Lord Justice when Sussex returned to England. Sidney carried on his brother-in-law's policy and continued the depredations the English had already begun by invading Ferical, where he attempted to subdue followers of the enemy chief, Donough O'Conor. When Sussex returned temporarily, he seems to have approved Sidney's courses. When he departed for Scotland, he again left the office to Sir Henry. Upon Queen Mary's death in 1558, Sussex was called back to England; he reappointed Sidney Lord Justice, and Elizabeth confirmed him in the office.

Because Sussex wished to remain at court, he urged Sidney's appointment as viceroy. Elizabeth, jealous of her dominion, resisted this arrangement, returned the earl to Ireland in August, 1559, and appointed Sidney lord president of the Marches of Wales.

Sir Henry transferred the vice-treasurership to Sir William Fitzwilliam, his brother-in-law, and returned to England. He established a residence at Ludlow Castle in Shropshire, which he considered "a happy place. . . , for a better people to govern or better subjects, Europe holdeth not."[8] Here he moved his family, and Robert, Ambrosia, Philip, and Mary undoubtedly met many Welsh aristocrats and gentry with whom they would deal in later life. Many Herbert clansmen would have made their acquaintance; perhaps, too, they encountered members of the Gamage family, from whose ranks Robert's wife was to come.

Although his duties were light and he spent much time at the court, Sidney seems to have governed wisely and with wit. Sir Francis Bacon relates an anecdote that provides an illuminating glimpse into the lord president's character. "Secretary Bourne's son," Bacon explains, "kept a gentleman's wife in Shropshire, who lived from her husband with him. When he was weary of her, he caused her husband to be dealt with to take her home, and offered him £500 for reparation. The gentleman went to Sir Henry Sidney, to take his advice upon this offer; telling him; that his wife promised now a new life; and to tell him the truth, £500 would come well with him; and besides, he sometimes wanted a woman to his bed. By my troth (said Sir Henry) take her home, and take the money; and whereas other cuckolds wear their horns plain, you may wear yours gilt."[9]

At the time of her accession, Sir Robert Dudley was aspiring to Queen Elizabeth's hand. Sir Henry supported his brother-in-law in these efforts, while Sir William Cecil opposed him and advocated an alliance with Archduke Charles of Austria. When, in 1561, the gossip surrounding Amy Robsart Dudley's accidental death cast a shadow on her husband's hopes, Cecil took the opportunity to remove Sidney to Wales for a short-lived rustication, on the pretext that he was needed there. But by April, 1562, Sidney was off on a diplomatic mission to the French court, where he unsuccessfully attempted to mediate between the rival Guise and Condé factions. Failing at this objective, he was sent to Scotland to propound the failure as the English excuse for postponing an interview between Elizabeth and Mary, Queen of Scots for a year, or until the French wars ended.

Sir Henry's career was at this stage when Robert was born. Before the boy was four years old, the father would be off again on the first of his three sojourns as lord deputy in Ireland, leaving much of the responsibility for raising his sons and daughters to his wife, Mary.

Fulke Greville describes Lady Sidney as a woman with spirit as noble as her ancestry.[10] Notably beautiful at the time she married, she was scarred by smallpox, which she contracted while she was nursing the queen. This happened in 1562, a year before Robert's birth, during the time that Henry was away on the French embassy. When her husband returned, he found her "as foul a lady as the smallpox could make her."[11] Henceforth, "shee chose rather to hide herself from the curious eyes of a delicate time, than come upon the stage of the world with any manner of disparagement."[12]

Mary Dudley Sidney provided for Philip and Robert a pedigree of greater substance than did her husband. She was descended from Edmond Dudley (d. 1509) and his second wife, Elizabeth Grey, heiress of the house of Lisle. Dudley held the titles of Viscount Lisle and earl of Warwick, and it was through him that Robert eventually could lay claim to them. Lady Mary's father, the duke of Northumberland, and her brother, Guildford, were executed in 1554, but several of her siblings survived to become influential figures at Elizabeth's court. Robert Dudley, created earl of Leicester in 1564, was, as the Queen's great favorite, the most powerful of the duke's children. His sister, Lady Warwick, and his sister-in-law, Lady Huntingdon, held intimate places in the queen's affection. As her confidantes, they were in a position to speak to Elizabeth for their nephews, Robert and Philip Sidney. Lady Warwick and her sister, Margaret, countess of Cumberland (mother of diarist Lady Anne Clifford), helped the two young courtiers when they could. Lady Huntingdon, Lady Mary Sidney's only surviving sister, was to be one of Robert's most persistent supporters during the grim factional infighting at Elizabeth's court in the 1590s.

Although Dudley's influence with the queen waxed and waned with the passions and politics of passing time, he was never out of Elizabeth's favor for more than a few short periods. His desire to marry Elizabeth inspired him to extreme and contradictory machinations. At one time, he sent Sir Henry to enlist the aid of the Spanish ambassador, De Quadra, a favor supposedly to be granted in return for Dudley's assistance in Spain's project to restore England to Catholicism. Later, he sided with the Puritans to block Elizabeth's marriage to Archduke Charles, but a few years further on, he fostered the agitation of the rebellious Catholic lords of the north in an attempt to oust Cecil, whose powerful influence against him prevailed and ultimately demolished Leicester's hopes for a match between himself and the queen.

By marrying Lettice, widow of Walter Devereux, earl of Essex, Leicester brought into the family the flamboyant Robert Devereux, his future rival for the queen's affection. Essex detested Leicester but found a friend in his cousin-by-marriage, Robert Sidney. He developed a relationship with Sidney that involved intermittent affection and patronage lasting from boyhood to near the end of the earl's life.

Despite their father's well-timed changes of heart and their uncle's mercurial loyalties, the Sidney sons were born into a nest of activist Protestants. Lawrence Stone asserts that the very success of Elizabethan Protestantism was due to the activities of a few peers, "notably the Earls of Bedford, Huntingdon, Leicester, and Warwick, and the irrepressible Duchess of Suffolk,"[13] all relatives or friends of the Sidneys. Robert's uncle, Henry Hastings, earl of Huntingdon, ran his household as "a Protestant seminary in miniature, with prayers, fastings, and catechisings. . . ," according to Stone. He filled the places he controlled with nonconformists, radical reformers, and Puritans. He founded a Protestant grammar school at Ashby and reorganized one at Leicester. He created four Protestant fellowships at Emmanuel, and he used his power as president of the Council of the North and as a leader in the High Commission in the North to plant Protestants all over northern England. The women in the family were equally influential in their support of the Protestant movement from the 1570s. Robert's aunt, Frances, countess of Sussex, refounded Sidney Sussex College as a seminary for the reformed religion. Catherine, duchess of Suffolk, Anne, countess of Warwick, and Catherine, countess of Huntingdon were active supporters of the cause, in conjunction with their associates, Elizabeth, Lady Russell, Grace, Lady Mildmay, Margaret, Lady Hoby, and Anne, Lady Bacon.[14]

Education had become a tradition in this company well before Robert and Philip's births. The Dudley brothers and Lord Huntingdon, especially, helped establish the Puritan patronage of universities and schools that proved so important in the growth of the Protestant movement. Leicester used his power as Chancellor at Oxford to influence large sections of the educational establishment to join the Protestant cause, and Burghley's tolerance of moderate Puritans at Cambridge allowed them to take control of that university.[15] The popularity of academic education among the gentry and peers produced an explosion of humanistic pedagogy that, led by scholars such as Sir Thomas Elyot, tended to exaggerate pure scholarship.

Standards for education in Robert's time were set out in Sir Humphrey Gilbert's scheme for a state academy where noble wards would be trained as administrators (1570).[16] Here the youth would study Latin and Greek grammar; logic and rhetoric for public speaking; current European political and military institutions; four modern European languages; natural philosophy; divinity (to teach obedience to the prince); civil law (for diplomacy); common law (for personal use and for service as a justice of the peace); arithmetic and geometry (for ballistics); cosmography and astronomy (to aid in map-reading and navigation); surgery; and medicine. Concommitantly, he would acquire the gentlemanly skills of horsemanship, shooting, fencing, playing the lute, dancing, vaulting, and heraldry.[17]

Lawrence Humphrey's similar but less arduous program[18] included study of the classical authors, especially Cicero; Erasmus' *Colloquies;* rhetoric and logic for conversation and argument; ethics from Isocrates, Deuteronomy, Ecclesiastes, Proverbs, Cicero, and Erasmus; politics from Aristotle; contemporary law and governmental institutions; arithmetic and geometry; geography and astrology (in moderation); and divinity from Calvin's *Institutes.*[19] Despite Ascham's condemnation of physical coercion, Tudor education was long and difficult, a tedious grind often enforced by corporal punishment.[20]

Robert's early training must have been no less vigorous than Philip's well-documented upbringing, although there is no mention that he was sent to the grammar school at Shrewsbury. Philip left for school only a year after Robert's birth. When, two years later, he matriculated at Christ Church, Oxford, Philip studied under tutors he would later recommend for his younger brother, Thomas Thornton, and Robert Dorsett. In 1572, Philip embarked on his two-year tour of the continent, making friends in intellectual and aristocratic circles to whom he would soon refer Robert.

Sir Henry's account books indicate that his younger children, Robert, Thomas, Mary, and Ambrosia, were placed together in the care of Robert Mantell and his wife, perhaps at Penshurst, instead of at the school at Shrewsbury. Early in 1573, Mantell laid out 1s. 4d. for a paper book for Robert's exercises at "the Schole," an institution that remains unnamed.[21] Robert's schoolmaster, a Mr. Thornton, received £5 in 1574,[22] while the child's stipend for the following year was £20.[23] The same account books afford a few tantalizing glimpses of Penshurst: passing references to payments "to them that played Robin Hood" and to "minstrels on Midsummer's Day,"[24] hints at clothes and gifts for the little ones—"a bow with arrows" for Robert and Mary, two pair of knit hose for Robert and "silk and egging to make him shirts," a pair of "crimson sattin hose," two pair, one purple, of canvas "slopes" (i.e., *slops:* wide, baggy breeches or hose).[25]

Dry accounts permit only a superficial impression of what Robert's boyhood was like. We do not even have a picture of him as a child. The painting that Fox Bourne mistakenly took to be a portrait of Philip and Robert as children has been shown to be that of Robert's sons, William and Robert, for the costumes in the painting titled "The Penshurst Boys" date the picture in the seventeenth century.[26] There apparently was a strong family resemblance between Philip and Robert; Languet remarked that the now-lost Veronese portrait of Philip "seems to me to represent some one rather like you than yourself, and at first I thought it was your brother."[27] This would suggest a picture of Robert as a smaller Philip, a slender boy with soft features and the Sidneys' inevitable auburn hair. Perhaps he had a clearer complexion than Philip's, whose face was marked by smallpox when he was about six.[28] This would have occurred in 1560 or, if he contracted it from his mother, in 1562, somewhat before Robert's birth. It is possible, then, that Robert could have escaped the disease's acnelike scarring.[29]

Whether or not he attended Shrewsbury, Robert surely received plenty of advice from his father. The best record we have of the elder Sidney's thoughts on the student's responsibility was addressed to Philip at Shrewsbury in 1566, but we can safely presume Robert heard much the same counsel as soon as he was old enough to understand. Sir Henry urged Philip to lift his mind to God and to pray daily at a fixed time. He should study when his master told him to, for the teacher knew how much time was sufficient for learning without damaging his student's health. Deference to the master was an exercise important to those who would lead, for one must know obedience to teach it to others. Philip was to be courteous and affable, keep his mind active, seldom drink wine, and be clean. "Let your Myrthe be ever void of all Scurilitee," Sir Henry advised in his letter to Philip, "for an wounde given by a Woorde, is oftentimes harder to be cured than that which is given with the Swerd." He must listen but not gossip, avoid swearing and ribald language, and think before speaking. In reading, he should mark the sense of his text as well as the words, and commit wise sentences and apt phrases to memory.[30] Since Sir Henry exhorted Robert to follow Philip's example, all his advice no doubt applied to the younger brother as well.

Although the Christ Church matriculation register shows that "Mr. Robert Sidney, *equitu filius, ex com. Cant.*," matriculated in May, 1574,[31] it appears that he did not go up to Oxford to stay until June, 1575. On February 2, 1575, Robert's fifteen-year-old sister Ambrosia died. Queen Elizabeth sent Sir Henry a kind letter of sympathy and invited little Mary to visit at court,[32] an offer that amounted to a command. Professor J. M. Osborn, in his biographical study, *Young Philip Sidney*, suggests that Robert and Philip joined their parents and sister on the queen's progess in June 1575.[33] If this were so, the occasion would have provided an early opportunity for Robert to make himself known at Elizabeth's court. However, correspondence between Philip and his old tutor, Robert Dorsett, which Osborn has translated from the Latin and printed in part in the same monograph, indicates that Robert must have gone to Oxford that month instead of accompanying his family on the progress. Dorsett, selected by

Philip to direct Robert's education, reported that the boy arrived in Oxford by June 3, and that he remained there until June 21, N.S. (New Style, equivalent to July 11, O.S., Old Style).[34] This is confirmed by Dorsett's accounts of 1575–76, which show that payment was made for Robert's admission to Christ Church on June 19 and that the boy remained there until August 19, when he left Oxford for the court in London.[35] Robert, then, was sent to Christ Church, accompanied by Edward Montague, Rowland Whyte, and the family retainer, Griffin Maddox, while his parents, Mary, and Philip proceeded to Elizabeth's traveling court.

Sir Henry had ended his second term as lord deputy in Ireland in 1571, and he passed the following four years at court and in Wales. By this time, he had made an ally of Sir William Cecil, who had come to agree with him on Irish topics. Although he received more thanks than he anticipated from Elizabeth, he thought himself ill-rewarded financially. In 1572, Lady Sidney asked Burghley to forestall her husband's rumored creation as a baron because they could not afford an offer with no added revenue to support it. Time proved that Sir Henry's earlier administration had been successful, and he was reappointed. In the first week of August 1572, he left London for Ireland, where he was to remain for three more years.[36]

With their father across the seas, the responsibility for Robert's education fell to Philip, at a time when, a polished young man of twenty-one, the older brother was actively campaigning for favor at court. Perhaps for this reason, Robert's higher education followed much the same pattern as Philip's. Correspondence with Dorsett at Oxford and later with Hubert Languet on the continent indicates that both tutors reported to Philip and followed his instructions about Robert. Robert and Philip shared a close fraternal attachment, a bond that appears not to have included the youngest brother, Thomas. Snatches of correspondence between the two older brothers reveal that Philip felt a deep tenderness and concern for Robert, and that he took his task of providing for Robert's education very seriously. If either brother took as much interest in Thomas, no indication of it survives.

Robert went up to Oxford bearing Philip's highest recommendations to their tutor, Robert Dorsett, who, by 1575, had attained the position of canon at Christ Church. Evidently having asked Dorsett to take charge of his brother, Philip especially commended Robert's "character and love of study," as Osborn puts it, and apparently asked Dorsett to take care of his cousin Edward Montagu and their Czech companion, Johannes Hajek,[37] as well as Robert.[38] A year-long correspondence ensued. A number of Dorsett's letters recording the boys' progress have been preserved at Christ Church, and they provide an enlightening description of Robert's personality.[39] Dorsett's aureate language describes the character of the adolescent Robert, his "mother's golden offshoot," in the most flattering terms. If Dorsett was being at all frank, Robert must have been something of a paragon.

Robert's three companions came from diverse social classes; the Sidneys' associates were of cosmopolitan origins and not restricted to the English gentry. A year older than Robert, the Montagu boy was the second son of Sir Edward Montagu of Boughton Castle, Northamptonshire. He was created Baron Montagu of Boughton in 1621, and, as a confirmed Royalist, served in Parliament and as Lord Lieutenant of Northamptonshire.[40] Johannes Hajek, who was about sixteen years old, had been introduced to Philip by Lobbet on the continent a year before. Philip had brought him to England when he was recalled at Easter, 1575, and continued to sponsor him for some time.[41] Robert's young servant, Rowland Whyte, accompanied them and studied with them under Dorsett's supervision.[42] Whyte, who may have been related to Philip's man, Harry Whyte,[43] grew to be Robert's most trusted companion and his agent at the English court.

Soon after the students arrived and established themselves at Christ Church, Dorsett sent word to Philip that he would cherish Robert because he was Philip's brother, because the boy was "worthy" of Philip, and "because I can not but love him for his dedication to integrity and to the love of letters." He promised to do all in his power to teach him and always to be guided by Philip's advice.[44] To aid him with the four boys—the three young gentlemen plus Rowland Whyte—Dorsett called upon his colleague John Buste, whom Osborn describes as "reliable but rather pedestrian."[45]

Philip must have returned a prompt answer to Dorsett's of June 3, 1575, for on the twenty-first the tutor acknowledged a letter from him, exclaiming over the great power of brotherly love and praising his own good fortune at having Robert with him. It was a pleasure to receive the boy, "for together with a quite polished mind he shows such gentle and moderate ways, together with a remarkable spirit and such gentle courtesy that it would clearly require a stony heart not to welcome the sense of proportion of such a gentle and tender nature." Languet also was to remark that Robert's character resembled Philip's. Any such similarity was to be carefully cultivated, and Dorsett promised to encourage the spirit Philip wished to see in the boy. "I shal not depart an inch from your judgment and counsel," he declared. Edward Montagu struck Philip as less polished than Robert, but Dorsett assured his correspondent that, with effort, care, and industry, both boys would be brought up to Philip's standards. Meanwhile, he forwarded a letter from Robert, hoping Philip would "judge it indulgently: practice will make future ones more fluent." For the time being, the boys' physical improvement would be moderate; later they were to throw the javelin more often. "The rest of the precepts in your letter," Dorsett concluded, "we shall diligently follow."

Exactly what these precepts were remains unknown. Philip's tutor, Hubert Languet, had recommended both volumes of Cicero's letters as a model for writing style, but had warned him to "beware of falling into the heresy of those who think the height of excellence consists in imitation of Cicero, and pass their lives laboring at it." Languet also approved the practice of double translation, rendering the original into English and then re-translating the result into Latin.[46] No doubt Philip passed this advice on to his younger brother. Languet further suggested Plutarch, but as for the Greek language, although it was "a beautiful study," he thought Latin more important for Philip's purposes.[47] He urged Philip to acquire at least a reading knowledge of German, in light of the frequent intercourse the English had with Germany and of the growing political power of the German states. Learning Italian, Languet regarded as sheer folly, since he believed the English had nothing to gain from Italy.[48] We know that Robert became rather fluent in German, probably as a result of Languet's advice. Like his elder brother, too, he ignored Languet's counsel on the subject of Italy and stubbornly learned the language, intending to tour the country.

Robert's training must also have been indirectly influenced by the philosophy of Shrewsbury's famous master, Thomas Ashton. Working from the teachings of Erasmus and John Colet, Ashton developed a pedagogy that emphasized action, service and utility, not knowledge for knowledge's sake. He combined religion and the classics, and selected his texts from authors who were politicians as well as thinkers: Cicero, Livy, Caesar, Isocrates, Xenophon. Like Languet, Ashton aimed to produce statesmen, educated leaders for whom philosophy was of use because it promoted correct action.[49]

Without doubt Philip's precepts for Robert's education reflected Languet's and Ashton's influence. Probably, too, he was familiar with the theories of Roger Ascham and Mulcaster. The latter's pronouncements came somewhat later (1581 and 1582) than Robert's stay at Oxford, and his pedagogy was aimed at a more bourgeois student than the scholars in the Sidneys' social class. Ascham began *The Schoolmaster,* however, the year Robert was born, and it was published posthumously in 1570, five years before Robert went to Oxford. Philip thus would have had time to digest Ascham's ideas and conceive of applying them to his younger brother. The general tenor of Philip's counsel probably did not change between the time Robert began his studies at Oxford and the time Philip sent him his famous letter prescribing the proper course for a young man touring Europe. He differed from Ascham in preferring plain Latin over Ciceronian, but like him, Philip recommended frequent writing exercises reviewing one's reading and observation, some study of science and mathematics, and performing on musical instruments, which, Philip advised, helped to assuage one's occasional melancholy. For exercise, he mentioned, in addition to music, horsemanship and practice with the sword and dagger.[50]

At any rate, the only tangible evidence about Robert's precise course of study comes from Dorsett's accounts, which indicate that the tutor bought a copy of Tully's *Offices* for Robert soon after he arrived at Christ Church. A year later the boy was studying logic out of "Valerius and Caesarius."[51]

Languet, who was less inclined to flattery than was Dorsett, was to deprecate Robert's early training. In the absence of any extensive records, the best one can guess is that Robert's training was directed, as was Philip's, at preparing him to be a statesman.

narrative

In October 1575, the plague struck Oxford and most of the university men fled. "Your flower of youths," Dorsett wrote to Philip, "and Edward Montagu were summoned by my Lord Montagu, with Buste and their two servants, Griffin and Hobson, and after spending a few days at the house of Kellsway, left for Northamptonshire." There, it was proposed, they would stay until the plague passed. The other two boys, Johannes Hajek and Rowland Whyte, were living with Dorsett, and he planned to send them to Kellsway or Northamptonshire whenever he decided which of the two places was most suitable.[52]

Robert escaped the epidemic in excellent health.[53] The Northamptonshire expedition, however, did not suit Philip's liking. He wrote to Dorsett to send Robert, Johannes, and Rowland to the court. Apparently concerned about the danger to the boys' health, Philip was taken by a great desire to see his brother, although he did feel the boy was well off where he was. Dorsett hoped Philip would arrange for Robert to make the journey on November 18, and "since they would have little time to return," he thought it unnecessary for Johannes and Rowland to join Robert and Buste.[54]

The plague continued into December, but the visit to the court was apparently delayed. On the December 1, Dorsett reported that Edward Montagu was considering leaving Boughton with his family, and that he wanted Philip to call the boys to court.[55] This request must have produced the desired result, for by the end of January the students had made the trip to court and returned to Oxford, which was now free of danger from the plague. Robert came back to his books with great pleasure and benefit, as did Montagu, but Johannes showed less enthusiasm. He "now thinks of nothing but the court," Dorsett reported. Apparently the boy felt that the best thing that could happen to him would be for him to be recalled to the court as soon as possible.[56]

So matters stood by the end of the first year of their stay at Oxford. Dorsett was pleased with Robert's intelligent and cooperative nature, and held out great hopes for the future of Philip's "little soulmate." "If he gets sufficient leisure from other activities to unfold the riches of his mind," he rejoiced, "it will bear some rich and rare fruits." Young Rowland Whyte also delighted Dorsett with his enthusiasm and his perhaps too-strenuous efforts to do the same work as Robert. The foundation for the lifelong friendship between Whyte and Sidney was already established, and one can imagine the two of them vying for Dorsett's attention and approval. Disappointingly, the Czech boy, Johannes, had not improved his attitude. He still longed for a place at court and showed small enthusiasm for scholarship. Exasperated, Dorsett indicated that he hoped that Philip would place him either at court or in his retinue, for, he noted with strained tact, "I should guess nature had not intended him for the discipline of higher learning."[57]

Robert spent most of his time in 1576 and 1577 at Oxford. He seems to have made a few unrecorded trips to Penshurst, Ludlow Castle, and the court, for Sir Henry remarked some years later about his middle son's frequent absences from Oxford.[58] Probably Robert visited his brother at court, where Philip continued to advance his fortunes.

The progress of Philip's career was to have effects on Robert's future that lasted long after the elder brother's death. Philip's friends became Robert's allies; his enemies, Robert's opponents; his interests, Robert's avocations. His successful endeavors on the continent and in the English court left an afterglow in which Robert would find his way with ease; his failures cast their shadows across Robert's future fortunes. His impression on his younger brother's development was so profound and so lasting that it can be argued that Philip's career became Robert's, and that as a young man Robert stepped into Philip's vacant boots and carried on in much the same direction his brother had begun. For these reasons, it cannot be amiss to review briefly Philip's activities during the period when Robert was studying at Oxford, even though abundant accounts of this segment of his life have been printed.[59]

Philip was in Ireland from July to September of 1576, when his friend Walter Devereux, earl of Essex, who was earl-marshal of Ireland, died suddenly of a mysterious ailment. Philip returned to England almost immediately thereafter, where he found the earl's death had improved the Devereux's standing at court; ten-year-old Robert, the new earl, was already one of the queen's favorites, and Lord Burghley had taken him into his protection and household. Marriage plans between Essex's sister, Penelope Devereux, and the old earl's chosen suitor, Philip, were broken off, probably because of the Sidney family's tenuous finances; nevertheless, the friendship Penelope and the young earl had developed with the Sidney brothers was to continue for some time.

Early in 1577, Philip was appointed ambassador to Germany, with a mission to congratulate and express condolences to the new emperor, Rudolph II, whose father, Maximilian, had died in October 1576, and to the new elector palatine, Lewis, whose father, Frederick, had also died in the same month. These two deaths had triggered crises in European politics. Rudolph, a Catholic, reversed his father's policy of religious toleration and immediately began to persecute the Protestants. In the Palatine, Lewis was violently trying to establish Lutheran doctrine and to extinguish the Calvinism his father had introduced, while his brother, John Casimir, championed the newly forbidden creed. Meanwhile, Don John of Austria, half-brother to King Philip of Spain, had recently come to terms with the southern provinces of the Netherlands, winning out over William of Orange's objections and warnings against Spanish treachery.

Philip's instructions left him more or less free to do as he wished in matters that seemed expedient to encourage a union of Protestant states and to stir them to action in their common defense. In February, he left for the continent, in company with the experienced Sir Henry Lee, Sir Jerome Bowes, and Fulke Greville, among others. At Louvain, he paid his respects to Don John, whom he impressed favorably despite his youth and inexperience. His meeting with Count Casimir at Heidelberg in mid-March gave Philip little reason to hope for the desired end of the dangerous feud between Casimir and his brother, Lewis, although he came away with a good opinion of the count, whose extremism he attributed to "mistaken conscientiousness."[60]

Having missed the Elector Palatine at Heidelberg, Philip joined Hubert Languet there and continued on to Prague in his company. In Prague, he encountered Emperor Rudolph, whom he urged to make peace at home and abroad and boldly warned against the dangers threatened from Rome and Spain, arguing for the necessity of a league of Protestant states to safeguard German religion and freedom from the Catholic league. When Rudolph failed to answer Sidney's appeal, Philip concluded that the emperor was treacherous, committed to the Roman Catholic cause, and "extremely spaniolated." After an interview with the dowager queen of France and the dowager empress of Germany, Sidney left Prague near the end of April.

Homeward bound, Philip met the elector, Lewis at Neustadt on May 1. He exhorted Lewis, as he had Casimir, to unite with his brother, and hoped he would desist from oppressing the Calvinists. Lewis responded that, although he personally had nothing against the Calvinists, he was bound to act as did the other German princes. Progressing on to Lauterberg, Philip again met and conferred with Casimir about the possibilities for organizing a general Protestant league and for lessening the Lutheran persecution of the Calvinists. Even the enthusiastic Sidney, however, could see that such a league was unlikely under the current circumstances of European politics.

Languet, who provided Sidney's strongest inspiration in his hopes for the Protestant league, left from Cologne to return to Prague, while Sidney, following new instructions from England, made his way to Gertruydenberg to convey the queen's congratulations to William of Orange on the birth of his son. He spent a week at William's residence at Dordrecht, during which time he established a friendship with the middle-aged Dutch rebel and stood godfather to the new baby. Bearing William's thanks to the queen and the Princess of Orange's gift to him of a "fair jewel," Philip left for London on June 2, where he arrived in good health and temporarily high in Elizabeth's favor.

With his star at its zenith during this trip, Philip was moving toward fulfillment of Languet's hopes for and cultivation of him as the future leader of the proposed Protestant league. In this project, he was supported by Sir Francis Walsingham and by the proponents of Admiral Coligny of France; the hope was that Lutherans, Calvinists, and Anglicans could be united in the crusade against the forces of Catholicism. On the continent, Philip had obtained the commitment of Casimir, Landgrave William, and the duke of Brunswick, but was disappointed by the elector Ludwig's lukewarm response. The landgrave of Hesse expressed sympathy with Casimir in the cause, and in May, 1576, he wrote to Elizabeth of his zeal for such a league.[61] Elizabeth, however, was less enthusiastic; it appears that she and Burghley regarded the scheme as the product of the radical Protestant faction. The queen may even have suspected Sidney's loyalty and feared the potential power he might develop as leader of a great continental combine.[62] Philip's ideology interfered with his practical judgment; as F. J. Levy has phrased it, "he was prepared to serve the queen only if she was willing to do God's evident will."[63] Not surprisingly, the distrust Sidney provoked in the queen made her unwilling to employ him or any of his persuasion.

The acquaintances and friendships Philip made during his continental tours later proved important to Robert's career. The connection with the House of Orange, for example, continued in Robert's friendship with William's son, Maurice, at whose side he was to fight in the Dutch civil wars. The Princess of Orange's affection for Philip was extended to Robert. In later years, she corresponded with Robert, exchanged gifts with him and his wife, and stood godmother to one of his children.

The shadow that fell over Philip's career as a result of his emergence at this time as an activist leader in an extremist cause, however, darkened not only his own career but also Robert's. After Philip's death, Elizabeth made it evident that the suspicion she had conceived for Philip extended to Robert. The eclipse of Philip's ambitions doubtless had something to do with Robert's continuing frustration during Elizabeth's reign.

While Philip was abroad, arrangements were being made in England for the marriage of Mary Sidney, the boys' only surviving sister, to Henry Herbert, earl of Pembroke. Their uncle, Leicester, who seems to have brought Mary to the queen's attention in 1575, had a great deal to do with making the match.[64] Sir Henry approved, although his finances at the time were so straitened he had to borrow part of the £2,000 dowry from Leicester. In addition, he gave the bride a cup worth £500,[65] the price of which he probably also borrowed.

The less-than-romantic match between the fifteen-year-old Mary and the forty-year-old Pembroke was ideal in terms of the Sidney family's political and economic ambitions. Pembroke's father—brother-in-law to Henry VIII by virtue of his second wife, who was Catherine Parr's sister—had acquired great wealth under Henry following the dissolution of the church lands. Like Sir Henry Sidney, the first earl underwent an abrupt conversion to Catholicism from Protestantism under Mary, and at Elizabeth's accession reverted to zealous Protestantism. He, too, had supported Northumberland, and had married his then sixteen-year-old son, Henry, to Catherine Grey, Lady Jane's sister, on the day of Lady Jane's marriage to Guildford Dudley. This union remained unconsummated, and the two were divorced after five weeks. The second earl's next wife, Lady Catherine Talbot, daughter of the earl of Shrewsbury, died in 1578.[66] A partisan of the Dudley faction and no doubt one of Leicester's intimates,[67] the earl was marvelously wealthy, owner of Baynard's Castle on the Thames in London and the stately mansion called Wilton in Wiltshire.[68]

Robert was the eldest male of the immediate family to attend the wedding, which took place on April 21, 1577. Leicester was not able to obtain leave for Sir Henry to return home for the event, and Philip was occupied on the continent. It was a gala affair, one that provided an occasion for Robert to indulge his taste in stylish clothes. His delight in fine material and elegant fashions was already well developed, and it was to remain one of his charming, if costly, foibles in the years to come. One did have to dress to match the dignity of one's position and of the occasion. The Sidneys' already respectable position was about to take on more substance with this match. If ever there was an occasion to dress up, surely the wedding of his pretty and intelligent young sister to the earl of Pembroke must have been it.

By the twentieth of the month, the bills were already coming in. For Robert's clothes "ayenst the maryadge of therle of Pembroke," Dorsett recorded that they had bought 4⅛ yards of white tufte taffeta, 4½ yards of white "jeyne ffustene" (i.e., twilled cotton cloth), black velvet, white satin, white sarsnet (a very fine, soft silk used chiefly for lining), and carnation velvet, for a total of £33 2s. 2d. Sir Henry noted that he would pay it in October, but reproached Dorsett for not specifying which garment the dry goods had been purchased for, and for whom. Henceforth, the bills were itemized. The white outfit trimmed in black and carnation velvet seems not to have sufficed for the occasion. In addition, Robert had made a French cloak of black velvet, a white satin doublet, "jerkin wise," a Spanish cape of black satin, and a doublet of carnation satin trimmed with carnation lace and two and a half dozen carnation buttons.[69] He must have cut a dashing figure, this handsome, gentle-natured youth: well dressed, cultured, and undoubtedly gifted with the self-confidence of the privileged young.

NOTES

1. Great Britain Historical Manuscripts Commission, no. 77, *Report on the Manuscripts of Lord De L'Isle and Dudley Preserved at Penshurst Place*, ed. C. L. Kingsford and William A. Shaw, 6 vols. (London, His Majesty's Stationery Office, 1925–66), 1:x. (This report is hereafter abbreviated *HMCD*. Please see List of Abbreviations, page   .)

2. Ibid.

3. *Dictionary of National Biography* (1921–22 imprint), s.v. "Sidney, Henry."

4. HMCD 1:x–xi.

5. Sir Fulke Greville, *Works in Verse and Prose Complete of the Right Honorable Fulke Greville, Lord Brooke*, ed. Reverend Alexander B. Grosart, 4 vols. (New York: AMS Press, 1966), vol. 4, *The Life of Sir Philip Sidney*.

6. These and subsequent details of Sir Henry Sidney's life are taken from the *Dictionary of National Biography*, subsequently abbreviated to *DNB*.

7. Mona Wilson, *Sir Philip Sidney* (London: Duckworth, 1931), pp. 23–24.

8. Great Britain, Public Record Office, *Calendar of State Papers, Domestic, Series of the Reigns of Edward VI, Mary, Elizabeth, and James I*, 13 vols., 2:98–99, Ludlow Castle, 1 March 1583, Sir Henry Sidney to Sir Francis Walsingham. (This series of the *Calendar of State Papers, Domestic* is hereafter abbreviated *CSP Dom.*)

9. Sir Francis Bacon, *The Works of Sir Francis Bacon*, ed. J. Spedding, 14 vols. (London: Longmans, Green, 1868–74), vol. 8, *Apophthegms New and Old*, p. 131.

10. Greville, p. 8.

11. *CSP Dom.* 2:98–99.

12. Greville, p. 8.

13. Lawrence Stone, *The Crisis of the Aristocracy* (Oxford: Clarendon Press, 1965), p. 734.

14. Ibid., p. 737.

15. Ibid., pp. 735–36.

16. "The Erection of Queen Elizabeth's Achademy in London for the Education of her Ma: Wards or Others the Youths of Nobility and Gentlemen," (London, 1572).

17. Stone, p. 679.

18. "The Nobles: or of Nobility," (London: T. Marshe, 1563).

19. Stone, p. 679.

20. Ibid., p. 680.

21. *HMCD* 1: 267.

22. Ibid., p. 257.

23. Ibid., p. 426.

24. Ibid., p. 268.

25. Ibid., pp. 267–69.

26. Alexander C. Judson, *Sidney's Appearance* (Bloomington: Indiana University Press, 1958), pp. 63–66.

27. Alexander Aspenwall Bradley, *The Correspondence of Philip Sidney and Hubert Languet* (Boston: Merrymount Press, 1912), p. 88, 11 June 1574, Languet to P. Sidney.

28. Judson, p. 71, citing Thomas Moffitt, *Nobilis, or a View of the Life and Death of a Sidney.*

29. Cf., Ben Jonson's *Conversations with Drummond* (London: R. V. Patterson, 1923), in which the playwright remarks that Philip's face was "spoiled with pimples."

30. Arthur Collins, ed., *Letters and Memorials of State,* 2 vols. (London: T. Osborne, 1746), 1:8.

31. "*Matricula Aedis Christi,* 1546–1636," Christ Church College, Oxford University manuscript.

32. *CSP Dom.* 1:494.

33. James M. Osborn, *Young Philip Sidney, 1572–1577* (New Haven: Yale University Press, 1972), p. 324.

34. Correspondence of P. Sidney and Robert Dorsett, Christ Church College, Oxford University MSS. Dorsett's letters are in Latin. I have used the typescript English translations, also located at Christ Church Library, commissioned and copyrighted by J. M. Osborn. Subsequent quotations from this typescript will be abbreviated "Christ Church Letters."

35. *HMCD* 1:268–69.

36. *DNB,* s.v. "Sidney, Sir Henry."

37. Philip's special charge, Hajek was the son of Dr. Thaddeus Hajek.

38. Osborn, pp. 312 *ff.*

39. See Osborn's interesting and enlightening commentary on this correspondence, pp. 313 *ff.*

40. Ibid., p. 312.

41. Ibid., pp. 242, 303–5, 312 *ff.*

42. Dorsett to P. Sidney, 21 March and 15 October, Christ Church Letters.

43. Osborn, p. 369.

44. Dorsett to P. Sidney, Oxford, 3 June 1574, Christ Church Letters.

45. Osborn, p. 312.

46. Bradley, p. 22. Languet to P. Sidney, Vienna, 28 January 1574.

47. Ibid., p. 29. Languet to P. Sidney, 22 January 1574.

48. Ibid., p. 35. Languet to P. Sidney, Vienna, 28 January 1574.

49. F. J. Levy, "Philip Sidney Reconsidered," *English Literary Renaissance* 2 (1972): 6–7.

50. Collins, 1:283.

51. Account (by Robert Dorsett) of expenses for Robert Sydney at Oxford and elsewhere, *HMCD* 1:268–69.

52. Dorsett to P. Sidney, Oxford, 15 October 1575, Christ Church Letters.

53. Dorsett to P. Sidney, 24 October 1575, Ibid.

54. Dorsett to P. Sidney, 31 October 1575, Ibid.

55. Dorsett to P. Sidney, 1 December 1575, Ibid.

56. Dorsett to P. Sidney, 24 January 1575/76, Ibid.

57. Dorsett to P. Sidney, 21 March 1575/76, Ibid.

58. Sir Henry Sidney to Robert Sidney, Baynard's Castle, London, [1581], *HMCD,* 2:95–96.

59. For the following résumé of Philip Sidney's movements, I am indebted to Henry Richard Fox Bourne, *A Memoir of Philip Sidney* (London: Chapman and Hall, 1862), Chapters VI–VIII (pp. 87–150).

60. Ibid., p. 117.

61. Osborn, p. 458.

62. Ibid., p. 499.

63. Fred J. Levy, p. 11.

64. *DNB*, s.v. "Herbert, Mary, Countess of Pembroke."

65. Bourne, pp. 130–31.

66. Ibid., p. 130.

67. *DNB*, s.v. "Herbert, Henry, Earl of Pembroke."

68. Bourne, p. 131.

69. *HMCD* 1:270.

[2]

Sidney's Career Begins

Shortly after New Year's Day, 1579, Prince Casimir came to England, seeking to abate the queen's annoyance over his mismanagement of a field maneuver in which he had Elizabeth's alliance. With him came Hubert Languet.

Languet visited England primarily to see his protégé, Philip. The Sidney family had spent Christmas, 1578, at Hampton Court, and Robert, who had quit Oxford at about this time, may have been with them. During the festivities that followed Casimir's arrival, Languet was pleased to see that Philip was in good favor with the queen, but he disapproved of the sycophancy of courtly life. He did develop warm friendships with Sir Henry, the young Countess of Pembroke, and Philip's friends Edward Dyer and Fulke Greville.[1] Philip took the opportunity to place his younger brother in his old tutor's care and send him off on a tour of the continent.

Robert and the Huguenot teacher left together for the Low Countries in February, accompanied by Fulke Greville, who was on a mission to Germany. As their parting gift,[2] the Sidneys presented Languet with a chain worth £45 15s, a token that reflected their high regard for the man. After a stormy crossing, the three arrived in Flushing about the end of the month.[3]

Sending a son to Europe was costly. Sir Henry gave Robert a stipend of £100 a year beginning at Easter, 1579, in addition to his regular annual allowance of £20,[4] yet the youth ran low on cash and had to have his brother's help to make ends meet. This expensive trip came just a year after Sidney had laid out some £2,500 for his daughter's marriage, and at a time when the establishment of his eldest son's career forced him to incur many expenses.[5] The custom of primogeniture made Henry's generosity in the matter of Robert's education all the more remarkable; frequently, all such opportunities and privileges were reserved for the eldest son. Sir Henry's financial circumstances were never much better than moderately sanguine—he had to borrow the cash for Mary's dowry, and the queen never reimbursed him adequately for his costs and time in Ireland. In this light, his concern that Robert be as well trained as Philip and that he have the same opportunities his older brother received speaks well for Sir Henry's liberality of spirit. He must have cared deeply for both boys, and the fact that he invested so heavily in the futures of both testifies not only to his paternal love but to his confidence in each boy's talent and skill. Perhaps he pictured them working together, as the Bacon brothers were to do. Whatever his vision of their future, Sir Henry's care for Robert went well beyond the demands of custom.

The European tour was the young English gentleman's finishing school. Conservative warnings against the alienating and demoralizing effects of exposing the young to the more sophisticated cultures on the continent, with their strange customs, skeptical attitudes, dangerous religious controversies, and new-fangled alternatives to the English elders' wisdom, were outweighed by the advantages of the experience. With the rise of the new diplomacy, the Renaissance administrator needed a working acquaintance with European languages, political systems, and social institutions. Earlier in the 1570s, at the time Philip went to Europe, continental tours were rare among Englishmen, but by the time Robert sailed for the continent with Languet, they had become somewhat more common.[6] Much could only be learned abroad: the arts of military command, fortification, siege warfare, tactics, and strategy were to be studied by example in the continental camps. The great royal courts could best be studied in person; that way a man could meet the personalities behind the pattern of Reformation and Counter-Reformation politics, and, just as important, make himself known to them. The physical accomplishments required of the cultivated gentleman—riding the great horse, fencing, dancing, music—were taught in great Parisian academies, and art, aesthetics, and antiquarian learning were available to those who were interested.[7]

In his 1578 letter to Robert, Philip had made his conception of what was to be gained in traveling around the continent clear enough.[8] The English gentleman toured the continent for one reason: to furnish himself with knowledge that would render him more valuable in the service of his country. In line with this single-minded purpose, Philip said the young traveler should compare the power of the various continental rulers with the Queen of England's. He should make note of the leagues formed by the European princes, of the comparative topography of each country, and how each government is supplied with revenue, fortifications, garrisons, and trained militia. Philip's choice of specifics for study was pragmatic; although more exotic cultures might be abstractly interesting, the gentleman-tourist should study those countries likely to have contact with England. Knowledge of faraway places, such as China, could be of little practical use to the future statesman.

In Germany, one should observe the outstanding system of administering justice; in France and Spain, study the governmental structure, and note how the leaders stood vis-à-vis the English in power and inclination. Flanders offered the best model for trade. As for Italy, Philip agreed with Languet that the Italians could offer little of practical substance to the

inquiring English traveler,[9] but he noted that they excelled in horsemanship, weaponry, and vaulting. Finally, Philip urged Robert to exercise some
discretion in his choice of friends, for "noe vessell can leave a worsse tast to
the licquor it containes, then a wronge teacher infectes an unskillfull
hearer. . . . Be sure therefore of his knowledge whom you desire to learne,
tast him well before you drinke to much of his doctrine, and when you have
heard it, trie what you have heard, before you hold it for a principle, for
one errour is the mother of a thowsand."[10]

The success of any individual grand tour depended as much on the
young man's temperament as on the tutor's skill and education. Languet
seems to have received a poor impression of Dorsett's and Buste's influence
on Robert, although he was not altogether without hope for the boy. "I
consider his natural disposition to be excellent," he wrote from Flushing in
his first letter to Philip since their parting, "but I still think you have not
taken such care as you ought, of his education. You have now given him so
much liberty, that it is not everyone who will find it an easy task to hold him
in command."[11] At fifteen, Robert appears already to have been a handful
for those in charge of him, and later gossip suggests he grew into a high-
spirited young man; indeed, he may have had reason to regret some of his
coltishness. Philip's tendency to melancholy seems not to have been one of
Robert's chronic failings, at least in his younger years. To keep him in
hand, Languet proposed to put him in the charge of Johann Matthäus
Wacker von Wackenfels, if the latter was available and would consent to it.
Philip had met Wacker in Padua. The author of a number of Latin dramas,
he was a diplomat and a statesman, and he had recently received a docto-
rate at the University of Padua.[12] If Wacker was not available, Languet
planned to take the advice of their learned friends, Lobbet and Sturm, in
choosing someone fit to superintend Robert's education.[13]

Languet lost no time in introducing Robert to European court life.
Within a fortnight, he had presented him to several eminent persons,
including the Prince of Orange and the great Huguenot soldier, François
de la Noue, who especially welcomed him. By this time, everyone was aware
that the Dudley prestige accompanied the Sidney sons when they traveled
abroad. In his earlier trips, Philip had left a trail of admirers who welcomed
any friend of his into their own affection. "There is hardly one of those
whom you have made your friends," Languet observed of the effect Philip
had on the Europeans, "who does not desire to obtain my friendship,
because he knows that you love me."[14]

At Antwerp, La Noue, known as *Bras de Fer* from the iron prosthetic he
wore to replace an arm lost at Fontenay in 1570, showed much kind interest in Philip's younger brother. "Full of courtesy, [he] showed [Robert]
every attention . . . as long as we were in the citadel."[15]

From Antwerp, Robert and Languet apparently went to Frankfurt,
and from there proceeded to Strasbourg, with a daylong side trip to Neustadt, where they paid their respects to the Prince, "for he had made
[Robert] promise him this when he was in Zealand."[16] They reached Stras-

bourg on April 28, and Languet immediately set to work on the problems of finding Robert lodging and a tutor. Consulting with his friend, Dr. Jean Lobbet ("Lobetius"), a learned jurist of Strasbourg, he discovered that a young gentleman who had been living with Dr. Sturm, whom Philip had met in 1577, had recently left, and Robert consented to the proposal that he take the youth's place under Sturm's roof. Robert was to pay ten talers a week for his own and his tutor's food and lodging. He might have lived more cheaply with a common citizen, but the accomodations would not have been as good. Languet observed that the townspeople indiscriminately admitted many boarders to the same table, and this led to disputes, particularly since, in that area, strangers were more likely to be insulted than were natives. Languet thought it better and safer that Robert live with a man whose guests respected their host's authority. Locating the tutor was less easy, and after a week of inquiry, Languet still had found no one in Strasbourg who satisfied them. Finally they engaged a young man named Peter Hubner on a temporary basis, on the condition that they could dismiss him after five months if they found a more fit tutor. Greatly in his favor was this Silesian's willingness to work for three Spanish crowns or five German florins a month, plus room and board, a wage Languet thought scarcely enough to allow him to buy adequate clothing.[17]

Robert's host, Johann Sturm, was an eminent Zwinglian scholar of Strasbourg. At the time Philip met him, he was rector of the academy. His pedagogical theories influenced Roger Ascham, and through him, he exercised some indirect influence on Ascham's pupil, Queen Elizabeth. In 1572, probably because of financial need, he became the English agent in Strasbourg. Although he was hostile to extreme Lutherans, his hospitality was generally extended to "all good men, and his home was the common Asylum of the Refugees . . . especially in providing for the French Protestants. . . ."[18] Living in the home of this experienced and knowledgeable Strasbourger must have provided Robert many excellent opportunities to meet members of Sturm's Zwinglian circle as well as numerous intellectuals and religious nonconformists passing through the city. One can imagine the English youth listening to much hot debate over religious and philosophical issues: Sturm had been involved in a theological controversy between the University with which he sided, and the Strasbourg pastors for some years, and the quarrel continued throughout Robert's stay.[19]

By May, Robert had gained more of Languet's confidence than he had when they arrived at Flushing. "His disposition pleases me more and more," Languet wrote, "and I am very glad there are no Englishmen here except himself and his servants."[20] There was a Scot in charge of one of M. Amelot's sons. Languet said he would not grieve at the Scot's departure, if it could be contrived. Perhaps drawing on these remarks, Mona Wilson portrays Robert's character in a less than flattering light, but her observations call for close examination.[21]

Wilson believes that, because of his deteriorating health, Languet regarded his responsibility for Robert as a burden. Robert, however, was left at Strasbourg in the care of Lobbet and Sturm, while Languet went on about his business. Most of his reports about Robert are secondhand, relayed through him from Strasbourg to Philip. Nowhere does Languet indicate that Robert was "less docile, respectful, and industrious" than Philip, nor that he "preferred the company of his English servants to that of the learned persons to whom he was introduced." To the contrary, Languet forwarded reports of Robert's good nature, talent, and industry,[22] and Sir Henry remarked with satisfaction on the positive news he received of his second son's character.[23] Languet's pleased remarks about the absence of Englishmen suggest that he believed that the presence of others of Robert's countrymen would be a distraction, an understandable prejudice. Then, as now, the tendency of students who find themselves in foreign countries to run in tight cliques cushioned them from absorbing as much as they might from the native culture in which they resided. They might fail to learn the language for lack of any need for foreign-speaking conversation partners, and they would tend to draw relatively few acquaintances and friends from the surrounding society.

While it is true that Robert considered a term of service with Casimir,[24] Philip had also considered joining the prince.[25] This yearning to follow the forces of a foreign prince must, if it was known to her, have done little to enhance Elizabeth's trust in either brother. Both young men regarded Casimir as a savior of the Protestant religion, reflecting their mentor's temporary admiration of him.

Records of Robert's movements stop for a year after May 4, 1579, a period that marks a hiatus in Languet's correspondence with Philip. Philip's and Sir Henry's letters to him in 1580 make it clear that he was as busy spending his allowance as studying. Probably he passed his time making friends among the German aristocrats and intellectuals, gaining some experience of European court life, listening to the constant word-of-mouth reports about the great conflicts in France and the Low Countries, and perhaps taking some short trips around the countryside.

Some hint of the nature of Robert's interests and studies appears in Philip's famous letter of advice, written in October, 1580.[26] Evidently, Robert had asked his brother's counsel on reading and writing history. Robert's commonplace books, compiled throughout his adulthood, reflect his fascination with the subject, and Philip's letter reveals that his interest began quite early. On historiography, Philip recommended that Robert read Jean Bodin, an avant-garde political philosopher who, in 1586, had written a critical study of history in an attempt to uncover the universal principles of law. Philip further recommended the chronological methods of Philip Melanchthon, Giovanni Tarchognota, and Languet, and stressed the importance of noting examples of virtue and vice, the rise and fall of great states, and the beginnings and endings of wars with the strategies used in them.

Bodin wrote in French; Tarchognota in Italian. We can surmise, then, that Robert was already familiar with these languages, as well as with Latin and the German he was learning at the time. Philip did not insist that Robert master an elaborate style of Latin; "so you can speak and write Latin not barbarously," he remarked, "I never require great study in Ciceronianism, the chief abuse of Oxford, *qui dum verba sectantur, res ipsas negligunt.*"[27]

Philip suggested a method of study for Robert that involved compiling tables of written notes on his reading, listing "wittie word[s]" or "sentences" or "similitudes" under appropriate logical headings. He particularly recommended that Robert set down his studies of the military and political arts in such a "table of remembrance," and that he note the special strength of each historian's method. Robert's commonplace books and other notebooks dated forty years later are organized in exactly this way.

Philip hoped Robert would not neglect the study of mathematics, noting that his tutor, Mr. Savill, was accomplished in that discipline. He stressed the importance of arithmetic and geometry, sciences important to the art of the sixteenth-century man of war, and he wished Robert would study the "mechanicall instruments" with which the Dutch excelled. He saw little need for his brother to understand more of astronomy, however, than was required for a basic grasp of the theory of the spheres. By this, Philip undoubtedly meant familiarity with the Ptolemaic system, for by the turn of the seventeenth century acceptance of Ptolemy's theories was still widespread among intellectuals. Donne was not unusual in his conservatism on astronomical topics.[28] Notwithstanding Philip's intercourse with Giordano Bruno, Robert's own poetry reveals that his understanding of cosmic theory was no more sophisticated than his contemporaries'.[29]

Never so unrealistic as to expect that all Robert's joy would rest in academic study, Philip urged his brother to "take a delight to keepe and increase your musick, you will not believe what a want I finde of it in my melancholie times." Osborn interprets this ambiguous remark as a confession that "Philip could not adequately assuage his melancholy by performing on an instrument, whereas Robert's training was such that he could."[30] Since a Renaissance man of his background would doubtless have been able to play an instrument with enough skill to relieve some frustration, this passage could also refer to a native musical talent in Robert. Robert enjoyed music all his life, patronized a number of musicians during James's reign, and is thought to have provided the lyrics to Dowland's *Musicall Banquet.* Probably his skill, even at this early age, was so refined that Philip enjoyed listening to him play, and particularly missed Robert's performances in melancholy moments.

Philip suggested that Robert augment his practice at horsemanship by reading "Grison[,] Claudio, and a booke that is called *La gloria del cavallo,*" which would help him to grasp quickly the skills of bitting, saddling, and "curing" horses. "Grison" no doubt was Federico Grisone, who in 1650 published *Gli Ordini de cavalcare,* and who may have produced a later work in horse care, *Scielta de Notabili avertimenti, pertinenti a Cavalli* (1571). "Claudio" may have been Claudio Corte, author of *Il Cavallerizzo* (1573). *La Gloria del cavallo* was a work published in 1576 by Pasqual Caracciolo.[31]

These references confirm the deduction made from Philip's recommendation of Tarchognota that Robert was fluent in Italian, and that he had a proficient enough reading knowledge of the language to grasp some very technical treatises.

As a final caveat, Philip urged that Robert practice in earnest at weapons, protecting himself with "thick capps and brasers." He told him not to dally at the business. He should practice with the single sword and the dagger. The exercise would increase Robert's strength, enhance his performance at courtly entertainments, and fit him to defend himself in an age when violence was commonplace and the duel was regarded as an acceptable device to uphold one's honor.

While Robert spent a year on the Continent, Philip's position at court was slipping. The previous year, he and Lady Sidney had successfully defended Sir Henry's Irish policy against Thomas Butler, Earl of Ormond and his supporters, but Philip's involvement in the controversy over Elizabeth's proposed match with Alençon was to have long-term negative effects on his own career as well as on his father's and his brother's. Alençon's agent, Jehan de Simier, had arrived during Casimir's visit and begun negotiating for the marriage. Faced with Leicester's opposition, Simier revealed to Elizabeth the Earl's secret marriage to Lettice Devereux, casting Philip's uncle into a temporary disgrace that permanently tarnished his influence with the queen. Lettice was forbidden ever to enter the queen's presence again and Lady Sidney relinquished her apartment at court.[32]

Philip's part in presenting the radical Protestants' arguments against the Alençon marriage, which he put before the queen in his celebrated letter of August, 1579, seems by its boldness to have suggested a certain hot-headed naiveté that identified him in Burghley's and the queen's minds with the forces of intemperate extremism. Following this frustration and the culmination of his rivalry with the Earl of Oxford in a noisy public squabble on a tennis court, Philip retired into voluntary rustication at Wilton, where he, his sister, and their circle of literary friends became the focus of a school of poetry that would produce some of the finest verse of the century.

Elizabeth's loss of confidence in Philip, and, by association, in Robert, undoubtedly had deeper causes than her distaste for the older brother's plain-spoken opposition to Alençon. Osborn hypothesizes that she suspected a Dudley plot in the pressure for a Protestant league.[33] Had Philip accepted William the Silent's offer of his daughter's hand when he was on the Continent, his connection with the House of Orange, his claim to the titles of Warwick and Leicester, and—if it matured to fruition—his position as a leader of a powerful international combine could have made him a threat to the security of her crown. If through his negotiations with William he became Lord Governor of Holland and Zealand, the Dutch might bestow sovereignty on him. Burghley seems to have concurred in this distrust.

The queen's suspicion seems to have extended to Robert, with dismal effects on the younger brother's prospects. Robert's appointment as Governor of Flushing, an office that belonged to Philip until his death, amounted to a kind of rustication, a backwater from which he did not escape until after Elizabeth died. All his requests for advancement were denied, his military achievements scorned or ignored, his personal initiative discouraged, and his aspirations frustrated. Although his ambitions were more personal and far less grandiose than Philip's, Elizabeth took no chances where Robert was concerned. She never raised him to the position at the court for which his inheritance and service qualified him.

A year after Robert established himself at Strasbourg, Languet reported to Philip that Lobbet suspected that the boy was planning to join Casimir's proposed expedition to France. Lobbet gathered this from Robert's "anxious enquiries of everyone he met, if they had any news on that head."[34] After Casimir's disastrous campaign in the Low Countries, Languet had come to distrust the prince and his unscrupulous counselor, Dr. Peter Butrech, who had been responsible for the alliance with the Ghent Calvinists. The atrocities Casimir and his Calvinist friends committed in Ghent—the sacking of churches, the burning of monks and friars in the marketplace, and the like—had given Languet some second thoughts that he had voiced to Philip during his 1579 visit to England. Because he believed Casimir had abused William of Orange's confidence, Languet devoted his remaining years to aiding and advising Orange, whom he now saw as the only hope for the Protestant cause in the Low Countries.[35] Recognizing that involvement with Casimir would be "certain destruction" for Robert, Languet advised Philip that any such plan must be prevented; he promised that he would write to Butrech and to Casimir if he found that Robert was contemplating anything of the kind. Then, in the first of several remarks that suggest that Robert's costs on the continent were more than the Sidney family finances could bear, Languet suggested that Philip send his brother at once to Leipzig, where he would learn German more easily than at Strasbourg, would be separated from other Englishmen, and would live at less expense. Lobbet was to be temporarily out of the city, which made Languet even less comfortable about leaving Robert alone in Strasbourg. The Frankfurt Fair was coming up, and that would be a good time to make arrangements to send Robert to Leipzig. No matter what, he concluded, Philip "must soon come to some determination about sending him a supply of money."[36]

Languet reiterated this need in his next communication to Philip (November, 1580). He intended to write, by the Antwerp merchants who were going to Frankfurt Fair, to Wechel to send Robert some money, for he was sure he had nothing left of what Philip gave him a year before.[37] If this was so, Robert had gone through a large sum of cash very quickly. In March, 1579, he had received a £240 advance on his yearly stipend of £100; he must have spent two and one-half years' worth of his support in eleven months.[38] Without funds, the youth would find Strasbourg a cold lodging. "Now that Dr. Lobetius has left," wrote Languet, "I fear there is no one who will take very great care of him. I know his host is a very poor man and cannot give him credit."[39]

This depletion of capital may have been one of Robert's reasons for contemplating joining Casimir's forces. Captains in Elizabeth's army made substantial livings off the graft that was commonplace in sixteenth-century military organizations, and that temptation, combined with the chance to win his own portion of glory in a Protestant battle against the Papists, must have been tempting for Robert.

By 1581, the Sidney family finances had reached a low point,[40] and Robert could not hope for more than just enough money to subsist on from home. By February 1580 he was running low; purchases such as the marten skins he sent his father[41] must have done much to exhaust his allowance. He got by until October 1580, when Philip wrote that he would gladly send him some money.[42] However, when their father had to send Robert additional funds, Sir Henry was furious at his extravagance. "All your money is gon," he wrote angrily, "which with sum wunder displeaseth me; and if you cannot frame your charges according to that proportyon I have appoynted you, I must and wyl send for you home. I have sent order to Mr. Languet for one hundryth poundys for you, whych is twenty pound more than I promysed you; and thys I looke and order, that it shal serve you tyll the last of Marche 1580. Assure your self I wyll not inlarge one grote, therefore looke well to your charges."[43] Robert knew that Philip, as the Sidney's firstborn son, stood to inherit the Sidney estates and possibly the Dudley fortune, while he might get little, if any, income by inheritance. His penury must have seemed a disturbing harbinger at a time when he was learning how much it cost to support himself in comfortable style.

Whether by improved finances or by fiat from his father and brother, Robert was dissuaded from marching off to war with Casimir. By October, he was doing well in his studies, having made progress in Latin and learned to speak German and Dutch.[44] Languet's friends in Germany praised Robert for "his goodness, his talents, and his industry in study." Since he was about to go to the Imperial Court, Languet recommended him to Aurelius, the French secretary there, who, because of his thorough knowledge of the court, could be of help to the young man.

Robert now determined to go to Italy. He arrived in Prague on October 31, 1580, passing through Nuremberg, Ingolstadt, Augsberg, Munich, and Regensberg. There he planned to spend part of the winter learning to ride in combat. After Christmas, he intended to go to Vienna and tour as much of Hungary as he could, including Cracow, if the Polish king went there. In spring, he informed his father, he was going to Italy and then into France. Meanwhile, he was keeping an eye out for "any good wars," as his brother had advised him, but so far had found none.[45]

Sir Henry disapproved of Robert's plan to visit Italy, reminding him of the danger Englishmen risked in touring a Catholic country. He preferred that his son not go there, nor to Spain, where the English were "under an inhibition," France, which was "in endless troubles," nor to the Low Countries, which were "in irrecoverable misery." He left the decision to Robert, however, whether he would return to England or spend the summer on the continent. If he preferred the latter, Sir Henry suggested he visit Moravia, Silesia, and Cracovia, and then tour Saxony, Holst, Pomerland, Denmark, and Sweden, after which he might embark from Hamburg to spend the winter with his father. Philip seems not to have opposed Robert's plans so completely, but we may gather from his 1578 letter of advice to Robert that he had his own reservations about touring Italy. He advised his brother that in Italy his greatest expense should be on "worthy men," not on householding. He evidently thought Robert was in more danger from his uneconomical habits than from Catholic animosity to touring Englishmen.

Instead of going to Italy that year, Robert returned briefly to England. The year 1581 was a difficult one for his continental hosts. In June, Sturm became embroiled in the university's controversy with the pastors of Strasbourg. After being condemned by the magistrates in the spring, he was deposed as rector of the academy on December 7.[46] Languet was ill, and he died in Antwerp on September 30, 1581. By then, Robert had been to England and returned to Strasbourg. Probably he spent the summer in England, which would have left little time for a tour of Italy and southern Europe. In a letter to Philip, Lobbet mentioned that "after his return from England Robert "stayed with us for a few weeks," leaving Strasbourg for Paris on September 26.[47] This suggests he had reached Strasbourg sometime late in August or early in September. Henry, Lord Cobham, who was then ambassador to France, mentioned Robert's arrival in Paris in a letter of October 10, 1581.[48] He probably remained in Europe, perhaps touring France, until Philip arrived in 1582, accompanying Alençon, now Duke of Anjou, to Antwerp.

When, in February 1582, Elizabeth managed to pack Anjou home, having postponed their proposed wedding indefinitely, she sent with him an entourage that included the Earl of Leicester, Lord Hunsdon, Lord Howard, Walter Raleigh, Fulke Greville, Edward Dyer, and Philip Sidney.[49] They were met at Flushing by the Prince of Orange, who accompanied them to Antwerp, where the courtiers spent two weeks in farewell festivities for Anjou. Doubtless, Robert met his brother, uncle, and friends either at Flushing or at Antwerp, and he probably returned to England with Philip in March 1582.[50] He certainly was in England by May 23, when Joachim Camerarius addressed a letter to him in London from Nuremburg.[51]

Little about or by Robert during the next few years has survived. He probably spent much time following Philip, who moved between the court, Wilton, Penshurst, Baynard's Castle, and Ludlow, fruitlessly seeking advancement. Proposals to send Philip to Ireland as his father's lieutenant and efforts to have him appointed to the Council for Wales failed. Robert also sued for an unnamed office in 1582,[52] but there is no indication that it was granted to him. Philip did receive a patent to share the Mastership of the Ordnance with his uncle, Ambrose Dudley, earl of Warwick, in 1583, and early that year, the same year he was knighted, he is listed among the "principal officers of the army" as General of the Horse.[53]

In 1583, Philip married Frances Walsingham, daughter of the secretary of state. For Robert, the value of this alliance with one of the most powerful men in the kingdom might be almost as great as it was expected to be for Philip. The union was also useful for Walsingham, in that it cemented his alliance to the earl of Leicester.[54] The groom probably now took up residence at Walsingham House or at Walsingham's country house, Barn Elms, for by Elizabethan custom the newlywed couple lived with the bride's parents until the husband had his own home. Although Penshurst was available, Walsingham House was in London and closer to the court, where Philip wanted to be. Robert no doubt visited Walsingham House and Barn Elms, too, and may now have been spending as much time there as at Penshurst, at Leicester's house, and in his sister's home at Wilton. During this period, one may guess that he passed his time quietly in the company of his friends and relatives, observing, learning, and making acquaintances among the English aristocrats and foreign visitors at Elizabeth's court.

At this time Robert undoubtedly conceived his interest in New World speculation. Years later, he would invest large sums in the Virginia Company and take an active part in the management of that organization. Now, he saw his brother's rising enthusiasm for the scheme to colonize America, and listened to Philip daydream about joining Sir Humphrey Gilbert's 1583 voyage to Newfoundland.[55] Gilbert, who drowned before the end of the trip, had served under Sir Henry in Ireland; his half-brother, Sir Walter Raleigh, was a friend of Philip and Edmund Spencer. Philip's brother-in-law, Christopher Carleill, was also among the group concerned in the enterprise, along with Sir Richard Grenville and Sir George Peckham. Philip's excitement about the possibilities inherent in the New World led him to obtain rights to as much as 3,000,000 acres of land there, and involved him in the adventures of Raleigh.[56] By 1585, however, his absorption with the crisis in the Low Countries took him away from his American ventures, as it developed, permanently.

On September 8, 1584, a wealthy Welshman, John Gamage, of Coity in Glamorganshire, died, leaving his estate to his young daughter.[57] After two weeks of frantic court intrigue the heiress suddenly married Robert Sidney. Since the queen was correctly expected to object, the marriage took place at the earliest possible moment, on September 23, 1584, in the Chapel of St. Donat's Castle, under the auspices of the earl of Pembroke.[58] The queen's messenger, who was sent to forbid the match, arrived too late, and Robert entered a marriage which, although hasty, matured into a long, happy union.

Soon after the marriage, Robert was elected to the House of Commons for Glamorganshire. Members as young as he, who was then twenty-one, were rare, and when they were elected, it was as the result of exceptional privilege. No doubt his marriage to the county's rich heiress had much to do with it. The local influence of Sir Henry Sidney, who was lord president of the Council in the Marches of Wales, and of his Welsh brother-in-law, the earl of Pembroke, must have helped.[59] Although Robert seems to have received little financial remuneration from the position—Pembroke promised to demand no charges from the county for his wages[60]—it was a sign of growing prestige.

Meanwhile, international events were coalescing into what seemed an apocalyptic crisis. Anjou's death, in June, 1584, caused renewed religious fighting in France, because the Huguenot Henry of Navarre now stood in line for the French crown. Catholic leaders in France swore never to be ruled by a heretic. Then, on June 30, William of Orange was assassinated. Conyers Read succinctly calls his death "a tremendous fact." The cause of the Dutch rebels was identified with Orange, and now that he was removed, Philip II and Parma seemed likely to crush the Dutch rebels. A Spanish victory would have disastrous consequences for England. Once the buffer of the Dutch rebels was gone, and it had been a thorn in Philip II's side that had distracted him from England for nearly twenty years, Elizabeth would find herself confronted with Spain triumphant, and with no alternative but to fight or to treat.

Sir Philip Sidney would have liked to see England attack Spain by sea. "To carry war into the bowels of Spain, and by the assistance of the Netherlands, burn his shipping in every haven as they passed along; and in that passage surprise some well-chosen place for wealth and strength: easie to be taken, and possible to be kept by us: he supposed to be the safest, most quick, and honorable consell of diversion. . . . [He] wisely considered, how Nature, to maintain that birth-right of [Elizabeth], had made all wars by sea far more cheap, proper, and commodious to her, than any expedition could possibly be."[61] War at sea was a new idea. The poor maneuverability of medieval and early Renaissance ships made it impractical, and until Drake led the English to sea against the Armada, the navy was used primarily for troop transport.

On June 29, 1585, a deputation from the Low Countries had audience with the queen at Greenwich, seeking aid against Philip II. They had already been refused by the French. They offered the sovereignty of the United Provinces to Elizabeth in return for her help against Spain. She declined the sovereignty, but agreed to send over an army of 5,000 foot and 1,000 horse on condition that at the end of the war the Netherlands should reimburse England for all expenses incurred in the services of the Low Countries. As security, the queen was to hold the cautionary towns of Flushing and the Brill, and the Castle of Rammekins. Leicester was expected to be the leader of the expedition and Philip was spoken of as the probable governor of Flushing.[62]

Robert joined the young noblemen hurrying to go with Leicester. One Wednesday in 1585, the young man wrote excitedly from Baynard's Castle to Sir John Norris, the colonel-general of the expedition: "My brother hath lett me know that you are well pleased to bestow a band of footmen upon me. If it please you to favore mee so much I will ever thinck my selfe greately beholding unto you and will take it for a greate good fortune that my first Aprentisage in soldiery hath bin under so worthy a Capten. . . . I shall never make you sorry. . . . The meanest soldier in your bookes shall not bee more obedient and serviccable unto you then myselfe."[63] Robert also obtained command of a troop of horse, as did Lords Essex, Willoughby, North, and Audley, Sir Thomas Shirley, and Sir Nicholas Parker.[64]

Meanwhile, Philip was about to set to sea from Plymouth after Sir Francis Drake's fleet. Only after two angry messages had been sent did the queen succeed in detaining him. Drake left for his crusade against the Spanish on September 14, leaving Sidney to return to Nonesuch to make peace with Elizabeth. Finally, on November 7, she signed a patent appointing Philip governor of Flushing and Rammekins and making Sir Thomas Cecil governor of Brill. On the sixteenth, he left Gravesend for Zealand, and on the twenty-second, he slogged ashore from the Rammekins, where he had been forced to land by ill winds, "with as dirty a walk as ever a poor governor entered his charge withal."[65]

There is some evidence that Robert crossed the channel in Leicester's train on December 10.[66] On January 6, he seems to have been billeted in the Hague; his name appears in a list of Essex's cavalry paid at the Hague on January 20, 1586. Shortly afterwards, he appears to have moved to Leiden.[67] If, as Fox Bourne states, Philip immediately placed him in charge of the Rammekins as his deputy, the position did not hinder him from traveling about the country with his band of soldiers, for it was customary for those in charge to assign their responsibilities to others and leave their places of command.

Leicester's regime in the Low Countries was marred by a series of fiascoes. His acceptance of the title of governor-general of the Low Countries, contrary to Elizabeth's orders, brought her wrath down upon him and on Philip, whom she saw as his advisor.[68] Her anger with Philip was such that she considered removing him from his office at Flushing.[69] Following the humiliation of having to surrender the Dutch title, Leicester alienated the Dutch leaders by meddling in internal Dutch politics and stirring up the Calvinist proletarian element against his rivals, the Arminian faction dominated by Olden-Barneveldt and Paul Buys. His machinations succeeded only in strengthening the opposition to him among men who controlled Dutch affairs.[70] On the battlefield, the glory he gained by successfully relieving Grave was tarnished when the Duke of Parma took Grave in May, Venloo in June, and Nuys in July. The only Anglo-Dutch achievement in early summer came with Prince Maurice's and Philip Sidney's capture of Axel. Leicester's troops were underfed, his finances confused, his officers angry. Any hope for support from the Dutch States General was slender and could only be expected to diminish.[71]

Robert appears to have suffered as much as the other English from the confusion, graft, and egotism. He and his men were no better paid than any others, and he experienced first hand, probably for the first time in his career, the effect of the government's neglect of men who, at best, lived on subsistence wages. In March, he wrote to his friend, Prince Maurice, from Berghen, entreating his attention in the matter of payment for the troops. The men were "cleane without money, eccepting the principall gentlemen, whoe to I ame sure woulde bee glad to receive some pay." The local prices were so high the soldier could not live on his pay, and the men were forced to forage from the villagers.[72]

Robert and Philip nevertheless performed admirably under these discouraging conditions. At Pigott, "Count Hollock and Robin Sidney overthrew a good cornett of horse of Camilles, beside Breda, kild and tooke 28 prisoners and horse."[73] Apparently, Count Hohenlo (called "Hollock" by the English) found it possible to fight at Robert's side despite his jealousy over the elder Sidney brother's appointment as colonel of the Zealand regiment of horse. Philip and Maurice took the town of Axel by surprise in July, and Robert very possibly was present there. They slaughtered the garrison of five to six hundred men, and by taking the city, which was on the southwest edge of the Scheldt estuary, they secured their hold on Sluys and Ostend.[74]

Count Hohenlo's vocal annoyance with the English in general and with Philip in particular continued to have repercussions into the summer. In July, Walsingham noted that the queen blamed Hohenlo's discontent over the colonelship on Philip, who she believed ambitiously sought it. "I see her majesty," he observed, "verry apt uppon every light occasion to fynde fault with him."[75] Less than a month later, Philip found himself involved in another Hohenlo quarrel, this time between the count and Edward Norris, the abrasive brother of Colonel-General John Norris. After an exchange of drunken words, Hohenlo commanded Norris to silence; when this failed, he hurled the cover of a cup into the Englishman's face.[76] Philip and the others present forcibly separated the two and ejected Hohenlo. Norris sent Philip to Hohenlo with a challenge a few days later, but before the duel could be fought, the squabblers were on the field of battle together before Zutphen.[77] There is no evidence that Robert was present at this episode, but wherever he was, he must have heard of it quickly and taken it as another demoralizing incident.

By August, Robert was with Philip before Arnhem, together with a cluster of aristocratic volunteers gathered about Sir John Norris.[78] When Leicester attacked Doesberg, a small fort on the east bank of the Yssel, the Sidney brothers and their comrade, the earl of Essex, distinguished themselves in action.[79] Ahead of them lay Zutphen. Of Philip Sidney's fall at Zutphen, so much has been written that little need be said here: how the 550 Englishmen came up against 3,500 fully equipped Spaniards; how Philip threw off his leg armor so that he might run an equal risk with his friend Sir William Pelham, who had not time to find his own, how the fifty English gentlemen fought like legendary cavaliers, how Philip's thigh was shattered by a musket ball where he should have been wearing armor.[80] A gesture that seems foolhardy to the twentieth-century mind was a heroic act in the sixteenth century, and Sidney was borne away from the scene of the battle in great honor, attended by the finest physicians, including Hohenlo's, and grieved over by the queen and the aristocracy of England. Notwithstanding, within twenty-five days he was dead of gangrene.

"The last scene of this tragedie," Philip's friend, Fulke Greville, wrote, "was the parting of the two brothers: the weaker showing infinite strength in suppressing sorrow, and the stronger infinite weakness in expressing it. So far did unvaluable worthiness, in the dying brother enforce the living to descend beneath his owne worth, and by abundance of childish tears, bewailed the publique in his particular loss . . . that Sir Philip—in whom all earthly passion did even as it were flash, like lights ready to burn out—recals those spirits together with a strong vertue, but weake voice; mildly blaming him for relaxing the frail strength left to support him; in this finale combate of separation at hand. And to stop this naturall torrent of affection in both, took his leave, in these admonishing words:

> Love my memorie, cherish my friends; their faith to me may assure you they are honest. But above all, govern your will and affections, by the wil and word of your Creator; in me beholding the end of this world, with all her vanities.[81]

Robert Sidney was knighted by Leicester for his valiant conduct at Zutphen on October 7, 1586.[82] It was small recompense for the loss of his brother.

Professor F. J. Levy suggests that Philip's education and training indicate he was being groomed to follow Walsingham's footsteps as a statesman.[83] Robert's education was very similar to Philip's. Although Languet did not personally attend the younger brother, Robert was placed in the care of eminent Protestant teachers on the continent, and the men in charge of his training clearly intended him to spend his life as a Calvinistic governor or administrator. Levy points out that Philip's career was hampered by his aggressive Protestant ideology; that while Leicester was protected from the queen's distrust by her sentimental affection for him and Walsingham by his own willingness to compromise, Philip enjoyed no such shelter. "There was," Levy observes, "a strong ideological tinge to Sidney's desire to serve his monarch." As a result, Philip and others who thought like him "were kept at court as ornaments, without any power to shape affairs." Levy recognizes this radicalism as perhaps the most telling reason Essex and his circle, including Philip, Robert, Fulke Greville, Edward Dyer, Henry Cuffe, and the Bacon brothers, failed to reach the ideological and material goals to which they aspired until after the death of Robert Cecil. In this light, it seems probable that had he lived, Philip would have encountered the same frustration that Robert did. Robert's career followed much the same path in which Philip's was already started. Both men were trained as men of action, both affiliated with Essex and the cause of militant Protestantism, both were relegated to the background as the result of Elizabeth's wariness. Philip's career and personality, both of which Robert as it were inherited, so colored the younger man's reputation that Robert was unable to free himself from it until the end of the reign. Although Robert was more careful about what he committed to paper, more wary in his dealings with those in power, less blunt than his brother, he seems not to have escaped the effects of Philip's rash letter to the queen attacking the match with Anjou nor of the Sidneys' unprofitable association with Essex until he was too old to build a career of great prominence.

NOTES

1. Bourne, pp. 173–75.
2. *HMCD* 1:259.
3. Bradley, p. 175. Languet to P. Sidney, Flushing, 27 February 1579. The *DNB* repeats Collins's error in dating Robert's departure in 1578. This incorrect chronology seems to be based on Collins' misdating of Sir Henry Sidney's letter to Robert as 25 March 1578 (Sir Henry Sidney to Robert Sidney, Baynard's Castle, 25 March 1578, Collins, 1:246–48). If, however, the letter from Robert to Sir Henry of 1 November 1580 (Collins, 1:285) is correctly dated, the father's letter must have been written after 1578. In his letter to his father, Robert announced his decision to go "next year" to Italy. Sir Henry responded with his disapproval of the proposal in the questioned letter. *HMCD* tentatively dates Sir Henry's letter in early 1581. Since there is no other reason to believe Robert visited the continent at the age of fourteen, a year before he made the passage with Languet, one may safely presume he first saw Flushing in February, 1579.
4. *HMCD* 1:258.
5. On the pervasiveness of corruption in Elizabeth's court, see John Ernest Neale, "The Elizabethan Political Scene," *Proceedings of the British Academy* (London, 1948), pp. 96–117.
6. Osborn, p. 3.
7. Stone, pp. 692–97.
8. Albert Feuillerat, ed., *The Complete Works of Sir Philip Sidney,* 4 vols. (1912; reprint ed., Cambridge, England: Cambridge University Press, 1962), 3:124–27. Feuillerat does not print a date for this letter, but Osborn (*Young Philip Sidney,* p. 117) places it in May 1578.
9. Languet to P. Sidney, 21 December 1573, Bradley, pp. 14–15.
10. Feuillerat, 3:127.
11. Languet to P. Sidney, Flushing, 27 February 1579, Bradley, pp. 175–76.
12. Osborn, p. 160.
13. Bradley, pp. 175–76.
14. Languet to P. Sidney, Antwerp, 24 September 1580, ibid., p. 200.
15. Languet to P. Sidney, Antwerp, 16 March 1579, ibid., p. 117.
16. Languet to P. Sidney, 14 October 1579, ibid., p. 83.
17. Languet to P. Sidney, Strasbourg, 4 May 1579, ibid., pp. 178–80.
18. Osborn, p. 91, citing Conrad Schusselberg, in Birch's *Bayle* 9:440n.
19. Ibid., p. 541.
20. Languet to P. Sidney, Strasbourg, 4 May 1579, Bradley, p. 180.
21. M. Wilson, p. 111.
22. See, for example, Languet to P. Sidney, 22 October 1580, Bradley, p. 206.
23. See, for example, Sir Henry Sidney to Robert Sidney, 25 March 1581, *HMCD*, 2:95.
24. Languet to P. Sidney, 6 February 1580, Bradley, p. 289.
25. Collins, 1:392.
26. Ibid., 1:283.
27. Bradley, p. 189. "Where, while they pursue words, they neglect the things themselves;" a blow at humanists who preferred form over matter.
28. See, for example, "A Valediction: Forbidding Mourning;" "Holy Sonnets: 5;" "The Sunne Rising."
29. See Sonnet 25 ("Yow that take pleasure in yowr cruelty"):

And when sunn like, yow in yowrself yow show
Lett mee the point bee, about which yow goe.

30. Osborn, p. 81.

31. Ibid., p. 81n.

32. Ibid., p. 503.

33. Ibid., p. 496.

34. Languet to P. Sidney, Antwerp, 6 February 1580, Bradley, p. 189.

35. M. Wilson, pp. 93–95.

36. Bradley, p. 189.

37. Languet to P. Sidney, Antwerp, 27 February 1580, ibid., p. 190.

38. John Leke's accounts, 30 September 1578 to 31 March 1579, HMCD 1:258.

39. Bradley, p. 190.

40. Osborn, p. 506.

41. Sir Henry Sidney to Robert Sidney, Ludlow, 28 October [1580], HMCD 2:94–95.

42. Philip Sidney to Robert Sidney, Leicester House, 18 October 1580, Collins, 1:283.

43. Sir Henry Sidney to Robert Sidney, Baynard's Castle, 1581, HMCD 2:96. The references to March 1580, must be a slip, either of Sir Henry's pen or of HMC's type. HMC's estimate that the letter was written in 1581, rather than in 1578, as Collins dates it, has much to recommend it. Robert was in Prague by November 1, 1580, and Sir Henry remarks that he approves of Robert's presence there. Robert did not leave England before February 1579, which negates Collins's date of March 1578, for the letter. We know he planned to go to Italy as early as November 1580. However, some shadow is cast on HMC's date by Sir Henry's remark that he is forwarding £100 to Robert, which he expects to last till "the last of Marche," 1580. Possibly HMC's date of 1581 is New Style (N.S.). Sir Henry reckoned the years in Old Style (O.S.) (January–March 25, 1580, = January–March 1581, N.S.). Even then, it is odd that in the same letter in which he berates his son's spendthrift habits he would promise to send the substantial sum of £100 to cover a three-month period. It is also curious in light of the fact that by the O.S. calendar, the year changed on March 25. So, from the vantage point of, say, January 1580/81, "the last of Marche" would have occurred in 1581; both by the old and the new reckonings. Perhaps by this phrase Sir Henry meant the last day of the year, March 25, 1580 (N.S.). Or possibly the letter was written late in 1580 (N.S.); Sir Henry remarks that he has received Robert's letters of 17 September and 9 November, and he probably would have responded to them before January. Even had he written as early as November 1580, though, the sum of £100 seems a large amount for a seventeen-year-old to spend in five months.

44. Languet to P. Sidney, Antwerp, 22 October 1580, Bradley, pp. 206–08.

45. Robert Sidney to Sir Henry Sidney, Prague, 1 November 1580, HMCD 2:95.

46. Osborn, p. 541.

47. Lobbet to P. Sidney, Strasbourg, 1 October 1581, ibid., pp. 541–42.

48. Great Britain, Public Record Office, Calendar of State Papers, Foreign Series, of the Reign of Elizabeth, 1558–1582, 16 vols., ed. William R. Trumbull (London: HMSO, 1863–1909), 15:336. (This series of the Calendar of State Papers, Foreign Series is hereafter abbreviated CSP For.)

49. Bourne, p. 251.

50. Ibid., p. 278.

51. Joachim Camerarius to Robert Sidney, Nuremburg, 23 May [1582], HMCD 2:99.

52. Robert Sidney to Edmund Molyneux, Greenwich, 1582, HMCD 2:99.

53. Bourne, p. 284.

54. Conyers Read, Mr. Secretary Walsingham and the Policy of Queen Elizabeth, 3 vols. (1925; reprint ed., Hamden, Connecticut: Archon Books, 1967), 3:423–25.

55. Bourne, p. 295.

56. Ibid., pp. 296–99.

57. Stone, Crisis, p. 660.

58. E. M. Tenison, Elizabethan England, 13 vols. (Royal Leamington Spa: issued for the author, 1933–50), 8:279n.

59. John E. Neale, The Elizabethan House of Commons (New Haven: Yale University Press, 1950), p. 317.

60. Ibid., p. 327.

61. Greville, p. 91.

62. Bourne, p. 312.

63. MS. St. Amand 8: fol. 69, Bodleian Library, Oxford, England.

64. Sir Clements R. Markham, *The Fighting Veres* (Boston and New York: Houghton, Mifflin, 1888), p. 84.

65. Bourne, p. 322.

66. Ibid., p. 323. Bourne states that Robert went over with Philip to Flushing and was immediately placed as Philip's deputy in charge of Rammekins Castle.

67. Jan A. van Dorsten and R. C. Strong, *Leicester's Triumph* (London: Oxford University Press, 1964), p. 129.

68. W. Davison to Leicester, London, 17 February 1585–86, in John Bruce, *Correspondence of Robert Dudley, Earl of Leicester,* Camden Society, no. 27 (London: J. B. Nichols and Son, 1844).

69. Walsingham to Leicester, Court, 28 March 1586, ibid., p. 192.

70. Read, *Walsingham* 3:158–59.

71. Ibid., 3:157ff.

72. MS Cotton Galba C:ix, British Library, London, England.

73. Leicester to Walsingham, 8 July 1586, Bruce, *Correspondence,* pp. 337–40.

74. Motley, 2:34ff.

75. Walsingham to Leicester, Barnelms, 11 July 1586, Bruce, *Correspondence,* pp. 342–45.

76. Leicester to Walsingham, Utrecht, 8 August, 1586, ibid., pp. 390–94.

77. Bourne, p. 339.

78. Motley, 2:43.

79. Bourne, p. 340.

80. See, for example, Bourne, pp. 341–46; Motley, 2:34ff.; Markham, pp. 940–96; M. Wilson, pp. 267–74; Greville, pp. 137–40.

81. Greville, pp. 139–40.

82. *DNB,* s.v. "Sidney, Robert, Earl of Leicester."

83. Levy, p. 17.

[3]

The Sidney Heir
Courtier, Soldier, Diplomat

The year 1586 brought much grief to Robert Sidney. Six months before his brother's death, he lost his father, and in August, his mother died.[1] Watching his brother die in agony must have given Robert more than enough cause for the "childish tears" Greville derides in his biography of Philip.

Robert's private losses were England's public losses. With the death of Sir Henry Sidney at the age of 56, no youth for a man of the time but still potentially useful, England lost an influential and uncharacteristically temperate provincial governor. Philip's death extinguished one of the brightest hopes of the English radical Protestants. At the same time, Leicester was mired in Dutch politics, making little progress at home with the queen while his meddling in Dutch internal affairs actively bred hostility to the English in the Low Countries. The progress of events in 1586, public as well as personal, must have appeared profoundly negative to Robert Sidney.

His new position as heir to the Sidney estate was a dubious blessing. Although he inherited large tracts of land from his father and brother, he also inherited their debts and the obligation to pay for their burials. Philip's funeral, delayed until February, 1587, while Robert and Sir Francis Walsingham struggled to satisfy the dead man's creditors,[2] was elaborate and expensive. Sir Henry's less extravagant funeral had already run to £1,541.[3] The costs involved in Philip's assuming office as governor of Flushing, including the payment due the gentlemen and yeomen in his train, remained to be paid by Robert. But, a year later, the Dutch had still not paid to the estate allowances they owed Sir Philip as colonel of the Zealand Regiment.[4] The charges mounted, while the available capital proved much smaller than the deceased man had apparently thought possible.

Philip provided in his will[5] that Robert and Walsingham pay his own and his father's debts by selling as much of the Sidney lands in Lincolnshire, Sussex, or Southampton as needed, and then bequeathed a complicated distribution of the remainder of the estate to his survivors. His widow, Lady Frances, was to receive half of his manors, lands, tenements, rents, rights, and reversions, with all the commodities appertaining to them, during her lifetime only. Thomas Sidney and his male heirs received as much land as was worth £100 a year, to be assigned by Robert or by the earl of Huntingdon, provided it not come out of the manor of Penshurst. If Lady Frances Sidney's unborn child was a girl, Sir Robert was to have all the remaining Sidney lands, plus, in the absence of any male heir of Thomas, the remainder of the lands bequeathed to Thomas after his death. This proviso was modified by the condition that Robert pay Philip's daughter, Elizabeth, £4,000 on or before Michaelmas, September 29, 1588, and, if the unborn child was female, that he divide an additional £1,000 between the two girls, to be paid by the same date. If the child was male and survived, Elizabeth was to have "two Partes of all my lands before bequeathed to my brother Robert Sidney" until she or her guardians received her portion of £4,000, and the male child would receive the rest of Philip's property by inheritance. As it turned out, the child was stillborn,[6] and so Robert shared half of the Sidney lands with Frances until her death.

Robert fell heir to the responsibility of paying off debts that Walsingham estimated at over £6,000[7] and dispensing the liberal gifts Philip specified in the will (See table 1). To their uncles, Leicester and Warwick, he was to give £100 apiece. For a servant named Stephen, who was imprisoned at Dunkirk, Robert was to provide £200 either as a ransom or, that failing, as a gift after his release, and he was to make every effort to have him freed. Five hundred pounds were to be paid to Philip's servant, John Uvedale, and £100 to Walsingham. Annuities worth over £200 yearly were set up for several of Philip's followers and servants. His finest jewel was to go to their sister, Mary; other jewels were left to Lady Huntingdon, Lady Warwick, Lady Leiceser, Lady Walsingham, the queen, and Sir Thomas Heneage. Philip's best sword went to Essex, and gifts of hangings and plate to Leicester.

Perhaps it is significant that Philip left his books not to Robert but to his friends, Dyer and Greville. Possibly he felt Robert was not enough the intellectual to appreciate them. However, even if Robert did not have the capacity to understand and treasure them, Mary, Lady Pembroke did. Probably this choice did not reflect Philip's opinion of his brother's intellectual vigor, but came from a generous impulse toward two of his closest friends and fellow poets.

Any remaining goods were to go to Lady Frances, who was to be the sole executrix of Philip's will. Writing thirty-five years later, Robert's accountant, Thomas Nevitt, stated that these goods, which included all the movables at Penshurst, were removed by Sir Francis in the widow's behalf, and that they were worth a total of £20,000.[8]

Much has been made of Walsingham's part in the payment of Philip Sidney's debts. Observing that Walsingham seems to have been made responsible in some way that is not clear for Philip's debts, Professor Read speculates that the consequences of Sidney's death aggravated the falling-out that had already begun between Walsingham and Leicester.[9] The secretary appealed to Leicester for assistance in the matter, claiming to have put out over £6,000, and he was refused. Walsingham said that Sidney's goods and lands would not suffice to cover his debts, and that the burial could not

TABLE 1

MONEY AND GIFTS DISPENSED BY PHILIP SIDNEY IN HIS WILL,
TO BE ASSIGNED BY ROBERT SIDNEY OUT OF HIS INHERITANCE

Source: Collins I:109–13

£ 6,000 ca.	Debts owed miscellaneous creditors (Walsingham's estimate)
4,000	Elizabeth Sidney
[1,000	Daughter unborn]
£10,000 – 11,000	
£ 100	Leicester
100	Warwick
200	Stephen, imprisoned at Dunkirk
20	Tristram Gibbs, a servant
10x	Gentlemen Servants in Ordinary arriving with P. Sidney in November (x)
5y	All other Gentlemen Servants (y)
5z	Yeomen arriving with P. Sidney in November (z)
3a	All other yeomen (a)
100	Francis Walsingham
500	John Uvedale
20	Ring for William Hungate
20	Jewel for Thomas Heneage
100	Jewel for the Queen
20	Mr. Marten, a surgeon
20	Ivert, the bonesetter
6 13s. 4d.	Roger, the apothecary
100	5 surgeons
10	Goodridge, a surgeon
10	Kelley, a surgeon
10	John, a surgeon
20	Another unnamed surgeon
20	Mr. Gifford, a minister
20	Mr. Fountain, a minister
£ 1,406 13s. 4d. + (10x + 5y + 5z + 3a)	

Annuities

£ 40/year	Henry Whyte
40	Henry Lyndley
40	Griffith Maddox
30	Philip Jordan and his wife
20 Mks (£13 10s.)	Adrian Molqueros
10	Richard Harte
30	[William] Temple
£ 203/year, approx.	
£11,609 – 12,609 +	*Total Cash Disbursements*

Gifts of Goods

Jewel	Mary Pembroke
Jewel	Lady Huntingdon
Jewel	Lady Walsingham
Jewel	Lady Leicester
Gilt Armor	William Russell
Books	Dyer and Greville
1 buck/year from Penshurst	Edward Wotton
Diamond Ring	Lady Huntingdon
Diamond Ring	Lady Pembroke
Diamond Ring	Lady Sussex
Jewels or choice of other goods worth £100	Lady Francis Walsingham
Ring worth £20	William Hungate
Jewel worth £100	Queen
Jewel worth £20	Thomas Heneage
Hangings, Plate	Leicester
Best Sword	Essex
One other Sword	Willoughby
Ring	Digby
Ring	Goodere
Land worth £100/year	Thomas Sidney

be performed "with the solemnity that appertaineth without the utter un-doing of his creditors."[10] Most scholars believe Walsingham assumed the entire debt.[11]

If Nevitt's retrospective accounts are correct—and in other matters concerning the will, such as the annuities, the widow's thirds, and Elizabeth's portion, they are substantially accurate—it may not be al-together true that Walsingham paid off Sidney's creditors out of his own pocket. Despite his protestations of hardship, Walsingham undoubtedly did remove several thousands of pounds worth of movables from Penshurst. Nevitt lists among his master's losses at Philip's death £500 a year in Lincolnshire sold by Sir Henry's executors, Walsingham and Lady Frances, to pay for Sir Henry's and Sir Philip's funerals and to pay their debts.[12] Legal complications surrounding these transactions later led to a long-drawn-out lawsuit between Robert and Lady Frances. Nowhere does Nevitt allude to Walsingham as a source of relief for Robert's indebtedness; his sole reference to the secretary of state involves the removal of the £20,000 worth of goods from Penshurst. If Walsingham and his daughter could have received even a fraction of this amount by selling these furnish-ings, they could have paid off the debt without extreme difficulty. Walsing-ham's plea to Leicester was in the nature of a dunning letter; there is no way to be certain how much he was exaggerating both the size of the debt and the degree of his own hardship. Read discounts at least one rumor, Dr. William Gifford's 1587 claim that Philip died indebted to the Flushingers for £17,000, as "ill-informed."[13] It cannot be said with certainty, then, that Robert abdicated his debts to Walsingham, who mysteriously consented to accept any such burden.

TABLE 2
ROBERT SIDNEY'S YEARLY INCOME, 1586,
FROM INHERITED LANDS AND OTHER SOURCES

Source: Nevitt; Philip Sidney's Will

Penshurst	£ 400
Lamberhurst	20
Mathersum	20
Salehurst	20
Brighting	10
Woodruff	250
Michelmarsh	70
Lands in Lincolnshire	200
Lands in Sussex leased by Mr. Pedway	20
Lands on Sussex Downs	80
	£1,090

Less

Widow's thirds to La. Walsingham	£ 274, approx.
Annuities specified in PS Will	203, approx.
	£ 613/year, approx.

Plus

Captain's Salary	145, approx.
Stewardship of Otford, etc.	7, approx.
Income from La. Sidney's Lands	600 (as of 1603)
	£1,365

Sir Henry Sidney estimated that his assets had dwindled by £30,000 by the end of his career, and complained that the queen never rewarded him sufficently for his services and expenses in Ireland and Wales.[14] Whether or not this was exaggerated, he appears to have retained a substantial estate. Despite the sale of the most lucrative tract of land his father had left him, Robert kept lands that brought in a total of £1,090 a year. After the widow's thirds and the annuities specified in Philip's will were deducted, he was left with £613 a year from his owns lands, plus about £600 annually from his wife's property (see table 2).[15]

However, Sidney did suffer a chronic shortage of ready cash throughout the remaining years of Elizabeth's reign. Rowland Whyte and Roger Seys, Sidney's lawyer, agonized repeatedly over their master's low funds; Sidney in turn complained to Barbara, and she complained to him that she did not have enough money to run their households at Penshurst and in London.

How can this be reconciled with the evidence that, despite the loss of the Lincolnshire lands, Sidney was left in 1586 with an income of approximately £1,200 a year from rents alone, excluding his captain's salary and income from other posts?

The explanation lies as much in Sidney's personal ambition as in the economic facts of late sixteenth-century England. At a time when inflation was steadily eroding the pound,[16] Robert was inclined not to save money and live frugally, but to spend liberally in pursuit of a stateman's career that, in view of his training and background, he had good reason to expect to be successful. The quest for advancement at court was a long, costly venture. Proper clothing had to be tailored for appearances in exalted circles. Nevitt estimates Lady Barbara's yearly expenditures on apparel averaged £300. Rowland Whyte, Sidney's agent at court and on the continent, had to be supported and paid for his efforts. Sidney's embassies to Scotland and France, accepted in hopes that his performance would win the queen's approval, were very costly and were paid for out of Sidney's pocket. Gifts had to be purchased for important friends—Sidney frequently forwarded tapestries, gourmet specialties, hounds, fruit, and tobacco from the Low Countries to figures such as Cecil, Herbert, and James VI.[17] Someone, usually Lady Sidney, had to reside in London to be close to the political scene while Sidney was overseas: this entailed the maintenance of two households, one in the city and one at Penshurst.

The cost of maintaining Penshurst alone is suggested by Nevitt's notation of the yearly payment for servants' wages, including the keeper of the park, the housekeeper, and the gardener, plus two liveries for two gentlemen: £180. The burden of supporting even a middling gentleman's family, household, taxation, estate management, gifts, and extraordinary expenses was breathtaking. The example of William Lord Cobham is instructive, for the Cobhams and the Sidneys were arch-rivals during the 1590s. As the two leading families of Kent, competing for local ascendency through the Parliament and the court, they probably had comparable life styles and expenditures. From 1591 to 1596, Cobham's household consumed £910 worth of food a year, of which £450, less than half, consisted of provisions in kind.[18] Between 1595 and 1596, Cobham expended a total of £4,229 on personal, household, and estate management.[19] If Sidney aspired to run in this company, his income of £1,200 would scarcely suffice.

So, he went into debt and threw himself into the competition for the lucrative positions at court.[20] His earliest patrons were his uncle, Leicester, and his sister-in-law's father, Walsingham. The latter seems to have aided him in his 1588 suit for a license to process a wide variety of skins and pelts into leather. In his written request, he emphasized the large sums he had lost at his brother's death, and asked the queen to grant him a twenty-one-year license to work the hides of sheep, lambs, goats, kids, bulls, horses, calves, and deer into leather pelts, and to export 300,000 of them, in exchange for an annual rent of £20.[21] Walsingham seems to have been cooperative in this suit, which began in May, 1588. "I do not dout but hee will bee my friend," he wrote to Lady Sidney.[22] The suit was successful, within limits; he was permitted to work all the specified skins into leather except calfskin, which was Stapleware; the government wished to maintain an ample supply for export should a peace with Spain be concluded.[23] Stapleware included goods monopolized by royal authority; in England, wool, sheepskins, leather, lead, and tin.

The secretary may also have had something to do with Sidney's acqui-

TABLE 3

COMPOSITION OF COMPANIES

Sources: Markham and Cruikshank

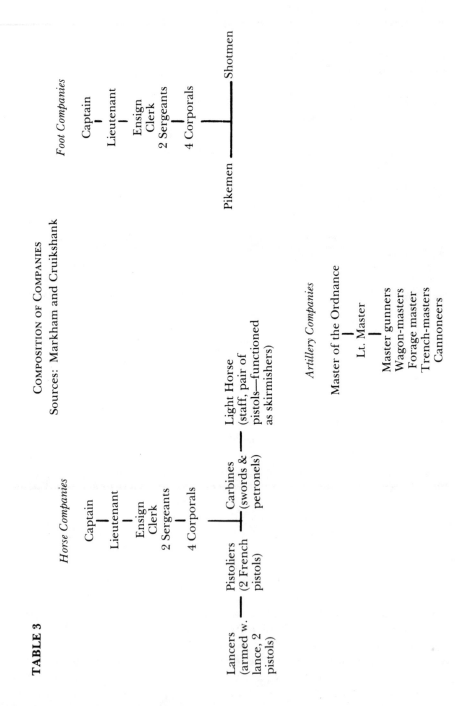

sition, a year earlier, of the stewardship of the honor of Otford and of the manors of Gravesend, Milton, and Swanscombe, with the keepership of Otford Park,[24] for which Sir Henry had applied unsuccessfully in 1573.[25] Although Robert makes no specific reference to Walsingham in connection with these stewardships, he was at court in 1587, when he wrote to his wife that Walsingham had been told Sidney had complained of him to the queen, and so he was staying at Richmond until he could persuade her to satisfy him that no such thing had happened.[26] He needed Walsingham's good will for support in projects such as the stewardships.

Exactly how much income these acquisitions added to his fortune is not clear. Probably the license in skins brought a fair return. The steward-ships had some value in terms of prestige and influence, but they were hardly lucrative. As keeper of the house at Otford, Sidney received 2d daily; of the gardens, 4d daily, and of the great park, £6 13s 4d a year.[27] If these figures are an indication of the fees associated with Gravesend, Mil-ton, and Swanscombe, the sum could not have been great.

Meanwhile, Sidney had been granted his own company of footmen at Flushing.[28] This charge augmented his income by about 8s. a day,[29] or approximately £145 a year, when he was paid, which was irregularly. As a captain, Sidney had command of and responsibility for a lieutenant, an ensign, a company clerk, two sergeants, four corporals, and about 150 foot soldiers. He was expected to see them adequately clothed, fed, and mus-tered for pay at the assigned intervals,[30] duties that he probably delegated to his lieutenant most of the time. The pay was minimal, but much lucre remained to be skimmed off by unscrupulous captains, who were in a position to profit by corrupt practices in the distribution of clothing, arms, pay, and victuals.

Although profiteering through abuse of the system was so common-place as to be routine,[31] we have no direct evidence that Sidney did nor that he did not rake in his own share of the illicit gains while he was in the Low Countries. His orders as governor of Flushing suggest the queen thought him trustworthy, for she commanded him to clean up the corruption there.

On the other hand, his close associates were less than pure; his uncles, Leicester and Warwick, amassed huge profits through the manipulation of their offices. Sidney seems to have been a good friend of Sir Thomas Shirley, and Rowland Whyte's sympathy for him is overt in his letters throughout the scandal that led to the treasurer-at-war's fall.[32] In balance, it is scarcely probable that Sidney alone among the English officers was im-mune to temptation. His official pay as a young captain likely represented only a fraction of the actual income from his military position, although we have no way of estimating the size of that fraction.

Sidney performed well and sometimes gallantly as a captain in the Low Countries. The task was not easy. The hardships the English troops faced are made clear enough in Sidney's March 1586 appeal to Leicester men-tioned above when his men had been mustered by the States General's commissioners, who had given no hint as to how, when, or even if the troops would be paid. They were without money, except for the principal gentlemen and all the garrisons in Brabant were foraging from the villagers.[33] Nevertheless, Sidney managed to persuade his underpaid and hungry men to follow him into battle and to fight admirably, even as hundreds around them were deserting. At Pigott, they joined Hohenlo and overthrew a cornet of horse, taking twenty-eight prisoners, and Sidney earned Maurice's congratulations and a knighthood at Zutphen.

Only one shadow fell over Sidney's reputation in these early years, part of the penumbra of suspicion cast over the English by Stanley and York's betrayal of Deventer and Aristotle Patton's treason against Gelder. A cornet in Sidney's service had been seen at Zutphen in conference with Tassis, and a rumor circulated that Sidney was about to sell out to Parma, as the others had done. Sidney was innocent, of course, although the cornet seems to have been corrupt; but the mere thought that a Sidney could betray the cause sufficed to produce a *frisson* of sensation.[34]

Leicester was Robert's special patron in things military during the two years following Philip's death. Leicester's and Walsingham's party, identified with the radical Protestant cause that advocated war with Spain on the side of the Dutch rebels, had been strongly opposed by the conservative faction, whose most prominent exponent was Burghley. Leicester and Burghley were often at loggerheads on questions of policy. Leicester and his followers believed English interests were so closely intertwined with those of Protestantism at large that Elizabeth's domestic and foreign policies should be shaped in reference to it. Burghley recognized that the religious factor was only one of many to be considered. "Burghley's partisans," Read observes, "were disposed to subordinate religious considerations to national ones; Leicester's national considerations to religious ones."[35]

Burghley and the conservatives had probably opposed Leicester's expedition to the Netherlands, and they certainly had opposed the appointment of Sir Philip Sidney as governor of Flushing, "presumably upon the grounds that if Leicester commanded, and Sidney, his nephew and Walsingham's son-in-law, held the most important Cautionary Town, the enterprise would be altogether too completely in the hands of the war faction.[36] Leicester chafed in frustration at the delays promulgated by the conservatives, while Burghley suspected Leicester was meddling in schemes to discredit him, involving the coinage of the English rose noble and double noble in the Low Countries. By 1586, events were going badly for Leicester. Having lost ground that summer to Parma at Grave, Venloo, and Nuys, his underfed and underpaid forces were shut up in garrison towns and on the verge of mutiny. His finances were in chaos, and the queen declined to advance him any more cash than she had estimated necessary for a strictly defensive war. His only hope for support, the States General of the United Provinces, gave him little encouragement.[37]

Leicester's machinations in the Low Countries following his massive blunder in accepting the governorship the Dutch had offered him earned him the animosity of the most responsible of the Dutch leaders. Recognizing that this aristocratic, theologically Arminian merchant class was naturally opposed by the predestinarian, democratic populace of the large cities, Leicester unsuccessfully attempted to pit popular leaders, including Reingould, Deventer, and Burchgrave, against his rivals in the States General. His meddling served only to intensify the opposition to him among the men who really controlled Dutch politics.[38]

Notwithstanding the earl's shortcomings as an administrator, Robert Sidney was ardent in his support of his uncle. Late in 1587, Sidney was in the Low Countries, corresponding with Leicester from Flushing. That year, Count Hohenlo, who frequently quarreled with Leicester, incensed the earl by publishing an attack on him.[39] Sidney seems to have entered the fray. He wrote to his uncle explaining the count had sent him word that he had heard Sidney was angry over the book, but that he would satisfy him if the young Englishman would come to him. The meeting took place, and Sidney's response was cool. Speculating that Hohenlo feared any answer Leicester might publish, he reported that the count had said he would gladly answer any points the earl would set down; that he had published the defense only to clear himself and not to touch Leicester's honor. However, Hohenlo insisted that if Leicester chose to print anything against him, he would be forced to produce his proofs and attestations of everything he put in his own book. Sidney responded that he was not privy to Leicester's plans, but that he thought if his uncle were too closely touched—and he understood he was—he probably would defend himself. It was too late now, he observed, for Hohenlo to ask Leicester's opinion of the book, but if he had allowed the earl to see it before its publication, as he had promised, he surely would have expressed his feelings in private. Sidney told his uncle that Hohenlo was "full of frivolous and childish excuses" and was worried about Leicester's response. To Hohenlo, he remarked that their relationship could no longer be as cordial as it had been. Sidney's loyalty to Leicester was such that he could not continue his friendship with the count under the circumstances. Indeed, he feared Leicester would be offended at the meeting he was describing, and he assured him, "I onely did it to see what I could learn out of him for your service and my fashion towards him could not promis him but little kindnes of my syde."[40]

Sidney's alliance with Leicester's party shows where his religious and political sympathies lay. The Leicester faction was taken with an aggressive brand of Calvinism, and that, combined with what we know of his upbringing, suggests that at the age of twenty-three, Robert's religious leaning was toward radical Calvinistic Protestantism. Religion and politics blended in the sixteenth century, and activists such as Sidney drew little or no distinction between the two. Throughout his life, he favored the hard line against Catholic recusants and other dissenters in England, for he saw them all as possible agents of Spain, each one potentially capable of acts that would betray England to Philip II and lead to the deaths of Elizabeth and most of her followers—himself included. In international affairs, he favored war with Philip before Spain got a chance to attack England, either directly or through Scotland or Ireland. He hoped Elizabeth would support the Huguenots in France and the Dutch rebels in the Low Countries, both to keep Spain as far from British shores as possible and in the hope that a Protestant combine could crush the Catholic powers and end the threat to "the religion" permanently. Elizabeth's tendency to hearken to the *politique* counsel of Burghley and her apparent reluctance to spare money and military materiel to her ostensible allies on the continent must have annoyed Sidney as much as it did his uncle.

Sidney seems to have maintained a dual allegiance with both Leicester and Walsingham. Although the two elder men shared a commitment to the radical Protestant cause, Read asserts that "they were at best never more than political allies and even that connexion appears to have been strained after Sir Philip Sidney's death."[41]

Sidney evidently had an unusually conciliatory nature and a gift for calming mutual suspicions between rivals. That he was personally charming from an early age is apparent in Dorsett's and Languet's remarks, and in the fact that he won over the hardened old warrior La Noue so completely during his grand tour. Hohenlo may have turned to Sidney in 1587 in an effort to repair the offense that he as well as the English felt he had committed against Leicester, and if this was his motive for requesting the meeting with Sidney, he must have believed the young Englishman had the charm and ability to conciliate the earl. If, as his letter to Leicester suggests, Sidney had managed to build a cordial relationship with the irascible Hohenlo at a time when his uncle was feuding with Dutch leaders of the count's faction, his tact must have been extraordinary. In later years, this characteristic manifested itself in his ability to maintain dual allegiance with two other antagonists, Essex and Burghley, and in the role he played in ending Essex's uprising.

Sidney's alliance with Leicester proved useful in his early career. Even in the midst of the squabble over Hohenlo's book, Leicester appears to have been politicking to install Sir Robert as governor of Flushing.[42] Lord Willoughby had succeeded Sir Philip in the post, and he was followed by Sir William Russell, who now wished to retire. Sidney wrote to Leicester that he did desire the position, and referred him to his services in the Low Countries as reasons why he should have the position, reminding him that he had performed well at Zutphen and elsewhere.[43]

These negotiations were interrupted by the events of 1588. When the Armada materialized off English shores, Sidney joined the courtiers and soldiers who had clustered around the queen at Tilbury. He left Barbara at Wilton with his sister, prepared to take flight. With a confidence he may not have felt, he reassured them in his letters. "For ought I can see my Lady of Pembroke neede not stir for any feare of the enemy," he wrote in August, "for I thinck hee will doe us no great harme this yeare." He still planned to bring Barbara to London that winter, he added, and he would have already sent her some money for that purpose, except that the sudden activity had spent all he had.[44] The next day, he was planning his wife's escape from the Spaniard. "If the enemy come not I will send for you, and if he doe I will send you money to provide for your going into Wales. . . ." Not wanting to frighten her unduly, he assured her that she "neede not dout that you will be taken on the sudden, for the ennimies will not bee heer so soone but that I shall have leasure to take order for you. . . ."[45]

Leisure was the last thing Sidney was granted when the crisis came, for Elizabeth dispatched him to Scotland with instructions to bring James VI over to England's side and keep him there. The Scottish situation remained ambiguous in the early part of 1588, with James appearing to vacillate between England and her enemies in Spain and France. Huntly and his followers were proven to be plotting with Parma to reestablish Roman Catholicism in Scotland and England, but James did little to discourage their intrigues. Although James may have been altogether in control, playing Catholic against Protestant to gain supremacy over the turbulent Scottish nobility, the English could not be sure of his strength or his private inclinations, and the court politics with which Sidney had to deal were mercurial.

Among the nobility, the pro-Spanish Catholic party, headed by Huntly, formed a powerful element whose strength was augmented by Elizabeth's impecuniousness. James needed money and coveted an English title, and it is probable that his tergiversations were designed to frighten Elizabeth into a concession. Elizabeth's strongest card in the game was the English throne: although the succession was James's by inheritance, there was no doubt that if Elizabeth preferred some other candidate, her Parliament would have established a new rule of succession. However, if James allied himself with Spain and Catholic France, he might have been able to conquer England and dethrone Elizabeth. Also a factor to be considered was the effect of James's claim to the succession upon Elizabeth's councillors and courtiers; none who expected to outlive his aging mistress would commit any act that would antagonize the future king.

Sidney was not sent to Scotland until the eleventh hour. He arrived in Berwick on August 24, and wrote to Walsingham of his safe arrival at Edinburgh on the thirtieth. He apparently was sent on rather short notice, although rumors that he would be the ambassador preceded him by over a month.[46] He wrote to Barbara that he was sent in such haste that he could not visit her before he left, but he hoped his embassy would be brief and he would be home within three weeks.[47] From Edinburgh, still unhappy that he had missed seeing her before his sudden departure, he wrote to her that he had arranged for her to receive whatever money she needed before he left.[48]

Meanwhile, William Asheby, who had earlier procured £3,000 for James from Elizabeth,[49] had been sent to the Scottish court early in July at the urging of Walsingham, who insisted that the enemy could harass the English more by employing 2,000 men and a small amount of cash in Scotland than by landing 30,000 men anywhere in the realm.[50] Asheby's instructions were unclear, but evidently he was to ply the king with fair words and promises. Possibly Walsingham advised him privately that if it seemed necessary, he had better not hesitate to exceed his instructions. When James did not appear satisfied with the promises proferred in their meeting of July 24, Asheby in desperation offered him an English duchy with the accompanying revenues, a pension of £5,000, a royal guard of fifty gentlemen to be maintained at the queen's expense, and a force of one hundred foot and one hundred horse to be maintained at the border. Accordingly, on August 5, James proclaimed his enmity to the Spanish and ordered up his forces to repel the invasion.[51]

Sidney's step-by-step instructions made it clear that, once the threat was past, Elizabeth had no intention of burdening herself with these costly arrangements.[52] First, he was to express the queen's great appreciation to James for his assurance to Asheby of Scotland's friendship and alliance with England, and he must thank him for his assurance of cooperation with Elizabeth in defense of Protestantism in both realms. Next, Sidney was to bring up the recent news that the Spanish fleet, having been forced from English, French, and Flemish coasts, had been seen around the northern islands off the coast of Scotland. He was to assure him that Elizabeth was sending him £3,000 sterling in gold for his defense against the threats of foreign invasion and internal dissension, and that she had directed the earl of Huntingdon, her lieutenant-general of the North, to assist James with both horse and foot, should Spain descend upon his realm.

Those messages delivered, Sidney was to remind James that abundant evidence demonstrated the Spanish king's intention to take over the whole of the British Isles. To better accomplish the conquest of Scotland, there was a plan afoot to render the tolerant king of Navarre ineligible to claim any right to the crown of Scotland or of England by excommunicating him. English intelligence had discovered that the Bishop of Dumblane and the Spanish ambassador, Mendoza, were soliciting the excommunication scheme with the Pope's nuncio in Paris. Furthermore, Elizabeth had been informed that Dumblane had asked Parma to send some of his forces to Scotland to assist the northern parts of the realm, where the Spanish faction expected they would be well received. To this remark, Burghley added the marginal note, "I dowt of this."

Sidney was also to let the king know that Elizabeth had reports that the Spanish ambassador in Paris had openly said James had "beguiled his master's expectation," but that Philip was not deluded; that he expected James to pretend a change of religion to gain his liberty, and that the Spanish king would take his revenge within a few months. Both Mendoza and the papal nuncio were publicly saying that Spain was confident of a large following in Scotland, and had named both the earl of Huntly and Lord Claud Hamilton as Spanish supporters. Under these circumstances— loath as Elizabeth would ordinarily be to interfere in another prince's affairs of state—Sidney was to relay to James the queen's recommendation that he take immediate action against the Spanish faction. Finally, Sidney should express to James Elizabeth's appreciation of the pro-English chancellor's efforts in maintaining the friendship between the two heads of state, and he should let John Lord Carmichael know that Elizabeth would not be ungrateful to him for his aid. With these instructions in hand, Sidney left for Scotland around August 20.

Professor Read thinks it significant that Sidney, rather than Lord Hunsdon's son, Sir Robert Carey, was sent to Scotland.[53] Most of the English courtiers, sure that James would succeed Elizabeth, were angling for his attention. As early as 1584, Hunsdon and Leicester were privately bidding for James's favor. For a number of reasons, Sidney was bound to please the Scottish king. "There could not have bene a gentleman sent hither," Asheby remarked, "more acceptable to the king, especially for the affection he bare to Sir Philip,"[54] upon whose death James had been moved to the point of writing an elegy.

While Sidney was en route, Walsingham shot off a letter of rebuke to Asheby, accusing him of making unwarranted offers to James. "You shall understand that I am sorry that you cannot so prevail as to have the said offers suppressed, seeing the standing upon them may work your undoing, without any profit to the King. . . . [The Queen] shall be made acquainted with the matter . . . and . . . I am very well assured that Robert Sidney—when her majesty shall be made acquainted with that strange and inconsiderate manner of dealing by the making of the said offers—shall receive sure direction to disavow that doing, and then there will be no way to justify her majesty but to try . . . you for transgression of your commission."[55] Before he received this letter, Asheby wrote to Walsingham that Sidney was expected shortly, "the only restoritive for the consumpcion that raigneth in these parts."[56]

Aware of the predicament into which he was riding, Sidney arrived at Berwick on the twenty-fourth and received his safe-conduct on the morning of the twenty-seventh.[57] Sidney reported to Walsingham that he would proceed to Edinburgh the next morning, where he understood "I shall find matters in some tickle terms," for the previous Friday, the earls of Huntley and Grayford and Colonel Steward had laid a plot to kill the chancellor, Sir John Maitland of Thirlstane. Steward was to do the deed as Maitland went in the night from the king's chamber to his own, but the scheme was thwarted when a gentleman warned the chancellor, who sent for Carmichael and an armed guard, and he reported the alarm to the king. Sidney had also heard there was much expectation at the Scottish court about what he brought with him, "and much assurance to those addicted to the Queen and the religion." No doubt moved by the specter of Asheby's disgrace, he asked that if the Spanish attack caused the queen to wish to extend her favors, he might have his instructions enlarged. He then made a request which reveals that, whether or not the queen had been informed of Asheby's offers, he was aware of them and knew his mission involved their retraction: "I desire greatly to have the contents of the letter Mr. Asheton [i.e., Asheby] carried, for I must make it the principal cause of the sending of me." He heard, too, that Lord Claud Hamilton had professed Protestantism, and decided that if he found this was so, he would have nothing to say against him.[58]

When Sidney arrived in Haddington on the evening of August 28, he found Asheby awaiting him with the news that James expected the £3,000 directly. Asheby had told the king Sidney was bringing it with him. Carmichael had already entreated Asheby for the money, for James could not pay the 300 soldiers he had mustered for his guard in expectation of receiving the money. Sidney thought the king needed cash desperately, for neither he nor his chancellor were safe without the guard. Placed in a difficult position—for of course he did not have the £3,000 with him—he decided the best course was to pretend no knowledge of the matter, unless he received word to the contrary from England. He hoped the queen had not specifically mentioned it in her letter.[59]

Two days later, he arrived in Edinburgh. Arthur Throgmorton, who was in Sidney's train, wrote to his benefactor, Walsingham, that "my lord ambassadour here maketh good chere and payeth deer."[60] Indeed Sidney probably was paying dear for the expedition. An Elizabethan ambassador supported himself and his elegant train out of his own pocket, with little or no reimbursement from the Crown. Nevitt remarked on the cost of Sidney's embassy to Scotland, at which time his servants' clothes were "lyned with hare cullered [i.e., brown or grey] velvett and trymed with hare culler and gould lace, which iorney," the accountant concluded, "was very chargeable unto you."[61] Undoubtedly at a loss for funds to sustain the show, Sidney requested Walsingham to procure his return after his instructions were delivered in almost every letter he sent home.

As soon as he arrived, Sidney forwarded to Walsingham a detailed report of his reception in Edinburgh. He was met on August 30 by Sir James Hume, Sir Robert Melvin, Carmichael, and many of the gentlemen of the court, and he was told he would have audience with the king the following Sunday. Sidney did not press for an audience sooner because he was hoping to receive further word from Walsingham regarding the £3,000, which the king "already thinks he has received," and for which he had already ordered Asheby to thank the queen. The king and his council assumed that Sidney had brought not only the money but also the queen's answer to James's other demands. "I will take knowledge of nothing and promise nothing," Sidney planned. "They shall not have through my speeches occasion to hope less than they have hitherto."

Sidney found the Scottish ministers "greatly perplexed," and one of them told him they feared some great trouble in the church, for "outrages" were freely committed, "the Papists so apparently manifest themselves." Although Huntly refused to subscribe to the Protestant religion, the king had effected a reconciliation between him and the chancellor. The reconciliation between the chancellor and Bothwell was thought to be genuine, and Bothwell was believed now to be well-disposed to James; Sidney thought "he may easily be won and only looks to be asked." Sidney had heard that the men Bothwell had mustered for the conquest of Lewis were not being paid in Spanish coin, and that Bothwell himself was not going on that expedition. "I think if he could be won it would not be amiss," he observed, "for the King favors him, he is valiant and much followed."[62]

Asheby also reported to Walsingham on the day of Sidney's arrival, saying he had received letters of the thirteenth and fourteenth from the secretary mentioning Elizabeth's offer of £3,000 to James. Avoiding mention of the fact that he had told James Sidney would arrive with the money in hand, he said he had followed Walsingham's orders to assure the king that Elizabeth would assist him with the means at her disposal against the Spanish attempts. James was "marvelously content" at the appointment of Sidney as ambassador, "for the affection he bears his name, and that he imagined that this favor proceeded from the Earl of Leicester and from [Walsingham], where of you may be sure he will not be ungrateful." He mentioned, too, that James had levied his guard upon the promise of the £3,000, and that if it had to be disbanded, the king would be in great danger.[63]

Sidney's audience with James fell on August 31, and the next day he wrote to Walsingham indicating that the king assured him he was an open enemy of Spain and had commanded that all assistance be given to the queen's fleet, and none to the enemy. Sidney told him that if the Spanish landed in Scotland, the queen would come to his aid with as much care for his state as for her own. He emphasized that the queen hoped he would keep in mind the news of Philip's designs against the Scottish and English thrones, reports of which had been confirmed by prisoners. James knew of the excommunication maneuver but had thought it directed toward the English throne. He expressed his scorn for Mendoza's remarks about him, and said that "the Kinge of Spains favors toward him would [have] bin like Poliphemusis to Ulisses, that he showld [be] the last man hee would eate."[64]

After Sidney left the king, he went to the chancellor and delivered the queen's letter to him. The chancellor pushed the matter of the promises made by Asheby of the £5,000 pension, the Duchy and its revenues, the personal guard, and the border guard. Lying diplomatically, Sidney claimed he had never heard of these offers until Asheby told him at Haddington "he had of his own authority made certen offers beyond his commission, and that he was much troubled withall." The chancellor suspected Asheby had been commanded to deny he had made offers by commission, and he recounted to Sidney the offers and the manner in which they were made.

Pretending great amazement, Sidney asked him if the king would "take hold of the sayde offers or no." The chancellor answered that he certainly would, unless some other offers of equivalent value were made. As though he were taking the chancellor into his personal confidence, Sidney announced that what he was about to say was as a private man and not as the queen's ambassador, for he knew nothing of the queen's intent; then he told him he thought it unfit for the king to insist on the offers, for it might seem he was taking advantage of a dangerous crisis to force the queen to do something she did not want to do, and that he knew the queen would not agree to anything she thought not fit.

Sidney began to explain why it would be unprofitable for James to insist upon Asheby's offers. "I fo[wnd] him very resolut towching the point of the duke[dom]," he reported, "and the lands which were the King's grandfa[ther's]." Still insisting that he spoke as a private man and as Asheby's friend, he remarked that the king would sooner offend in demanding too much than would her majesty in giving too little. The decayed condition of Sidney's letter obscures some of the meaning, but it appears that the chancellor thought the fault lay with the commissioners of both sides, and that Sidney managed to mollify him somewhat during their exchange.

The young ambassador imagined that the chancellor did not know he was reporting their interview to Walsingham. Maitland insisted that he wanted to do "all good offices," and Sidney thought he could, for he was the only man who consistently influenced the king in matters of state. However, Sidney judged that the king had to be pleased somehow, or he would be forced to change his course, for the factions at the Scottish court continued to work against him, and the chancellor survived only by James's favor.[65]

The next day, Sidney had more to report. That morning, Carmichael[65] visited him and spoke with him at length about Asheby's offers. Carmichael was not buying a word of the English story that Asheby had acted unofficially; "there was never a wise man in Scotland," he told Sidney, "that would be perswaded that an imbassador authorized by a prince would or durst make any such offers without having commission for them." Sidney repeated what he had told the chancellor, insisting that he had known nothing of the offers until he had entered Scotland, when Asheby himself told him he had made the offers on his own authority. "But," Sidney observed, "I find they take this answer for very small paiement." Perhaps in defense of Asheby, he added that the reasons the Scots gave for why the offers would profit James made him think they must have instigated the matter themselves.[66]

In the afternoon, Carmichael returned with a series of new promises and arguments from the chancellor. If Asheby's offers were honored, he claimed, James could assure the queen that he was henceforth free of any alliance with foreign princes, and that he would commit himself to follow any course the queen desired. Addressing himself to Asheby's offers, Carmichael claimed that James desired not so much his own profit as to suppress resentment among his own subjects at the proposed alliance with England. If only he could show them that he had a dukedom in England, he did not care if he received any revenues with it. As for the personal guard, Carmichael said that if the queen expected to secure James's loyalty, she must take care to make him his own master, and not let his great men rule him as they pleased. The one hundred men and one hundred foot along the border would be more useful for England than for Scotland in restraining the depradations of the local thieves.

Sidney listened to this recitation and then asked what would become of Scotland if Asheby's offers were not granted. Carmichael answered darkly that James would be forced to do certain things in spite of himself, and that it would not be without the deaths of Carmichael and "far greater persons"—meaning, Sidney thought, the chancellor. Carmichael insisted that the money that was promised was expected. Sidney replied that he had nothing in his commission about it, and, since Carmichael did not press him further, he said no more. Sidney apparently thought Carmichael was asking for a bribe. He observed that the man was poor and some help would profitably be bestowed on him, and that at base Carmichael's protestations of affection for Elizabeth were believable. Sidney added that Lord Claud had professed himself Protestant as reported, but he remained "inwardly a papist and a practiser."[67]

Sidney's insistence upon the need to make a concession to James had some effect in England, for Walsingham wrote to him on September 1 that the queen would send James £3,000. Sidney was glad to receive that news, "for since they have had knowledge of it, I find them not so hard bent upon the offers as they were before." The chancellor was gone from the court for a day or two, but before he left, Sidney spoke with him again about Asheby's offers and urged him not to press for them. Time, he suggested, might make the queen grant more and the king demand less. He thought the Scots intended to insist on the title, but they might abandon their demands for the guard and the men at the frontiers if they were given more money. Sidney believed the king and the chancellor were both inclined toward the English cause. Although opposing factions caused endless friction, Sidney observed that James was so thoroughly committed to the Protestant religion that it would take a powerful cause to make him change.[68]

Reporting on another development, Sidney wrote that Lord Scroope had written and asked him to request the king to send a warden or officer to meet with him, for since Maxwell's imprisonment and Lord Angus's death, justice was in great disorder on the Scottish side of the border. Scroope intended to go himself to see that order was established. In communicating this to the king, Sidney advised him in Elizabeth's name to take care for his own safety, and to keep an eye on Huntly and Lord Claud, who were known to have received the Spanish ambassador's promise of aid. James assured Sidney that he had sent agents to sound out the Catholic noblemen, and that within a month he would deal with them.[69]

On September 4, 1588, while these negotiations were taking place, Leicester died. Walsingham wrote to Sidney three days later[70] that the queen had not yet been acquainted with his proceedings with James, for she was so grieved at the lord steward's death that she would let no one have access to her. However, the lords who knew of Sidney's dealings, especially Chancellor Fortescue, approved of them. The English hoped that on delivery of a sum of £2,000,[71] which the Scottish seemed to need more than titles, they would not insist so peremptorily on Asheby's offers, "which will never be effected, unto what so ever shew they make [of] running forraine courses." Walsingham thought James should count himself satisfied if the queen could be persuaded to honor him with the Garter. If James let himself be alienated from the English, Walsingham observed, he would lose the claim he had to the English crown.

It was not yet known, he wrote, what arrangements Leicester had made for the disposal of his goods. He died suddenly, contrary to his physician's expectations, and it was thought the conveyance he made of most of his land before going to the Low Countries was "to lead to uses," and that he bestowed the rest of his property on his illegitimate son, Robert Dudley.

Robert Bowes was promptly sent to convey the £3,000 in gold from the earl of Huntingdon to James. Bowes met Carmichael near Berwick on September 9, paid him the cash, and forwarded the receipt to Burghley.[72] Sidney left Edinburgh immediately afterward. He wrote to Walsingham from Berwick on the eleventh that he had obtained the king's leave to depart upon receipt of the news of Leicester's death. He was hurrying to the court, and he asked Walsingham to direct him by letter where to meet him, "for I would bee glad not to come openly into the court so soddenly after my lordes departure."[73]

Sidney left a good impression behind him, despite the abruptness of his withdrawal. James wrote to Elizabeth in praise of the young ambassador who had successfully talked him out of holding the queen to some promises that would have been most profitable to him. "The sudaine pairting of this honorable gentleman, youre ambassador, upon thaise unfortunatt and displeasant neuis of his onkle, has mouit me of the more haist to trace theis few lynes unto you; first, to thanke you, as well for the sending of so rare a gentleman unto me, to quhose brother I was so farre beholden; . . . I pray you most hairtly, that in any thing concerning this gentleman fallen out by the death of his onkle, ye will have a favourable consideration of him for my sayke, that he may not have occassion to repent him of his absence at suche a tyme. . . ."[74] Asheby also remarked on Sidney's warm relationship with James, who apparently would have been pleased to continue entertaining the ambassador indefinitely. "The King was mervelouse sorie," Asheby said, that "he had suche occasion so suddenlie to depart, meaning to have killed all his buckes in Fauckland if he had taried."[75] James sent letters after Sidney, ordering Bowes to see they were delivered at the English court.[76] In light of the rather unpleasant nature of his mission, his conquest of James must be added to the evidence of Sidney's tactful and ingratiating character.

Sidney arrived in London September 16,[77] and found his countrymen in high spirits after the defeat of the Armada. His own news added to the general celebration. Camden says the "publique rejoycing was increased by the arrival of Sir Robert Sidney, who being come out of Scotland, assured her Majestie that the King of Scots embraced most affectionately the Queene's friendship, made sincere profession of the true Religion, and would defend it with all his might. . . ."[78] Sidney's report of James' comparison of Philip II to Polyphemus particularly delighted the English.

Sidney accomplished more than merely insuring James's support of Elizabeth against the Spanish, which, since James was in better control of matters than he seemed, may never have been in real doubt. Sidney was despatched to a foreign court at the last minute during a dangerous crisis not only to secure James's pledge of loyalty, but to back the queen out of some intemperate promises that had been accepted by the Scots in good faith. This he was supposed to manage without alienating James. By accomplishing his purpose smoothly and quickly, he strengthened his country's defensive position while he freed Elizabeth from an onerous obligation. Had England been forced to honor Asheby's promises, the Crown would have had to carry the burden of paying 250 soldiers, plus their officers, plus the proposed £5,000 pension—which would have come to £75,000 over the fifteen years Elizabeth continued on the throne—plus the revenues associated with the dukedom. Too, the grant of a duchy to a foreign potentate would have been less than popular among the English, and it would have given added ammunition to the pro-Catholic faction. Sidney extricated the queen with a payment of only £3,000, and he seems to have augmented James's good will in the bargain.

Sidney's Scottish embassy was an important milestone in his career. James did not forget his affection for him, and as soon as the king was in a position to aid Sidney, he granted him the peerage Sidney sought fruitlessly from Elizabeth and secured him a comfortable office. Unfortunately, Elizabeth lived for another decade and a half, so that by the time Sidney was in a position to profit from his sovereign's favor, he was too old to take full advantage of it. Had he been in 1588 in the position he suddenly acquired in 1603, he might have built a career of more lasting memory in English history.

NOTES

1. M. Wilson, pp. 256–57.

2. Bourne, pp. 355*ff.*

3. Stone, *Crisis,* p. 784, citing MS Lansdowne 50, fol. 88, British Library, London, England.

4. M. Wilson, p. 279.

5. Printed in Collins, 1:109–13.

6. Bourne, p. 352.

7. M. Wilson, p. 278.

8. Thomas Nevitt, "Income and Expenses of the First Earl of Leicester, 1622," Additional MS 12066, n.p., British Library, London, England (hereafter cited "Additional MS 12066").

9. Read, *Walsingham* 3:167.

10. Walsingham to Leicester, Barnelms, 6 November 1586, Bruce, *Correspondence,* pp. 456–57.

11. Read, *Walsingham* 3:168; M. Wilson, p. 278; Osborn, p. 516.

12. Additional MS 12066.

13. Read, *Walsingham* 3:170.

14. Osborn, p. 5.

15. Additional MS 12066.

16. Stone observes that the Phelps-Brown index of prices of consumables more than doubled between 1560 and 1640 (*Crisis*, p. 273).

17. *HMCD* 2:278, 279, 437, 440.

18. Stone, *Crisis*, Appendix XXIV (n.p.).

19. Ibid., Appendix XXII (n.p.).

20. See ibid., pp. 467 ff, for an enlightening discussion of "the explosive demand for office under the Crown in the decades after 1585. . . ."

21. MS Lansdowne 58, item 76, British Library, London, England.

22. Sidney to Lady Sidney, London, 24 May 1588, *HMCD:* 2100–2101.

23. MS Lansdowne, item 77, British Library, London, England.

24. Dudley and De L'Isle MSS, U 1475 070/1, Kent Archives Office, Maidstone, England (hereafter abbreviated KAO De L'Isle).

25. Captain C. Hesketh, "The Manor House and the Great Park of the Archbishop of Canterbury at Otford," *Archaeologia Cantiana* 31 (1915): 1–24.

26. *HMCD* 2:100.

27. Rowland Whyte to Sidney, 10 November 1599, *HMCD* 2:412.

28. Great Britain, Public Record Office *List and Analysis of the Calendar of State Papers, Foreign*, 3 vols. (London: HMSO, 1964–   ), 1:21 (hereafter abbreviated *L & A CSP For.*).

29. Additional MS 5753, British Library, London, England. Sources vary on the pay of captains at this time. Markham, writing in 1888, puts it at £1,680 a year. Additional MS 5753 records that it was 8s. a day (£1 = 20s.; 8 × 365 divided by 20 = £146). SP 84/46, fol. 46 mentions a rate of 42s. a week (£109.2 a year). Probably the average pay for an ordinary captain who had no other income was between £100 and £150 a year.

30. Markham, pp. 54–56.

31. See, for example, Charles G. Cruickshank, *Elizabeth's Army* (Oxford: Clarendon Press, Oxford University Press, 1966), pp. 134–43 and pp. 150–53; Markham, passim; Great Britain, *Acts of the Privy Council* 17:446; Read, *Walsingham,* pp. 1–3, passim; for discussions of the enormous proportions of the corruption within the English military organization.

32. *HMCD* 2:266ff., correspondence of Whyte to Sidney.

33. Sidney to "Excellency," Berghen, 1 March [1586], Cotton Galba C:ix, British Library, London, England. The date on the binding of this manuscript is 1596, but that is probably not the date of the letter. Leicester was the only correspondent Sidney addressed as "excellency" except Prince Maurice, for whom the letter is manifestly not intended; Leicester died in 1588.

34. Motley, 2:181.

35. Read, *Walsingham* 1:ix.

36. Ibid., 3:116.

37. Ibid., 3:157.

38. Ibid., 3:157–58.

39. *Verant woordinge van P. Grave von Hohenloe teghens zerkere Vertooche ende Remonstrie by den Grave van Leycester als Gouverneur der vereenichen Provincen zhedaen senden heeren Staten General der selves Provincian,* etc. (Leyden, 1587).

40. Sidney to Leicester, Flushing, 20 December 1587, MS Cotton Galba D:ii, fol. 274, British Library, London, England.

41. Read, *Walsingham* 3:428.

42. *CSP Dom.* 2:336.

43. Sidney to Leicester, Flushing, 31 December 1587, MS Cotton Galba D:ii, fol. 288, British Library, London, England.

44. Sidney to Lady Sidney, "At Camp," 5 August 1588, *HMCD* 2:101.

45. Ibid.

46. [R. Douglas] to [Archibald Douglas], the Scottish ambassador, [1588, ca. July 12], Great Britain, Historical Manuscripts Commission, no. 9, *Calendar of the Manuscripts of the Most Honorable the Marquis of Salisbury, K.G., Preserved at Hatfield House,* p. 378 (Hereafter abbreviated *HMC Salisbury*).

47. Sidney to Lady Sidney, at Wilton, [August 1588], *HMCD* 2:101.

48. Sidney to Lady Sidney, Edinburgh, 2 September 1588, ibid., 2:102.

49. Read, *Walsingham* 3:341.

50. Ibid., 3:321.

51. Ibid.

52. Instructions for Sir Robert Sidney, [August] 1588, Great Britain, Public Record Office, *Calendar of Scottish Papers* 9:604–6 (Hereafter abbreviated *Cal. Scot. Papers*).

53. Read, *Walsingham* 3:340.

54. Asheby to Walsingham, Edinburgh, 25 August 1588, *Cal. Scot Papers* 9:600.

55. Walsingham to Asheby, 22 August 1588, ibid., 9:599.

56. Asheby to Walsingham, 22 August 1588, ibid., 9:599.

57. Sidney to Walsingham, Berwick, 27 August 1588, ibid., 9:601.

58. Ibid.

59. Sidney to Walsingham, Haddington, 28 August 1588, ibid., 9:602.

60. A. Throgmorton to Walsingham, Edinburgh, August 30, 1588, ibid., 9:602.

61. Additional MS 12066.

62. Sidney to Walsingham, Edinburgh, 30 August 1588, ibid., 9:603.

63. [Asheby] to Walsingham, Edinburgh, 30 August 1588, ibid., 9:603–4.

64. Sidney to Walsingham, Edinburgh, 1 September 1588 (original decayed in several places), ibid., 9:607–8.

65. Ibid.

66. Sidney to Walsingham, Edinburgh, 2 September 1588, ibid., 9:608–10.

67. Ibid.

68. Sidney to Walsingham, Edinburgh, 7 September 1588, MS Harley 7004, fol. 18, British Library, London, England.

69. Ibid.

70. Walsingham to Sidney, 7 September 1588, *Cal. Scot. Papers* 9:611–12.

71. *Sic.* Read (*Walsingham* 3:339), quoting directly from the original (Cotton MS Caligula D.i, fol. 339), which was damaged by fire, interprets this figure as £5,000. Probably it refers to the £3,000 finally conceded to James.

72. Robert Bowes to Burghley, [10] September 1588, Great Britain, Public Record Office, *Calendar of Border Papers* 1:333 (Hereafter abbreviated *Cal. Border Papers*).

73. Sidney to Walsingham, Berwick, 11 September 1588, *Cal. Scot. Papers* 9:613–14.

74. James IV to Elizabeth I, September 1588, Bruce, *Letters of Elizabeth and James VI*, pp. 54–55.

75. Asheby to Walsingham, 12 September 1588, *Cal. Scot. Papers* 9:614.

76. Bowes to Walsingham, 13 September 1588, *Cal. Border Papers* 1:333.

77. Sidney to Lady Sidney, London, 16 September 1588, *HMCD* 2:101; cf., Robert Bowes's account, [September 1588], *Cal. Border Papers* 9:620.

78. William Camden, *Annales*, 3 vols. (London: H. Lownes, 1625–29), I:iii:286.

[4]

Assuming Office
The New Governor of Flushing

Whatever glory accrued from the Scottish adventure was short-lived. Back home, Sidney found his services as ambassador to James VI did little immediately to advance his fortunes. Once the excitement surrounding the Spanish attempt against England subsided, he was still faced with the problem of how to advance himself at court, a challenge complicated by the death of the queen's old favorite, whose patronage had been too important for Sidney to lose so early in his career. Nor did he inherit much from Leicester's estate: the legacy was tied up for years by legal attacks from the earl's putatively illegitimate son, Robert Dudley.

Sidney's appointment in 1589 to the governorship of Flushing meant he had to carry on his courtly efforts at long distance. His career was bifurcated between 1589 and 1603: on the one hand, he played his role as military governor with competence and occasional brilliance, while on the other, he carried on his struggle for advancement at the English court, either in person or through his agents and patrons. Because of this dichotomy and the complexity of each hemisphere of his career, I will treat the decade and a half between Sidney's appointment as governor and the queen's death in two sections. Sidney's attention was at all times divided between Zealand and England. His efforts to advance his reputation and prospects at home, which took place simultaneously with the events of the next three chapters, will receive detailed discussion following chapter 6.

Sidney's instructions, set down by the Privy Council in July, 1589, make clear what was expected of him in his new post.[1] He was to deliver several reassurances to the waiting burghers, who no doubt were anxious to see what changes the new administration would bring. These included a promise to continue the practice, proposed and instituted by Sir Philip Sidney, of allowing merchants who carried the governor's written testimony that they were residents of Flushing to trade in English dominions as though they were the queen's own subjects. He also was to assure the burghers that the soldiers would behave in an orderly way, and indeed,

Sidney's orders charged him to see that no offense was committed against the Flushingers either by his own soldiers or by any other English subjects.

Sidney was responsible for maintaining the routine watch and ward and for keeping track of all strangers who passed through. He was to ensure that the gospel was preached and common prayer exercised daily, and men not on duty were required to attend public religious services each day. Sidney was also told to guard against the influence of and prohibit the meetings of "Sectaryes, as Annabaptystes, Lybertines, and soche lyke . . . soe her Majesties subjects may not be infected by them."

Sidney was given his own copy of the articles contained in the Contract between England and the United Provinces regarding the authority accorded for the town's government. Walsingham, who composed Sidney's instructions,[2] drew the new governor's attention to the fact that the garrison originally had only six bands of one hundred fifty footmen apiece, which the queen paid separately from her army of five thousand foot and one thousand horse stationed in the Low Countries. There were ten foot bands in Flushing in 1590.[3] Any companies above and beyond the original six garrisoned at Flushing were part of the auxiliary to her army, and therefore, Walsingham emphasized, appointments of their officers and captains belonged to the general of the queen's army. Nevertheless, as long as these auxiliary companies were stationed in the town, Sidney had authority to command them to observe the garrison's ordinances and to defend it the same as his own ordinary companies. If any captain of the auxiliary bands committed a capital offense or a crime calling for his dismissal, Sidney was to refer the matter to the queen's lieutenant and general of her forces for disposition.

The queen ordered Sidney to bring a halt to the captains' practice of padding the companies by bribing "townsmen, artisans, tipplars, or soche lyke which did no service." In this way, the captains collected the pay, victuals, uniforms, and arms for nonexistent men, which enabled them to pocket substantial sums above their meager salaries. After notifying the men that the queen was determined to stop the fraud, he was to assist her treasurer (Sir Thomas Shirley, who proved to be one of the arch-abusers of the queen's system), her muster masters, and their commissioners (none of whom were immune to temptation) in an effort to secure accurate musters records, to determine that no pay, allowances, or supplies were distributed for absent men, and to see that allowances for dead pays (pay continued for men no longer in active service) were not exceeded.

Sidney's instructions give a good indication of the manifold nature of his responsibilities. As governor of the garrison, his rank approximated that of a regimental colonel (see table 4, "Organization of the English Army"), except that he accounted directly to Burghley rather than to the general of the army in the Low Countries. Ranking below him in the garrison were a lieutenant-governor, a sergeant-major, corporals, the company captains, a varying number of companies approximately one hun-

TABLE 4

ORGANIZATION OF THE ENGLISH ARMY
Sources: Markham, pp. 54–66; Cruikshank, pp. 47–53

General
Council of War:
Lord or High Marshall (second-in-command)

General or Lt. Gen. of the Infantry

General of the Horse
— Wagon-master
— Forage-master

Treasurer of War
— Provost Marshall
— Victual-master
— Judge-marshall
— Staff of sub-treasurers and clerks
— Muster-master-gen.
— Muster-masters

Master of the Ordnance
— Lieutenant
— Master-gunners
— Wagon-masters
— Trench-masters
— Cannoneers

Scout Master — Quarter-Master-General
— A guard of light horse
— A staff of vant-curriers (runners or scouts)

Sergeant-Major-General — Provost Marshall
Sgt.-Majors

Regimental Colonel
— Lt. Colonel
— Sgt. Major
— 4 Corporals

Company Captains (ca. 200 men per company)
— Lieutenant
— Ensign
— 2 Sergeants, each leading 2 squadrons
— 4 Corporals
— About 20 men in each squadron
— Drummers
— Preacher
— Cannoneer

dred sixty men strong plus his own company of two hundred, a chaplain, a surgeon, and miscellaneous other minor officials. In addition, the governor of Rammekins was nominated by and was responsible to Sidney. He occasionally had to arrest and sit in judgment upon the mischief-makers, both military and civilian, who surfaced in his domain. He regulated trade activities and helped in distribution of goods and pay to his men. As a diplomat, he attempted to maintain amicable relations with the burghers, with the officials of the States of Zealand, and with the representatives of the States General of the United Provinces, sometimes under difficult conditions. He also served to some extent as an intelligence agent; his letters to Burghley indicate that he functioned as a conduit of information to the home government, transmitting much general news and some secret and sensitive intelligence. He frequently expressed his personal judgment about the men and intrigues in European politics. That he was not discouraged from doing so suggests that his opinion was of some value to the English policymakers.

Situated near the sand dunes on the south edge of Walcheren Island at the mouth of the western Scheldt estuary, Flushing was a key to the Netherlands in that its position controlled access to Antwerp. A major point of embarkation for voyagers to and from England, it was one of the prime trading ports in the Low Countries. The power that controlled it commanded Zealand's main gateway to the sea, the source of the country's strength. The English, the Dutch, and—perhaps belatedly—the Spanish recognized this. The fact became unmistakable when on April 6, 1572, Flushing made itself the first town to throw off Spanish rule and raise the tricolor of William of Orange.[4] Alva had erred in failing to complete the citadel of Flushing while he attempted to finish the one at Antwerp; Sir Roger Williams speculated that had the Spanish first finished the citadel of Flushing, Zealand would never have revolted.[5] The citizens, supported by the semipiractical navy called the Sea Beggars (Les Gueux), conspired against Spain and hanged the Spanish governor, Pacheco. The Prince of Orange, Count Ludowick, and Sir Thomas Morgan, as well as the Walloons and the Flemings rallied behind the Flushingers, and they succeeded in expelling the Spanish from the town. Rotterdam, Schiedam, and Gouda quickly joined the rebels; the native garrisons turned from Alva to Orange, and "the people, hungry, unemployed, and ripe for revolt, were rising everywhere."[6] The revolt of Flushing signaled the beginning of success for the United Provinces in their struggle against Spanish domination. As Juan de Vargas observed in a report to his king, even if the Low Countries could be conquered by force, "on ne pourrait les conserver sans tenir Flessingue."[7]

The town was fortified behind a wall and a moat that ran along its landward boundaries to the north and west. The wall, built in 1489 by Philip the Good, duke of Burgundy,[8] was originally broken by five gates, one of which was removed in 1586 to accommodate a new haven. The Water Gates of Head Port allowed entry to the Old Haven, a man-made channel constructed in 1319 under William the Good, count of Holland.[9]

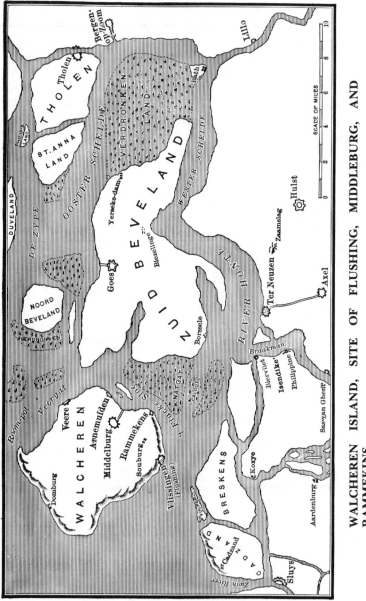

WALCHEREN ISLAND, SITE OF FLUSHING, MIDDLEBURG, AND
RAMMEKINS
Source: Markham, facing page 46

The Gevangen, or Prisoner's Port, opened onto the sand dunes along the north shores. Middleburg Port, exactly opposite the Water Gates, led to the Middleburg highway, and Rammekins or Blaauw Port gave access to Fort Rammekins and the neighboring farm village of Ritthem. Contained within the wall were two canallike harbors. To the northwest ran the Old Haven, surrounded by the older parts of town, where the prison, the marketplace, the brewhouse, the church, and the guesthouse were located. The governor's house overlooked the New Haven, a comparable harbor that branched to the east and was bordered by a district named "The New Town." Directly next to the governor's house stood Prince Maurice's mansion. Graced by five formal gardens, it commanded a view of the sea, the New Haven, and the fortified town that was the prince's partrimony from William of Orange. The only major structure outside the wall was the gunpowder house: it was built a respectful distance up the road to Middleburg.

When Antwerp was restored to Spain, Elizabeth agreed to help the United Provinces by sending them 5000 foot soldiers and 1000 horsemen; in return, the towns of Flushing and the Brill were offered to her as security. Elizabeth made it clear that she preferred money to the sovereignty of the United Provinces, which the Hollanders also offered her in return for her assistance. Zealand objected to the proposition that Flushing be offered as a cautionary town. Although it was deeply mortgaged for the debts of William of Orange, it formed a large portion of what had been left to his son, Count Maurice. As long as his elder brother, Philip William, remained a captive in Spain, Maurice styled himself Marquis of Flushing and Kampveer, and derived prestige as well as revenue from his rights in the town. Too, the States of Zealand were unhappy about converting their commercial capital into an English city.[10] Knowing the English queen's unpredictability, the Dutch feared that once she possessed the town she might use it to win a favorable peace settlement between herself and Spain.[11] After some delay, the Dutch overcame their discomfort and entered into the bargain the English desired, making Flushing a British garrison town until 1616. Eventually, they contracted to pay off a debt of £800,000 to the English Crown in annual payments of £30,000 to relieve the queen of expenses related to auxiliary troops and the cautionary towns, and to furnish men and ships should England be invaded.[12] Sir Philip Sidney became the first English military governor of Flushing, followed by Lord Willoughby and Sir William Russell. Sir Robert, succeeding Russell, was the last English governor and held the post until James restored Flushing to the Dutch.[13]

Sidney officially replaced Russell, who retired for personal reasons, on August 12, 1589. However, he did not arrive in Flushing until May 6 of the following year.[14] Meanwhile, the direct administration of the government remained in the hands of the lieutenant governor, Sir William Borlas,[15] a commander experienced in the wars of the Low Countries.[16] Borlas seems to have antagonized the Dutch and annoyed Sidney. In October 1589, he was defending himself both against rumors that he allowed armed ships to lie within the town and against Sidney's low opinion of his competence. That he was married to a Dutch woman, he argued, did not make him the less qualified to serve as lieutenant-governor.[17] Perhaps in his anxiety to prove he was not overly lenient with the Dutch, Borlas committed some errors that were to cause Sidney considerable difficulty in the months ahead. On January 25, 1590, Flushing ships captured one of three Dunkirk warships, with ninety-three men aboard. Borlas claimed the ship was the admiral of the Dunkirk fleet and, on February 3, he had forty or fifty of her mariners executed. He also encouraged the execution of some soldiers from Gravelines for their part in a massacre that took place in Sir Philip Sidney's time.[18] Repercussions from these incidents dogged Sidney's administration for some time.

Sidney finally took his oath of office at Flushing on Sunday, May 24, 1590, according to the terms of the contract. All the members of the States of Zealand assembled for the occasion and threw a great feast in his honor. They asked him to sign a declaration concerning his commission and a copy of some points of admonition regarding the faults they felt were being committed in the English government of the town. Sidney promised to try to correct these problems, but said it would take time.[19] In their papers, which Sidney forwarded to Burghley, the States General and the Council of State proposed eleven articles:

1. That the money paid to the garrison be paid only to English subjects and the six foreigners permitted in each band, and not include any dead pays or men absent from their posts;

2. That the auxiliary companies in Flushing, above and beyond the five cautionary companies there and the six at the Rammekins, be at the Council of State's service;

3. That musters be held when commanded by the Council of State and according to the established orders, and that superfluous dead pays not be allowed;

4. That good discipline be kept and the men not permitted to range about the country or behave in a rowdy manner;

5. That the governor dismiss all freebooters;

6. That the governor not grant safeguards to those in enemy-occupied territory or passports and safe-conducts to pass to and from the enemy;

7. That the governor allow the appointed Dutch officers to collect convoys and licenses on goods imported from England and elsewhere;

8. That Rammekins in particular not impeach ships passing the castle;

9. That everyone except the governor's household members pay imposts on wine, beer, etc., according to the treaty, and the English officers quit exempting themselves and cease brewing their own beer;

10. That the governor not meddle with police matters proper to the town or the country;

11. That the governor conduct himself according to the treaty, main-

tain amicable relations with the States General, the Count of Nassau, et al., without giving ear to those who had offended the States.[20]

Sidney thought this list was meant to illustrate to him the faults the Dutch felt had been committed before his arrival, and he believed they were content with his answer that such problems could not be dealt with in haste.

However, he sought the advice of Sir Thomas Bodley, English ambassador at the Hague, about the eleven articles. Bodley supported the Dutch in all but the second and third items. Most of the articles reflected agreements that had been made under the treaty. Some, he said, had come to be "usurped daily," and Bodley agreed that the Dutch grievances were justified. About the second article, Bodley confirmed that the auxiliary companies were at the States' disposal, but he suggested the treaty be "understood" in light of the fact that the cautionary companies were incomplete, so that the town's safety might not be compromised. The difficult matter of the musters orders had never been settled to everyone's satisfaction, and Bodley remarked that he hoped Buckhurst would see to it.[21]

One of the new governor's most urgent problems was to build and maintain friendly relations between the queen's government and the Dutch, two entities that frequently worked at cross-purposes. Complicating that were the commonplace abuses of English officers in muster and victualing practices mentioned in the States' eleven articles, plus the pervasive paranoia the English suffered where the people of the Low Countries were concerned, aggravated by the ongoing negotiations for peace with Spain. Naturally, Sidney did not want to find himself in the predicament of the late Spanish governor; even less did he care to face the humiliation of being ejected by force from the town. He believed the Dutch were capable of placing him in either position, given enough provocation. He knew just as well that the enemy coveted the strategic town and could at any time attempt to take it by deception or force. About June 13, he received word of a plot against Flushing[22] that pro-English Dutchmen at Berghen said was probably occasioned by desire for revenge for Borlas's execution of the Dunkirk pirates.[23] Rumors of an impending peace treaty between England and Spain kept Sidney in continual discomfort, for he feared, with some justification, that the Dutch would regard such an agreement as perfidy and retake the cautionary towns.[24]

Sidney turned for suggestions to Sir George Gilpin, the English agent at the Hague and secretary of the Society of Merchant Adventurers' Staple at Middleburg,[25] and to Sir Thomas Wilkes, the English agent in the United Provinces. Wilkes could offer little constructive advice. He disliked the Dutch, a people he thought "as hedstrong as so many bulles," ungrateful, and wanting in judgment.[26]

Gilpin, a loquacious man and one favorably disposed toward his Dutch hosts, advised Sidney "to give these men good words and not to contend with them."[27] His advice, urging the importance of observing the treaty and of keeping the Council of State well-informed, concurred with Bodley's. Gilpin observed that the town's fortifications were in decay, and remarked that he hoped Sidney would arrange promptly for their repair.[28]

This matter had not escaped the new governor's attention. Directly after Sidney's arrival, President Valck had indicated that the States would take care of repairing the fortifications, and on May 26, Sidney wrote that the States of Zealand had agreed to repair both Flushing's and the Rammekins'. By mid-June, there was still no sign of work beginning, although the townsmen did start a church for the English that Sidney expected would be finished the following year.[29] The question of whether the Dutch were to rebuild the fortifications, and, if so, when they would get to it, developed into a conundrum that went unresolved until the end of Sidney's administration.

One of Sidney's earliest vexations concerned the auxiliary companies garrisoned at Flushing. Theoretically, they were at the States' disposal, and Sidney was to send them forth when requested by the Dutch. However, he was uncomfortable with this arrangement, because he felt unable to defend the town with only the cautionary companies. Burghley and the lords of the Privy Council ordered him to comply with the Dutch demands, provoking from him a speedy protest. In one of his first letters to Burghley from Flushing he explained at length the reasons for his reluctance.[30] There were only five cautionary companies, too small a garrison for such an important place. Russell had not felt secure with fewer than twelve companies; with only twelve, Sidney believed he would govern "precariously." The town was large, and the English had many gates and *corps de garde* to keep. If the Dutch drew out the auxiliary companies, Sidney feared he might not get them back.

Burghley wrote back on June 3, informing Sidney that he was required to release the auxiliary companies at the States' command. "Since I see yt is your Lordship's mind," Sidney responded unhappily, "I will not contrary the Counsel of State if they send for some of the auxiliary companies, though I remain of one opinion still."[31] He continued to worry about his ability to defend the garrison in the absence of the soldiers, and he dragged his feet about sending them forth. Late in July, Wilkes reported that he had heard of "a sharp Lettre" recently written to Sidney from the Council of State about the two auxiliary companies under Sidney's command. He suggested that, unless it was unavoidable, the governor forbear from visiting the Hague, for he would surely be importuned about the Dutch demands if he appeared in person.[32]

Sidney grew more determined. The Dutch were convinced the queen had concocted a secret treaty with Spain, and he was afraid for the safety of Flushing. He suspected that they sought to weaken the garrison so they could take it back if necessary, for they believed the queen could use it to force them to do as she wished. He refused to send any companies out of the town "lest they [the Dutch] might find a way to turn me out and afterwards say indeed they ment it not, but since yt was done they could not remedy yt." The Council of State had, as Wilkes had heard, sent him a "peremptory" letter, but, Sidney said, "as long as the[y] fight with pen and inck I will have a sheele of paper ever ready for them." In his answer to the Dutch, he gave no ground at all.[33]

The Dutch were as suspicious of Sidney's motives as he was of theirs. President Valck, Peter de Rich, and an unnamed third man were deputed to meet with Sidney, and they questioned three points of his letters patent. First, they resented the queen's terming the place "*our* town of Flushing;" Sidney said there was no such word in the letters and it must have been the fault of the copyist. They took exception to the queen's granting Sidney authority over those who entered the town, including strangers of all types; according to the Contract, they said, he was to govern only the garrison and leave the rest to the town magistrate. Sidney assured them that he understood he was to observe the treaty and that he would not meddle with anything beyond his charge, unless he saw an occasion that affected the garrison's safety. The Dutch were uncomfortable, too, with the queen's order that Sidney obey any direction from her or the Privy Council; they inferred that he might be commanded to do something contrary to the treaty. Sidney answered that if he acted against the treaty's provisions, the Dutch knew where to take their complaints. If he acted by warrant, he added, they should appeal to the treaty's markers. He was in Flushing at the queen's pleasure and was bound to obey her command.[34] By and large, Sidney handled his own and the Dutch suspicions much as Gilpin suggested: with "good words" and as little open contention—or cooperation—as possible.

Sidney found the town undersupplied with powder, arms, money, men, and provisions, a problem that became chronic. Borlas was already entreating Sidney, before he came over, to make some arrangement for arming the soldiers.[35] Sidney asked the Privy Council for troop reinforcements as soon as he arrived, requesting one hundred fifty to two hundred men to replace those absent or unfit at Flushing. He urged that the new men be better chosen than the present ones, who, besides being unfurnished with arms and clothing, were "men of all sorts of ill life. . . ."[36] Early in 1591, soldiers were levied in several shires and put into bands of one hundred fifty to be sent to Flushing.[37]

At the same time, Sidney began his interminable series of requests for arms and powder. Under the new orders established in 1589, the captains, who had formerly provided these items, were no longer able to do so. Merchants, Sidney thought, were unfit to be the exclusive dealers in arms, for they were not expert enough in the matter. He himself did not have sufficient credit to supply the garrison with powder, and he also needed arms—muskets, corselets, pikes, etc.[38] According to the Contract, the States were to furnish the cautionary towns with powder;[39] naturally, the home government was reluctant to rush these supplies to Sidney, when they might be needed if England were again attacked by foreign invaders.

Sidney dealt with the States for powder, but, by June 12, 1590, had received no answer. He wrote to Wilkes to solicit them for it, but since he knew those negotiations would take time and the need was urgent, he requested some powder for the interim from the home government, which he promised to return when the States furnished their share.[40] When he received Burghley's letters of June 13 reporting the rumor of a Dunkirker attempt against Flushing, he again (June 23) requested powder and complained of the slowness of dealing with the States.[41] Burghley apparently assured him he would attempt to procure a supply, but a month later, all the powder in the old store was spent and no fresh powder had arrived from England, nor had any order for it appeared. Sidney was forced to use his own and some of the merchants' credit to acquire some powder; so, he remarked, the English would not need to send over more than three additional lasts of powder.[42]

The problem of the soldiers' lack of clothing was no less vexing than the powder shortage. In the winter of 1589, Borlas begged Sidney to obtain help from Walsingham and Burghley regarding the men's lack of shoes. They were ill-clothed in the cold weather, and they complained daily. Borlas hoped the government would correct these shortcomings before Sidney came over.[43] It did not.

Ideally, Sidney's men were to receive supplies of clothing twice a year. The regulation winter outfit for a private was supposed to include a cassock, a doublet, a pair of cloth breeches called "venetians," a hat, two shirts and collars, three pair of stockings, and three pair of shoes. In summer he was to have a canvas doublet lined with white linen, a pair of venetians of Kentish broadcloth, also lined with linen, two shirts and collars of Holland cloth, two pair of leather shoes, two pair of coarse wool stockings, and a hat. The more elaborate officer's costume consisted of a doublet of Milan fustian faced with taffeta, a pair of broadcloth venetians trimmed with silk and lined with cotton and linen, and a pair of worsted stockings; in winter, a broadcloth cassock lined with baise and faced with taffeta was added.[44]

By the end of Elizabeth's reign, the provision of clothing was mostly in the hands of merchants under contract, and during the first decade of Sidney's administration, these arrangements were in transition. The resulting confusion and incompetence provided plenty of opportunity for graft, both to merchants and to military officers. In 1588, the treasurer-at-war, Sir Thomas Shirley, who was Sidney's friend, was still involved in supplying uniforms. About that year, some merchants offered to take on the responsibility of providing the clothing in the Low Countries. The Privy Council decided to commission some of them to provide goods at reasonable rates and deduct the money to pay for them from the soldiers' wages. General Willoughby was ordered to see that the captains collected no graft from these distributions.

By 1589, Uriah Babington and Robert Bromley, who continued to operate into James's reign, were supplying clothes to the Low Countries. They complained that Dutch customs authorities were illegally charging the usual import duties on clothes destined for use by the English troops.

After sending a strongly worded note to the burgomaster of Flushing, the Privy Council apparently received some redress for this grievance.[45] Several captains complained about these arrangements between the government and the merchants. They claimed that the clothing was not as good as the standard outfits provided by the Wardrobe Office—that they were made of inferior material which wore out too quickly and shrank, that the stockings were too short, that the shoes were badly made. They wanted material sent from England and outfits made on the spot to the soldier's measure. Shirley, however, replied that the merchants were supplying adequate goods and that the captains were meddling because they hoped to lay hands on the troops' uniform allowance.[46]

Another arrangement new at the time Sidney took office was the contract for John and Thomas Bolton and Richard Catcher to supply clothing to the Low Countries at a fixed rate per head. They were to manufacture up to £1,000 worth of goods every fifteen days until the whole amount was provided; the Crown would pay on delivery. Thomas Catcher, Richard's brother, contracted to carry the goods abroad at £1,000 a year. Summer clothes were to be delivered in May and winter supplies by mid-October. They put up a bond of £1,000 as security and had three reputable citizens vouch for them. This offer saved the government a substantial amount over the rates paid to previous merchants.[47]

Sidney, as he noted in his letter to Burghley of June 10, 1590, was averse to allowing merchants a monopoly in the supplying of clothing and arms to the men.[48] However, if distribution of the uniforms was inefficient, it was largely the fault of the captains. Many complaints reached the Privy Council from the Low Countries that the captains were retaining uniforms and lining their pockets at the soldiers' expense. The privates themselves habitually sold their spare clothes.

To discourage abuses in the supply of uniforms, the Privy Council ordered that the captains cease distributing clothing, a responsibility that was now to be carried out jointly by the merchants' agents and an official of the Crown. No soldier not a full member of a company, nor any who did not keep watch and ward, was eligible for a uniform; thus, enlisted men occupied in part-time civilian jobs in the garrison towns were disqualified.[49] The precautions necessary for distribution of clothing and other supplies in the Low Countries reflect the large-scale fraud prevalent there. Regulations were tightened, for example, when it was revealed that the earl of Warwick, Sidney's uncle, had been liberally embezzling official funds in his position as Master of the Ordinance Office. Essex, who succeeded the deceased earl in that capacity, was exhorted not to imitate Warwick's corrupt practices.[50]

Keeping his men supplied with decent food was as much a problem to Sidney as supplying them with usable clothes and arms. As with the clothing, victuals were supplied through private contractors. The victualler's existence, however, was somewhat less certain than the clothing merchant's, for the soldiers were expected to buy their own rations out of their pay of 1s. 8d. a day,[51] which was frequently in arrears. When the men were unpaid, so was the victualler, who was then forced to live on credit, if he could stay in business at all. Complaints against the merchants were frequent. Before Sidney came over, Borlas reported that the bread available to the troops was too musty to be eaten.[52] Captains in the Low Countries accused the merchants of charging the army 30 percent more than the market value of their goods, while providing food so poor it undermined the men's health. In addition, the merchants were guilty of selling food to the enemy; smugglers exported goods to the enemy from garrison towns, sometimes shipping whole cargoes to the opposite side.[53] The English government made several attempts to discourage these illegal exports. In 1591, the Privy Council found that large quantities of grain were being sent to the Low Countries without license and freely sold in the garrison towns. They authorized the victuallers to confiscate any such grain and sell it, half the proceeds going to the Crown and a quarter each to the victualler and to the commander of the town where the grain was discovered.[54]

Professor Cruickshank, in his detailed study of the question, finds nothing to be said for the private supply of the army's victuals. "It was clearly intolerable. If only because of the irregularity with which the army was paid, the burden of financing the purchase of food was too much for private individuals. Even had the army been paid regularly and the victuallers been able to recover their money at reasonable intervals, the dangers of competition between them for the available supplies and of smuggling food to the enemy remained."[55]

The Privy Council attempted to meet these problems by entering into agreements with the merchants that made them more and more responsible to the Crown, enabling the lords to keep better track of the movement of the supplies and transferring more of the financial burden to the government. In the mid-1580s, they appointed as victualling commissary for the garrison town a man with whom Sidney and his agent, Rowland Whyte, were to have many dealings, George Lester. For the first time in the history of the English army, the government established in the Netherlands permanent food stores consisting of wheat, cheese, butter, and beer, which were to be systematically used and replaced. Any surplus was to be sold to private citizens. This made for a reserve greater than the minimum required for the army's ordinary use.[56] In 1589, an agreement was established between Sir Thomas Shirley, William Beecher, George Lester, and others for victualling the forces in the Low Countries. Beecher and Lester were to provide stores of good corn, butter, cheese, etc. in the garrisons of Flushing, Brill, Bergen-op-Zoom, and Ostend, which they would sell to the troops at market value. In return, Shirley agreed to procure for them within one year license to transport to Holland and Zealand four thousand quarters of wheat and four thousand tuns of beer, for which the merchants were to pay only the ancient customs.[57] This contract was renewed indefinitely in 1591.[58]

Ideally, Sidney's men were to be supplied with a staple diet of loaf bread or biscuit, butter, cheese, and beer, supplemented by such other items as oatmeal, peas, beans, pork, bacon, fresh or salt beef, dried cod, ling, and herring. The private paid for his victuals and drink out of his daily wage, and, in 1598, the cost of his daily allowance of one pound of bread or biscuit, three ounces butter, six ounces cheese, and three-quarters pint oatmeal came to four and one-half pence. Beer was considered an essential, for water could cause disease. In the Low Countries, the allowance was as much as half a gallon a day.[59]

The Privy Council's efforts to cut down on the graft involved in the distribution of food and apparel naturally met with resistance in the garrison towns. The Flushing magistrates protested the 1589 establishment, usually called the "new orders," which provided that each soldier be paid two shillings in cash and eight pence in bread baked and issued by two English bakers (instead of the previous cash wage of 2s. 8d.), as a breach of the town's privileges. Lester denied that the English bakers had yet been authorized to supply the garrison, but said that when the magistrates forbade the burgers to bake for the victualler, he of course had to employ others. The burghers profited greatly from the garrisons, he claimed, and they had no right to interfere with the form of the queen's pay to her men.[60]

Similar protests against the new orders were raised by the captains. They all stood to lose illicit income, to which they had become so accustomed that they regarded it as their due, as a result of restrictions on and revisions of the distribution systems. For a time, the Flushing captains refused to obey the new orders, and, in September 1589, the orders had to be temporarily suspended until the matter could be settled with the magistrates, whose protests added fuel and support to the captain's resistance.[61] Sidney reestablished the orders in October, over the continued resistance of the captains and the magistrates.[62] The establishment of new musters orders in January of the following year provoked more aggrieved protest from the Flushing officers, who felt disgraced by the implication in the printed articles that they were guilty of fraud and theft.[63]

Sidney had a difficult task mediating between the English government and his angry captains. He read the musters orders to the captains, but deferred their publication while he communicated to Burghley the captain's request that he commend their faithfulness and obedience to the queen. On January 13, he sent his sergeant-major, Captain Sampson, to speak privately to Burghley about the new orders, but, having heard nothing by February 6, he wrote that the orders had been established in the garrison. He and the other governors, he declared, would obey any of the queen's orders, but these last removed all trust and credit from them. He still had heard nothing on February 15 and so he wrote asking if his letters had been delivered. Finally, on March 4, Sampson arrived with Burghley's letter of January 31, informing Sidney that the queen was displeased that he had shared his opinion of the new orders with the sergeant-major. Sampson, Sidney replied, was discreet, and as sergeant-major, he had no company of his own and so had nothing to do with the captain's profits and losses. He had sent him because "letters cannot reply," and because Sampson thoroughly understood everything.[64] Protests of the magistrates and the men at Flushing notwithstanding, the new orders were established by the middle of 1590.

A related matter to which Sidney had to attend as soon as he arrived in Flushing was the problem of Captains Wingfield and Randolph's debts to the local merchants. In 1586, the muster-master, Digges, had put their two companies into the States' pay without the knowledge or approval of the States General. As a result, debts amounting to about £687 had accrued— which neither the Dutch nor the English government was willing to pay.[65]

Sidney's sympathies were with the Dutch creditors, and he wished the Privy Council would satisfy them, for the dispute was causing trouble for his government. The debt, he said in May 1590, was "to many poor artificers who say they are undone by it, and the towns' officers allege that according to the contract the queen is bound to pay the garrison of Flushing and therefore they are not to be turned over to the States."[66] The Privy Council replied that Wingfield and Randolph's creditors should apply to the States for redress, since the captains were in their pay when the debts were incurred.[67] The States insisted that the queen should pay off the debts, and Sidney was convinced they would not pay willingly. Meanwhile, he reported, the creditors came to him daily, complaining that they would be ruined without a quick resolution of the matter, and he confirmed that most of their substance was indeed tied up in the debts. Urging the importance of preventing discontent among the Flushing residents, Sidney asked Burghley and the Privy Council to order Wilkes to deal with the States.[68]

The States did not attempt to prove Wingfield and Randolph's companies had been in the queen's pay, but instead relied on her promise by the Contract and by Sir Philip Sidney and Davison that the English companies in Flushing would be at her charge.[69] In the papers from Valck that Sidney forwarded to Burghley, Zealand claimed the two companies in question had been included in the treasurer's accounts from October 29, [1585] to April 12, 1586, as part of the English auxiliary troops in the queen's pay. Leicester attempted to transfer them to the States' pay on the latter date, without informing either the States General or the Council of States of this move. The men remained in Flushing and never served the States.[70]

The matter remained unresolved throughout 1590, while both governments procrastinated. Sidney entreated the English in favor of the Dutch merchants. "I am so earnestly requested by Captains Wingfield and Randolph's creditors," Sidney wrote to the Privy Council in September, "that I present once more their suit. I know the men are very poor and some have been forced to sell the residue of their goods for want of being paid. In truth they are very much to be pitied for they willingly trusted their goods when the companies needed them."[71] Burghley instructed Bodley to tell the States General to relieve the dependents of the deceased creditors who were importuning both governments, suggesting that if the Dutch would yield a portion of the money, the queen might contribute something out of charity. Muster-Master Digges offered to show how the queen could pay without prejudice to herself by offsetting the sum against the thousands due the States by Shirley. Bodley believed the town of Flushing had already partly satisfied the victuallers, and he suspected the deputy's plea on behalf of the victuallers' widows was a ploy to recover their money from the queen.[72] In November, Sidney wrote to Burghley again, this time in French, supporting the creditors' suit for repayment.[73] The two governments continued to procrastinate throughout 1590.

Although Sidney might have been as much motivated by a desire to silence the Dutch creditors' bothersome complaints or to please the Flushing magistrates as by any sense of justice or charity, he had little reason to fear his private correspondence to Burghley and the Privy Council would be read by the Dutch. He could have assured them he would support their suit while taking the approved stance before his English superiors. Instead, he chose to oppose his government's policy on the matter. The queen and her counselors had no intention of making good the debt incurred by the two companies. To Sidney, however, the livelihoods of the men who had been caught up in this fiasco were of greater value than a few hundred pounds sterling.

Yet another imbroglio between the two governments was in progress when Sidney arrived in Flushing, and he was immediately called upon to deal with it as best he could. The Dutch merchants were in the curious habit of doing business with whomever would pay for their goods. They harbored no compunctions about dealing with the Spanish or with the Dutch in enemy-occupied provinces. The English regarded this practice as counterproductive and did all they could to interfere with and block any such traffic.

When, in June 1590, Burghley told Sidney about a trader said to be carrying munitions out of Flushing to Spain, the governor identified him as a Middleburgh dealer, but was unable to move against him without a specific complaint. A Flushinger offered to inform the English of this illicit trade, asking one-third of the spoils of the intercepted ships.[74] Little came of that proposal, and the practice continued unabated. When Sir Martin Frobisher and Sir John Hawkins intercepted some Dutch ships that summer, the uproar issuing from the States General was so furious that the Privy Council had to let Sidney promise the Flushing and Middleburg magistrates that restitution would be made.[75]

Sidney by and large resisted his home government's efforts to interfere with the illicit traffic, probably out of reluctance to anger the Dutch and concern that he might not be able to hold the town if Zealand rose against the English there.

In the fall of 1590, Burghley and Nottingham ordered Sidney to have his water bailiff search six flyboats that were loading military supplies at Flushing and that they suspected were carrying it to Spain. He was to confiscate any contraband, examine the shippers on their corporal oathes, and answer any Dutch protest with the response that Philip II could not put his navy to sea without the provisions he received from the United Provinces.[76]

Sidney used the fact that he was in the field with Maurice when the letter arrived to delay action for about ten days, and then, stressing the loyalty of the Flushingers to the English, he protested that the States would regard forcing a Dutchman to a corporal oath as a breach of the Contract, and that, in addition, the Contract forbade English officers to meddle with the town's merchandise and government.[77]

Only the *Hare* and a few other grievously suspect ships were searched, and nothing of importance was found.[78] The English government wanted a further search at Flushing, and Sidney again protested the unseemliness and danger of these investigations, which aggravated the Dutch animosity toward the weak English garrison. He sent instructions to his lieutenant-governor, Borlas, to use discretion and avoid violent confrontations.

Borlas, meanwhile, had already discovered three small ships freighted for Bayonne and insisted on searching them. When one of the three was found to be carrying cordage, her men claimed they had a safe passport and argued that the queen should not forbid them this trade, which was customary in Dutch and common in English shipping, until she made others quit it. Knowing the poor strength of his own garrison, Borlas backed down, thinking it best not to meddle with the Dutch in Sidney's absence.

The Dutch custom of trading with the enemy was a recurring problem to Sidney's administration. [Edward] Burnham reported that shipping with a great store of cordage and other war supplies left for Spain from Flushing daily. The States refused to stop it, and the only hope was to intercept it en route. To the mystification of the English, licenses for merchants to go into any part of enemy territory were common. As a result, Antwerp and other hostile dominions were as well furnished with fresh fish and victuals as in peacetime.[79]

In 1595, the Zealand government itself attempted to bring a halt to the practice, not out of any sense of its illogicality, but because the Spanish, to Dutch annoyance, had seized all the Dutchmen's goods and account books in Spain. Sidney did not know what Holland would do, but the Zealand government requested him to stop any disobedient merchants by force.[80]

A year later, the Privy Council wrote to Sidney regarding two hundred ships which, although nominally en route for Rochelle, were bound for Spain. They had been forced by contrary winds to put in at Rammekins. Sidney was to determine the number of ships in the convoy, their origin, and their destination, and to hold them there unless their master would agree to come to England and sell his grain in that country. If he refused, Sidney was to acquaint the Council of State with the matter in the queen's name and try to persuade them to order the ships to England.[81] When Sidney reported that he was unable to determine whether they would come to England, or whether they were really headed for Spain, the Privy Council instructed Sir H. Palmer to lie in wait for them, detain them, and insist they bring the grain to England, where they would be paid a good rate for it.[82]

Sidney wrote to Cecil that he had forwarded the Privy Council's letters to Captain Browne in the Rammekins with orders to delay all ships laden with grain in the vicinity of the castle. He went to Middleburgh and met with the Council of the States of Zealand on the morning of January 27, delivering to them the queen's request. They responded with the disingenuous explanation that the ships could not be bound for Spain, because none left their harbor laden with grain except those who guaranteed they would unload in places friendly to the Dutch cause. Theirs was a country of free traffic, they said, and therefore they could constrain no one. The council suggested that Sidney meet with the merchants and urge them to go to England, where, if they were assured of selling their goods, they would willingly go. Observing that the merchants, to save the security they had put up to guaranty their conduct, might go to the places they had agreed to visit and then proceed straight to Spain, Sidney asked the councillors to consider the damage the trade was causing Zealand and England. Their own sailors who had come from there had reported that Spain's fleet was in such need of wheat that it could not put to sea unless Philip II received provisions from the Low Countries. He asked the council to use its authority with the merchants and shipmasters, but his arguments and pleas accomplished nothing. So, he sent for some of the shipmasters, and, pending their arrival, he commanded Sir William Browne to detain all ships put in by the contrary winds.[83]

Sidney thought it dangerous for the queen to use violence without first consulting the States General, for the Contract did not specify the action she requested. Knowing the Dutch would never agree to allow arrest in their harbors, he thought the queen's best course was to waylay the ships in the narrow seas. There was no other means but the English artillery to force them to stay, and that method, Sidney observed, would cause much hurt. Dutch resentment over Flushing's and the Rammekins' interference could prove dangerous to the garrison, since the places were so weak and undersupplied. He remarked that if the queen decided to make a move not justified by the authority granted the English in the treaty, she ought to do it on the high seas, where the action would not be highly visible.

The matter grew increasingly complicated as the Dutch refused to cooperate and Sidney attempted to stand firm. A week after he advised Cecil against the efforts to delay the ships at Flushing, he reported to Burghley that the wind had improved, the merchants had made their peace with the States of Zealand, and that President Valck and another member of the council had come to him demanding to know what Sidney proposed to do with the ships now that Zealand had discharged them. He replied that he had delayed them by order of the Privy Council and showed them the lords' letter. He explained that he was not to let the ships pass unless the States opposed him, in which case he knew the queen would not want him to use any violence; so, if they opposed his arrest, he felt that by letting them know the queen's will he had discharged his duty. Valck offered a number of reasons why they could not have the ships stopped in their harbors, particularly that news of it would dry up their commerce. Sidney answered that the queen expected him to obey in this matter.

The Zealanders argued that a delay of the ships violated the Contract and Sidney's oath of office. This failing to move him, they tried to defer the matter until they could confer with the States General. Sidney responded that he had no authority to deal with the States General, but only with the Zealand government. Their insistence on their innocence in the matter elicited from the governor the observation that there was no point in praying God to overthrow their enemies, since when He had cast them down, the Dutch would raise them up again themselves.

It was concluded, as Valck and the others had resolved from the beginning, that Zealand would not agree to forceable stoppage of shipping in the haven at Flushing. They informed Sidney that they would answer the queen and take responsibility for the matter on themselves, and they discharged him. Sidney seems to have given way. Despite a rumor that reached Gilpin in the Hague that the Castle of Rammekins had opened fire on the ships,[84] on February second and third, while Sidney was conferring with the Dutch in Middleburgh, the ships sailed from Flushing.[85] If the queen or Privy Council wanted to command it, he promised in his report, he would try another time to detain future shipping by force, but as things stood, he advised the queen against such a course, because of the discontent it would cause in Zealand.[86]

The Privy Council perceived this outcome as a result of Sidney's failure to perform his duty according to their orders, and he took the brunt of the lords' displeasure. In response, he produced a list of the reasons behind his actions. First, he pointed out that he was not furnished with sufficient authority to do more than he had, nor, in fact, could he have done more without extreme risk. He had been ordered to delay the ships, to request their masters to go to England, and, if they refused, to go to the Council of the States of Zealand and to request them, in the queen's name, to send the ships to England. This was exactly what he did, as he could prove by his own and Cecil's correspondence. No one gave him any charge, in the event the States did nothing, to do anything on his own; rather, Cecil concluded his letter of instruction to Sidney with remarks about the trust the queen reposed in the States. Sidney could find no authorization in Cecil's letter to warrant him to restrain the ships forcibly. Since his reasoning failed to persuade Valck and Zealand's Council of State, and they discharged him under their own hands, Sidney could not see what else he might have done without exceeding his commission.

While it was true that he would "never be discharged of a commandment of Her Majesty but by Her Majesty herself . . . ," he said, "in such cases I am to expect an absolute commandment." Sidney believed he had received no such absolute command. Even had he been given sufficient authority, it was still beyond his power, as poorly as Flushing was provided, to detain the ships against their masters' wills. The ships were not in the town's haven, but between Flushing and the Rammekins. He had only two means to stop them: to remove their mariners, sails, or rudders, making them unable to put to sea (impossible for him to effect, since the English were outnumbered and out-armed by the Dutch seamen), or to use the town and the castle's artillery to intimidate them. He might have damaged or sunk a few of them in this way, but the rest would have gotten through, and besides, that course would have enraged the townsmen. In any such extremity, the States of Zeland would side with their own countrymen.

Sidney pointed out that the fury of the Dutch, and especially of the Flushingers, had been made abundantly clear when "Having no assurance of any help on earth, they durst in a time of a Duke of Alva, cast out their kings garrison, discharge the Artillerye upon his ships, and hange up his officers." With three thousand Dutch mariners in the town and almost twice that many on the ships, Sidney hardly felt in a fighting mood. "If the Queen persists in her resolution," he added, "I beseech you to procure me her letters signed by her own hand, commanding me to use all means warlike or other to effect her will. . . ." He was convinced that without such authorization, the States would see any forcible action against them as a violation of the Contract, a hostile act with Sidney as its instigator, "and I may be called afterwards to answer with my heade, for havinge bin the worker without sufficient warrant of a breach in such a time as this of a League between her Majesty and these contreyes."[87]

The furor died down without immediate consequence to Sidney, but he had not heard the last of the corn ships débâcle. In August 1597, when another fleet of sixty to eighty ships was driven into Flushing, he was again ordered to halt them there, but the messenger was delayed by foul weather and did not arrive until the ships had moved on. The queen reminded him of his earlier "scruple" in stopping the ships, and Sidney again felt called upon to defend himself, on much the same grounds that he had already presented.[88] If the queen insisted on hindering this shipping, he suggested she send eight to ten warships to lay in the narrow seas to sink some and confiscate others as examples. Flushing and Rammekins were not equipped to block the fleet without reinforcement from home. Besides, he added, less grain than the English believed was passing from Zeland to Spain.[89]

Sidney's relations with the burghers of Flushing and the Zealanders at large were somewhat ambiguous. On the one hand he was uneasy about his ability to defend the garrison and suspicious almost to the point of paranoia about the motives of the Dutch, who he evidently believed were ready to eject him on the slightest provocation. On the other, he formed a number of friendships among the Dutch, and at times he displayed real respect and amity for the people of the Low Countries. His sympathy for the small Dutch merchants caught up in the machinery of England's and the United Province's institutionalized parsimony has already been discussed, and his desire to avoid antagonizing his Dutch hosts is clear in his handling of the corn ships affair.

Cautious as he was in his dealings with them, Sidney seems to have felt more sanguine about the Dutch than did many of the English officials in the Low Countries. Leicester's opinion of the Lowlanders was notorious. Bodley thought they were a sour people and remarked that it was "not possible to draw wine out of vessels full of vinegar." He believed their show of friendship to England was unreliable, and said he "did never yet perceave any harty good Will, in any one of this People, either towardes her Majestie, or any one of our Nation."[90] Sir Thomas Wilkes's opinion was hostile. Sir John Throckmorton, one of Sidney's lieutenant governors, spoke of "cunning and subtle practices against his Majesty's (James I) estate here,"[91] while he was amazed at the free way in which the Dutch spoke their minds about James's relations with Spain.[92]

The Dutch, for their part, were no less suspicious of the English. Stanley and York's betrayal of their charges had given them no reason to believe the Englishmen were better than the general run of humanity. They feared Elizabeth would conclude a treaty with Spain, to their infinite disadvantage, while the English suspected the Dutch alliance would last only as long as it was profitable to the United Provinces. Both sides expected to find perfidy everywhere. Sidney's reluctance to send out the auxiliary troops when the States asked for them "has made them think I nourish all diffidence with them," he observed, so that when the joint effort to take Sluys was unavoidably delayed, the Dutch "imagined it was some practice of mine to hinder the coming of soldiers into those quarters."[93]

To allay their fears, Sidney responded with 120 men from Flushing when Count Maurice invited him to join him in the field, contravening Burghley's order that he stay in town. When the English troops moved en masse, the Dutch feared the soldiers would spoil the countryside,[94] and the capitulation of Gertruydenberg in 1593 again raised the specter of possible treason. Sidney was anxious over the withdrawal of English troops to aid the French king following that loss, and he was keenly aware of the Dutch fear that betrayal might be pending at Flushing or Ostend. As Motley observed, Dutch trust in the characters of men like Norris and Sidney, loyal and intelligent and brave as they might be, "was no more implicit than it had been in that of Sir William Stanley before the commission of his crime."[95]

Under the circumstances, the friendships Sidney developed and the trust he built with individual Zealanders were rather remarkable. He especially like Jacques Gelley, the Burgomaster of Flushing, whose daughter was consecutively married to two English captains there.[96] Sidney heartily recommended Gelley to the home government when the burgomaster was deputed to England to negotiate with the Privy Council in his suit for licenses to transpor beer to Flushing. In 1596, a warrant for Gelley and Peter de Walcher to export to Flushing one hundred tuns of beer was granted "at the request of Sir Robert Sidney, Governor of Flushing."[97]

Sidney told Burghley he knew of no man in Flushing as devoted to the queen as Gelley, and reported that the burgomaster promised there would be no practice against the queen. Gelley vowed to let Sidney know of any such stirrings, and he was in a position to know about everything that went on. Burghley's favor and assistance to him while he was in England, Sidney urged, would ingratiate him and encourage others to place more faith in the English.[98]

Sidney also appears to have liked President Valck, "the principal man of this Province." He remarked that Valck was "well affected to the queen's service," and that he always found him helpful.[99] He felt a particular affection for the old friend of the Prince of Orange, Philip Marnix van St. Aldegonde. "There is no man that were a fitter servant for your Majesty, in these contreys than he," he wrote to the queen, "and I persuade myself it were nothing impossible to winn him."[100] He mentioned his "very good acquaintance" with St. Aldegonde and thought he was "free from all practices." St. Aldegonde asked Sidney to recommend him to the queen, and, said the governor, "since I knew he was suspect I decided to do little by little."[101]

Sidney generously supported the merchants of Flushing and Zealand in their suits to the English government. In 1590, English privateers attacked and spoiled some Flushing ships, causing large losses and damages to the local traders. Sidney sent letters with the deputations of both towns requesting that the queen grant their suit for restitution of their goods. He was gratified to hear from Burghley that the queen was well inclined toward their cause.[102]

In 1597, Sidney supported Flushing over various other towns that were pressing suit to have the staple of English cloth. If the queen would grant it to Flushing, it would assure the town to her. The people would grow rich and thankful, and, he wrote, it "will give your Majesty some profit from this town, since you complain of getting none from it."[103] Rowland Whyte delivered Sidney's letters and a petition to have the English merchant adventurers come to Flushing,[104] but he said nothing further about the proposal in his surviving letters.

The Flushingers welcomed Sidney and his men in their own way. They built a church for the English in Flushing, which was completed, except for the windows, in 1592. Every province was to donate one window for the building, and the uppermost was left for the queen to bestow, if she pleased. The town felt it was showing "a great dutifulness" to the queen in offering the principal window as a monument to her, and they earnestly entreated Sidney to find out if it pleased her.[105] Nothing more appears in the State Papers, Foreign or in other Sidney correspondence regarding this matter.

Sidney, despite Borlas's fears to the contrary, seems not to have thought that fraternization with the local people made a man unfit for responsible positions within the garrison. A number of his subordinates were married to women of Zealand or other provinces with no diminishing of Sidney's trust in their loyalty. Borlas had married a Dutch woman, and Sir William Browne, who succeeded Sir Edmund Uvedall as lieutenant-governor, also had a Dutch wife.[106] Captain Arthur Randolph married Jacques Gelley's daugther, and, when he died, she took Captain Fleming as her second husband.[107]

Many of Sidney's friends came from the upper classes of Dutch society. Louise de Coligny, Princess of Orange, was godmother to Sidney's eldest son, William.[108] Sidney and Lady Sidney carried on a cordial correspondence with her until the end of her life. Her son, the illustrious Count Maurice, declared his affection for Sidney and made him his comrade-in-arms. When Sidney was planning to bring Barbara and several of their children over to Zealand, Maurice offered to lend the family his house in Flushing. They were invited to come whenever they pleased, and to occupy *"tout le quartier d'enhault,"* one of the lower rooms, and any part of the garden they liked, leaving only enough room for the concierge and for the Princess of Orange, who might choose to visit.[109]

This alliance with the House of Orange aligned Sidney with the Calvinists and against the Arminian party of Barneveldt, with whom Maurice fell out and came to oppose implacably. It was perhaps inevitable that Sidney's sympathies would lie with the Calvinist party, the one his uncle, the earl of Leicester, had supported. At any rate, the affiliation proved to be the "correct" one in times to come, for James I conceived a distaste for Arminians, which he was undoubtedly pleased to find shared by Sidney, his foremost expert on Netherlands politics.

NOTES

1. "Instruccions given by the Lordes and others of her Ma: privy counsell to Sr. Robert Sidney Knt, to take the charge and government of the towne of Flushing there," MS Cotton Galba D.v., fol. 42, British Library, London, England; Great Britain, Public Record Office, *Acts of the Privy Council*, 43 vols., 1542–1682, 15:421–27. (Hereafter abbreviated *PC*.)

2. *PC* 17:426. The copy of the contract was "signed by the hand of me, the Secretary."

3. *L & A CSP For* 2:111.

4. Dame Cicely Veronica Wedgwood, *Biography of William the Silent* (New Haven: Yale University Press, 1944), p. 135.

5. John X. Evans, *The Works of Sir Roger Williams* (Oxford: Clarendon Press, Oxford University Press, 1972), p. 82.

6. Wedgewood, p. 135.

7. Juan de Vargas to Philip II, Paris, 12 December 1577, in Philip II, King of Spain, *Correspondence de Philip II sur les affaires des Pays-Bas*, 5 vols., ed. M. Gachard (Brussels: Librairie Ancienne et Moderne, 1848–79), *2me partie*, 1:154. ["One could not retain them without holding Flushing."]

8. Markham, p. 75.

9. Ibid.

10. Motley, 1:286 *ff.*

11. Read, *Walsingham* 3:98.

12. Markham, p. 269.

13. Sidney was never appointed governor of the Brill. Sir Thomas Cecil held the post in Sir Philip Sidney's time, followed by Lord Burghe (1587) and Lord Sheffield, who resigned in the winter of 1597/98. He was succeeded by Sir Francis Vere, whose brother, Sir Horace Vere,

followed him in 1609 and held the post until the cautionary towns were returned to the Dutch. See J. Payne Collier, ed., *The Egerton Papers,* Camden Society, no. 12 (London: J. B. Nichols and Sons, 1840), pp. 270–71.

14. *L & A CSP For.* 1:121, 131.
15. Ibid., 1:121.
16. Collins, 1:298n.
17. *L & A CSP For.* 1:126.
18. Ibid., 1:108
19. Sidney to Burghley, Flushing, 26 May 1590, SP 84/37, fol. 174, Public Record Office, London, England. (Public Record Office, State Papers Foreign, Holland [vol. 84] is hereafter designated "SP 84;" State Papers, Foreign, France [vol. 78] designated "SP 78;" State Papers, Foreign, Holland and Flanders [vol. 83] designated "SP 83.")
20. *L & A CSP For.* 1:132–33.
21. Collins, 1:305.
22. Sir Thomas Heneage to Sidney, Court, 13 June 1590, *HMCD* 2:107.
23. *L & A CSP For.* 1:132–33.
24. Ibid., 1:135.
25. Ibid., 2:112.
26. Collins, 2:305; *HMCD* 2:109.
27. *HMCD* 2:107.
28. Ibid., 2:105–06
29. Sidney to Essex [*sic.;* however, the letter is endorsed "To my Lo. Burghley. . . ."], Flushing, 14 May 1590; Privy Council to Sidney, 6 October 1589, in William Murdin, *A Collection of State Papers Relating to the Affairs in the Reign of Elizabeth from 1571 to 1596: Transcribed from Original Papers (etc.),* 2 vols. (London: W. Bowyer, 1759f, 2:642–43.
30. *L & A CSP For.* 1:131; Sidney to Burghley, Flushing, 10 June 1590, SP 84/37, fol. 155; Sidney to Burghley, Flushing, 10 June 1590, SP 84/37, fol. 268.
31. Sidney to Burghley, Flushing, 12 June 1590, SP 84/37, fol. 272.
32. Collins, 1:305, Thomas Wilkes to Sidney, Hague, 22 July 1590, *HMCD* 2:109.
33. Sidney to "My Lord," 29 July 1590, SP 84/38, fols. 113–14.
34. Murdin, 2:642–43.
35. *HMCD* 2:104.
36. *L & A CSP For.* 1:131–32.
37. *CSP Dom.* 3:3, [14] February 1591.
38. Sidney to Burghley, Flushing, 10 June 1590, SP 84/37, fol. 268.
39. *L & A CSP For.* 1:131–32.
40. Sidney to Burghley, Flushing, 12 June 1590, SP 84/37, fol. 272.
41. Sidney to Burghley, 23 June 1590, ibid., fol. 302.
42. Sidney to Burghley, 29 August 1590, SP 84/38, fols. 226–27.
43. Collins, 1:394; Borlas to Sidney, Flushing, 22 November 1598, *HMCD* 2:104.
44. Cruickshank, pp. 92–93.
45. Ibid., pp. 95–96.
46. Ibid., p. 96.
47. Ibid., pp. 97–98.
48. SP 84/37, fol. 268.
49. Cruickshank, pp. 98–99.
50. Ibid., p. 123.
51. Warrant to Sidney for pay of his company of 100 soldiers (1585), Additional MS 5753, fol. 278, British Library, London, England.
52. *L & A CSP For.* 1:128.
53. Cruickshank, pp. 78–79.
54. Ibid., p. 81.
55. Ibid., p. 80.
56. Ibid., pp. 86–87.
57. *CSP Dom.* 12:275, [?] July 1589.
58. Ibid., 3:4, 18 January 1591.
59. Cruickshank, p. 88.
60. *L & A CSP For.* 1:124.
61. Ibid.
62. Ibid., p. 127.
63. Ibid., p. 122.

64. Ibid.
65. Ibid., 2:117.
66. Sidney to [Burghley], Flushing, 14 May 1590, Murdin, 2:642–43.
67. L & A CSP For. 1:134.
68. Sidney to Burghley, Flushing, 10 June 1590, SP 84/39, fol. 1.
69. L & A CSP For. 2:123.
70. Ibid., 1:134.
71. Sidney to Privy Council, 1 September 1590, SP 84/37, fol. 1.
72. L & A CSP For. 2:123–24.
73. Sidney to Burghley, 10/20 November 1590, SP 84/39, fol. 209.
74. L & A CSP For. 1:134.
75. Privy Council to Sidney, 26 July 1590, PC 19:347.
76. L & A CSP For. 2:118.
77. Ibid., 2:118–19.
78. Ibid.
79. Ibid., 1:119.
80. Sidney to Essex, Flushing, 8 August 1595, Murdin, 2:688.
81. Privy Council to Sidney or Uvedall, 23 January 1596, PC 26:441.
82. Privy Council to Sir Henry Palmer, ibid., 26:446.
83. Sidney to Cecil, Flushing, 27 January 1596/97, SP 84/54, fol. 41.
84. Ibid.
85. Sidney to [Cecil], Flushing, 17 February 1596/97, ibid., fols. 72–73. Internal evidence suggests this letter was addressed to the Privy Council and not, as PRO speculates, to Cecil. Note Sidney's references to his readers as "your honors," and a reference in his letter to Cecil to his answer to a letter from the Privy Council forwarded by Cecil (Sidney to Cecil, February 18, 1596/97, SP 84/53, fol. 78).
86. Sidney to Burghley, 3 February 1596/97, SP 84/54, fols. 55–56.
87. Sidney to [Cecil], Flushing, 17 February 1596/97, ibid., fols. 72–73.
88. Sidney to Cecil, Flushing, 17 August 1597, SP 84/55, fols. 89–90.
89. Sidney to Cecil, Flushing, 8 August 1597, ibid., fol. 165.
90. Bodley to Sidney, Hague, 10 March 1591/92, HMCD 2:125.
91. Throckmorton to Sidney, Flushing, 27 February 1611/12, HMCD 4:22–24.
92. Throckmorton to Sidney, Holland, 30 August/9 September 1590, SP 84/70, fol. 100 v.
93. Sidney to Burghley, Buchoven, [25] September 1590, SP 84/39, fol. 80.
94. Sidney to Burghley, Flushing, 25 July 1592, SP 84/45, fol. 252.
95. Motley, 3:267.
96. Sidney to Burghley, Flushing, 25 July 1592, SP 84/45, fol. 104; Gelley to Sidney, 28 June 1601 [n.s.], HMCD 2:520.
97. CSP Dom. 4:288, 30 September 1596.
98. Sidney to Burghley, 18 December 1590, SP 84/40, fol. 53.
99. Sidney to Cecil, Flushing, 2 September 1596, SP 84/53, fol. 47.
100. Sidney to Elizabeth, Flushing, 20 November 1590, SP 84/39, fols. 228–29.
101. Sidney to Burghley, 1 January 1590/91, SP 84/41, fols. 8–9.
102. Sidney to Burghley, Flushing, 21 November 1590, SP 84/39, fols. 230–31; Sidney to Burghley, 18 December 1590, SP 84/40, fol. 55; Sidney to Burghley, 18 December 1590, ibid., fol. 94; Sidney to Burghley, 18 December 1590, ibid., fol. 96; Sidney to Burghley, 18 December 1590, ibid., fol. 98; Magistrates of Flushing to Queen Elizabeth, 19/29 December 1590, ibid., fol. 68.
103. Sidney to Burghley, Flushing, 28 July 1592, SP 84/40, fol. 68.
104. Whyte to Sidney, Strand, 25 January 1597/[98], HMCD 2:313.
105. Sidney to Queen Elizabeth, MS Cotton Galba D. xiii, fol. 146, British Library, London, England.
106. Browne to Sidney, Flushing, 16 October 1602, n.s., HMCD 2:600.
107. Sidney to Burghley, 3 February 1596/97, SP 84/55, fol. 56.
108. Sidney to Lady Sidney, Hague, 22 May 1592, HMCD 2:127.
109. Count Maurice to Sidney, Hague, 3 April 1592, ibid., 2:126.

Military Exploits in the Low Countries

As soon as Sidney was established in his governorship, he and Maurice began to plan an attempt on the town of Sluys. Probably this scheme especially appealed to Sidney because his brother and Essex had incurred the queen's displeasure by their involvement in the earlier loss of the town to the enemy. Sluys, located in the estuary of the Zwin River, had strategic importance as the foreport of Bruges. If the plot succeeded, it would help insure the safety of Ostend, where Sir Edward Norris feared a siege. In June 1590, Sidney went to Berghen, partly to act as Essex's deputy at the christening of Sir Thomas Knowles's child, but more particularly to confer with a gentleman about the surprise of Sluys. He had heard reports that recent flooding had deepened and improved the harbor, making it possible for large ships to approach the very walls of the town; for this reason, he thought Sluys would make a better prize for the queen than Ostend.[1]

The allies made their move late in July. Sidney and two hundred men from Flushing met Count Maurice, Sir Francis Vere, and eight hundred soldiers in the field. Unfortunately, heavy rains and great floods all over the provinces so hindered their efforts that the action did not take place.[2] This anticlimax was the more embarassing because the Council of States had written to Sidney while he was in the field, requesting two companies from Flushing, a demand Sidney could not fulfill, under the circumstances. He was also unable to respond to Sir Edward Conway's request for help in the surprise of Nieuport. Sidney and the count consoled themselves by sending two hundred Flushing soldiers into Flanders, where, after burning and spoiling the countryside, they brought back various beasts and some quantity of booty.[3]

In the spring of 1591, Maurice and Sidney revived their hopes for the conquest of Sluys. Their secret plans were communicated to Burghley via Captain Sampson. After conferring with Maurice and Vere, Sidney was to have the place viewed by observers from Flushing. He went to Holland for two weeks in late March and early April and there discussed the scheme with Maurice and Bodley. Enthusiastic about the plan, the count agreed to send men from Berghen and other places. Sir John Norris also liked the

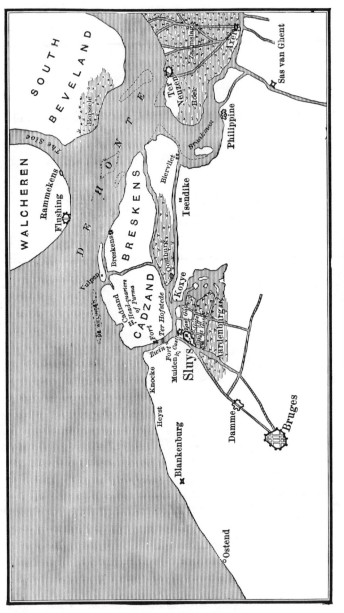

THE SIEGE OF SLUYS
Source: Markham, chapter 9

idea and thought it a fit occasion to bring the band for Brittany to Flushing. Sir Thomas Morgan agreed to send four companies from Berghen and planned to go himself.[4] The home government, however, was less sure about the scheme than were the field commanders, and Burghley sent back a message to that effect with Sampson. The captain did not arrive until March 4, however, and the troops were already on the move before Sidney received Burghley's letter.

It was another failure. This time they could not blame their lack of success on the weather, for the wind, the tide, and the moon were all in perfect concurrence. "[W]e failed," Sidney reported, "because the boats on which success depended were negligently insufficient, which when I discovered it I would proceed no further but brought the troops back again."[5] Burghley found this explanation thin and demanded to know more. Sidney referred him to Sir Thomas Baskerville, who had been on the scene and could inform the lord treasurer better in person than Sidney could in writing. He hoped Burghley would not blame him more "then is ordinarily done to undertakers of enterprises," and would bear in mind the unexpected difficulties of such endeavors.[6]

Later in the summer, Burghley inquired again why Sidney did not go forward against Sluys when he was in the field near Bruges, and Sidney had to explain that any effort against the town had to be done by surprise rather than by force.[7] Sidney complained to Burghley that he had heard that the queen and the lord treasurer blamed him for the Sluys failure, although others had done worse. He was annoyed by these reports and decided he would deal no further in any such enterprise unless commanded, although, he added, the Sluys scheme remained as feasible as ever. Burghley wrote back reassuring Sidney of his continued favor, and claiming he had defended Sidney to the queen. He never discontinued his friendship to anyone, Burghley said, without telling him the cause. Sidney was not to believe rumors about his attitude.[8]

While the enterprise against Sluys was in progress, Maurice, Sidney, and Vere were concocting a similar scheme against Dunkirk. The count hoped Dunkirk would provide him the foothold he desired in Flanders. It would ensure safe traffic out of the Low Countries and entry into Flanders where the French and allied troops could assist each other. Maurice was keeping his plans very secret, and, as of October 10, 1590, he had made only Vere, the Admiral Nassau, and Sidney privy to them. He asked Vere and Sidney to go with him to make a personal inspection of the place. Reporting on this development to the home government, Sidney expressed his wish that the English could claim some of the glory of the proposed triumph, despite Maurice's having kept his plans a close secret until he chose to impart them. However, Sidney thought it not too late for the queen to second Maurice with some forces out of England, "for then it will be thought that this matter was undertaken on the hope of them." With great relish, he contemplated the discomfiture of Parma at the loss of Dunkirk, and speculated that the duke would be drawn out of France to

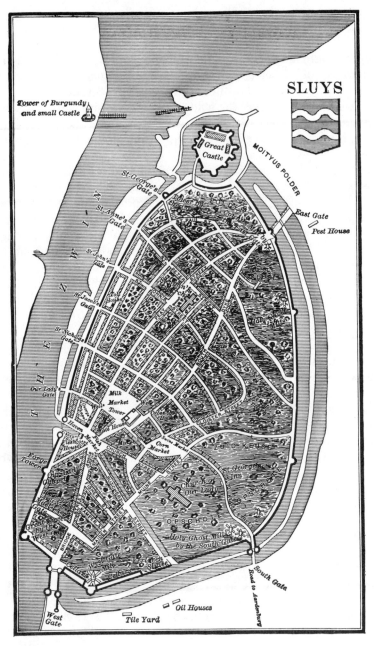

SLUYS
Source: Markham, facing page 104

Flanders, where, given enough men, the English and Dutch could easily withstand him. If the Dunkirk enterprise succeeded at the same time as the proposed English attack on Bois-le-Duc, it would "amaze the Spaniards greatly."[9]

These sanguine plans went forward, but the project was delayed by foul weather. The English at home apparently caught Sidney's enthusiasm, for Burghley ordered him to recommend Sir Francis Vere for the governorship of Dunkirk, even though the Dutch had already promised it to Meetekerke.[10] In mid-October they moved against Dunkirk, with no more success than they had in the Sluys enterprise. Meetekerke either had not reconnoitered or not remembered the place well, and they were discovered as they attempted their surprise. As they were going to view the town, the count of Solms was shot in the face, Vere through a foot, and Meetekerke through both feet. At that, the Anglo-Dutch allies thought better of their plan and retreated.[11]

The queen expressed her impatience with Sidney's absences from his post while he engaged in these fruitless adventures. Burghley defended him and earned Sidney's thanks. Sir Robert hoped the lord treasurer would continue his patronage. He hoped "that I be not forced to continew stil within the wales of Flushing since the going sometimes abrode among the men of war is very requisite for the service of this place. . . ." Experience with the forces that might harm Flushing, Sidney argued, would show him how to avoid causeless fears or overconfidence. Nor could he afford to be an utter stranger to Maurice and the other men of war, for that would increase their suspicion of him.[12]

Nevertheless, Sidney was stung by the disapproval he received or sensed from home. A year later, early in March of 1592, the count of Solms made an attempt against Sluys that Sidney described as identical to his own enterprise. Solms had no more success than Sidney. "I hope her Majesty will now thinck that the fault of missing was not propre unto me," he wrote to Burghley, "but that other men may that way have as goodluck as myself." Sidney was irked that the Dutch had kept the matter secret from him, so that he did not even know about it until a week after the fact. Since he had already led a similar enterprise, he thought courtesy demanded he be included in this one. "[I]ndeed it is a wrong among men of warre, one to take the others actions out of his hands and as it were seeke to reape the frute of the others labors." The more he thought about it, the angrier he grew, and by the time he reached the end of his report to Burghley, he had worked himself into quite an indignant state. The Dutch had usurped his right to participate in the Sluys exploit, he felt, because of their petty jealousy and suspicion of the English. They really did not want English help; in fact, they would just as soon have Sluys in the enemy's hands as in the queen's. Their motive in hiding the maneuver from him, Sidney theorized, was their fear that he would find a way to undermine it out of personal envy; of course, he added, they would deny any such jealousy and say his surmise stemmed from spite. Their behavior showed a contempt for the queen as well as for him, one which "they would not have offered to the meanest governor of theyr own in the Land."

Hearing of the assembly of their troops, Sidney had asked for a reason but was put off. He pointed out to the Dutch that since he was there by the queen's commission he expected to be told in due time of any assembly of soldiers in the vicinity of Walcheren Island—to no avail. It was a menacing precedent, he observed to Burghley, for if the Dutch were plotting against Flushing, they could muster their troops "under our noses and we in the town would be none the wiser." The situation underscored the importance of supplying and manning the garrison adequately: Sidney wanted the queen to keep twenty-two companies in the town and provide them with ample powder and arms. He was convinced such a show of potential force would remove a great number of the irritations the English suffered at the hands of the Dutch. He proposed, the queen sent him an ersatz letter, signed by her own hand, commanding him to look into rumors that the States and the Flushingers were doing things that might endanger her garrison. With this in hand, he thought, his authority would be enhanced and he might be able to have the matter redressed. Still, he added, until the garrison was stronger, he would have no choice but to take any answer the Dutch gave him.[13]

If any such letter from the queen was issued, no trace of it survives, and Flushing certainly was not reinforced to a total of thirty-three thousand men. Probably Sidney simmered down after he had sent his tirade to Burghley. He seems to have reconciled with the Dutch quickly, and soon he was back in the field beside Maurice and Vere.

In 1592, the States decided to try to relieve Friesland and Groningen of the Spanish presence by attacking the enemy garrison in the north. Parma was occupied in France, leaving Count Mansfelt as his deputy and Verdugo in command in Friesland. The States opened their campaign with the siege of Steenwyck, between Deventer and Groningen in the northern corner of the province of Oversell.[14] Maurice invited Sidney to join him at the Hague with as many troops as he could assemble.[15] On May 7, Maurice and his allies made camp before Steenwyck[16] with an army of more than six thousand foot and fifteen thousand horse.[17] After extensive preparations, the battery began on the afternoon of June 3 [O.S.],[18] and ten days later a ravelin on the west side was captured.[19] However, the walls were so strong that Maurice finally had to resort to mining. Explosive charges were planted at strategic places, and at dawn on June 23, the army assaulted the town, to the accompaniment of the blasting charges. A series of attacks defeated the garrison's defense, and on the fifth of July the defenders marched out. Maurice lost six hundred men and was wounded, as were Sidney, Sir Francis Vere and Sir Horace Vere, Captains Lambart and Buck, and one hundred fifty-two of their men.[20]

Sidney's moment of glory came at the battle of Turnhout. In the autumn of 1597, Archduke Albert's army, commanded by the count of

Barras, had encamped its four thousand infantry and six thousand cavalry at the village of Turnhout, some twenty miles south of Breda. Evidently they were waiting for a chance to make some attempt against the Dutch. Sir Francis Vere, conferring with Barneveldt at the Hague, suggested the allies strike first, and about the end of December, Maurice began secretly to collect a force at Gertruydenberg for that purpose. Five thousand foot and eight hundred horse, with two demicannon and two field pieces, were assembled there under Governor Heraugière of Breda. Vere brought an English regiment and Sidney joined them with three hundred men from Flushing. Count Hohenlo commanded the States' cavalry, with Marcellus Bacx under him. Broderode and Solms brought men from various garrisons, and Sir Alexander Murray came with a Scottish regiment.

At daybreak of Thursday, January 23, 1598, the four divisions marched out of Gertruydenberg, their cavalry at their flanks. Six ensigns of foot were in the van under Maurice, followed by seven hundred under Sidney's command, and eight ensigns of foot under Vere. Murray and his Scots brought up the rear. They marched twenty-four miles in one day, reaching the village of Ravels, three miles from Turnhout, two hours after sunset. Spies reported that the enemy was still camped at Turnhout, without entrenchments and unaware of the allies' approach. The men ate a hasty meal and settled down to spend the dark, cold night trying to rest. Maurice, Sidney, and Vere camped together, their cloaks wrapped around them like sleeping bags to protect them from the frozen ground. Maurice was unable to sleep and began pacing around and lighting fires of straw near the *corps du garde*. Realizing they would get no rest around him, Sidney and Vere retired to a barn full of soldiers, where they were able to sleep briefly.[21]

At three or four o'clock in the morning, the army rose and built a huge fire, an activity that unnerved the soldiers who thought a surprise of the enemy was planned. At seven, they marched toward the enemy. Vere led a band of musketeers against some Spanish soldiers who were breaking down a bridge to delay the English. Sidney joined him with another group of musketeers and some horse. Together they took the bridge and in a fierce fight held the Spanish at bay. The access for horses was so bad that Hohenlo judged it impossible. He was about to turn back when he got news that Sidney and Vere were heavily engaged in their skirmish, and that the water was passable for horses. Within the hour, Maurice ordered the English to come forward; they pushed the enemy to a heath about three miles from Turnhout.[22]

Sidney, spotting Hohenlo as he came up with half the horsemen, left Vere to inform him of what had happened and encouraged him to charge the enemy. The Count hesitated to attempt such a difficult operation. "And trulie had [Sidney] not seen further into their [the Spaniards'] amazement then the Count did," wrote a contemporary observer, "that happie victorie which God gave this valient attempt, had not been that day achieved." Sidney convinced Hohenlo to attack and then returned to Vere's side,

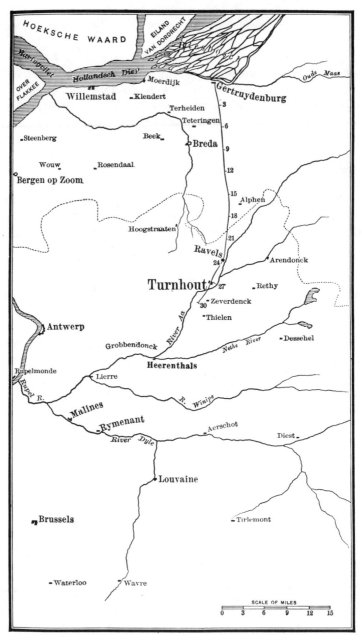

THE FIELD OF TURNHOUT
Source: Markham, facing page 256

"whereupon Sir Robert Sidney and Sir Francis Vere together with Captaine Edmondes, a Scottish Captaine, charged home upon the reregard
and drave the mustetiers upon their owne pikes, from whence arose the
beginning of the victorie." Hohenlo charged the enemy's horse, "and they
not abiding the charge, he fel upon the vangard, where the overthrow was
by a few horse most fortunately seconded."[23]

The enemy was routed and their infantry batallions destroyed. Three
hundred of the four-thousand-man force were killed, six hundred taken
prisoner, and thirty-eight ensigns were captured. Their commander, the
count of Varras, was slain in action. The allies lost about ten men, having
fought the whole action with fewer than eight hundred horse; the infantry
never came up. That evening the army rested at the village of Turnhout,
and the next day the castle of Turnhout capitulated without a struggle.[24]

The news of the victory was joyously received in England. Sidney's and
Vere's reputations waxed large. The queen wrote personally to Sidney
congratulating him on the increase of his reputation at Turnhout, although she tempered her praise with a suggestion that he tend to business
closer to home.[25]

Several months later, a play depicting the overthrow appeared on
stage. Rowland Whyte heard of it and wrote Sidney that "all your names
were used that were at yt, especially Sir Francis Veres, and he that plaied
that part got a beard resembling his, and a watchett satten doublett, with
hose trimed with silver lace."[26] A day later, on the afternoon of October 29,
Whyte got a chance to attend the play and "saw Sir Robert Sidney and Sir
Francis Vere upon the stage, killing, slaying, and overthrowing the
Spaniard. There is," he added, "most honorable mention of your service in
seconding Sir Francis Vere. . . ."[27]

Ironically, this "happie victorie" marked the end of Sidney's friendship
with Sir Francis Vere. Up until the battle of Turnhout the men had been
on cordial terms.[28] After the battle, Sidney and Vere rode together in a
spirit of good comradeship to Willemstadt, where Sir Robert was to continue by water to Flushing. Both wrote official dispatches home, which they
sent by one of Sidney's captains. "I gave him my letters to read," Vere
reports, and "then to one of his captains to deliver in England: but my
letters were held back; and his, which were far more partially written,
delivered. Which art of doublement changed the love I had so long borne
him, into a deep dislike that could not be soon digested."[29] In truth, Sidney
gave Vere his due in his report and even laid the victory to Vere's credit.[30]
Vere, however, never believed Sidney meant him anything but mischief,
and the incident bred a lasting rancor on both sides. Years later, Sidney
haughtily characterized Vere "as one whose business I meddle nor make
not withall, thogh I know he troubles himself much about me."[31]

Sidney's reputation suffered more than once from the misapprehen-
sions and unjust accusations of others, and each time it happened, he seems
to have been stung. After the Sluys and Dunkirk affairs, for example, he
remarked icily to Burghley that he was unwilling to enter into any new

matters or make any promises to Maurice, for "I hear the Queen says I have meddled with many things which have neither been wisely begun nor carried."[32] One such misunderstanding had dangerous repercussions, and only with great protest and detailed explanation was Sidney able to keep his good name intact.

In June 1600, he had accompanied Maurice into Flanders. The enemy, taking note of the count's arrival, marched with their whole army to greet him. They suddenly appeared on the sands before Nieuport. Maurice was taken unawares, not having expected the archduke to be able to gather his mutinous army so quickly. The deputy of the States General at Ostend had received intelligence that the archduke's rebellious men had been contented and were on the move, and sent Maurice several letters urging him to retire without chancing a battle, but now the choice was out of his power. His men were exposed in and around the haven of Nieuport, and there was no access to the town except at low tide, which was not due for several hours. The enemy had cut off their passage and was advancing on them. With no means of escape, their only hope lay in forcing their way through the Spanish forces. The archduke, however, was overconfident, and, said Sidney, "theyr arrogancy was iustly punished." Expecting Maurice to flee by sea, which was an impossibility, the archduke sacrificed his advantage by going after the prince rather than forcing him to attempt an attack on the Spanish army. The result was a two-hour fight that ended in a Spanish rout. The archduke "was forced to provide for himself by the goodness of his hors, wherein he was accompanied by the greatest part of his cavalry." The Spanish infantry was slaughtered and its commanders killed or taken prisoner.[33]

It was a glamorous battle and a great triumph, but unfortunately, Sidney was not there to share in the glory. Surveying the situation, he realized that the future safety of the States depended on the battle's outcome. He had come with no men and no command in Maurice's army, and he was unprovided to go into battle. He knew his place was at Flushing, which would be in danger if the Dutch lost at Nieuport; so, he withdrew from the fight and sped back to his post. At the time, he felt some misgivings about this decision, knowing how it would be construed by his enemies. "Already I have bin blamed for venturing to much," he remarked as he reported the incident to Cecil, "and if now for being respective I bee also disliked, I trust the day wil one day come wherein I may show that onely the care of my duty, made me doe as I did."[34]

His fears were justified. In under ten days the gossip was flying at the English court. Rowland Whyte must have felt under siege. "I long to hear from yourself," he wrote to Sidney; "many inquire the cause of your absence [from Nieuport]." One of the Lord Chamberlain's gentlemen told Whyte he had heard Sidney and La Noue had retired to Ostend because Prince Maurice refused to give them commands in the army.[35] Vere was reaping the harvest of glory from the battle, and little credit was being given to Maurice.[36] The rumours grew more and more elaborate. Vere's followers reported that Sidney was there all the time. Others claimed he was involved in the beginning of the fight, but that he withdrew from the skirmishing to accompany Maurice into the thick of the battle. Still others said that Sidney returned to Flushing in anger over having no command. Whyte hoped Sidney's aunt, Lady Huntingdon, would speak to Elizabeth in Sir Robert's favor, "for she governes the Queen, many howres together very private."[37]

Sidney soon wrote to Whyte to provide him with the explanation for his conduct, and observed in a letter to Cecil that, despite his triumph at Nieuport, Maurice had not been able to win a foot of ground and was being forced to retire without accomplishing anything more. Sidney hoped this made it clear that he had good reason to look to his charge, for, he remarked, he understood there was some talk about his leaving the army, "wherein I had not so much to do as the most ordinary man that draweth pay."[38]

Cecil responded with his approval of Sidney's decision, and Sidney's friends came to his defense. Lord Nottingham, who was high admiral of England at the time, spoke to the queen, showed her a letter from Sidney, and explained the governor's reasons for retiring to Flushing. She was well satisfied and publicly praised Sidney's discretion.[39] Meanwhile, before he could have received Whyte's report of his exoneration, Sidney heard what was being said by the gossipmongers at court. He shot off a scorching letter to Cecil. He was glad Cecil approved his reasons for leaving the battle of Nieuport, but he wanted it made clear that duty, not fear, made him return to Flushing. "[I]f there bee any man that doth say I did it out of passion not out of iudgment, in any worthy occasion where wee shall meet together, I will make it seen that the hilt of my sworde shall be more advanced than the point of his."[40]

He evidently suspected specific men of maligning his reputation, and he was ready to run them through. He ordered Whyte to report on Sir Walter Raleigh, Lord Cobham, and Sir Robert Drury, a captain in the Low Countries who earlier had been frustrated in an attempt to gain a company under Sidney. Whyte protested that he had been "very wakeful both by my self and your good friends to understand what [Drury] shuld say of you; but I cannot learn that he said any thing that might offend you . . . neither did [Cobham] or [Raleigh] say anything to your dishonor that I can heare of."[41] Whyte must have been anxious to avoid bloodshed, for his letters abruptly turned conciliatory and soothing in tone; he assured Sidney that "all of the best sort say that you had great reason to doe as you did, and not to be in such an army as a private man."[42] A few days later he insisted again that all men of honor and discretion approved of Sidney's return from the battle, and those who spoke against him were only "some base fellows of [Vere's] followers."[43] Essex sent for Whyte to inquire about Sidney's actions and, hearing Whyte's report, "approved, and protested . . . that yt had bene dishonorable for you to be comanded by hym to whom you first gave honor in the warrs."[44]

In the end, Sidney's honor was upheld. Sidney was particularly grateful for Cecil's ready support. "I do not leave to acknowledge myself very much honored by you, that it pleases yow to iudge iustly of mee," he wrote, "since I find not the like measure of others, and in discharge of that debt I doe vowe an arme and a sworde ready to defend anything that may concern your cause, in any occasion."[45] It was even said that Sidney had reconciled with Vere, but since Vere's followers seem to have been the source of much underhanded gossip, it is difficult to believe the truth of this.

That Sidney departed out of cowardice is unquestionably not a possibility, considering his past record of daring on the battlefield. Sidney claimed he left because he knew his place was at Flushing and because he was not equipped to go into battle. Too, he seems to have been in the habit of riding with the prince with no intention of doing battle, but simply to enjoy his company and to reconnoiter the countryside. This custom made it probable that he had no armor, adequate weapons, or properly trained horse with him. Unlike his brother, Robert seems to have recognized the futility of sacrificing his life in a noble gesture by charging unprepared into a pitched battle. Had he died or been taken prisoner and, as appeared likely, Maurice had gone down in defeat at Nieuport, Flushing would have been thrown into confusion. The Dutch might have capitulated to the Spanish, and the queen's cautionary towns would have been turned over to the enemy. A chain of events such as this would have destroyed Sidney's reputation, and the contemplation of even posthumous dishonor was more than he cared to consider.

Whyte, Essex, and others at the English court seem to have believed Sidney left because Maurice offered him no command in his army, and they clearly approved this ground for the decision.[46] Perhaps some such motive was in Sidney's mind, but the fact that he did not accompany Maurice with the intention of fighting indicates that his explanation to Cecil can be taken at face value. He showed a certain moral courage in declining to make a display of chivalric heroism and taking the mundane course of duty, knowing he would be criticized for doing so. Reports that have described the colorful exploits and intemperate decisions of men like Sir Philip Sidney, the earl of Essex, and Sir Walter Raleigh make good reading but, upon reflection, leave one amazed at their folly. Sir Robert's appraisal of the danger at Nieuport and his sensible, accurate appreciation of his own position were, if lacking in dramatic flair, practical interpretations leading to the only rational decision he could have made in the circumstances.

By 1600, the war had begun to resolve itself in favor of the Dutch. Spain's soldiers were mutinying and Maurice was in control almost everywhere. Sidney accompanied the Prince on one of his triumphant marches and described the scene as fort after fort yielded to the States' army. In June, they took Oldenborow, which had already been abandoned, proceeded to Bredenay, a strongly fortified place that had also been abandoned, and then to Bruges, which they took without the loss of a single man.[47] In September 1602, Sidney was with Maurice before Grave when the town was surrendered to the Dutch. He observed how poorly provided the garrison's eight hundred men were, and reported that the Spanish troops were daily disbanding for want of money.[48] After 1603, Sidney was rarely in the Low Countries, and he stopped following Maurice personally in the wars.

Although he was eager and daring enough in his youth, Sidney did not have the makings of a great soldier. He enjoyed the company of military men—his friendships with Maurice, Vere, and Hohenlo evidence that. But his character was perhaps too temperate, too conservative to permit him to run the risks that, as much by good fortune as by valor or intelligent strategy, brought these men their reputations as battlefield geniuses. His refusal to go ahead with the Sluys enterprise when he saw the inadequate boats that had been supplied illustrates this cautious turn of mind. He was not cowardly, but neither was he foolhardy. Too, he seems not to have been expected to perform the duties of a field commander; the queen more than once complained of his forays with Maurice and said she wanted him to stay at his post. That he often accompanied Maurice into the field unarmed and without men reveals that he went into the field with little intention of performing any miracles of valor. Indeed, with the exception of men like Vere, Williams, and Norris, the English showed little military distinction in their involvement with the United Provinces at this time. It was a Dutch show, and men of Sidney's rank were more often audience than players.

NOTES

1. Sidney to Burghley, Berghen, 15 June 1590, SP 84/37, fol. 272.
2. Sidney to Burghley, Middleburgh, 12 August 1590, SP 84/38, fols. 167–68.
3. *L & A CSP For.* 2:114–15.
4. Ibid., 2:99–100.
5. Sidney to Burghley, 16 March 1590/91, SP 84/41, fol. 251.
6. Sidney to Burghley, March 15[90]/91, SP 84/44, fol. 175.
7. Sidney to Burghley, Flushing, 8 July 1591, SP 84/42, fols. 192–95. The editors of *L & A CSP For.* seem to be in error when, on pp. 99–100, they connect the skirmishing around Damme and Bruges mentioned in this letter with the spring attempt on Sluys. This confusion perhaps stems from the incorrect placing by the PRO of Sidney's March, 1590/91 letter (SP 84/44, fol. 175) among later correspondence.
8. *L & A CSP For.* 2:100.
9. Sidney to Burghley, Flushing, 10 October 1590, SP 84/39, fols. 131–32.
10. Sidney to Burghley, Flushing, 23 October 1590, ibid., fols. 164–64.
11. Ibid.
12. Sidney to Burghley, Flushing, 29 October 1590, ibid., fols. 181–82.
13 .Sidney to Burghley, 6 March 1592, SP 84/44, fols. 135–36.
14. Markham, pp. 181–82.
15. Maurice to Sidney, Hague, 8 May 1592, N.S., *HMCD* 2:126.
16. Markham, p. 182.
17. Sidney to Burghley, Camp before Steinwick, 21 May 1592, SP 84/44, fols. 318–19.
18. Sidney to Burghley, Camp before Steinwick, 13 June 1592, ibid., fol. 320.

19. Markham, p. 183.

20. Ibid., pp. 183–84.

21. Ibid., pp. 255–56.

22. *A True Discourse of the Overthrowe Given to the Common Enemy at Turnhaut,* (London: Peter Short, 1597), n.p.

23. Ibid.

24. Markham, pp. 260–61.

25. Queen Elizabeth to Sidney, 15 February 1596/97, SP 84/54, fol. 64.

26. Whyte to Sidney, Strand, 26 October 1599, *HMCD* 2:406.

27. Whyte to Sidney, Strand, 27 October 1599, ibid., 2:408.

28. See, for example, Vere's bantering letter to Sidney, 8 February 1596/97 (*HMCD* 2:231) and Sidney's admiration of Vere in his letter to Burghley, 26 September 1591 (SP 84/43, fols. 39–40).

29. Sir Francis Vere, *The Commentaries of Sir Francis Vere, 1657,* in *English Books, 1641–1700* (Ann Arbor, Mich.: University Microfilms, 1961–), p. 81.

30. Sidney to Cecil, SP 84/54, fols. 30–34 [Incomplete].

31. Sidney to Cecil, Flushing, 2 June 1600, SP 84/60, fol. 53–54.

32. Sidney to Burghley, Flushing, 19 July 1591, SP 84/42, fol. 240.

33. Sidney to Cecil, Ostend, 25 June 1600, ibid., fols. 179–81.

34. Ibid.

35. Whyte to Sidney, Court, 5 July 1600, *HMCD* 2:471–72.

36. Whyte to Sidney, Court, 7 July 1600, ibid., 2:472.

37. Whyte to Sidney, 2 July 1600, ibid., 2:472.

38. Sidney to Cecil, 16 July 1600, SP 84/60, fols. 239–40 [Incomplete].

39. Whyte to Sidney, Nonesuch, 8 August 1600, *HMCD,* 2:476.

40. Sidney to Cecil, Flushing, 27 July 1600, SP 84/60, fols. 244–45.

41. Whyte to Sidney, Nonesuch, 8 August 1600, *HMCD* 2:476–77.

42. Ibid.

43. Whyte to Sidney, "The Black Boy in the Strand," 16 August 1600, ibid., 2:477–78.

44. Whyte to Sidney, Court, 21 August 1600, ibid., 2:478.

45. Sidney to Cecil, Flushing, 27 July 1600, SP 84/60, fols. 244–45.

46. Whyte to Sidney, Nonesuch, 8 August 1600, *HMCD* 2:246.

47. Sidney to Cecil, Osten, 17 June 1600, SP 84/60, fol. 165.

48. Sidney to Cecil, Camp at Grave, 6 September 1602, SP 84/62, fol. 201.

[6]

The Administration of Flushing

When Sidney was not in England, in the field, or visiting Middleburgh or the Hague, he passed his time in the routine management of the garrison. A fair picture of his day-to-day responsibilities can be gleaned from two sources: his own letters to Burghley and Cecil, and his lieutenant-governors' correspondence with him. Sidney's deputies, Borlas, Uvedall, Browne, and Throckmorton, described their daily undertakings in much greater detail in their reports to him than he did in his reports. The governor juggled the concerns of Dutch politicians, English and Dutch merchants, the townspeople, the soldiers, and the home government, trying to keep everyone contented and to maintain the peace with as little friction as possible. Religion, controversy, intelligence, military transport, law enforcement, local justice: all came within the province of the governor's reponsibility.

Sidney's authority was well defined in his instructions, but it was subject to erosion. Once he had established the compass of his power, he had constantly to fight off encroachments from other empire builders. This ongoing struggle appears most clearly in the repeated squabbles over Sidney's own companies in the Low Countries (of which he was the nominal captain) and over the disposition of the captaincies of the companies under him at Flushing.

When he took over the governorship, Elizabeth granted him the horse band belonging to the previous governor, Sir William Russell, which was stationed at Berghen. The income from this position was to defray the substantial personal charges involved in his government.[1] Russell thought he would be permitted to retain it.[2] Another captain, who was also named Russell, had commanded it for years; he complained, saying the company was weakened by the transfer because the men were loyal followers of Sir William Russell, and because under the new orders it would be impossible to maintain from Flushing a horse band at Berghen.[3] Sidney responded that he needed the income, for his expenses far exceeded the queen's allowance, and that the company had been granted to all his predecessors. He begged for Burghley's favor and apparently received it, for on August

1, 1590, he wrote thanking the Lord Treasurer for his positive answer.[4] Sir William Russell was promised a foot band at Berghen, and the Privy Council finally ordered the Governor of Berghen to deliver the horse band to Sidney's lieutenant, which he did, "without suffering the soldiers to disperse into any other band or to make away with either horses, arms, or furniture."[5]

This small victory by no means resolved Sidney's difficulties over the horse company. In 1593, the company, along with companies under Sir Francis Vere, Sir Nicholas Parker, and Sir John Pooley, were broken up; some of the men were sent for service in Brittany and some were cashiered. Three years later, the States and Prince Maurice requested the queen to reorganize Sidney's and Parker's companies, perhaps at Sidney's suggestion.[6] Gilpin and Caron were enlisted in this effort. The Privy Council ordered Gilpin to deal with the States at the Hague about the matter, and Sidney told him they had earlier made some resolution in favor of Sir John Pooley, which Gilpin thought would help their case. However, he felt the Council of States would be extremely conservative; he noted that they allowed their own captains something for horses lost in actual service, but were not inclined to make allowances in other circumstances.[7] In January 1596/97, Sir Thomas Wilkes wrote to Sidney that a warrant for the horses had been delivered to Rowland Whyte, who had "discretely travailed" for the governor.[8] At the end of the month, the Privy Council issued an open warrant granting Sidney's suit for an allowance to replace his forty-three lost horses; Sir Thomas Shirley was authorized to allow him £8 8s per horse, for a total of £529 4s.[9]

The matter went on into 1597, however, with Gilpin struggling with the Dutch at the Hague and Whyte and Noel Carol laying siege to the English government. Lady Barbara procured Lady Warwick's aid, and she received the queen's promise that the horse company would be made up. "While the grass grows," said Sidney, skeptically invoking an old equestrian proverb, "the horse starves."[10] Caron asked Essex and Cecil's help in the matter and set forth a scheme to accomplish it without charge to the queen. Whyte, whom Sidney had authorized to spend as much as £200 in pursuit of the horses, attempted to bribe a friend of Cecil's with an offer of a "fair set of hangings . . . and two coach mares for his wife." Whyte thought these "gratuities" were "honorable and very necessary . . . seeing you know the power [Cecil] hath to do good and harme."[11] Evidently the unnamed friend offered Cecil the hangings; the latter declined, politely protesting his willingness to further Sidney's suits.[12] Essex was approached, and he said it had to be done by petition to the Privy Council; however, he advised Caron to stand firm on his request that the queen reinforce the horse company at her own expense.[13] At last the suit was granted, and on May 19, Whyte wrote that a warrant for the lost horses was being issued to William Meredith, paymaster of the forces in the Low Countries.[14] After seemingly endless bickering, harassing, arguing, bribing, and begging, Sidney finally had his way in the matter of the horse companies.

Meanwhile, he was engaged in a different power struggle, this one over his authority to dispose of the cautionary companies under his command at Flushing. In the fall of 1596, Captains Arthur Savage and Thomas Baskerville were to be transferred to France, leaving their companies at Flushing. Baskerville and Savage felt they should be allowed to keep their captaincies in absentia. The queen thought not; she intended to dispose of them in her own way. Neither did Sidney think the two captains were entitled to keep the Flushing companies; but, since both companies were cautionary, he understood he had the right to dispose of them. Sidney's instructions made it clear that he had no say over the appointments of the auxiliary companies stationed at Flushing. Although his orders did not specify in so many words that he had control of the captaincies of the cautionary companies, they did establish his immediate command over the companies and implied that his authority over them was all-inclusive. Precedents set in the other garrisons supported Sidney's claim.

Whyte was the first to sense trouble brewing when, on September 21, 1596, he heard Baskerville and Savage would be made to forego their companies, and that the queen was bestowing Baskerville's on his brother, Nicholas, and Savage's on Sir John Sheldon. He could see that Sidney's interest in the bestowal of the cautionary companies was being ignored, and because Essex was preferring Sheldon to the place, he feared Sidney would be overruled.[15] Matters developed quickly, and, long before he had time to receive word from Sidney, Whyte decided he had better make a move to protect his master's prerogative.

Whyte's labors, reported in detail in his letters to Sidney, show what was involved in pressing suit at Elizabeth's court. A review of his activities in this case make clear how important was the play of personalities and, by extension, how much more effective Sidney's own presence at the court might have been in the effort to advance his career.

Contriving to have an audience with Essex on the morning of September 24, Whyte asked the earl if it were true that Baskerville and Savage were to lose their companies because of their employment in France. He pointed out that the companies were cautionary and therefore by rights Sidney's to dispose of, and he begged Essex not to allow the governor's authority and reputation to be prejudiced. Sidney had kinsmen and followers of his own who had spent much time hoping for preferment whenever any companies fell within his power to bestow. Whyte reminded Essex that Sidney had once given away an auxiliary company, but was overruled and the company was bestowed otherwise "very unworthely."[16] He expressed his concern that, without Essex's support, Sidney would be humiliated again, even though he had the right to bestow the cautionary companies.

Essex confirmed the truth of the rumors, and explained that the queen had given Sheldon a company which Essex had previously given to Sir Samuel Bagnall; for this reason, she had promised the next vacant company to Sheldon. When she heard of the two Flushing companies, she announced she would bestow Savage's, for which Sir Robert Drury had been suing, upon Sheldon. Baskerville had asked her to allow him to cede his to his brother. Savage, meanwhile, was unwilling to part with his company, but if he was to go into France he would have to. Essex assured Whyte of his love for Sidney and that he would protect the governor's authority. Whyte, however, was not so sure, for he knew Essex was in some disgrace over the Calais journey, and that the queen had said he owed her £68,000 for that expedition. "My lord," he wrote to Sidney, "there is nothing but informing and divising means of crossing; but surely my lord of Essex gives great attendance here and is most careful to please and observe her Majesties humors."[17]

Whyte next approached Burghley, still having had no time to receive word from Sidney. Obtaining access to Sir Robert Cecil, Whyte argued for Sidney's rights to bestow the companies. Cecil proclaimed his affection for Sidney and said he would never deal in anything that might prejudice the governor's right or credit. He advised Whyte to go to Essex.

Having already visited those quarters, Whyte proceeded to Lady Warwick and asked her to let him know if she had heard anything. She told him the queen saw no reason why the two captains should have companies in both countries, and therefore would dispose of them otherwise. However, she thought there was some hope that they might still keep them.

Baskerville and Savage were making a mighty suit to the Privy Council to keep the companies, protesting that their allowance of 10 s. a day was too small to maintain them in the wars of France. The lords were responding with fair promises and thought their demands reasonable, but the queen disagreed. Whyte guessed that she would give their companies away as soon as they were gone.[18]

Two days later Whyte heard that Baskerville's allowance was increased to 15 s. a day and Savage's to 20 s.; he thought this indicated that they would not keep their companies, although they remained convinced that they would. The controversy gained currency at the court, and some evidently felt Sidney would retain his rights in the matter, for Whyte reported that a number of men had asked him to help them obtain one of the companies from Sidney, for a price: £200 in hand and another £100 at the end of six months. Whyte assured them that Sidney did not customarily sell companies.[19]

As soon as Sidney got word of these tergiversations, he wrote to Cecil, first assuring him of his respect, admiration and loyalty; "the world knows the power you have either to hinder or to advance," he said, echoing Whyte's admonition. He asked Cecil to remind the queen that she had already given Sidney the right to bestow the companies. Lord Burgh, he pointed out, had given away two cautionary companies over the past two years by virtue of the same power, and Sidney himself gave Savage his company.[20]

He also wrote to Burghley and to the Privy Council, beseeching their favor. The council replied that the queen's grant to him was very firm and good, and they thought his requests reasonable. However, since Elizabeth reserved the power to bestow certain places, they did not know how to advise him. They agreed with him that the absence of captains from their charges was undesirable, but said under certain circumstance it could not be helped.[21]

The matter remained uncertain into November, when Thomas Lake advised Sidney that little was happening at the court. Finally, Sidney seems to have asserted his rights, for, on December 2, he informed Burghley that he had given Savage's company to Captain John Fleming, "as being one of the five cautionary companies and therefore in my gift."[22] Nicholas Baskerville apparently succeeded to his brother's place with no further argument.[23]

The maintenance of supplies adequate to defend the garrison was another recurring concern. Sidney repeatedly importuned both governments to provide his troops with the powder and munitions they needed to function as soldiers. As they had in other matters, the Dutch and English administrators bounced the problem back and forth, neither government willing to take on the expense if the other could be induced to pay. The shortage of powder and other supplies, as we have seen, was one of the first difficulties Sidney encountered when he took over the post. He managed to persuade the English government to send over four lasts of powder, eight thousand weight of match, and four fodders of lead by October 1590,[24] but whenever he ran short he had to beg for more or try to obtain it from merchants on his own credit. He used every conceivable occasion to remind Burghley and Cecil that Flushing needed adequate supplies; each rumor of plots afoot against the town elicited from Sidney a new request for supplies or reinforcements, as did the brouhaha over the corn ships and every *frisson* of antagonism among the Dutch. The powder supplied in 1590 seems to have lasted about a year. By October of the following year, he needed more. He received a small amount by December and forwarded to Burghley an account of its distribution, but he asked the lord treasurer to arrange for more powder to be sent soon.[25]

The low levels of provision at Flushing aggravated Sidney's suspicion of the Dutch. Their successes in the field aroused his fear that their self-confidence would lead them to feel they could survive independently of the queen and to desire to be free of "the yoke they think themselves under." Sidney thought the Contract involving the cautionary towns was such a burden to the Dutch that, when they no longer thought they needed Elizabeth's help and she was preoccupied in France or elsewhere, they would not hesitate to attempt to retake the towns by force. He emphasized the importance of providing the towns against unexpected mischief, especially Flushing, "which is indeed far more worth then all the rest besydes, and yet more slenderly provided for then any of them."

The States had refused to allow more auxiliary companies in Flushing than were already there; naturally, Sidney remarked, for "if ther were but one Englishman in the town they would wish half of him out." In April

1592, Flushing badly needed munitions of all sorts; twice since Sidney had arrived the garrison had been without a grain of powder for days, and the treasurer's deputy would not disburse a farthing's worth, claiming he had orders to the contrary. If this became known, Sidney feared, the Dutch could shut up the English garrison "like so many lambs." He asked Burghley either to send more or to tell the queen he could not account for the town without it. "My honor as well as my life," he protested, "is at stake."[26]

This plea seems to have worked some effect. In July—three months later—two lasts of powder arrived. Sidney expressed his gratitude to Burghley, but reminded him that the town would continue to need powder. If Flushing were besieged, he noted, the garrison would spend more powder in a day than they ordinarily used in two months.[27]

So it went, year in and year out. Sidney or his lieutenant-governors were forced to devote their best eloquence to elaborate, repetitious prayers to the home government: letters calling for supply appeared in 1595, 1596, 1597, 1600, and 1601,[28] all expressing the same worry that Sidney first put on paper in 1590. In fairness to the English administration, however, it must be noted that maintaining the cautionary towns placed a heavy burden on the queen's treasury. Further, the year 1588 had shown the English that their enemies were capable of launching an attack against the island that could be repelled only with the grace of God and the help of a North-Atlantic storm. After the Armada, Elizabeth had reason for her reluctance to export powder that she might need for defense at home.

Dr. William A. Shaw, in his introduction to volume 3 of the Dudley and De L'Isle papers, constructs a carefully documented defense of Elizabeth against Motley's portrait of "a niggardly queen, chaffering over half pence and torn between an insular statesmanship and a womanly passion for Leicester." Shaw argues that the treaty bound the Dutch to carry costs which, despite their affluence as a merchant nation prospering from the wars, they repeatedly tried to foist off on Elizabeth; that Henry IV was "a cynical tricky diplomatist, never true to his word, steadfast only in his selfishness, always begging from Elizabeth, always deceiving her;" that Prince Maurice, though a courageous and patriotic man, was mentally limited to the Netherlands and "when the question came of honoring the bond to Elizabeth he was as shifty and as unprincipled as Barnevelt himself."[29]

Sidney's correspondence and evidence outside the Dudley and De L'Isle papers tend to support Shaw's contention; the governor was frequently rejected in his efforts to make the Dutch honor their commitments and forced to beg his own government for whatever provisions it would or could send him. The costs of the war in the Low Countries must have been burdensome to the English government. Walsingham signed an estimate in 1585 placing the total annual sum at £125,856 8s,[30] and Gardiner estimated that, on James's accession, the yearly costs of maintaining the garrisons in the Low Countries was £24,000, a figure that may have grown by about £1,000 a year thereafter.[31] One contemporary account calculates the costs of the cautionary garrisons at over £4,000 for a three-month period.[32] In March 1591, the sums allowed for the army stationed at Flushing and the Brill, plus an additional seventy-six hundred foot and four hundred lance in the Low Countries, came to £120,626 8s. 4d., exclusive of charges for apparel and "other extras."[33]

Nevertheless, it remains difficult to accept Shaw's picture of Elizabeth as, alone among the Protestant allies, "true to her word, faithful to her principles, unbreakable in her courage, prodigal of her treasure, careful not of money but only of the blood of Englishmen."[34] Elizabeth, Walsingham, and Burghley were certainly no less versed in Machiavelli than were Barnevelt, Maurice, and Henry IV, and the English government was not less devious nor more pristine than the United Provinces'. An accurate picture no doubt lies somewhere between Motley's and Shaw's. Much of Elizabeth's policy involved playing off the French and the Dutch against Spain in a prolonged, deliberate effort to keep Philip II occupied on the continent; naturally, careful management of her funds was to her interest in these intrigues. The English government could not afford the immense sums the war in the Low Countries involved, and, as Motley observed, Elizabeth could see for herself the United Provinces' apparent wealth. Sidney begged for money and supply in letter after letter and was told to ask the States for it; in turn, the States insisted that Elizabeth had contracted to pay for her garrison in Flushing. The conclusion is that neither state intended to carry more of the costs of the war than it had to.

The point is illustrated again in the matter of the fortification of Flushing. As we have been, the Dutch, represented by President Valck, assured Sidney when he first arrived that they would repair the decayed fortification around the town and build new ones where needed. This project dragged on into James's reign, with delays and vacillations right up to the time Flushing was returned to the Dutch. The building was delayed in 1596, resulting in prolonged negotiations between Gilpin and the States of Zealand and the States General. Even after Gilpin succeeded in having the States General order Zealand to proceed with the fortifications, they delayed returning to work into 1598.[35] Maurice claimed the cold weather interfered with the project and promised to remedy the situation,[36] but when the matter dragged through the spring, the summer, the fall, and then another winter, even the patient Gilpin was disgusted. He suggested Sidney write to Burghley to deal with the States and to tell them "roundly" of the slackness, "that long syded fellowe Van Den Werck being one of the chief that love to feede men with delayes."[37]

When James succeeded to the English throne, the burgomasters at Flushing promised that all things would continue as before, apparently including the building on the fortification.[38] In 1605, plans were drawn up to build a new dock, which the burgomasters claimed would strengthen the town; however, Lieutenant-Governor Browne reported that he still could not get them to fortify the town entirely.[39] In the spring of 1606, some of the fortifications were damaged by heavy storms;[40] rebuilding was under way throughout the summer of that year.[41] Browne reported more delays and promises from the States of Zealand in 1607, and evidently construction only proceeded under constant prodding by the lieutenant-governor and other English agents in the Low Countries.[42] This routine continued for years. Browne died in 1611—he complained of the town's weakness and the Dutch procrastination just a few weeks before his death[43]—and his successor, Sir John Throckmorton, had no more luck moving the Dutch to haste than did Browne.

In 1612, Sidney, styled Lord Lisle after 1605 and governing for the most part in absentia after James's accession, visited Flushing and saw for himself the state of the fortifications. "I perceive," he wrote to Sir Ralph Winwood, then English ambassador at the Hague, "there is nothing done by Monsieur Barneveldt with the States about our fortifications. . . ,"[44] and in the following year, when he was again in the Low Countries, he noted that little more had been done, nor did it appear that anything would be accomplished in the near future.[45] Throckmorton continued to solicit the repair of the fortifications throughout 1614,[46] and so it went until 1616, when the town was returned to the Dutch and the English were finally relieved of the problem.

Shaw suggests the long-standing Dutch reluctance to reinforce the garrison and their habitual delays were the result of mutual suspicions between the Dutch and the English, fostered by the French, who underhandedly schemed to keep the Dutch at war to tie Spain's hands. The United Provinces regarded James's peace with Spain as a betrayal. Their resentment and suspicion gave the English officers in the garrison good reason to fear an insurrection and to urge the strengthening of their defenses.[47]

Certainly mutual distrust existed, but it was not exclusive to James's reign. Sidney had to deal with it from the beginning of his governorship. We have already seen the nature of Sidney's efforts to maintain some equilibrium in his handling of the States' eleven points, of Wingfield and Randolph's debt, and in the matter of the Spanish trade. Sidney and other English officers feared the Dutch reaction to any English peace negotiations with Spain. The States distrusted Elizabeth and suspected she might conclude a secret treaty, and the English garrisons in the cautionary towns feared that any confirmation of the Dutch suspicions would end in their downfall.

When, in 1592, the queen proposed to send 2500 men into France, including four companies from Flushing, Sidney protested that their absence would weaken his defense against the Dutch, who, he claimed, were ready to take Flushing the minute the English backed off. He had heard it was being said in England that "Flushing may be kept with a whyte rodd," but, Sidney remarked, unless they had the rod of Mercury, which brought sleep to all men, they knew little of Flushing and did not have its interests at heart. Sidney now saw that the Dutch attitude toward the queen had changed since the English had first entered Flushing. They blamed the loss of Gertruydenberg on the English; they resented English hindrance of their free traffic and the spoiling of their ships by English privateers. However, Sidney thought they would not be willing to have the English companies removed nor to break off the Contract with Elizabeth, for "it is one of the principal chains that hold these provinces in union together and one of the best graces they have with the princes abroad."[48] Nevertheless, the troop movements took place over Sidney's protest, and he was convinced that the Dutch were offended and made more suspicious of England's motives.[49]

Sidney was as unhappy at the prospect of an Anglo-Spanish peace as were the Dutch, both because he thought it contrary to the interests of his country and because he feared it would incite the Dutch to retake Flushing forcibly. "[I]n the ruins of the towne," he ruminated, "my self must needs be buried."[50] He urged the queen to retain the towns in her 1599 negotiations with Spain, since they were all that remained, after so many years of war, of her trouble and expense. He feared the Spanish would eventually regain Flushing if Elizabeth abandoned it to the Dutch, and they would use it as a stronghold to harass England. He advised Elizabeth to grant the inhabitants of the cautionary towns freedom to trade and traffic in Spanish dominions, for, he urged, this was the cord that would bind the trader nation to Elizabeth and confirm its loyalty to her.[51]

One of the most direct ways Sidney had of maintaining a peaceful equilibrium between the Dutch and English at Flushing was to keep his own men in line, restraining illegal and disruptive activities within the garrison. This was not always an easy matter, and Sidney and his lieutenant-governors handled it with varying degrees of success, depending on their own personalities. The men who were levied to serve in the Low Countries were not often "of the better sort." Their patience was tested by below-subsistence wages, poor food and clothing, and monotonous duty in a cold, wet, and only marginally friendly country. Nor could they have been inspired to ideal behavior by the examples set by their superiors, who, although they may not have invented the concept of white-collar crime, certainly carried on the tradition with verve and ingenuity.

Squabbles between the enlisted men and the townspeople or the Dutch seamen occurred with moderate frequency. Sidney described a couple of such "iarrs" between his men and some local soldiers, which he of course blamed on the insolence of the mariners. Once a bailiff committed one of a number of riotous sailors to prison; his fellows promptly rescued him by main force. Sidney agreed to cooperate with the town magistrate in the matter but used the occasion to remind Burghley that the town needed "no less than twelve companies well chosen with good and discrete Captens" to insure against the depradations of arrogant sailors.[52]

Desertion was another common problem. Men absented themselves not only to escape the army, but often to join allied units where the pay and living conditions were better. During one rash of desertions, Uvedall complained that the Dutch and Scottish captains entertained their troops so well they would soon get all the men from Flushing. He tried to bring a stop to it by allowing none of the men to go through the gate.[53]

Justice, when it was administered, seems to have been severe and peremptory in the garrison. Late in 1592, Sidney sent word to his lieutenant-governor, Uvedall, to arrest one Borchensho (or Burchinshaw), who had been embezzling pay from the companies. Uvedall, obtaining Burchinshaw's papers by a ruse, moved swiftly and nabbed him at the very instant he was embarking from Flushing. A court of the Flushing officers convened, and, after hearing him confess to taking pay from every company, concluded he should lose his ears, a sentence which was promptly executed. He was then shipped off to confront the Privy Council in England, over the protests of his friends in the Low Countries. Uvedall, was most pleased with this small victory for justice, and thought it "a matter done on so good grounds as howsoever his best friends take het, they cannot chous but aloue well of het."[54]

Sidney and his lieutenants resisted allowing anyone from outside the garrison to stand in judgment over their men. Once in 1596, for example, the States asked Browne to produce a couple of men, Devill and Lanche, to answer some accusations against them. Browne responded that he would imprison them at Flushing, and, if the Dutch would sent their accusations and a deputy, he would meet with them and they should have satisfaction as the cause required. He regarded it as an infringement on Sidney's authority to send soldiers to the Dutch "to be justised by them."[55]

Maintaining some order among the enlisted men was simplicity itself compared to the task Sidney faced in trying to control the irrepressible abuses of his enterprising captains. They were furious, at the orders of 1590 designed to bring a halt to their crooked dealings in the mustering procedures. Sidney relayed their outraged protests of innocence and loyalty to Burghley, but nevertheless insisted that the new orders be followed. His behavior did not make him popular among the officers. "I have always been the first in observing all new orders," he told Burghley, "which has procured me the dislike of my own and many other garrisons." The captains resented being forced to accept the orders when the other garrisons refused to do so, and they believed they might have successfully resisted them had Sidney cooperated.[56]

Whether or not Sidney was observing the new orders as meticulously as he claimed, the Privy Council sent off stern letters at the end of 1591 to Sidney and to Burghe threatening to remove the two governors if the musters orders were not severely executed. The measures so far taken were not working; the companies recently sent into France had arrived "so weake as noe one companie can nomber half the men for whom paie hath been delivered, and some but 50 or 60 for a hundred and fiftie. . . ." The queen asked the Dutch States General and the Council of State to have a special regard for the companies in the cautionary garrisons and to inform the governors of abuses. Sidney and Burghe were ordered to take musters at the States' request and to act upon the new orders to their utmost ability.[57]

Sidney and his officers found this Dutch mustering of their troops particularly galling. The governor expressed his annoyance to Burghley when the States' commissioners held a muster early in 1592. They wanted to leave only one company on the walls, but Sidney insisted on two. The rest were shut up in a church to be counted, which Sidney regarded as a dangerous precedent. The men could hardly hold the town against the Dutch, he pointed out, if they could be locked up whenever the States said so. The States' intention might be unknown to the English, and Sidney thought the States should not be made privy to the garrison's strength. Surely, he thought, some other course could be taken against abuses.[58] The queen and her council seem to have thought not, for the new measures, ineffectual as they may have been, remained in force.

One feels a kind of reluctant sympathy for the captains' self-serving practices when one reflects upon the even more blatant larcenies of the merchants who served the garrisons in the Low Countries. These have been admirably described by Cruickshank. A mercantile mafia preyed on the queen's forces overseas with relative impunity. Even Burchinshaw, who appears to have been a merchant, was not put out of commission when Uvedall arrested him in 1592. Two years later he was making more trouble for Sidney's government, claiming to have involved Sir Edmund Uvedall in some of his nefarious dealings.[59] And evidently this same Burchinshaw joined with William Beecher, another merchant, to inform on Sir Thomas Shirley, causing a great scandal and permanent disgrace for the treasurer-at-war.

Beecher and his partner, George Lester, supplied victuals to Sidney's garrison. As early as 1590, they were accused of brazen malpractice, but they continued in business throughout the decade. Captains at Berghen and Flushing, citing their "inordinate desire of gayne," claimed they were responsible for substantial losses and that they sold goods meant for the queen's forces to the enemy. They accused the merchants' agent, a Mr. Cox, of extorting £25 to £30 out of every £100 in bribes to guarantee his delivery of the goods destined for the companies.[60]

Sidney complained that his captains were criticized for their relatively small misdeeds while the merchants continued to handle the soldiers miserably and "monstrously deceaved" the queen. He reported that they frequently sold apparel to others for one-half to two-thirds the sums they made the queen pay. They bragged in their letters (which Sidney had available for Burghley's perusal) that they got £40,000 out of the blood of the poor soldiers, while the captains, reproached excessively for their co-zening, were not permitted to arm their own companies. Arms provided by the merchants were "scarcely good," the merchants refused to repair defective goods, and everything they delivered was outrageously overpriced.[61] He begged Burghley to persuade the Privy Council to bring a halt to these practices, to little avail. In 1601, the Privy Council had to inquire into another incident, when George Harvey delivered eight hundred muskets and callivers for the queen's store, of which fewer than one hundred sixty were serviceable. Harvey dodged the responsibility by blaming the defects on the merchants, giving substance to Sidney's earlier complaint.[62]

As the captains' felonies overshadowed the misdemeanors of the enlisted men, so the villainy of the officers in the upper echelons dwarfed the captains' crimes. The most notorious example is that of Sir Thomas Shirley, the treasurer-at-war, whose immense illegal profiteering was exposed in 1597, largely by means of the earless Burchinshaw's informing. Sidney managed to escape implication in the affair, but it was a close call, for he and Rowland Whyte had had many dealings with the treasurer.

After he had attacked Shirley, Burchinshaw turned on Beecher and Lester, delivering to the queen a tract entitled "A Discovery of Lester and Beechers Practices. . . ." He named Rowland Whyte in this exposé, accusing him of smuggling a large quantity of gold for Beecher, hidden in a portmanteau of stockings. Whyte declared his innocence, but he heard Burghley had conceived such a bad opinion of him that he suggested Sidney consider employing "one that were well thought of, for the good of your own service."[63] He did remember that Beecher asked him to deliver a portmanteau of stockings to his man, Joseph Waring, but he insisted he never knew what else—if anything—was in it.[64] Apparently, he and Sidney succeeded in convincing Burghley of his innocence, for Whyte was never relieved as Sidney's agent, and he soon was active again in promoting the governor's business in England.

When he was in Flushing, Sidney spent much of his time collecting and forwarding news and intelligence to the government at home. Almost every letter to Burghley or Cecil contains reports on Parma's and Maurice's movements, current developments on the Dutch political scene, rumors of rumors. He received much of his information in writing from Bodley, Wilkes, and Gilpin; a good deal more of it seems to have come from intercepted mail and from conversation with the Flushing and Middleburg officials, Maurice, and passing merchants. When he was in England, his lieutenant-governors performed the same function, passing on news to him that he presumably communicated in his own name to his superiors. Very little escaped his notice. He learned of the Polish peacemaking efforts in 1597 from the Polish ambassador himself, Paulus Dzinlinsky, "a very precise papist and a great favorer of the Jesuit's faction."[65] He was usually aware of the condition of the Spanish army: whether it was suffering a dearth of food;[66] when it was preparing to besiege a city;[67] when it was in mutiny.[68]

Some of the information he forwarded was more in the nature of intelligence than news. Now and then, he caught wind of some plot, as when Lieutenant-Governor Browne interviewed an errant Scotsman who reported a scheme to set fire to Flushing, a promise to kill the queen made to Count Fuentes by an English Jesuit, and another scheme set afoot by Sir William Stanley to procure the lord treasurer's death.[69] Part of the governor's job involved interrogation of passing strangers, which gave Sidney an occasional opportunity to unearth a valuable informer. One gentleman offered to tell all about some merchants he had traveled with and observed carrying munitions into Spain. Sidney sent him directly to Burghley to report in person.[70]

A Dutch sailor who had escaped the Spanish galleys gave Sidney detailed information on the Spanish and Dutch shipping at Lisbon, St. Lucar, St. Anderas, Naples, and Oporto, and reported that Spain intended to launch its fleet against the Isle of Wight in the winter of 1597.[71] He remained alert for more news of the fleet, and in November he was able to report the loss of twenty-eight Spanish galleons off Cape Finistre,[72] and in December that the seventeen ships for St. Lucar that joined the Lisbon fleet were so weak and ill-manned that no Spanish army could set forth that year.[73]

Warily, Sidney watched the six galleys and a fleet of smaller ships that were observed at Sluys in the summer of 1599; naturally, he feared they would try to take Flushing or attempt a similar enterprise.[74] He was delighted to report that one of the galleys went around as it left the harbor at Sluys,[75] and described an allied attack on them that seems effectively to have put them out of commission.[76]

Sidney was approached by those who would have liked to corrupt him, but he proved steadfast in his loyalty to the queen. The most notorious of the tempters was Hugh Owen, the fugitive Welsh activist who was later involved in the Gunpowder Plot. Owen made a couple of unctuous advances to Sidney, claiming he had known and loved Sir Henry and offering his friendship, hostilities between their sovereigns notwithstanding. He forwarded a bribe of two writing tables, some small gifts for Barbara, and a pair of unusual bracelets, and offered Sidney any service within his power, reserving his duty to his master, the King of Spain.[77] Sidney graciously thanked him for his letter, told him he could not accept his gifts—which he forwarded to Burghley[78]—and mockingly remarked he would be willing to do him any pleasure, "my duty ever reserved to her Maiesty, to whome at the last I would you would remember how much you owe."[79]

That evidently discouraged Owen, for little more came directly from him. The queen had disliked Sidney's dealing with Owen unadvised, but, with Burghley's help, he seems to have escaped her displeasure.[80] He thanked Burghley for his advice in the matter and asked him to see to it that Barbara never found out Owen's gifts were meant for her.[81] This brush with dishonor was easy enough for Sidney to escape unsullied. Meanwhile, though, a more persistent character was trying to deal with him.

Patrick Sedgrave first surfaced in November 1590, when he wrote to Rowland Whyte enclosing a letter for Sidney. The reason he gave for contacting Whyte was that he did not want it known that he was writing to

Sidney; he planned to put Whyte in the compromising position of go-between for himself and the governor, and promised him a passport to Antwerp.[82] Sidney must have felt either a chill of apprehension or a moment of ironic amusement as he read over Sedgrave's clandestine letter, which began "Right worshipful and dearlie beloved friend, Sir Robart, albeit not hitherto so known unto you as I hope to be. . . ." Sedgrave claimed to have developed a friendship with Sir Henry and Lady Mary Sidney in Ireland, whence he came. Because of his deep affection for the Sidneys, he offered to provide Sidney with "a great means for you to please the queen and advance your living (which I am sorrie is so much diminished)," and asked him to send word by the messenger who had brought the letters when he would send Whyte.[83]

Sidney sent Sedgrave's letters to Burghley with the first favorable wind, assuring the lord treasurer that he had never heard of Sedgrave nor could he imagine what he meant. Fearing delay might cause some complication, he answered the letter promptly, and he showed his response to Sir Francis Vere. He did not send Whyte, however, for he was known in Antwerp and would be noticed there, and besides, his presence there might cause suspicion among the United Provinces.[84]

Sedgrave may have come from the Irish family of Segraves of Dublin. Sir Henry Sidney had done business with Christopher and Walter Segrave in the late 1560s and early 1570s; they were merchants trading with the English in Ireland. However, there is no indication that Sir Henry was a great friend of either man.[85] Sir Robert thought he was the nephew of a man who had once served his father and brother.[86]

Sidney heard nothing from either Burghley or Sedgrave until December 3, when he received a communication from the lord treasurer telling him the queen was pleased he had lost no time in the matter but disliked his imparting his reply to Vere. Sidney had to apologize and assure them his letter contained nothing but an acknowledgement of receipt of Sedgrave's letter, his reasons for not sending Whyte, and a request that he deal with someone other than Whyte. He promised to discuss the matter no further with Vere.

Sedgrave was so insistent on Whyte, of whose loyalty Sidney was sure, that the governor suspected he intended to try to corrupt him, but he thought if the Irishman were sincere he would not quibble over who was sent to deal with him.[87] By the tenth, he had heard from Sedgrave, who reported that the duke's return meant their matter must be deferred while he and his friends were employed in some service. Sidney thought he still seemed "earnest and affectionate." Sedgrave insisted on Whyte, but Sidney was unwilling to send him on such a dangerous mission, even though Burghley approved his going.[88]

Sedgrave came over to Flushing in person at the end of January, 1591/ 92, and briefly outlined his scheme. Since "letters . . . do run many hazards," Sidney told Burghley he would not commit the matter to paper, except to say it involved "the matter of the greatest importance of all these contreys," alluding as it developed to Antwerp. He asked for leave to go to England to discuss Sedgrave's offer with the lord treasurer in person.

Naturally, this effort to provide himself a short vacation from Flushing failed, and the queen ordered him to send the details by letter. When Sidney did so, in March, 1592, he expressed his growing reservations. Sedgrave had told him of a sergeant-major in Antwerp named Antonio de Sayaveldra, who had decided to use his position to gain some profit from the queen. He wanted a sum of money (mentioned in an earlier Sidney letter, now lost), one-half the spoils and ransoms made, and assurance for himself and his comrades of a safe dwelling in England or Ireland, where he wished to be allowed to buy some land to be enjoyed peacefully by his followers and their posterity. He also requested they have the liberty of their religion without constraint by any law to the contrary, and the queen's protection from the king of Spain and his agents. In return, he would deliver Antwerp to the English, which he could do because he had the keeping of the ports in the governor's absence. However, since he knew Philip was preparing to attack England that summer, he wished to delay the enterprise until he saw the outcome of that endeavor. As security, de Sayaveldra offered to deliver to Sidney his eldest son, a ten-year-old child.

Sidney was suspicious. He thought Sedgrave delivered the story rather poorly, and besides, de Sayaveldra was a native Spaniard who would not have been placed in his position unless his superiors had reason for trusting him. Nor was he convinced any segeant-major had so much authority. He also doubted the offer of the boy as security, and noted that Sedgrave seemed unsure whether de Sayaveldra even had a son. It struck him as odd that de Sayaveldra wanted the matter kept secret from the States, for he was sure the town could not be taken without them; even with them, he remarked, "the matter halts with every legg." He told Sedgrave that he had some reservations, and that since so many accidents could hinder such an enterprise, it would be unreasonable for the queen to disburse so much money in advance. Sedgrave said he would discuss it with de Sayaveldra and forward an answer.

Sidney described Sedgrave as "a regular prest" who had dwelt for some time in Lorraine and come to the Low Countries planning to enter England with the Spanish armada; since then he lived in Brabant on a pension of thirty crowns a month from the Spanish king. That he was a priest particularly aroused Sidney's distrust. Sidney's suspicions were aggravated when Sedgrave asked him if he was sure he wanted to anger the king of Spain at a time when Philip was about to launch another attempt on England. He mentioned a list of Englishmen slated, with their families, for execution if Spain prevailed, and said Sidney's name was on it. The governor replied that if he were afraid of Philip, he would not have come to Flushing. Sedgrave then said he knew Cardinal Allen would be glad if Sidney would convert to Catholicism, and spoke of what earldoms and lordships and authority he might have in England if he would befriend the king. Finally recognizing that this tack was enraging Sidney, Sedgrave assured him all he wanted was his best welfare, but the governor was not deceived. He told Burghley he would have imprisoned Sedgrave then and there and sent him to England, but since he had promised the man a safe return, he felt bound to let him go.[89]

The queen was not pleased when she heard of this encounter; she seems to have disliked Sidney's efforts to deal with Sedgrave on his own. In a letter now lost, Burghley must have expressed her annoyance in strong terms to Sidney, for on April 4, the governor replied, in a letter that might almost be termed cringing, that he was amazed she took offense, for he was following her orders. He knew nothing of the proposal Sedgrave intended to make until they met in person, for Sedgrave would never put it on paper. Burghley and the queen wanted Sidney to try to capture the Irishman, but he thought now that it was apparent the plot was failing. Sedgrave would hardly put himself into a vulnerable position again.[90]

Meanwhile, Hugh Owen was in the background. An English spy whom Sidney referred to in cipher as "M.M." had been dealing with Owen, and suggested Sidney try to negotiate with him.[91] This "M.M." may have been one Mody, whom Sidney also mentioned in connection with Owen as assuring the governor that Owen could be drawn to do the queen some service. Sidney knew only that Owen was "an ill man to the state" and wished to have nothing to do with him.[92] When he rejected Owen's offer, made through Mody, the queen apparently was annoyed that he fumbled an opportunity to capture him.[93] Evidently, Burghley suspected some complicity between Owen and Sedgrave, and in the midst of the governor's dealing with the latter, ordered Mody to approach Sidney about again trying to lure Owen into their hands. Sidney was less than enthusiastic; he did not like Mody, and he was convinced Owen meant only to corrupt him and to betray Flushing to the Spaniards.[94]

Sidney's and Burghley's misgivings proved correct. In April 1592, a Reinold Bosely wrote to Cecil that while he was employed by the queen overseas, he learned Owen and Sir William Stanley planned to employ an ex-servant of Sidney, William Whipp, to renew his relationship with Sir Robert and obtain a print of the keys of Flushing.[95] At almost the same time that this report came in, Sedgrave was trying to reassure Sidney by sending him intelligence about Spain's planned "mischief" in the Low Countries, which Sidney forwarded to Burghley.[96] Their suspicions were confirmed the following year, when Griffin Jons and Henry Walpole were induced to confess their involvement with Owen and Sedgrave. Jons said that Owen had met with him in Brussels and told him to approach Rowland Whyte and commend him to his master, "of whom we have good hope," and to have him relay to Sidney that the Spanish agents could help him improve his state.[97] Walpole said Owen knew Sedgrave had been dealing with Sidney, and also stated that Owen had tried to corrupt Lord Burghe to surrender the Brill.[98]

Sidney had not heard the last of Sedgrave. In September 1595, the man again approached him. Sidney forwarded his letter to Burghley. If he could see a way to catch Sedgrave without breaking his word, Sidney said, he "would make him see that he had addressed his commodities to a very ill merchant." However, he was unwilling to deal with the other side without the queen's direct commandment, under the circumstances, and, he added cryptically, because of "the alliance I have in Spaine."[99] Sir Robert Cecil wrote in reply that the queen, while sympathizing with his disinclination to deal in the matter, thought his Spanish alliance a "poor scruple," and said that an honest man need not feel constrained to keep his word to a dishonest one.[100]

Burghley and the queen wanted Sidney to promise Sedgrave safe conduct to and from Flushing, and, once the priest was inside the town, to capture him. Sidney flatly declined to break his word. With an unusual degree of self-assertion, he told Burghley that "how worthy so ever [Sedgrave] may be to have promised broken with him, I thinck myself unworthy to doyt." He would give his life but not his honor to the queen's service.[101]

A few days later, Sedgrave, now operating under his matronymic, Fitz James, wrote to Sidney reiterating his affection and asking for a passport for himself and his servant from Middleburgh to Flushing. Sidney sent him one, but by October 22 had heard nothing from him.[102] In November, he forwarded a letter from Sedgrave at Antwerp and asked Burghley if the queen wanted him to send for him. He had sent back Sidney's passport because it did not assure his return. Evidently, Sedgrave was still trying to intimidate him with the Spanish king's enemies list.[103] In mid-November Sidney received another letter from Sedgrave, which convinced him that his principal motive in coming to Flushing was to make sinister offers.[104]

This seems to have marked the end of Sidney's dealings with Sedgrave; it is the last mention of the fugitive Irish priest in the governor's correspondence. Sidney was not temperamentally suited for spy work. His sense of personal integrity was too strong to permit of dirty tricks and long chains of underhanded machinations. He might have done his country a service by deceiving Sedgrave, but for him the loss of his self-respect was too high a price to pay.

As governor, Sidney was in a position to use his influence in favor of those who applied to him. He immediately procured a position, for example, for Rowland Whyte, who appears as Clerk of the Ordnance at Flushing in 1589.[105] Many appealed to Sidney for patronage. One of the first was Lewis Lewknor, who had been living on the continent and wished, in 1590, to return home to England.[106] Walsingham and Vere had given him safe conduct, but Sidney was at first unsure of how to deal with him and asked Burghley for advice in the matter.[107] The lord treasurer must have felt favorably inclined, for Lewknor was allowed to come over and Sidney recommended him as "a proper civil man" who could report at length about matters on the enemy side.[108]

Sidney was called upon to use his influence in an intriguing variety of causes. There were routine matters, such as recommending a Captain Spring be given a company in Flushing[109] and considering suitors to take the place of the terminally ill marshall of Flushing.[110] He was asked at least twice to speak on behalf of Flushingers captured by the Turks, in the hope that he could influence the queen to intercede for them. John Everett, son of Captain Everett of Flushing, master of a Flushing merchant ship, was kidnapped in 1596 en route from Venice to London and, with his entire company, enslaved in the Turkish galleys. They claimed they were subjects of the queen and were told that if this were confirmed, Everett and his men would be freed. Sidney urged the Privy Council to move the queen to write to the Turks herself or order her ambassador to procure their release.[111] Two years later, a Cornelius Jansson, who was an inhabitant of Flushing but was born in England, needed Sidney's help. He had been a prisoner in Barbary for the past fifteen months, where his kidnappers had given him to the king of Morocco, who refused to release him for any amount of money. An English merchant at Flushing took pity at his plight, but failed to secure his release with a £2,600 bribe. Sidney earnestly requested Cecil to persuade the queen to write to the king of Morocco to procure Jansson's freedom.[112]

On some occasions, Sidney was not moved to sympathy by his suitors. In 1597, the Irish who had served under the traitorous Stanley grew discontent with their leader and decided they wanted to return to the English side. They sent as their spokeswoman Abisag Marrit, the English wife of one of the Irishmen, Richard Devinis. She assured Sidney of their willingness to serve England and asked him to help them obtain a pardon from the queen. Sidney sent her over to Burghley, promising her he would do whatever the queen wanted. However, he told Burghley, "I would rather bring them all to the gallows, then to [the queen's] favor." He could not forgive their betrayal of Leicester, and doubted they would ever be true to the queen. He thought they could not be trusted to stay in England, and if they got to Ireland they would do more harm in a day than they could do in a year in the Low Countries. He suggested the queen employ them in "som desperat action," which if achieved would be to her advantage and if failed would be "the loss of so many bad fellowes." If they performed some extraordinary act that would alienate them from the enemy, it might atone somewhat for their villainy, Sidney suggested, but otherwise "I am of the opinion that it were better news for her Ma: to heare they were all dead, then that they were yealded unto her service."[113]

The queen evidently concurred, for the woman was sent straight back, and Sidney, pleased to find Elizabeth had approved of his proceedings, set forth the proposition that the Irish should prove themselves worthy by performing some act that would demonstrate their repentance. Asked what service they might do for the queen, he hinted that Stanley's blood might wash away their faults. Abisag Marrit departed, promising to procure some resolution within three or four weeks and leaving Sidney to devise some impossible exploit for her comrades to perform.[114]

The Irish must have lost interest in the effort, for nothing more concerning the matter appears in Sidney's letters. His determination to
squeeze some revenge from the ostensibly repentant Irish troops throws a
less than heavenly light on his character. He was capable of using his
influence to serve his own prejudices and bitterness. That he was not
alone—for the queen herself seems to have approved his scheme to send
the men to their destruction—does not erase the fact that he could simply
have denied the woman's suit and never soiled himself with a murderous
scheme.

On other occasions, Sidney inclined toward mercy and forgiveness.
When he was in England in 1600, he began a suit to Cecil in behalf of a Mr.
Copley, whom he described as his kinsman, carried out of England as a
child by his father. Copley's mother, formerly "a great papist," had con-
verted to the English faith and Sidney thought Copley would, too. At any
rate, since he was removed from his country so young, he could not be
blamed for any practice against the queen and, once he was returned
home, he would deserve to be pitied rather than suspected. Cecil promised
to obtain Copley's pardon in return for what seems to have been a bribe of
£500.[115] In July, however, Cecil backed off, and told Whyte that although
he would advance the suit, he would not initiate it. Whyte suggested that
Sir John Stanhope be approached. Whyte could not understand Cecil's
sudden reluctance. He thought Sidney would do best not to insist, but
should either make a smiliar offer (of £500) to someone else or write to the
queen himself asking for Copley's pardon.[116] There is no evidence either
that the sum was offered by Copley through Sidney, acting as a go-
between, or that Sidney expected to receive a still larger bribe from Copley
in return for the pardon. Sidney was apparently willing to go to some
trouble and expense on Copley's behalf, and it is unfortunate that the
outcome of the suit is not recorded in the surviving correspondence. Some
years later, Sir William Browne reported the blasphemous and anti-English
speeches used by one Copley "lately sent into England by [way of] the Brill
by our Ambassadour out of the Hague," but nothing positively identifies
this man with the Copley Sidney had championed.[117]

Preferment within the garrison was customarily influenced by nepotism and favoritism. Familiar names kept popping up in the rolls of the
privileged, as Sidney and his friends procured places for their relatives at
every opportunity: Gamage, Sidney, Browne, Vere, Throckmorton.[118]
When one finds no trace of a son, cousin, nephew, or brother-in-law of Sir
Edmund Uvedall on the Flushing payroll one wonders if he died in disgrace or merely without male heir. Naturally, the governor's sons, William
and Robert, received companies of their own even before they came of age.
Other Sidneys populated the garrison: Captain John Sidney and Sir
Robert's cousin, Sir Harry Sidney, were only two among many. When Sir
William Browne died in 1611, the young Robert Sidney was given his
company, and William was primed to take over as lieutenant-governor.[119]
Unfortunately, William also died within the year, leaving Robert as Vis-

count Lisle's eldest son. Robert held an important position in the garrison until the town was handed back to the Dutch, when he was made colonel of the English regiment remaining in the Low Countries.[120] Throckmorton's son was received into Viscount Lisle's company in 1612, and the lieutenant-governor hoped it would be a first step in the young man's advancement up the ladder of command in Sidney's government.[121] Sir William Browne's cousin was made a lieutenant and his nephew an ensign to Sir John Sidney.[122] Browne's son, who apparently was not of age, was given a company when his father died. The proceeds were to go to the impoverished widow during the boy's minority. Who was to perform the work of leading the farmed-out company is not specified.[123] When Sir John Sidney died, his brother Philip was standing by to take over the company, and William Browne suggested that, if Sidney did not wish to give it to him, the way to turn him down with the least discontent was to bestow it on his own son, Robert.[124]

Curiously, Sidney was not able to procure the place he wanted for his brother Thomas as governor in the Castle of Rammekins. He attempted to do so early in 1590, but was turned down with the explanation that the queen intended to place a Mr. Lane there.[125] His indignant letter to Burghley protesting the failure of Thomas's suit and insisting on his own prerogative there condemned the government's ingratitude: "neyther the wars that he hath seene nor the parents he is come of can recommend so much as to the Castle of Rammekins. . . ." He ended his complaint on an injured note, remarking that he hoped "my government since my coming hether hath not been given any occasion of blame, and therefore I beseech her Ma: most humbly, and your Lordship that I may not be dealt withall as if I had offended."[126] It was to no avail, and Thomas did without the post.

By their own characters, the four lieutenant-governors Sidney appointed to run Flushing during his frequent absences reflect to a large extent on Sidney's nature. Too, because he governed in absentia as much as possible, their activities frequently determined the color of his administration. Their dispatches to the governor often provide a clearer view of Sidney's function at Flushing than does his own writing. For these reasons, some study of their correspondence is important in order to understand the governor's duties. In conjunction with Sidney's reports to the home government, their letters define the never-ending problems of pay, of powder and supply, of fortification, and of discipline with which they had to deal.

The first of the four, Sir William Borlas, was a holdover from Russell's time. Shortly after Sidney's arrival, Borlas had to defend his reputation against certain rumors questioning his loyalty, perhaps because of his Dutch wife. He wrote to Walsingham of his unhappiness over Sidney's negative opinion of him.[127] The queen seems to have decided he should be replaced, but he somehow convinced Sidney of his worth, for in January 1591, the new governor wrote in his defense to Burghley. Sidney thought it would be an "unrecoverable disgrace" to displace Borlas unconvicted of any faults. He was truly sorry for the man and considered him a loyal servant of the queen, undeserving of the censure he was fighting.[128] Apparently the matter did result in Borlas's removal; however, he successfully defended himself in the end. In May, a letter from the Privy Council came to Sidney authorizing Borlas's reinstatement as a soldier, "having sithe his repaire hither so sufficientlie satisfied bothe her Majestye and their Lordships as that he now retorneth her Highness' and their Lordships' good likings. . . ."[129] Sidney, relieved for his lieutenant's sake, told Burghley he trusted Borlas's service would confirm all his recommendations.[130]

Little time was left for Borlas to prove himself, for in the fall of 1591, he died.[131] Sidney appointed in his place Sir Edmund Uvedall, a man of some experience in the Low Countries. Listed in 1589 as lieutenant-colonel of Lord General George Willoughby's regiment,[132] Uvedall impressed Sidney as "a gentleman I dare answer for, who [will] discharge all duties belonging unto the place. . . ."[133]

Uvedall filled the position adequately for several years, standing in for the governor when Sidney was in England and France between 1592 and 1595.[134] In 1595, however, he fell into disgrace over a new involvement with Burchinshaw, the man whose ears he had ordered shorn several years earlier, and he returned to London to defend himself that fall. While Uvedall was there, he gave Whyte some reason to suspect that he was underhandedly politicking for advancement behind Sidney's back. Whyte discreetly inquired of Burghley's secretary, Mr. Mainard, if this were true. Mainard denied it, observing that if Uvedall were doing so, he would make enemies of his best friends. He asked Whyte if there were some bad feeling between Sidney and Uvedall, and Whyte told him there was not.[135] If Uvedall had any such intention, it evidently was abandoned; in 1596, Browne reported that Uvedall did not intend to quit the lieutenant-governorship.[136]

Uvedall, however, was absent on and off throughout 1596, and Sir William Browne took command while both the governor and the lieutenant-governor were in England. In May and August he seems to have been at his post briefly, but Browne governed the rest of the time, until Sidney returned in August.[137] In 1597, Uvedall left Flushing for England again; Browne took command in July, in the absence of both men. In October, Sidney wrote to Burghley on another of Uvedall's departures for London, asking that the lord treasurer treat him favorably.[138]

Sidney nowhere explains the reason, but Browne seems gradually to have replaced Uvedall as lieutenant-governor. The exact circumstances of Uvedall's withdrawal remain obscure, but by 1597 Browne was acting as de facto lieutenant-governor. Early in 1598, he is addressed as "commander of the garrison,"[139] and in May of the same year, he wrote asking Sidney, "if I must remayne here," for "a more ample confirmation or commission," and for a letter signifying his official position to the States of Zealand.[140] Evidently he received it, for he remained as Flushing's lieutenant-governor until his death in 1611. As for Uvedall, whatever the reasons for his removal, he was still in England's service in 1602, when a warrant was granted to pay him £156 5 s. 5 d. ½, the amount due him and his company of 150 men for service in 1597, because of his "good service" as lieutenant-governor and for losses sustained when, at an unnamed time, he was taken prisoner.[141]

In Browne, Sidney found an excellent lieutenant. Long experience in the Low Countries made him knowledgeable in both military affairs and in local customs. He had served in the Low Countries from the beginning of the English involvement there, and Sir Philip Sidney had entrusted him with the surprise of Gravelines in 1586, where he was taken prisoner. He later distinguished himself in a number of other actions.[142] He was strongly pro-Dutch—his wife was Dutch—but he had no illusions about the Lowlanders' politics. He was aware at all times of the need to strengthen the garrison, more to protect it from a Dutch or French takeover than against Spain. Always alert to news and gossip, he filled his loquacious correspondence, particularly after James I's accession, with information now valuable to students of early seventeenth-century European history. Even the secret negotiations on the Spanish side did not escape Browne; he caught wind, for example, of the transactions between James and Philip's agent, Don Fernando Giron, and recorded them in his letters to Lisle.[143]

Morale in the garrison deteriorated steadily following James I's accession, both because of eroding living conditions and because of Dutch resentment of the new English king's peace negotiations with Spain. In Lisle's more or less permanent absence, Browne managed to hold the garrison together under difficult conditions. His sympathy with the Dutch and his distrust of the Spaniard account partially for his success. He must have also had a winning way with the captains and the enlisted men, for the contrast between his administration and his successor's is made manifest in the relative scarcity of disciplinary problems he reported.

Browne, whose health had been deteriorating for several years, fell terminally ill in 1611. He was in much pain between February and the time of his death in May. Seeing the end in sight, he begged Lisle to make some provision for his wife and six children, who he expected would be left in poverty without the governor's aid.[144] When he received no answer, he wrote complaining of Lisle's neglect. The viscount responded with a letter brought by a special servant, which greatly comforted him. Throckmorton, who was sergeant-major at the time, sent a sanctimonious letter to the governor remarking that this gracious act inspired all who served under Lisle to honor and love him.[145] Browne confessed that the governor's "kyndness in sending to mee and the expressing of your affection by letter did dryve me into a passion of teares."[146]

Browne soon lost faith in Lisle's affection. In March, he reproved the governor for the emptiness of his good and noble words. Although Lisle protested his devotion to Browne, he had done nothing to fulfill his assurances that the lieutenant-governor's family would be cared for. Browne complained that others who had followed the wars had advanced much further than he; that had he chosen to follow someone else, he too would have had better fortune. Lisle had not so much as arranged for Browne's son to succeed to his father's company; perhaps he intended to give Lady Browne one or two hundred pounds, "butt I beeseech hour Honour be not offended if I speake plainly: my wife nor myne after death shall never be indetted for such a consideration, nor I fedd with such verball promyses, unless I may be assured in my life whereunto I may trust."[147]

Throckmorton and Nicholas Blocq, the English agent at Flushing, could see that Browne was dying. Blocq wrote to Lisle begging him to give Browne a final and favorable response to his letters desiring some provision for his children; "I can see that your Honour's irresolution aggravates his malady."[148] Throckmorton frankly wanted Browne's position and told Lisle so. Furthermore, he did not wish to see Browne's son get the deputy governor's company; he wanted that for himself, too. "My lord," he complained, "to suffer a separation to made of the [deputy governor's] company from the entertainment of the place and the command were to bring it so lamely to me and the disgrace of it would be such that neither I nor any worthy man could undergo it with reputation."[149]

Browne died in May and Sir John Throckmorton took his place. We do not know if Browne received any further assurances of the governor's affection, but Lisle did make some provision for Browne's young son. Throckmorton would not tolerate the bestowal of Browne's company upon anyone but himself. However, the death of Sir John Sidney the previous fall made it possible for Lisle to reshuffle the deck to everyone's temporary satisfaction. Sir John's company went to his own son, Sir Robert. Sir Robert Sidney's vacant company went to Browne's son, and so the deputy governor's company was left for Throckmorton.[150] Lady Browne visited the governor in England, where she obtained, in addition to the company, a pension of £100 for the rest of her life.[151]

Lisle had not heard the last of the Browne family, however. Lady Browne continued to press for her rights and to demand that he fulfill his promises to her late husband. Lisle's attitude toward her is obscured by Throckmorton, who detested her and whose hostile observations are almost the only source of information about the matter. Apparently, the viscount meant to have her evicted from the house she had occupied with Sir William, much to Throckmorton's glee,[152] but later he seems to have changed his mind and allowed her to stay on.[153] A year after Browne's death, Lisle spoke contentedly of his stay with Lady Browne when he visited Flushing;[154] so he must not have been influenced by Throckmorton's characterization of her as "a malitious despitfull woman."[155]

Sir John Throckmorton was Lord Lisle's least happy choice of the lieutenant-governors who served at Flushing. His character was abrasive, tactless, and not a little arrogant. When he conceived a dislike for someone, he was capable of much petty meanness, as when he wrote to Sidney vituperating against Browne's widow. From the start he provoked hostility. He demanded to know the contents of a letter Lisle had sent to Captain

Yonge, who answered him in "the most scornful manner." Throckmorton lost his temper and was unable to command any respect from Yonge; the sergeant-major, who was himself embroiled with Throckmorton, had to speak to the captain sharply to stop the squabble.[156] He had a propensity for alienating the people whom he needed on his side: Lisle's daughter, Lady Mary Wroth, early expressed her lack of sympathy for him,[157] and Lady Lisle liked him no more than her daughter did.[158]

He must have made a wonderfully pompous figure: at the height of King James's quarrel with the Dutch over Vorstius, for example, he proposed his scheme "to bring the King out this Labryrinth of [the Netherlanders'] malice." In his secret plan, England would induce France, Germany, and Poland to recall all their students from the University of Leyden "to prevent the corruption of their minds," thereby bringing the offending university to the brink of collapse and forcing the town to expel the heretics and schismatics.[159]

The hallmark of Throckmorton's tenure was his quarrel with Sir Michael Everarde, the sergeant-major of Flushing. Throckmorton had entertained a long-standing scorn for Everarde, who did not hide his own disdain for the lieutenant-governor. They quarreled in 1612, when Everarde defended his friend Miles Hart in a matter that Throckmorton thought was not the sergeant-major's concern. Throckmorton complained to Sidney, not failing to put in a few bad words about the man's "blasfemmy . . . .imperious fashion of commaunde. . . , debaushedness. . . , and . . . contempt and negleckt of me."[160] This minor tiff was soon blown all out of proportion, with Throckmorton threatening to court-martial one of Everarde's men, who had delivered a letter from the sergeant-major to Lisle without the lieutenant-governor's passport, and with Lady Browne and Lady Mary Wroth taking Everarde's side.[161] Finally, Lisle had to send for Everarde and inquire into the matter himself. Throckmorton was offended, of course, and complained that the governor was unfairly handling the matter by his letters and by requesting Everarde's presence.[162] Nevertheless, Lisle managed to effect a temporary reconciliation and the waters were calm for a few months.[163]

The squabble over Hart, however, was only the start. Two years later, the pair's simmering hostility boiled over during a drunken brawl in which Everarde took on Throckmorton's brother-in-law, Captain Thomas Amyes, and his friend, Captain Ferdinando Carey, in the State House at Flushing. When Throckmorton interfered, Everarde, blind with rage and drink, shrieked, "it is you whoe art the cause of all this. Have at thee!" and attacked the lieutenant-governor with his poignard. He would have killed Throckmorton had Sir John Fleming and Burgomaster de More not tripped him; as it was, he managed to deliver a blow to the leg that Throckmorton said lamed him. Throckmorton then ordered Everarde held under house arrest in his lodging until it was seen whether Carey, who had been stabbed in the belly, would live or die. Everarde exclaimed that he would never be taken prisoner by the likes of Throckmorton, raced to his dwelling with the lieutenant-governor's men after him, roused his kinsman out of a sound sleep, and with him held off his antagonists at sword point from the top of the steps. Finally, after a struggle, he was overpowered and arrested.[164]

Throckmorton saw his chance to destroy the sergeant-major. He, Amyes, and Carey deposed in the ensuing court-martial that Everarde's attack had been wholly unprovoked.[165] They rallied everyone they could think of to their cause, including the magistrates of Flushing and William Zoete (Admiral Haultain), who had been witnesses. Even Lady Dorothy Throckmorton was persuaded to complain about her brush with widowhood.[166]

Everarde admitted he was so drunk he could scarcely remember the episode, but he recalled enough to produce a version somewhat different from Throckmorton's. The sergeant-major claimed Carey made an insolent remark and threw the first blow. Everarde said he tried to attack Carey with his poignard, but that Amyes grabbed him, pinned him down, and beat him while Carey threw "at least a dozen trenchers" at his head. The Admiral Haultain and the Flushing burgomasters entered and broke up the fight, followed by Throckmorton, who, by his scornful manner and refusal to listen to Everarde's side, enraged the sergeant-major. Everarde confessed he threw himself upon the lieutenant-governor, but he believed he had not stabbed him, because Fleming immediately wrenched his poignard away from him. He was also convinced that Carey was not mortally wounded, for he was lively enough that day to lead the attack against Everarde's quarters. Everarde expressed his remorse, admitted he was at fault, and said he was ready to accept any punishment that Lisle—but not, he emphasized, Throckmorton—chose.[167]

Lord Lisle had a difficult task judging which of the two versions most closely approximated the truth. Throckmorton had the weight of his office plus the testimony of his friends to lend credibility to his report. However, some of the witnesses the lieutenant-governor insisted on calling gave testimony that supported Everarde's story. Admiral Haultain was noncommittal, but he said that when he tried to reconcile the two men, the lieutenant-governor would hear nothing of it; "le Lieutenant Governeur n'y a voulu entendre jusques à ce que Vostre Seigneurie fût advertie du fait."[168] The Flushing magistrates went further, producing a narrative that paralleled Everarde's.[169] Whatever the truth of the matter, Everarde could not win. Even though Lady Mary Wroth, Lady Browne, Chaplain Thomas Pott, and the Flushing magistrates sided with him,[170] Lisle removed him from his position, while Throckmorton crowed that he was lucky to escape with his life.

Throckmorton's problems reveal the difficulty of managing a garrison full of highly charged personalities. The successful governor had to possess tact and intelligence as well as a commanding demeanor. Clearly, Lisle was blessed with these qualities. The men and officers of Flushing had always to deal with the daily tensions of garrison life. Living conditions were crowded, and the enlisted men were paid subsistence wages. The English soldiers had to cope with the boredom of military life as well as with the growing hostility of the Dutch, who liked the English less the further peace negotiations progressed. Yet neither Sidney nor Browne ever allowed the garrison's psychological tension to erupt in this way. Everarde had been in Flushing at least as early as 1605,[171] but Browne never indicated that he had trouble exacting the appropriate respect and obedience from him. Without doubt, Everarde was a hothead and a heavy drinker, but Throckmorton's arrogance seems to have aggravated his already bad temper. Throckmorton could not handle the man, and his ineptness resulted in an outburst that factionalized the garrison, disgraced the sergeant-major and the entire company before the Flushing magistrates, shattered Everarde's career, and added to the demoralization of the captains and lieutenants.

One wonders why Lisle tolerated Throckmorton, after the man's marginal competence became obvious. Several reasons probably worked together. The simplest was ordinary friendship; Sir John's eldest son, evidently named after the governor, was Lisle's godson.[172] Too, once James had established himself, the new Viscount Lisle was kept busy at court; perhaps he no longer cared so much what happened in the garrison, as long as he did not have to live there. Lisle's eldest son died in 1612, a loss which must have distracted the viscount from duties that he had already assigned someone else to perform. Nor could Lisle have been unaware that morale at the garrison was sinking. Possibly he felt that no one else could do better under the deteriorating circumstances.

Presumably, Lisle picked men whose points of view approximated his own. Their opinions very probably echoed the governor's: for example, Browne was strongly but not naively pro-Dutch and implacably anti-Spanish, as was Sidney. Following this line of thought, it is possible to deduce from Browne's and Throckmorton's attitudes that Lisle, while he was not a Puritan himself, was not unsympathetic to the Puritan cause. Both Browne and Throckmorton inclined in that direction. Browne's sympathies are manifest in his admiration for Thomas Pott, the chaplain of the Flushing garrison, who, when he first arrived, Sir William described as preaching "every day better than the other," and characterized as "an honest, zealous, and learned man."[173] At the death of Pott's colleague, Mr. Daniel, Browne advocated keeping Pott on alone, with no other preachers to interfere with him: "He hath taken much pains and done much good in this garrison," Browne wrote to Lisle.

Pott characterized himself as a Puritan when he requested that he not be given the place by himself, but that another minister be chosen to succeed Mr. Daniel from among the "woful ruins" of the suspended Puritan clergy of England. He went on to request the introduction of elders to assist the ministers and to propose that the English church join with the Classis of Walcheren, for better correspondence between themselves and the Zealand Church.[174] He also attacked the custom of making the soldier take an oath that he would do his duty in watching and warding,[175] a stance to which he clung despite steadfast opposition. Even Browne had to admit that Pott was "too vehement in many poincts," and when he learned Lisle meant to send over a second preacher to replace Daniel, he requested he might be "not so extreme Puritan" as Pott.[176]

Throckmorton could not tolerate any deviation from regulations, as Browne apparently had. He was bothered by Pott's attack on the oath and by the minister's habit of exhorting the soldiers from the pulpit to refuse it, and yet he had to agree that both the soldier who took it and the officer who signed it were in danger of being forsworn. As usual, he turned to the governor, asking Lisle to revise the oath according to Pott's demands.[177] He was infuriated when Pott presumed to express some sympathy for Everarde, but the minister continued in his position until Flushing was returned to the Dutch. Although Throckmorton claimed to have fallen out with Pott over the oath,[178] until the Everarde affair he had found the preacher "extraordinarily well disposed in the business of his office."[179]

During all the time he was at his post, Sidney barraged London with requests for leave from Flushing. His incessant pleas for a few months here or there, plus Rowland Whyte's and Barbara Sidney's indefatigable bargaining and pleading in his behalf, have given rise to the mistaken impression that Sir Robert was chained to his post, pining to be home and denied in his reasonable quest for occasional relief from his duties. Careful examination of his movements between 1589 and 1603, however, reveals a very different picture. Between the time of his succession to the governorship on August 12, 1589 and the date of Elizabeth's death, March 23, 1603, Sidney spent sixty-eight months in Flushing and ninety-one and three-quarters away from the garrison. That is, out of just under fourteen years, he spent five and two-thirds at his post and seven and two-thirds away from it.

The impression we have of a rusticated Sidney made prisoner of his post by a heartless queen is no doubt grounded in Sidney's genuine concern, which was reflected in his own and in Whyte's correspondence, that his absence from the court was harming his chances for advancement. His loneliness, boredom, and frustration are made clear by the tone as well as the frequency of his pleas for leave.

In August 1595, for example, he began to plan his strategy to obtain a new leave on the very day he left Margate for Flushing following a two-and-a-half year stay in England.[180] Within three weeks of his arrival, he sent Whyte to Burghley and Essex to begin a suit for his leave, and, in his first letter to Cecil, begged the lord treasurer's son to advance the suit.[181] He did not go to his post for almost nine months after he was awarded the governorship, and within a few months after his first arrival, he was already asking permission to visit England.[182] He presented every conceivable reason why he should be in England: his health, his finances, the Sedgrave affair, the needs of his family, the death of Lord Huntingdon, and the illness of his aunt, Lady Huntingdon. He rallied his wife, his aunts, lady Rich, Lord Admiral Nottingham, Burghley, Fortescue, Buckhurst, Essex,

TABLE 5
SIDNEY'S PRESENCES IN AND ABSENCES FROM FLUSHING, 1589–1603

Source: *HMCD* 2, passim

	Time at the Garrison	Time Away
August 12, 1589–May 7, 1590: Out		8.75 mo.
May 7, 1590–September [1], 1590: In	3.75 mo.	
September [1], 1590–September [30]: Out		1
October [1], 1590–December 8, 1592: In	26.25	
December 8, 1592–August 3, 1595: Out		31
August 3, 1595–January 12, 1596: In	5.25	
January 12, 1596–August 29, 1596: Out		6.50
August 29, 1596–March 4, 1598: In	18	
[January-February 1596/97: Out]		[1]
March 24, 1598–August 4, 1599: Out		16.50
August 4, 1599–October 30, 1600: In	14.75	
October 30, 1600–March 23, 1603 (Death of Elizabeth): Out		29
	68.00	93.75

Approximate total: 13.47 years
Approximate total time in Flushing: 68 months or 5.66 years
Approximate total time out of Flushing: 93.75 months or 7.81 years

Sir John Stanhope, and anyone else who would give ear to his cause, and bombarded the queen with requests for his leave from every direction. At one point, Elizabeth lost patience with his demands and turned him down with a flippant remark,[183] but evidence shows she allowed him to govern in absentia well over 50 percent of the time.

Sidney's most strenuous efforts to obtain leave occurred in 1597, when Essex and his friends were politicking to raise Sidney to new heights. Essex had put up Sidney's name for the Warden of the Cinque Ports in opposition to the young Lord Cobham, who felt by rights he should inherit it from his recently deceased father. Sidney's presence at court might have done much to advance that suit; naturally, Cobham's party did all they could to keep him safely consigned to his post. Whyte and Lady Barbara made a series of fruitless efforts to have Sidney called home. Sidney's gift to Cecil of a cast of Barbary hawks,[184] Lady Warwick's conversations with the queen,[185] and Burghley's intercession[186] failed to overcome Cobham's opposition. Sidney and Whyte sensed that the leave was being "purposely crossed,"[187] and this was confirmed when Lady Warwick discovered the queen had been convinced he was making over £2,000 a year off his governorship and his horse and foot companies, that he further lined his pockets by "intercourse of marchants to and fro," and that it was unsafe to leave Flushing without a governor while Lord Burghe and Sir Frances Vere were absent from their posts at the Brill and Ostend, for the enemy had designs against the islands at the mouth of the Scheldt for the winter of 1597. All these obstacles Rowland Whyte perceived as "purposely found out to hinder your coming" and wrought by Lord Cobham.[188] Despite this, leave was granted to Sidney on October 9, but, to Whyte's amazement, it was revoked on the twenty-second because Sir Edmund Uvedall was away from Flushing.[189] Whyte was embarrassed and incredulous, but not as astonished as Sidney when the same thing happened again less than three months later. Sidney could scarcely believe that with "a Lord Treasorer . . . , and a principal secretary to be the movers of yt, and an Earle of Essex and a Lord Admiral to further yt," the queen could respond to his suit with dilatory answers as she had.[190] He finally obtained his leave in March 1598, after the Cinque Ports had been bestowed on Cobham and the furor had quieted down.

The stridency of Sidney's unsuccessful pleas for leave during this crucial period no doubt has given rise to the conception that he was endlessly confined to Flushing much against his will. Even though he spent three years two months at his post between August 1595 and October 1600, he spent almost two years away from it during the same time—unfortunately, not at moments when he might have been able to speak for himself to advance his career at court.

It is true that during some of his absences from Flushing he was engaged elsewhere on the queen's business. However, these missions, such as the 1594 embassy to France, might have been expected to effect his advancement, something he did not believe would result from remaining at his post.

Sidney cannot be blamed for wanting to absent himself from Flushing. The duty was routine, repetitious, and frustrating. It was a job that could be handled by yeomen soldiers such as Browne and Uvedall. Sidney had a sophisticated liberal education meant to prepare him for an elevated and sensitive position in the English government, and he had been groomed by his parents and his aristocratic relatives for a career in diplomacy or upper-level administration. He was a competent but not a brilliant military commander; he would never compare with Vere or Norris on the battlefield. Flushing represented a backwater for Sidney. His only hope for personal advancement lay at the court.

NOTES

1. *L & A CSP For.* 2:113.
2. *CSP Dom.* 12:330.
3. *L & A CSP For.* 1:137–38.
4. Ibid., 2:113.
5. Ibid., 1:138.
6. [1596] Memorandum, *HMC Salisbury* 13:603.
7. Gilpin to Sidney, Hague, 5 September 1596, *HMCD* 2:216–17.
8. Sir Thomas Wilkes to Sidney, London, 17 January 1596/97, Ibid., 2:229–30.
9. Open Warrant to Sir Thomas Sherley, Knt., Treasurer-at-Wars, 26 January 1596/97, *PC* 26:431.

10. Sidney to Lady Sidney, 1 March [1597] *HMCD* 2:258.

11. Whyte to Sidney, Strand, 13 April 1597, ibid, 2:264.

12. Whyte to Sidney, 16 April 1597, ibid., 2:266.

13. Whyte to Sidney, 27 April 1597, ibid., 2:272; Whyte to Sidney, 8 May 1597, ibid., 2:276.

14. Whyte to Sidney, [19 May] 1597, ibid., 2:280–82.

15. Whyte to Sidney, Court, 22 September 1596, ibid., 2:217–18.

16. A reference to Captain Rowle's (or Roels') company, which, in 1592, Sidney had given to Captain Inge, provost-marshal at Flushing. Sidney's appointment was overruled and Captain Purley was placed in charge of the company. See Sidney to Burghley, Flushing, 16 February, 1591/92 (SP 84/44, fol. 116) and Sidney to Privy Council, Flushing, 8 March 1592 (SP 84/44, fol. 1592).

17. Whyte to Sidney, Strand, 24 September 1596, *HMCD* 2:219–20.

18. Whyte to Sidney, 26 September 1596, ibid., 2:220–22.

19. Whyte to Sidney, Penshurst, 28 September 1596, ibid., 2:222–23.

20. Sidney to Cecil, Flushing, 2 October 1596, SP 84/53, fols. 76–77.

21. Dated 31 October 1596, *PC* 26:290–91.

22. Sidney to Burghley, 2 December 1596, SP 84/53, fol. 186.

23. *HNCD* 2:306 *ff.* See references to his position and activities.

24. *L & A CSP For.* 2:117.

25. Sidney to Burghley, 3 December 1591, SP 84/43, fols. 284–85.

26. Sidney to [Burghley], 18 April 1592, SP 84/44, fols. 246–47.

27. Sidney to [Burghley], Flushing, July 1592, SP 84/45, fol. 87.

28. See, for example, Sidney to Burghley, Flushing, 22 October 1595, SP 84/51, fol. 203; Browne to Sidney, 2 April 1596, *HMCD* 2:208–10; Uvedall to Sidney, Flushing, 20 May 1596, ibid., 2:214; Gilpin to Sidney, Hague, 2 December 1596, ibid., 2:227; Sidney to Burghley, Flushing, 1 April 1597, SP 84/54, fol. 155; Sidney to Cecil, Flushing, 31 July 1597, SP 84/60, fols. 250–53; Sidney to Cecil, Flushing, 21 August 1601, SP 84/61, fols. 242–43.

29. *HMCD* 3:lxxvii.

30. [December] 1585, *CSP Dom.* 12:164.

31. Samuel Gardiner, ed., *Parliamentary Debates in 1610. Edited from Notes of a Member of the House of Commons, Camden Society*, no. 81 (London: J. B. Nichols and Sons, 1861), 10:xii.

32. Item CCLXVIII, 26.1, *CSP Dom.* 6:89.

33. Dated 24 March 1591, ibid., 3:22.

34. *HMCD* 3:lxxvii.

35. Browne to Sidney, 2 April 1596, ibid., 2:208–10; Gilpin to Sidney, Hague, 10 November 1597, ibid., 2:304; Gilpin to Sidney, January 1597/98, ibid., 2:308; [States General?] to States of Zealand, 24 January 1598 [N.S.], ibid., 2:309; Gilpin to Sidney, Hague, 16 January 1597/98, ibid., 2:310; Gilpin to Sidney, Hague, 24 January 1597/98, ibid., 2:312; Gilpin to Sidney, Hague, 27 January 1597/98, ibid., 2:314; Gilpin to Sidney, Hague, 10 February 1597/98, ibid., 2:318–20; Gilpin to Sidney, Hague, 20 March 1597/98, ibid., 2:332; Gilpin to Sidney, Hague, 28 March 1597/98, ibid., 2:333.

36. Gilpin to Sidney, Hague, 2 December 1596, ibid., 2:227–28.

37. Gilpin to Sidney, Hague, 28 March 1597/98, ibid., 2:333.

38. Browne to Sidney, Flushing, 2 October 1603, ibid., 3:65.

39. Browne to Sidney, Flushing, 6 May 1605, ibid., 3:159.

40. Browne to Lisle, Flushing, 21 March 1605/06, ibid., 3:254.

41. Browne to Lisle, Flushing, 15 June 1606, 3:282; Browne to Lisle, Flushing, 2 July 1606, ibid., 2:288.

42. Browne to Lisle, Flushing, 9 February 1606/07, ibid., 3:349; Browne to Lisle, Flushing, 29 August 1607, ibid., 3:397; Browne to Lisle, Hague, 18 September 1604, ibid., 3:402.

43. Browne to Lisle, Flushing, 31 January 1610/11, ibid, 3:250.

44. Lisle to Winwood, Flushing, 12 September 1612, Great Britain, Historical Manuscripts Commission, *Report on the Manuscripts of the Duke of Buccleuch and Queensbury*, 6 vols (London: HMSO, 1809–1926), 1:112.

45. Lisle to Winwood, 22 August 1613, ibid., 1:143.

46. Throckmorton to Lisle, 10 July 1614, SP 84/70, fols. 15–16; Throckmorton to Lisle, 27 July 1614, ibid., fol. 37.

47. *HMCD* 4:xvii.

48. Sidney to Burghley, Flushing, 14 July 1592, SP 84/45, fols. 93–95.

49. Sidney to Burghley, Flushing, 21 September 1592, SP 84/45, fols. 93–95.

50. Sidney to Cecil, Flushing, 21 August 1601, SP 84/61, fols. 242–43.
51. Sidney to Elizabeth, Flushing, 24 December 1599, SP 84/44, fols. 200–202.
52. Sidney to Burghley, Flushing, 21 January 1591/92, SP 84/44, fols. 1–2.
53. Uvedall to Sidney, 19 March 1592/93, HMCD 2:133–34.
54. Uvedall to Sidney, 16 December 1592, ibid., 2:129; ibid. 2:131–34, passim.
55. Browne to Sidney, 24 January 1596, ibid., 2:208.
56. Sidney to Burghley, Flushing, 6 October 1591, SP 84/43, fols. 80–82.
57. Dated 19 December 1591, PC 22:137.
58. Sidney to Burghley, Flushing, 20 January 1590/91, SP 84/44, fol. 49.
59. HMCD 2:135; pp. 167–80 passim.
60. Complaint to the queen, with copies of letters from Sir Nicholas Parker, Sir Conyers Clifford, Sir Francis Vere, Captain John Burke, Sir Matthew Morgan, and Lieutenant Loveman to Cot revealing Cot's extortionate demands, 1590, SP 84/42, fols. 175–77.
61. Sidney to Burghley, Flushing, 20 March 1596/7, SP 84/54, fol. 134.
62. Privy Council to Sidney, Sir John Peyton, and Lewis Lewknor, PC, 31:439–40.
63. Whyte to Sidney, 24 February 1597/98, HMCD 2:325.
64. Whyte to Sidney, 25 February 1597/98, ibid., 2:326.
65. Sidney to Burghley, Flushing, 16 July 1597, SP 84/55, fols. 22–23.
66. Sidney to Cecil, Flushing, 4 August 1597, SP 84/55, fol. 80.
67. Sidney to Cecil, Flushing, 31 October 1597, SP 84/55, fols. 197–98.
68. Sidney to Cecil, Flushing, 5 January 1599/1600, SP 84/60, fol. 7
69. Browne to Sidney, Flushing, 21 January 1596 (enclosure), HMCD 2:207.
70. Sidney to Burghley, 22 July 1590, SP 84/38, fol. 86.
71. Ibid.
72. Sidney to Burghley, Flushing, 15 October 1596, Additional MS 4122, fol. 53; Sidney to Essex, 26 November 1596, Additional MS. 4122, fol. 132, British Library, London, England.
73. Abstract of Intelligences, CSP Dom. 4:326.
74. Sidney to Nottingham, Flushing, 12 August 1599, SP 84/59, fol. 23 [PRO incorrectly lists this letter as addressed to Cecil, but Sidney, in a nearly identical letter to Cecil of the same day, states that it was meant for Nottingham]; Sidney to Cecil, 12 August 1599, SP 84/59, fols. 25–26; Sidney to Cecil, 27 August 1599, SP 84/59, fol. 44.
75. Sidney to Cecil, Flushing, 2 September 1599, SP 84/59, fols. 50–51.
76. Sidney to Cecil, Flushing, 22 September 1599, SP 84/59, fols. 72–73.
77. Hugh Owen to Sidney, Brussels, 3 November 1591, CSP Dom. 3:119.
78. Sidney to Burghley, Flushing, 17 December 1591, SP 84/43, fol. 284.
79. Sidney to Owen, Flushing, 8 November 1591, SP 84/43, fol. 182.
80. Sidney to Privy Council, Flushing, 15 January 1591/92, SP 84/44, fol. 33.
81. Sidney to Burghley, Flushing, 17 December 1591, SP 84/43, fols. 284–85.
82. Patrick Sedgrave to Rowland Whyte, Antwerp, 9 November 1590, SP 84/39, fol. 203.
83. Sedgrave to Sidney, Antwerp, 9 November 1590, SP 84/39, fol. 203.
84. Sidney to Burghley, 20 November 1590 (2 letters), SP 84/39, fol. 226; fols. 228–29.
85. HMCD 1:242, 423, 424.
86. Sidney to Burghley, Flushing, 3 December 1590, SP 84/40, fols. 11–12.
87. Ibid.
88. Sidney to Burghley, Flushing, 26 January 1591/92, SP 84/44, fol. 62.
89. Sidney to Burghley, Flushing, SP 84/44, fols. 151–55.
90. Sidney to Burghley, Flushing, 4 April 1592, SP 84/44, fols. 203–4.
91. Sidney to Burghley, Flushing, 5 February 1591/92, SP 84/44, fol. 100.
92. Sidney to Burghley, Flushing, 10 November 1591, SP 84/43, fols. 185–86.
93. Sidney to Burghley, Flushing, 3 December 1591, SP 84/43, fols. 284–85.
94. Sidney to Burghley, Flushing, 4 April 1592, SP 84/44, fols. 203–4.
95. Reinold Bosely to [Cecil], 7 April 1592, CSP Dom. 3:209.
96. Sidney to [Burghley], Flushing, 18 April 1592, SP 84/44, fols. 246–47.
97. Confession of Griffin Jons, [4 January 1593/94], HMC Salisbury 13:509.
98. Confession of Henry Walpole, 13 June 1594, CSP Dom. 3:52.
99. Sidney to Burghley, Flushing, 12 September 1595, SP 84/51, fols. 134–35.
100. Cecil to Sidney, Nonesuch, 21 September 1595, SP 84/51, fol. 159.
101. Sidney to Burghley, Flushing, 10 December 1595, SP 84/51, fols. 272–73.
102. Sidney to Burghley, Flushing, 22 October 1595, SP 84/51, fol. 203.
103. Sidney to Burghley, 12 November 1595, SP 84/51, fol. 203.

104. Sidney to Cecil, 13 November 1595, SP 84/51, fol. 233.

105. *L & A CSP For.* 2:111.

106. Lewis Lewknor to Sidney, Brussels, 4 June 1590, *CSP Dom.* 12:307.

107. Sidney to Burghley, 12 June 1590, SP 84/37, fol. 372.

108. *L & A CSP For.* 2:113.

109. Sidney to Burghley, 29 August 1590, SP 84/38, fol. 222.

110. Uvedall to Sidney, 22 February [1592/93], *HMCD* 2:131.

111. Sidney to Privy Council, Flushing, 26 November 1596, SP 84/53, fol. 170.

112. Sidney to Cecil, Flushing, 1 October 1599, SP 84/59, fol. 90.

113. Sidney to Burghley, Flushing, 4 July 1597, SP 84/55, fol. 6.

114. Sidney to Cecil, 23 July 1597 [incomplete], SP 84/55, fol. 41.

115. Sidney to Cecil, Flushing, 15 July 1600, SP 84/60, fol. 231.

116. Whyte to Sidney, 26 July 1600, *HMCD* 2:474; Whyte to Sidney, 27 July 1600, ibid., 2:474–75; ibid., 2:478–81 passim.

117. Browne to Lisle, Flushing, 7 July 1608, ibid., 2:5.

118. Ibid., 2:2, 3, 4, passim.

119. Winwood to William Trumbull, Hague, 3 May 1611 (O.S.), in Great Britain, Historical Manuscripts Commission, *Report on the Manuscripts of the Marquess of Downshire*, 4 vols. (London: HMSO, 1924), 3:71.

120. List of Officers of the Regiment 27 April 1616, *PC* 34:515.

121. Throckmorton to Lisle, Flushing, 11 December 1612. *HMCD* 5:54.

122. Ibid., 3:294, 366, et passim.

123. Throckmorton to Lisle, Flushing, 11 December 1612, ibid., 5:68–69.

124. Browne to Lisle, Flushing, 3 October 1610, ibid., 4:253.

125. *L & A CSP For.* 2:125.

126. Sidney to Burghley, Flushing, 26 March 1590/91, SP 84/41, fol. 50.

127. *L & A CSP For.* 1:126.

128. Sidney to Burghley, 17 January 1590/91, SP 84/41, fol. 50.

129. Privy Council to Sidney, 24 May 1591, *PC* 21:154.

130. Sidney to Burghley, Flushing, 12 June 1591, SP 84/42, fol. 134.

131. Sidney to Privy Council, Flushing, 10 September 1591 (2 letters), SP 84/43, fol. 3 *ff.*, and fol. 240.

132. Dated 4 September 1589, *CSP Dom.* 12:282.

133. Sidney to Burghley, Flushing, 10 September 1591, SP 84/43, fol. 22.

134. *HMCD* 2:128–60, passim.

135. Whyte to Sidney, 19 October 1595, ibid., 2:128–60.

136. Browne to Sidney, [1596], ibid., 2:211.

137. Ibid. 2:206–17, passim.

138. Sidney to Cecil, Flushing, 6 October 1597, SP 84/55, fol. 163.

139. Whyte to Sidney or Browne, 18 March 1597/98, *HMCD* 2:332.

140. Browne to Sidney, Flushing, 9 May 1598, ibid., 2:254.

141. Warrant to pay Sir Edmund Uvedall . . . , 1602, Additional MS 5753, fol. 289, British Library, London, England.

142. Collins, 2:3n.

143. Browne to Lisle, 6 December 1608, *HMCD* 4:87; Browne to Lisle, Flushing, 7 January 1608/09, ibid., 4:95.

144. Browne to Lisle, Flushing, 19 February 1610/11, ibid., 4:253.

145. Throckmorton to Lisle, Flushing, 19 February 1610/11, ibid. 4:253.

146. Browne to Lisle, Flushing, 19 February 1610/1611, ibid. 4:253.

147. Browne to Lisle, Flushing, 13 March [1610/11], ibid., 4:256–58.

148. Blocq to Lisle, Flushing, 6 April 1611 (N.S.), ibid., 4:261.

149. Throckmorton to Lisle, Flushing, 27 March 1611, ibid. 5:68.

150. Throckmorton to Lisle, Flushing, 3 October 1610, ibid. 568.

151. John More to Trumbull, London, 18 July 1611, *HMC Downshire* 3:109.

152. Throckmorton to Lisle, Flushing, 15 May 1611, *HMCD* 4:268.

153. Throckmorton to Lisle, Flushing, November 1611, ibid., 4:298.

154. Lisle to Lady Lisle, Flushing, 13 August 1612, ibid., 5:59.

155. Throckmorton to Lisle, Flushing, 13 February 1611/[12], ibid., 5:15.

156. Throckmorton to Lisle, Flushing, February 1611/12, ibid., 5:17–18.

157. Throckmorton to Lisle, February 1611[12], ibid., 5:15.

158. Throckmorton to Lisle, 21 July 1614, SP 84/70, fol. 27.

159. Throckmorton to Lisle, 13 March 1611/12, *HMCD* 5:30–31.

160. Throckmorton to Lisle, Flushing, 29 January 1611/12, ibid., 5:6–7.

161. Throckmorton to Lisle, Flushing, 25 January 1612/13, ibid., 5:80.

162. Throckmorton to Lisle, Flushing, 20 February 1611/12, ibid., 5:18–19.

163. Throckmorton to Lisle, Flushing, 22 February 1611/12, ibid., 5:19–20.

164. Ibid., 5:187–97, passim.

165. Throckmorton to Lisle, 27 April 1614, ibid., 5:194; Sir John Fleming to Lisle, 26 April 1614, ibid., 5:189; Thomas Amyes to Lisle, 26 April 1614, ibid., 5:191.

166. Lady Throckmorton to Lisle, 27 April 1614, ibid., 5:190.

167. Sir Michael Everarde to Lisle, Flushing, 26 April 1614, ibid., 5:192–94.

168. Admiral Haultain to Lisle, Middleburgh, 6 May 1614 (N.S.), ibid., 5:201.

169. Certificate by the Burgomaster, Echevins, and the Council of Flushing, Flushing, 16 April 1614 (N.S.), ibid., 5:204.

170. Pott to Lisle, Flushing, 16 April 1614, ibid., 5:190; Everarde to Lisle, 6 May 1614, ibid., 5:204; Throckmorton to Lisle, 6 May 1614, ibid., 5:282.

171. Everarde to Browne, Camp, [September] 1604, ibid., 3:202.

172. Throckmorton to Sidney, Flushing, 9 December 1604, SP 84/70, fol. 193.

173. Browne to Lisle, Flushing, 22 June 1605, *HMCD* 3:173.

174. Pott to Lisle, Flushing, 8 May 1607, ibid., 3:173.

175. Pott's paper of scruples concerning the soldier's oath; in a letter from Throckmorton to Lisle, Flushing, [2 July 1611], ibid., 4:313.

176. Browne to Lisle, Flushing, 10 December 1607, ibid., 3:441.

177. Throckmorton to Lisle, Flushing, [2 July 1611], ibid., 3:312.

178. Ibid., 5: 323, 324, 338–40, 381–83, 385, 386.

179. Throckmorton to Lisle, Flushing, 18 August 1611, ibid., 5:316.

180. Sidney to Lady Sidney, Margate, 3 August 1595, ibid., 2:159.

181. Sidney to Burghley, Flushing, 25 August 1595 (2 letters), SP 84/41, fols. 110 and 112.

182. *L & A CSP For.* 2:115.

183. E.g., Sir John Stanhope to Sidney, *HMCD* 2:120.

184. Sidney to Cecil, Flushing, 3 September 1597, SP 84/55, fol. 115.

185. Whyte to Sidney, Richmond, 4 October 1597, *HMCD* 2:293.

186. Sidney to Burghley, Flushing, 28 October 1597, SP 84/55, fol. 187.

187. Sidney to Lady Sidney, Flushing, 21 March 1597, *HMCD* 2:253–54.

188. Whyte to Sidney, Richmond, 4 October 1597, ibid., 2:293.

189. Whyte to Sidney, 9 October 1597, 13 October 1597, and 22 October 1597, ibid., 2:294–97.

190. Sidney to Cecil, Flushing, 13 January 1597/98, SP 84/56, fols. 25–26.

[7]

Sidney at the Court of Queen Elizabeth I

Sidney's ambitions were not unreasonable in light of his background and training. He desired four things: a secure, prestigious position, influence, money, and an office that would keep him in England. These he sought to obtain by seeking employment that would show his worth, by bringing himself to the queen's attention, and by associating himself with members of the ruling court factions, who he hoped would use their influence to help him.

His mission to Scotland in 1588 had demonstrated his diplomatic skills. In 1593, he was again selected to go abroad, this time as ambassador to Henri IV, who had recently determined, to the dismay of the Protestant community, that *"Paris vaut une messe."* Lady Sidney seems to have felt small enthusiasm about the journey; Sidney sent her a series of letters explaining why he could not refuse the nomination. It would be costly, for the ambassador had to transport and support himself and a swarm of servants and attendants, entertain nobly, and hand out fine presents to the appropriate people. However, as Stone observes, men of birth regarded such assignments as moral obligations as well as opportunities for advancement.[1]

"Sweet Barbara," Sidney wrote to his wife, "be not greved with my jorney. They that live in the world must be subject to such imploiments and however it be chargeable it will be honorable."[2] Sidney was confident that the mission would bring some reward, although Lady Sidney apparently expressed her concern that it would bankrupt them. He assured her that he had borrowed £1,000 from Essex on excellent terms. "You are married, my deer Barbara, to a husband that is now drawn so into the world and the actions of yt as there is no way to retire myself without trying fortune further.... And I do not dout but this imploiment will bring me some good requital, or if yt do not, it must and shalbe the last ever I wil under take."[3]

Henri's conversion caused serious concern in Protestant circles, where it was feared that it portended major disaster for the cause in France. It might also mean Elizabeth would lose one of her buffers between herself and Spain. Sidney accordingly was sent to deal with the king in favor of the French Protestants; one of his missions was to confer with the ministers of the church there about their course of action, their demands to the king, and his answer. The queen orally told him to remind Henri that she had always defended the Protestants in France from his predecessors and to warn him that she would not now forsake them,[4] although he was to assure him of her desire to continue her friendship with him. He evidently was expected to learn what he could of the king's real, as opposed to professed, religious inclination and of his plans for the future regarding marriage, the Prince of Condé, the House of Lorraine, and relations with the Pope. He was also to deal with Henri about the question of English succor for Brittany, which the king greatly needed in his war campaign.

Henri had been raised a Protestant by his mother, Jeanne D'Albret, Queen of Navarre, and in 1568 he fought with the Huguenots under Coligny. He succeeded to the throne of Navarre in 1578 and married Margaret de Valois. The Saint Bartholomew Massacre, in which Sir Philip Sidney nearly lost his life, took place on the day of the wedding; Henri saved himself by a feigned conversion to Catholicism. For the next four years, he was forced to live at court, but in 1576, he escaped, renounced his new faith, and took the leadership of the Huguenot armies. When, in 1584, the death of Francis, Duc D'Anjou, left the throne to Henri, he was opposed by the Roman Catholic House of Guise and the Holy League. Guise and Henri III were both assassinated in 1589, and Henri IV succeeded to the French throne. The League, supported by Philip II of Spain, continued its opposition, and, although he made progress in the provinces, Henri was unable to take Paris. In 1593, he finally took his friends' advice and reconverted to Roman Catholicism, convinced it was the only way to unite the kingdom. The following year he was to be crowned at Chartres and take Paris; in 1596, he would end the war with the Holy League, and 1598, the war with Spain. The Edict of Nantes in the same year was to grant religious freedom to the Protestants, and Henri was to rule France in relative tranquillity, aided by his minister Maximilien de Béthune, until his assassination in 1610.

If speed was important, the start of Sidney's mission was ill-starred. He received his orders in October 1593, but not until February 8 of the following year—hours before Henri's coronation—did he have his first audience with the king. He was delayed by bad weather at Dover for almost a month. Winter tempests made it impossible to sail across the Channel—one ship that tried foundered, losing all the baggage and most of the horses and men of Colonel Shirley and Captain Wingfield.[5] On the twenty-sixth, Sidney and his train attempted to embark but were forced back before they had gone ten miles.[6] Sidney's man Foulckes was in a bark that disappeared into the storm. Sir Robert feared that, unless he had made it to Flushing, he must have been lost.[7] They tried again three days later without success,[8] and on January 2, 1593/94, they were forced back to Dover a third time.[9] Sidney grew more impatient: "God rid me quickly out of this place, I am ecceeding weary of yt," he complained.[10] He began to worry how he would accomplish his mission, as news came in that the truce was broken in

France, that Henri had gone to Senlis or Compiège, and that the duke of Bouillon had left the king to make war in Champagne. This turn of events would make his negotiations most troublesome. He was not equipped to follow Henri to war, and besides, he anticipated that the war would provide Henri with many excuses. He feared the deputies of the Protestant religion, who were meeting with the king to discuss their cause, would have disbanded, and he wondered what the queen would have him do if they had.[11] He was concerned that the queen's order to remind the French king that she would not abandon the Protestants in his country would offend Henri, who might demand to see his commission to make such a threat. He asked Burghley under what specific circumstances the queen wanted him to deliver this message, and requested some written authority for it. He also reminded Burghley and the queen of the Order of the Saint Esprit, which every New Year's Day renewed its oath to extirpate Protestantism; perhaps, he proposed, the king could be urged to alter this oath or abolish the order and resurrect in its place the old Order of Saint Michel.[12]

At last Sidney got away from England. On the morning of January 9, he and his friends in the *Tramontina* caught sight of Dieppe, where Foulckes, to Sidney's delight, was waiting for him, having survived the storm and successfully made the passage to France at the time his master had been forced back to Dover.[13] Sidney wrote to Burghley promising to hurry to the king and apparently contacted Thomas Edmondes, the English agent in France, arranging to meet him at Gisors and asking him to speak with the duc de Bouillon about the mission.[14] In Dieppe, where he spent almost ten days, Sidney was kindly entertained by the governor, M. de Chiettes, who promised him a convoy to Nantes and planned to accompany him part of the way in person. He conferred with the ministers of the church at Dieppe about the state of their cause, and saw documents enumerating their demands and the king's answers. The assembly of the Deputies of the Religion was beginning to break up, and Sidney feared that, although about thirty-five of them were still together, they would be gone before he could reach them. The Dieppe ministers hoped to learn that the king was secretly inclined to the Protestant cause, and Sidney expected to be able to send Burghley a clear impression of Henri's sympathies after he met with him. He had heard that the king planned to move to Senlis or Meuse, and feared Henri would have left Nantes by the time he reached the town.

Sidney left Dieppe to follow Henri to Nantes on January 18,[15] leaving part of his company behind for want of some horses lost in Foulcke's stormy passage. He sent his coachman back to England, for he was unable to take his coach along.[16] The day before he departed, he wrote to Burghley requesting clarification of some new instructions he had received from home, regarding the town of Brest. The place was in some danger, as was all of Brittany, and apparently Elizabeth was proposing that Henri put up the town in return for her aid in securing that province. It was the first Sidney had heard of the idea, and he could scarcely believe it was serious.

He reported rumors of a thirty-thousand-man Spanish army at the frontiers, against which Henri could not prevail without English help. Sidney hoped Elizabeth would aid the French, fearing she would lose the investment she had already made if Henri lost.

The ambassador arrived in Nantes on the twenty-sixth, aware that his coming was "greatly apprehended, both of the king, the papists, and some of the Protestants." Henri expected Sidney was bringing complaints and demands he could not grant, with no hope of succor from the queen, which at the moment he desired "infinitely." His pro-Catholic counsellors feared the queen's request would incline the king to do too much for the Protestants, or if not that the queen would promise the Protestant party aid against Henri. The Protestants, meanwhile, were in a turmoil, some saying they should be satisfied with the Edict of 1577, and others arguing that the king's promises were empty and that the edict hurt their cause as much as it helped, for it restored the mass to all the towns where it had been banned. The Protestant deputies, hoping the queen's mediation would help their cause, sent their agents to thank Sidney for her interest and to vow their service to her. For all Sidney could tell, they demanded no more than that Henri carry out his promises, and they hoped the ambassador's presence would exert pressure on him to do so. Sidney expected to see Henri on the twenty-seventh, in the company of either Mme. d'Angoulême or the duc de Montpensier. He anticipated, however, that the pro-Catholic counsellors would delay the meeting until more of their number could be present. Everyone was treating him very courteously, including the Cardinal and the chancellor; most of his time had been consumed in giving and receiving compliments. He recognized, however, that many of Henri's counsellors were "infinit adversaries of the cause of the religion and seeke by all meanes the extirpation of yt;" currently they were advocating that each large town which capitulated to Henri exile its Protestants. Sidney found Edmondes a great help in these labyrinthine politics, and, although Edmondes wanted to return to England for a few days, the ambassador felt he could not do without him.[17]

Sidney missed seeing Henri at Nantes, because the Admiral, hearing the enemy was approaching, raised the siege there.[18] He left Nantes on the twenty-ninth and headed for Senlis, hoping to find the king there, but when he arrived he heard that Henri was already en route to Chartres. He proceeded to that city, where Henri was expected in two or three days; it was thought that his stay would be brief. There, Sidney heard news of the capitulation of Lyons. The Protestant deputies let him know his presence and evident haste to see the king had helped them to obtain many of the promises that had been made to them.[19]

At last Sidney had his first audience with Henri, on February 8, almost a month after he had landed in France. The meeting was short and mostly taken up with the formalities of exchanging greetings and discussing the siege of Orléans. The king was very busy preparing for the ceremonies surrounding his coronation, but Sidney expected to have another audience the following Tuesday. Certain that Henri needed Elizabeth's aid to reduce the provinces to his obedience, he feared the king would be defeated by the Spanish army without some English succor.[20] By that time, though, despite the excitement of finally speaking with the king, Sidney was weary of chasing around the French countryside. He had Essex campaigning for his return, and, in a letter full of news to the earl, he reminded him to keep pursuing his revocation.[21]

The date of the proposed second meeting fell on Shrove Tuesday, and so Sidney's audience was postponed until Wednesday. Toward evening on Tuesday, however, the king went hawking and invited Sidney to join him. They talked in general of the state of French affairs. The next day, the king sent a dozen of his gentlemen to accompany Sidney to his cabinet, where the two spoke together for a couple of hours. After the customary exchange of assurances of affection between the two sovereigns, Henri got directly to the business of the three thousand English foot soldiers he desired. When Sidney answered according to his instructions, which contained no specific resolution concerning the troops, the king showed "some alteration in his countenance," but thanked the queen for her promise not to abandon him. He explained that it was not his fault the queen's troop had lost time in France, for his failure to meet with Essex had been occasioned by the duc de Bouillon's report that the mercenaries would mutiny without his presence, which he found true, for when he reached them they had already marched five or six leagues backwards. Nevertheless, the English troops had not been idle; under the Marshall of Biron they had taken Gournay and Caudebec, two places that needed to be held before they could lay siege to Rouen. As for the lengthy period Henri had delayed joining the queen's forces in Brittany, the king pointed out that he had sent more of his own troops to join them than he had agreed to, and remarked on the notorious weakness of the queen's troops, which never came up to the numbers they were supposed to contain. Asked what forces he could put into the field, Henri said that, with the three thousand English troops, he would have a total of fourteen thousand foot, including six thousand Swiss and five thousand French, plus five to six thousand French horse. He did not expect the enemy to have over eighteen or twenty thousand troops. To the queen's proposal about Brest, Henri responded that although its governor professed to be his servant, if he imagined the king was about to give the town's government to any other Frenchman, much less to the Queen of England, he would instantly yield to the Holy League. Claiming he had no power to let Elizabeth have Brest, Henri told Sidney he would write to her to explain why. Sidney then presented the queen's request in favor of the Protestants, and Henri replied that he would continue to protect them. Unlike the late king, he said, he intended to fulfill his promises. Sidney observed that Henri's council and officers would put up obstacles, and the king replied that if any such thing happened, he would set it right if complaint were made to him. He also claimed he would not ally himself with the Pope, who had proven himself "more Spanish than the King of Spaine himself."[22]

Meanwhile, Sidney regarded as his principal mission assisting "them of the religion," a complicated proposition. The king had granted as much as he could by the Edict of 1577, and was little by little yielding a few other points, granting the Protestants liberty in specific towns. The zeal of some, however, was causing offense and sectionalism, so that Sidney could scarcely find two leaders in agreement. He intended to keep trying to determine how they might employ him to their common good, so at least they might have no cause to complain of the queen's lack of favor toward them or of her servants' lack of diligence. Sidney thought the French Protestants' fate depended on the king's disposition and that they had nothing to fear from Henri.

Now that he had discharged his commission, Sidney wanted to return to England. Hoping to prompt his recall, he mentioned in his report that Henri had asked for the queen's advice about some problems which "confound his judgment" and had told Sidney to discuss them with her on his return. He wanted to leave as soon as the king returned to his army. He was, he said, not able to follow the king in the field, for his health was not up to par and he was running out of money.[23] He wrote to Lady Sidney on February 20 that he expected to leave the king within ten or twelve days and planned, if he could land at Rye, to see her en route to the court.[24]

The queen had other plans, however, and a week later she sent Sidney instructions to deal with Henri further in the Brest affair. Using as a lever the three thousand English troops the king wanted, he was to insist she only wanted to hold the town for its security and would return it to him at his request as soon as Brittany was assured. She had found the governor of Brest well-disposed to the king and to her proposition, and was convinced Brittany could not be won unless Brest was thus assured. Sidney was to urge the king to agree, emphasizing the costs the queen had already contributed to his cause and his need for her continued aid.[25]

On the day this letter was being written, Sidney sent word to Burghley that the king had invited him to join him at Saint Denis with some of the French council. Sidney's observations led him to believe the Protestants would be satisfied with the provisions of the Edict of 1577 and that the king was disposed to execute it, despite the obstacles thrown up by his council and parliament. The duc de Nevers was returning from his mission to the Pope, so offended that he was calling Rome the "Sea of Babilon" in his letters. It was thought that on his return, Henri would establish the Protestants and set up a patriarch in France. Turning to military matters, the council had asked Sidney to let the queen know that Henri had six thousand Swiss paid for six months, beginning in January, and another four thousand paid for the entire year. The king had also made a deal with a merchant of Luca to obtain enough cash to pay three thousand foot and six hundred light horse, and, in addition, he would entertain twenty companies of men at arms, including six to seven hundred horse that would remain with him at all times. With the three thousand Englishmen Henri hoped to obtain from Elizabeth, they expected not only to make headway against the Spanish army, but to be able to send fifteen thousand Swiss into Brittany to make up the number of forces the king had promised to send there. More aid was arriving from the Low Countries, which had already sent their agent, Calvaert, to discuss succor and the Protestant cause with the king.[26]

Sidney had not received the queen's letter of the twenty-seventh by the time he arrived in Nantes on March 2. The fact that Sidney was sending regular dispatches although he had received nothing from England since January 21 caused the French to suspect that he had a secret commission against the king's cause. He reported that he was traveling in the company of the duc de Monpensier and Catherine de Bourbon, who had shown him a letter from Henri telling of his good hopes of taking Paris. Sidney thought the queen would be approached about a league against the king of Spain that would include France, the German princes, and the United Provinces.[27]

Sidney found the king at Saint Denis, fully occupied with the Paris project. Henri had just hanged a trumpeter of the duc de Maines who had been carrying letters to the count de Brisac warning of the enterprise against Paris and was now, Sidney reported in cipher, treating with Brisac and expecting to win him over. News came as Sidney was writing to Burghley that Rouen had capitulated and, he observed, the French people were daily inclining more and more toward Henri. Nevertheless, the king had sent two of his men to Sidney asking him to tell Elizabeth that he continued to need her help against the Spanish army. Henri wanted the queen to know her help would, in addition to allowing him to defend himself against the Spanish, enable him to send twenty-five hundred Swiss to Brittany. Despite the siege he was about to lay to Paris, the king planned to go in person to the frontiers to investigate the state of affairs there, and he needed some resolution from England so that he might decide what to do. From other sources, Sidney had heard that if the queen failed to aid Henri in this crisis, he would not look to her again. Urging her to support Henri, Sidney added that many Protestants were saying the only way to assure their safety was to strengthen Henri with pro-Protestant forces. Having received no word from England, the ambassador felt in a difficult position, for he was unable to answer the king and the council's repeated inquiries for news from Elizabeth.

Henri asked Sidney to ride with him to Senlis. Sidney agreed, but said he could go no further, because he was not prepared to follow an army. Edmondes had gone to England and Sidney hoped he or someone to take his place would be sent back quickly, for he was unable to continue in France himself.[28] He evidently intended to accompany Henri on March 8,[29] but four days later the king entered Paris and took it without the loss of any French blood. The people, in what Sidney thought "one of the strangest actions ever," welcomed the king. M. de Brisac opened the port through which three thousand of Henri's men entered peacefully, and the Spaniards were made to agree not to resist the king. They left the town in less than an hour; the city was not spoiled in any way, and, Sidney wrote in his dispatch to Burghley, on the day of the capitulation the shops were already open. Only the Bastille remained to be taken, and, five days later, it yielded by composition. Sidney, amazed at the degree to which the state of French affairs had so "exceedingly changed" since his arrival, remarked hopefully to Burghley that it would be better for him to describe the events to the queen in person rather than by letter.[30]

Sidney remained in Paris until after the Bastille was taken, still having heard nothing from home since he left Dieppe. He must have received permission to return to England by March 22, however, for on that date he wrote to Lady Sidney that he intended to start homeward within four or five days.[31] He reached the English court on April 8,[32] three months after he had landed at Dieppe. In a memorandum, he reported Henri's principal messages. The king wanted to know the queen's inclination toward the idea of an offensive and defensive league; if she did not care for it he would not risk the disgrace of publicly proposing it to her and being refused. He also wanted the queen's advice about the Prince of Condé, who he feared would be forcibly brought up a Papist if brought to Henri's court or, if left where he was, might be used against him. He assured Elizabeth that he would never enter any treaty with Spain without her knowledge, the Spaniards being the only ones among his enemies whom he could not forgive. He hoped for her aid in his revenge against them as well as in the reduction of the House of Lorraine. Henri insisted he would treat the Protestants as he himself would wish to be treated, and "that in his soul he maintains the profession he first did and will never alter." He promised to establish as much liberty for the Protestant practitioners as he could, adding that the best means to establish them was to give him enough assistance to assure he would not be overruled. Everyone was urging that he marry, he said, but he did not know what match to make; so far, the Duchess of Lorraine and Philip II's daughter, the Princess of Tuscany, had been suggested. However he decided, his bride would have the liberty of public exercise of religion in all places except Paris.[33]

The embassy to France was one of the highlights of Sidney's career. It provided him with valuable diplomatic experience and made him expert in French affairs. The personal goodwill between Sidney and Henri seems to have lasted a number of years. In 1596, for example, Sidney planned to send the king some hunting hounds that he had earlier promised him.[34]

In that year, Sidney was sent again with the queen's messages to Henri. Calais was in Spanish hands and Henri asked for Elizabeth's aid in retaking it. Sidney met the king at Boulogne on April 21 and presented Elizabeth's proposal that Calais go to her in return for her assistance. Henri refused. Embarrassed, Sidney suggested he pledge Calais to the queen for her lifetime. Henri refused that suggestion, too. Sidney proposed a pledge of one year and was again turned down. After a three-hour interview, he departed, assuring the king that Essex would arrive before Calais with eight thousand men despite the answer, apparently having forgotten that he had said at the beginning of the encounter that the troops had been forbidden to march until the king returned a favorable answer to the queen's proposal.[35] In light of Sidney's alliance with Essex, who in the following year attempted to secure more than one advancement for him, it is possible that this commitment was based on another of the earl's intemperate promises. When Essex proved unable to fulfill it, Sidney would have been forced to pretend an uncharacteristic carelessness.

Both these adventures were, as Sidney's accountant put it, "very chargeable." The 1594 mission had required the purchase of twelve suits of apparel: one sable-lined cloak alone cost £250. The cost of his pages' and footmen's suits came to at least £300, above and beyond that of his servants' liveries. These charges, combined with the cost of his 1598 mission and £500 he paid to take part in a masque at the earl of Derby's wedding, forced Sidney to sell his lands upon the downs in Lincolnshire and land in Sussex leased to Mr. Podway, which had brought him a yearly income of £220.[36]

Sidney's hopes that the embassy to France would be rewarded with advancement at Elizabeth's court were never fulfilled. By 1598, it had become clear that his expenditures and efforts in behalf of the English state were getting him nowhere. In that year, rumor had it that he would attend the marriage of Henri's sister as Ambassador Extraordinary, but he did not go.[37] In 1601, he declined to accompany Sir Robert Cecil when the secretary was appointed Ambassador Ligueur to France.[38] For the rest of the time Elizabeth occupied the throne, he made good his promise to Lady Sidney that he would undertake no more costly employments if the early ones did not bring him some recognition.

It is possible that as late as 1595 Sidney envisioned a military career for himself. In December, he had been nominated for the place of Vice-Chamberlain, and Sir Walter Raleigh, who wanted the position, asked Lady Sidney if it were true that Sidney was coming over from Flushing for that purpose. Rowland Whyte reported that she answered that her husband had never sought the place, for it was "very contrary to the course of liffe you [Sidney] chiefly delyte in which was soldiers. . . ." It was a very fit place for Raleigh, she said, and she hoped that after so long suing for it and so many mighty friends aiding him, he would get it.[39] This may have been a disingenuous answer; if Sidney's rivals knew he sought the office, they would try to hinder him by delaying his leave from Flushing. A couple of years later, for example, Sidney's leave had already been signed when the queen remarked that she had promised the vice-chamberlainship, which was again open, to Sidney, and so Sir John Stanhope would not get it. Sidney's leave was subsequently cancelled. "You see," Whyte wrote in frustration, "this was cause enough to keap you away."[40]

Not until 1597 did Sidney begin working in earnest for advancement at court. In that year, the death of William Brooke, Lord Cobham left vacant the wardenship of the Cinque Ports. The office became the object of a power struggle between Essex and the Cecils. The Cecil candidate was Henry Brooke, the new Lord Cobham, whose father had been Burghley's friend and whose sister was Sir Robert Cecil's wife. As Read puts it, the honor of England's two major parties was engaged; "the wardenship virtually carried with it the Lord Lieutenancy and the primacy of their [Sidney's and Cobham's] native county, Kent."[41] Even before Cobham's death in March, Essex had nominated Sidney to the Cinque Ports.

There is some question as to who was more enthusiastic about the scheme to place Sidney in the wardenship, Sir Robert himself or Essex. Some scholars have suggested the idea was exclusively Essex's, one that grew to be an obsession with him, while Sidney never took it very seriously.[42]

However, it would appear from correspondence between Whyte and Sidney that, contemplating the possibilities as he sat in Flushing, the governor worked himself up to a high pitch of optimism. That Cobham was terminally ill was clear to everyone by February. Sidney ordered Whyte that month to begin his suit for the place, and the two laid the plans for their strategy in their letters. Whyte was not as carried away as Essex and Sidney seem to have been. "If you mean to be a suitor, I do not see what way to devise," he admitted. He discerned that Sidney must make a private motion to the queen before Cobham's death if he was to have any hope of obtaining the place, and suggested that Essex was the fittest man to do so.[43] Accordingly, Sidney wrote to Essex to tell him he wished to stand for the place and hoped for the earl's support, while Whyte approached him in person. At the same time, Sidney began to ask the queen to grant him a leave of absence.

Essex's answer must have raised Sidney's hopes further. The earl proclaimed he would support none other than Sidney for the place, for which no one was as fit. The only other candidate was Henry Brooke, "who," Essex declared, "of all men is the unfittest, and such hath his base villanies bene towards me, which to the world is to well knowen, that he shalbe sure never to have yt, if I can keape him from yt."[44] Meanwhile, Lady Sidney was recruiting support for her husband by inviting Lady Sussex and the earl of Southampton to be godparents to the Sidneys' new baby, Bridget.[45]

Other news was less encouraging. The queen, no doubt influenced by Cobham's party, refused to allow Sidney to come over at this time, when his presence at court was crucial. "We are so credibly informed," she explained, "of many Plotts laid for ye surprise of yt place as we can not dispence with your services." She promised to reconsider after a short time.[46] Young Cobham met with the queen daily, and his father expressed his wish that his places, especially the Cinque Ports, go to his sons.[47] Worse, the brouhaha over the Spanish shipping in the Low Countries arose at this time, and Whyte reported Elizabeth was irate that Sidney had disobeyed her command to halt the ships going to Spain. Essex defended Sidney, and

Cecil read to the queen the governor's letter of explanation addressed to the Privy Council. This seemed to mollify her somewhat, for she said he was a very fine gentleman with many good points—but, she added, his "mynd was to much addicted to the presence chamber. . . ."[48]

At about this time, Sidney may have committed a serious indiscretion. One of Essex's followers reported to Whyte that he had seen two letters sealed with the Sidney arrowhead, directed to two of the queen's maids, and that the knight who was to deliver them had carelessly allowed them to be seen.[49] Hilton Kelliher and Katherine Duncan-Jones take this as a clue to Sidney's amorous activities,[50] and suggest that Rowland Whyte's reference to the queen's remark about Sidney's "youthful toyes"[51] also alludes to some romantic liaison. If this is true, he certainly chose the worst moment to indulge himself.

However, Sidney could instead have been soliciting the ladies' aid in his political cause. Although Bacon remarked that the maids of honor were "like witches," in that "they could do hurt, but they could do no good," they did draw the attention of courtiers who, with varying degrees of success, applied to them and even bribed them to advance their suits with the queen.[52] When Lady Katherine Howard was sworn of the Privy Chamber in September 1599, Whyte remarked that her presence greatly strengthened the Cecilite party,[53] with whom her husband, Lord Nottingham, was associated. Two months later, Barbara Sidney appealed to the countess, who, along with Lady Huntingdon and Lady Warwick, agreed to support Sidney in his current appeal for leave.[54]

Whyte's remarks about Sidney's reputation for levity do not date the incidents on which the queen's impression was grounded, nor does Whyte specify the nature of Sidney's behavior. In February, 1599/1600, Whyte reported the queen had said "that now all your youthful toyes were out of your brain, you wold prove an honest man. . . . The least toy is here made powerful to hynder any mans preferment."[55] Several days later, he wrote that Nottingham had "removed out of her Majesty's mind all those idle opinions, the malice of the time had grounded in her of your youthful lightness."[56] The "youthful toyes" could have taken place at any time; Whyte may have been referring to some coltish behavior that occurred in Sidney's youth. His allusion to "the malice of the time," however, suggests the 1597 opposition to Sidney, during which, no doubt, his enemies made use of all the gossip at their disposal, whether or not it was based in reality.

As the elder Cobham sank, the rush to acquire his worldly offices grew more intense. Henry Brooke stood for the Cinque Ports and the Lord Lieutenancy, both of which, Whyte asserted, were wished for Sidney by "gentlemen of Kent." If Essex was able to do anything, he added, they would find out now.[57]

Essex was splendid in his self-assurance. "I am resolved yf his Lordship do teake himself to another world to deal earnestly and confidently for you," he wrote to Sidney. "I know Lord Brooke doth resolve to try both his credit with the queen and all his frendes in this cause. But I will protest unto the queen against him, and avow that I will think it is the reward of his slanders and practice against me, yf the queen should lay honor upon him."[58]

Cobham died about midnight on March 6. Early the next morning, Essex spoke with Elizabeth in Sidney's behalf, urging her to give the governor the Cinque Ports.[59] The queen responded that Sidney was too young and would be absent in Flushing too much to administer the post. Essex insisted. Sidney's qualifications as a soldier, said the earl, suited him better than Cobham for the place, and he was born and lived in Kent; further, though he had no title, his virtue made him as noble as Cobham.[60] Elizabeth held firm. She would not wrong the new Lord Cobham, she declared, by bestowing the wardenship on a man whose station was inferior to his. Essex soared into a rage at what he interpreted as a personal insult. If that was the case, he announced, he would stand for the place himself. He told Burghley he hated Cobham for his villainy, that there was no worth in the man, and that if the queen graced him, "I may have just cause to thincke myself little regarded by her."[61]

His ego was now launched on a fantastic voyage; once the thing was set in motion, there was no stopping it. He stood for the Cinque Ports himself, and the queen told him flatly that Cobham would have it. With an elaborate display of injured honor, the earl prepared to leave the court, but Elizabeth recalled him to her presence and made him Master of the Ordnance, which mollified him.[62] Sidney's rivals were not soothed, however; they rose up against him to block his advancement in any direction.

Sidney continued his pursuit of the Cinque Ports. He wrote to Burghley, who he knew was supporting Cobham, to explain his reasons,[63] and asked Lady Warwick to try to influence Essex in his favor again. She responded that she was sure Cobham would have the post, and Whyte perceived that she was afraid to have it known she spoke for Sidney in the suit. No one else cared to become involved in the fracas, either. Lady Huntingdon said she could not assist him in the Cinque Ports project until the outcome of her own suit for a lease for her jointure appeared. Stanhope was too obliged to Cobham's party to dare speak for Sidney.

Sidney persisted. He sent Whyte with a letter to Essex, who advised that Lady Warwick was the best to deliver it. Lady Warwick excused herself by saying she was about to leave for North Hall, and sent Whyte to "40," whose identity remains undeciphered. From him, Whyte turned to Stanhope, who told him the wardenship was already granted to Cobham; Whyte did not bother him with the letter. He next approached Lady Huntingdon at Baynard's Castle, and found she would have nothing to do with it either. Returning to court, he sought out another unidentified friend, "15," who suggested he take the letter to Lady Rich. At last he found a favorable reception; Lady Rich took the letter without reading it, assured Whyte of her loyalty to Sidney, and promised the letter would reach the queen by March 19 or 20.[64]

These continued efforts proved fruitless. Sidney could not so much as obtain leave to come home, much less the wardenship of the Cinque Ports. Even he began to realize that all his suits were being "purposely crossed," and he wrote to Barbara that, if the leave for which he had been suing since the beginning of the Cinque Ports effort were denied, she was to tell their friends they would ask their favors at some later date and join him at Flushing. Discouraged by his and Essex's defeat, he remarked that he could "not but see the extreme inequality betweene others and me.[65] Whyte was convinced that Sidney's leave had been crossed because he had challenged Cobham, and even feared the queen's unwillingness to let Sidney keep his horse company was occasioned by Cobham's opposition.[66] By March 25, it was almost certain Cobham would have the Cinque Ports, and on April 3, the rumors were confirmed. Cobham was even given Sir Thomas Shirley's vacated company in the Low Countries, which Sidney had requested for his nephew.[67]

One wonders why Sidney ventured his fortune in such a forlorn project. In retrospect, the whole idea seems foolish. For Sidney, who was untitled, to take on the Lord Cobham and to oppose himself to the party with which his superior, Lord Burghley, was linked by affection as well as by kinship seems strangely self-destructive. Perhaps Essex's confidence and mad enthusiasm gave Sidney, distanced from the realities of court politics as he was in Flushing, some reason to hope for success. Too, many at the court probably recognized that Sidney's military experience fitted him well for the wardenship and thought that the aristocracy in his ancestry and the important commands his father had held were as high a recommendation as Cobham's peerage. Nevertheless, Whyte had sensed disaster ahead as early as the day after Cobham's death. Little good for Sidney could be expected, he realized, when an inherited title was more respected than "the virtuous and the worthy," and he begged Sidney "to determine to live within your compass and get out of debt, for I fear it will be long ere any advancement be laid on you for your good."[68]

Sidney's correspondence suggests that, about the year 1596 or 1597, he was seized with the desire to escape Flushing. Around this time he involved himself in a flurry of projects for advancement, of which the Cinque Ports fiasco was only the most noisy. He began campaigning for a peerage, for employment in France, for a position on the Privy Council, for the vice-chamberlain's post. In October 1597, he was proposed as lord deputy of Ireland, a dubious honor he deftly avoided. Later he made suits for the presidency of Wales, the governorship of Jersey, and a place in the army in England. He felt that he was insufficiently rewarded for nearly a decade of service in the Low Countries. Whyte told Lady Warwick to mention to the queen that Sidney was "not so wedded to Flushing but that [he] would leave it" when the queen thought him worthy of service near herself, and that by being tied to Flushing Sidney lost reputation in the wars, while others whom he had once commanded were now employed in greater matters.[69] Despite the queen's conception that Sidney was pocketing £15,000–£16,000 a year or more,[70] expenses at Flushing were high, and the burden of maintaining separate households there and in England was more than Sidney could bear. Lady Sidney could hardly make ends meet, and Sidney was finding it difficult to provide her with an allowance of £10 a week.[71]

Sidney's rivalry with Cobham was longstanding; the Sidneys had been competing with the Brookes for local ascendancy in Kent at least since Sir Henry's time. In 1592/93, with the earl of Pembroke's help, Sidney had been elected knight of the shire to serve in the House of Commons from Glamorgan.[72] In 1597, he was elected the first knight of the shire from Kent; Cobham's nephew and heir, Sir William Brooke, was elected with him in the second place, much to Cobham's annoyance.[73] Whyte reported that Cobham was much grieved to see the chief place given to Sidney by the people's acclamation,[74] and an attempt was made to have a new election in Kent because of Sidney's absence.[75] John Ernest Neale explains the reasons behind Cobham's distress: much prestige was assigned to the first of the knightships of the shire in Elizabeth's time, and to secure the second place "might be only less hard to bear than total defeat."[76] The Cobhams' agitation against Sidney seems only to have caused them more trouble, for, when the names for Kent were read in Parliament, only Sidney's was announced. Secretary Cecil asked if Kent did not have another knight, and, said Whyte, it was whispered in his ear that Sir William Brooke was outlawed.[77]

In this light, Lawrence Stone's observation that the warden of the Cinque Ports, by virtue of his office, had influence over five seats in the House of Commons, is most revealing (*Crisis*, p. 621). The man who took the Cinque Ports would also gain political ascendancy in Kent.

If Sidney was rejected for the wardenship of the Cinque Ports because Cobham had a title and he did not, the logical course was to obtain a peerage. Early in October 1597, rumors were flying that new peers would soon be created, and Sidney's name was prominently mentioned.[78] Whyte was hard at work soliciting Sidney's friends at court to support his master's suit for a baronage. Cecil told him he thought there would be no new creations until Essex returned to court. Lord Admiral Howard, who was created earl of Nottingham on October 23,[79] promised his assistance in Sidney's effort. Roger Manners told Whyte it was true there was some talk of creating barons, but, for reasons unknown to him, Sidney was not named. He promised to discuss the matter with Burghley and Cecil.[80] Essex made another of his extravagant promises to Sidney, vowing he would have him made a baron during the 1597/98 Parliament. Sidney wanted the peerage so much he urged Essex to go forward with the pursuit of the baronage even if it meant not pushing his concurrent suit for the post of vice-chamberlain.[81] Whyte thought his master had made an error in judgment when he heard of this; he called it "strange" that Sidney would give up his pursuit of the vice-chamberlainship so that he might be a baron, for this was exactly what Sidney's enemies most desired.[82] Sidney, preferring the barony over all his other ambitions, said he would not like to aim at too

TABLE 6

SIDNEY'S PEDIGREE, SUBMITTED TO ESSEX IN THE SUIT FOR BARONY, 1598

Sources: *CSP Dom.*, 12:269:70

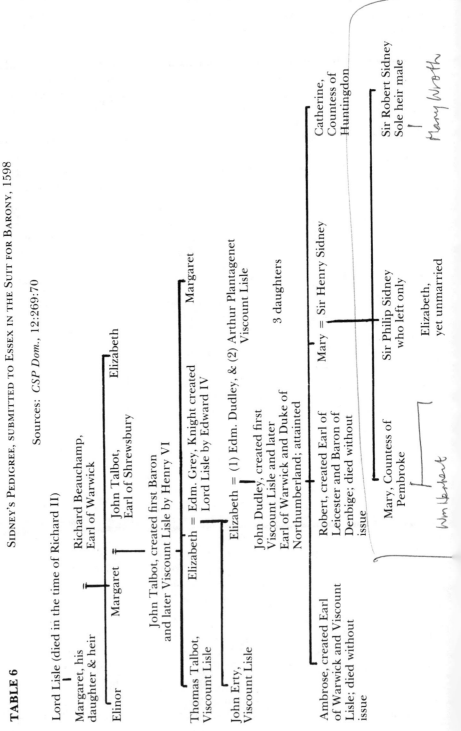

many marks and hit none. He told Essex he did not believe Cecil truly supported him, "for all his faire words," and he feared the secretary would turn the queen against him in both the vice-chamberlainship and the barony. He had heard Cecil had promised to support Sir Edward Wotton's suit for a barony, and Sidney was aware of the Cecils' concern for Lord Cobham, who did not care to see Sidney elevated to Cobham's own rank.[83]

These were politic words. As Earl Marshall, Essex was the man to whom Sidney had to submit his suit for the peerage. He did so early in 1598, presenting a pedigree that showed his descent from the House of Lisle and the earls of Leicester and Warwick, and he demonstrated that he was the sole surviving male heir to these titles. This he accomplished with a written declaration emphasizing that he was the heir, through his female relations, to Warwick, Leicester, and Lisle, and that the title in the past had descended through women. He included a reminder of his merit: "I have, since I was eighteen yeeres old, never bin out of her Maties service, either in her court, or her warrs, or imployments to forren princes, and have had, and have as great charges, as are ordinarilie incident to gentlemen of my qualitie. . . ." Trusting his suit would not seem arrogant, since he was only asking what had so often been granted to his ancestors, he wrote that he pretended no right to the title, but sought the queen's favor only by grace of his nearness of blood to the peers. To underscore the modesty of his request, he directed Essex's and the queen's attention to the fact that, despite the elite titles his grandfather and uncles possessed, "I content myself with making sute onlie for the title of Lisle. . . ."[84]

Elizabeth agreed that Sidney was deserving enough, but some conservative element in her character kept her from granting a baronage to him or to anyone else. "But . . . what shall I doe with all these that pretend to titles?" she asked Essex when he approached her with Sidney's suit. "I could be willing to call hym and one or two more, but to call many I will not. And I am importuned by many of there frends to doe yt."

"Madame," said the earl, "let their titles be first examined by me. I will not doubt but to fynd cause to keape them backe, and lett the fault be myne."[85]

That would not do. Elizabeth told Essex she would discuss it with Burghley. Soon, Sir Robert Cecil asked Essex to favor Sir Edward Wotton's suit for a baronage; he responded that if Cecil would join him in his efforts to have Sidney called first, he would agree to support Wotton's suit.[86]

Stone observes that the number of peers was falling during the last years of Elizabeth's reign; he attributes this, among other reasons, to her essentially conservative character. He speculates that her resistance to new creations may have been motivated by fear of the kind of aristocratic factions that surfaced in the rebellion of the northern earls of 1569 and in the Ridolfi Plot of 1571. Whatever her reasons, she maintained her resistance in the face of the rapidly changing social conditions of the late sixteenth century and of increasing pressure from all directions. Nothing came of Sidney's and Wotton's suits until after the end of her reign.[87]

At the same time that he was trying to obtain the peerage, Sidney hoped to obtain the office of vice-chamberlain. Henry Carey, baron Hunsdon, had been lord chamberlain since 1585; at his death in 1596, he was succeeded by his son George, the second baron Hunsdon. It was possible that a vice-chamberlain would be appointed; many aspiring young men sought preferment, chief among whom were Sir John Stanhope, Sir Walter Raleigh, and Sir Robert Sidney. Whyte seems to have thought it probable that Sidney would get the post. He wrote encouragingly in October 1597, that the queen had said she had promised it to Sidney.[88] However, Sidney's rivals were conspiring to keep him away from the court, which was where he most needed to be if he was to effect any of his suits. Stanhope joined the Cobhamites in this conspiracy,[89] and Sidney's leave was delayed indefinitely. Essex supported Sidney for the post, as he did in the suit for the peerage and the Cinque Ports. Through his mediation, Raleigh was persuaded to give up his suit.[90] Essex expected to make Sidney vice-chamberlain in February 1598, but that month Whyte observed that Sir Henry Leigh, possibly at Burghley's and Cecil's urging, was encouraged to stand for the post. Whyte feared that, although Essex was firm in his support of Sidney, the earl might not oppose Leigh.[91] In March, Sidney was unexpectedly granted leave, causing speculation that he would be chosen vice-chamberlain, although some said he was "too young and too amorous to be conversant among the ladies." There was also some speculation that he would be sent as lord deputy to Ireland.[92] Although in May rumors were still trickling back to Sidney's lieutenant-governor in Flushing that Sir Robert would be made vice-chamberlain or placed on the Privy Council,[93] nothing came of either possibility. When Hunsdon fell ill in 1600, another flurry over the vice-chamberlainship arose, but Elizabeth left the place empty; "there have been so many suitors, that Her Majesty will hardly be drawn to bestow it," Whyte observed, "and she will not discontent many."[94]

The question of why Sidney failed in so many efforts to gain advancement between 1596 and 1598 is open to speculation. The most obvious reason is simply that he was not at court, and the cause behind that circumstance was vigorous opposition by the Cobhams. The Cobham party, annoyed over Essex's and Sidney's extravagant suit for the Cinque Ports, effectively blocked Sidney's leave until it was too late for the governor's presence to do him any good at court. Perhaps it is also significant that the fall of Sir Thomas Shirley, treasurer-at-wars in the Low Countries, took place during this period. The scandal cast a shadow over the queen's entire staff in the Netherlands, and made it easy for Sidney's rivals to convince Elizabeth that the governor of Flushing was raking off enough extraneous income to reward him for his work. In 1597, too, Whyte had been implicated in the Shirley fiasco by Burchinshaw; although he escaped censure, some lingering onus may have remained. Also at this time there was the uproar over the corn ships bound for Spain. Sidney's failure or refusal to detain them at Flushing, as we have seen, antagonized the queen.

Anthony Esler, in *The Aspiring Mind of the Elizabethan Younger Genera-*

tion, calls the last half of the queen's final decade on the throne "the bot-tleneck years," and suggests that Elizabeth consistently refused to advance any of Sidney's contemporaries for psychological reasons. It is difficult to find any explanation beyond the queen's character to account for Sidney's and his contemporaries' failures to eke out even one barony between them, nor for the continued emptiness of the vice-chamberlain's post. Between the queen's advancing age and the factionalism at court, few men of Sidney's age and rank could expect much relief from their frustration. Rowland Whyte said as much when, observing "the fashions of the Court"; he discerned that "the way to preferment [is] very difficult; I mean for men of your [Sidney's] sort. Besides, there is in her Majesty no great inclination to bestow any place that falles unles meere necessity occasioned it for the good of her service."[95]

With the situation at home looking so hopeless, Whyte suggested to Essex that Sidney be made general of the two thousand men waiting to go into France in the spring of 1597. Essex thought it not a fit command for Sidney.[96] Three years later Lady Warwick mentioned to Whyte the possibility that Sidney might be sent into France, but Sir Henry Neville was chosen.[97] Rumors that he might be employed in France persisted until 1601,[98] but nothing came of them.

Sidney did well to miss one opportunity, the position of lord deputy of Ireland. When Lord Deputy Burghe died in October 1596, Sidney and Sir William Russell were each nominated to succeed him. Whyte thought Sidney would be better off where he was than in Ireland, unless he could manage to keep the governorship of Flushing in absentia.[99] Russell refused to go, and Whyte hoped that Sidney would not be saddled with the job, which he called "a faire way to thrust you on to your own destruction."[100] Dudley Carleton remarked to his friend John Chamberlain that, when Sidney and his wife were at court in March 1598, he was by common voice proclaimed deputy of Ireland.[101] Fortunately, Charles Blount, Lord Mountjoy was named to the onerous post instead, and Sidney escaped the dilemma of having either to offend by turning it down or to accept another difficult, dead-end position.

In the fall of 1599, Sidney's brother-in-law, the earl of Pembroke, fell ill. Whyte expressed to Lady Warwick Sidney's desire to succeed Lord Pembroke as lord president of Wales, and she suggested he apply to the lord admiral. Nottingham told Whyte that people would dislike seeing anyone who was not a peer in the place, and since he had recently approached the queen in another matter for Sidney, he could not deal with this one. The matter of a peerage was a curious objection, for Sidney's father had held the position. Annoyed, Whyte reminded Nottingham of Sidney's descent from the duke of Suffolk through his father and from the duke of Northumberland through his mother.[102]

At this time, factional infighting at the court was fierce; Whyte observed that Essex and Cecil hated each other and the earl was said to be using "dangerous words." Nottingham, who was associated with Cecil's party, had grown very powerful and exercised perhaps as much influence with the queen as Leicester once had. Whyte, fearing the presidency would be bestowed on no one who was associated with Essex's faction, devised a stratagem that he hoped would improve Sidney's eligibility. Sidney was to write to the queen herself and tell her he desired the post his father had held. Then he should write to Burghley and offer him Otford Park in return for his support. At the same time, Whyte was to suggest to Nottingham, as though it were his own idea, that he marry his niece to Sidney's nephew, Lord Herbert. If Sidney could obtain a leave and, while in England, could succeed in inducing Herbert and his mother to accept the proposal, it might advance Sidney in Nottingham's esteem and, through him, with the Cecil faction.[103]

Pembroke recovered and brought a halt to these intrigues.[104] Whyte now hoped the earl would agree to resign the presidency to Sidney while he still lived; this, he thought, was Sidney's only chance to get the office.[105] Young Lord Herbert, who at the moment was enjoying some popularity at court, longed to have his uncle Sidney at home and agreed to try to persuade Pembroke to resign the office.[106] The negotiations continued in this vein. Pembroke proved willing enough to let his brother-in-law have the office, if Sidney had enough strength at court to carry it off. Whyte could think of no way to garner enough power but by an alliance with Nottingham; he also knew Sidney would do well to ingratiate Lord Buckhurst. By February 2, 1599/1600, Whyte was sure that if Sidney could procure the queen's grant, the office would be his.[107] This Sidney evidently was not able to do, for he did not obtain the office and the aging Pembroke continued as president of Wales.

In the spring of 1600, Sir Francis Vere quarreled with the States General, and Sidney conceived some hope for advancement through the Dutch government. If he were offered Vere's place as commander of the English forces in the Netherlands, Whyte hoped he would "accept yt, for it wilbe a latter to clime to honor here, where honor comes lamely on."[108] Rumor circulated at court that Vere was displaced and Sidney given his command, which offended Cecil, who remarked ominously that Sidney was "to wise" to take on such a position without conferring with the queen.[109] The queen considered sending Vere to Ireland to relieve the ailing Mountjoy, but said nothing about Sidney commanding the English troops.[110] This hope, like the others, died in obscurity.

Sir Anthony Paulett, the governor of Jersey, died in the summer of 1600, and, although it was almost certain Sir Walter Raleigh would be granted his place, Sidney made a desultory effort to obtain the position. However, Nottingham declined to support him, telling Whyte that matters were too far gone and the queen had promised it to Raleigh.[111] The competition narrowed to Raleigh and Sir William Russell, and Sidney dropped out of the running.

In the closing years of the decade, court factionalism grew even more bitter and, even before Essex's fall, party alignments shifted. Two principal parties had dominated the English court in the 1590s, Essex's and Cecil's. At the end of the decade, William, Lord Cobham, who had been associated with the Cecil party, gained enough power to break away and form a third faction, the Durham House group.

Sidney was necessarily affiliated with Essex at the beginning of his career, although from the start he attempted to maintain amicable relations with Burghley and Cecil. He was tied by blood, friendship, and training to the earl's faction, which represented the intellectual heritage of Leicester, Walsingham, and Sir Philip Sidney—the extreme Protestant faction of the 1570s and 1580s. Most of those we now regard as members of the Sidney circle stood with Essex's party, including Robert, Lord Rich; Roger Manners, earl of Rutland (who married Sir Philip's daughter, Elizabeth); and Sir Edward Dyer. Also associated with Essex were Leicester's influential sisters, Lady Huntingdon and Lady Warwick; Lady Penelope Rich (Lord Rich's wife and Sir Philip Sidney's "Stella"); Edward Somerset, earl of Worcester; Charles Blount, Lord Montgomery; Lord Henry Howard; John, Baron Lumley; Henry Wriothesly, earl of Southampton; and Henry Percy, earl of Northumberland.

Sidney knew that while Burghley and Cecil were ascendant, his alliance with Essex compromised his aspirations for advancement. In 1596, Burghley had openly told Sir Thomas Bodley that he so disliked the earl that "he had very great reason to use his best means, to put any Man out of Love of raising his Fortune, whom the Earl with such Violence, to his extreme prejudice, had endeavored to dignifie. And this, as he affirmed, was all the motive he had, to set himself against me [Bodley] in whatsoever might redound to the bettering of my State, or encreasing of my Credit, and countenance with the Queen. . . ."[112] Sidney must have taken note of this, for in that year and in the preceding one he discreetly asked Burghley for his patronage, remarking that his great friends had never fulfilled the expectations he had placed in them.[113]

Cecil's party represented the realists who were not so fervent in their religion or their philosophical commitment that they would not adjust their ethics to fit the times. Until 1600, the Cecilites included Cobham and his henchman, Sir Walter Raleigh; also with Burghley were Leicester's old enemy, Thomas Sackville, Lord Buckhurst; Gilbert Talbot, earl of Shrewsbury; Charles Howard, earl of Nottingham; Thomas Howard, later created earl of Suffolk; Henry Howard, earl of Northampton; Thomas, Lord Gray; Sir George Carew; and Sir John Stanhope.

Although Burghley never granted Sidney unequivocal support during Essex's lifetime, the lord treasurer was not altogether hostile. He promised Sidney his favor in 1591, and, within limits, he delivered it. He protected Sidney following the Sluys failure and the corn ships fiasco, and defended his reputation during the controversy over his departure from the Battle of Nieuport. He repeatedly aided Sidney in his efforts to obtain leave from his post, and explained to the queen the necessity for Sidney to accompany the military men of the Low Countries in their jaunts through the provinces.

Certainly, until the mid-1590s, Sidney leaned heavily on the earl for patronage and advancement at court. In 1591, when Sidney's lawyer, Roger Seys, aspired to the attorneyship of the Marches of Wales, he asked Sir Robert to recommend him to his friend Essex.[114] By 1594, Sidney still spent most of his time at court in Essex's company; in September of that year, for example, he reported to Lady Sidney that he expected the earl's arrival at court to speed his business there. A month later, he planned to accompany Essex to the Lord Mayor's feast in London.[115] From the Low Countries, Sidney sent Essex gifts of boar pie, which Whyte reported were much commended for their "well seasoning." Interestingly, however, at the time he sent one pie to Essex in 1595, he sent three to Burghley.[116] When their son Robert was born, the Sidneys invited several prominent members of the Essex faction to take part in the christening. Lady Rich agreed to be the boy's godmother, and Lords Compton and Mountjoy were his godfathers. Among the guests were Lady Cumberland, Lady Essex, Lady Dacres, their daughters.[117]

At least as early as 1595, however, Sidney and Whyte began to understand that all hope for advancement could not be vested in Essex. In November of that year, Whyte observed that the earl was "mightelie crossed" in all his projects; Bacon had not received the solicitor's place, and a "deadly unkindnes" was breeding between Essex and Burghley. That month a tract titled *A Conference on the Next Succession to the Crown of England* appeared; it demonstrated that blood alone was not the only claim to the throne and surveyed the claims of all who might be eligible.[118] Elizabeth regarded it as a piece of sedition. It was dedicated to Essex, a circumstance that threw the earl into temporary disgrace. Moreover, Whyte reported a growing hostility between Essex and Sidney's brother-in-law, the earl of Pembroke.

When Sidney obtained leave to return to England late in 1595 upon the death of the earl of Huntingdon and Lady Huntingdon's subsequent illness, he had not Essex to thank, but Burghley and certain key members of the Cecil faction. Whyte noted that Sidney was "much beholden" to Burghley for his good reports of him. Lord Admiral Nottingham, Stanhope, and Cecil were responsible for Sidney's release from Flushing that year, and Whyte said that Sidney owed them thanks for their assistance.[119]

During the next four or five years, Sidney maintained an equivocal position. On the one hand, he wished to curry favor with the Cecils, but on the other, he dared not alienate Essex. Writing to the earl in his capacity as lord high marshal, from which position he could influence any suit for a peerage, Sidney swore he had no faith in Cecil's affection. "I do not only beleeve that he prefers others in his affections before me but that he doth not for all his faire words unto me assist me at all."[120] But just a few months later, Sidney thanked Cecil for honoring him with the title of "an extraordinary frend" and pledged his loyalty and willingness to return the secretary's favors.

The Sidney family's long-standing rivalry with the Cobhams for local primacy in Kent gives particular significance to Essex's 1597 nomination of Sidney for the wardenship of the Cinque Ports. When, in 1600, Cobham split away from the Cecilite party, it was only natural that Sidney would move closer to that group, which now represented his rival's opposition. By 1602, Sidney was fully reconciled with Buckhurst, who had proved a loyal Cecil follower, and had obtained Buckhurst's sanction of his grant of Otford manor as well as an extended lease of Leeds castle.

That Essex's prestige and possibly his sanity were slipping became increasingly evident as the century closed. In July 1598, the earl quarreled with Elizabeth over the appointment of a lord deputy in Ireland. When he proposed one of his enemies for the onerous post, a squabble arose that ended with the queen striking Essex on the ear and dismissing him from her presence with the imprecation that he go and be hanged. This dispute marked a major break in their relationship. The following month, shortly after Burghley's death, Essex involved himself in Southampton's secret marriage to Elizabeth Vernon, one of the queen's ladies-in-waiting. This incensed the queen further, and the reconciliation that took place was only superficial.[121]

In March of the following year, Essex accepted an appointment as governor-general of Ireland, knowing failure could ruin him. Events went badly for him there, and when he made his famous return to England, unbidden, dramatically appearing in Elizabeth's bed chamber on the morning of September 28, 1599, he fell into a new disgrace. He was charged by the queen's council with disobedience in leaving Ireland without leave, with sending presumptuous letters to the queen, with acting contrary to his instructions, with intruding into the queen's bed chamber, and with knighting too many of his followers. On October 1, he was confined to York House, where he was kept in complete seclusion.[122]

Whyte watched these developments with trepidation. On October 2, he wrote to Sidney warning him to beware of any connection with Essex and advising him to cultivate the friendship of Cecil, who had a good opinion of him at the time. Whyte thought Essex could not be trusted, and urged Sidney not even to write to him.[123] As Essex sank deeper into disgrace, Sidney worked to extricate himself from his influence. Ten days before the Star Chamber issued its declaration of the earl's offenses (November 29), Sidney wrote to Cecil expressing his hopes that the lack of an answer from the secretary to one of his earlier letters did not indicate any displeasure with him, and beseeching the favor Cecil had often promised. Sidney swore he would perform anything the secretary wished of him, and hoped to be granted leave from Flushing.[124] On December 26, well before Essex's loss of his state offices, Sidney revealed his conviction that the earl could no longer help him when he remarked in a letter to Cecil that he could "not imagine after so violent a fall soon to see him clime again."[125]

Sidney continued to seek Cecil's favor after Essex was brought before a court, dismissed from all his state offices, and imprisoned at Essex House during the queen's pleasure (June 5, 1600). Early in August, shortly before Essex was set at liberty, Sidney wrote to Cecil disclaiming his affection for the earl. He felt he had nothing to fear from Essex's fall, and claimed that the earl "made it apper, notwithstanding his specious show of frendship unto mee, that he did not desyre to ioine mee unto him in any of his actions." Concerned that Essex's and his own enemies would attempt to use the earl's fall to implicate and ruin him, Sidney appealed to Cecil to "keepe mee from wrongfully taking part with his il fortunes, since he did never make mee take part with his good fortune."[126]

Naturally, Sidney could not foresee Essex's final act of melodramatic self-destruction, even if he sensed that the earl was mentally unbalanced. However, by switching his allegiance to Cecil somewhat before the eleventh hour, he established himself in a relatively safe position, one that was secure enough to protect him from ruin when Essex' rebellion came. Had he continued steadfast in his loyalty to the earl—weak though that alliance had become—he might have followed him to destruction and ended his life in 1601 with others of Essex's friends, on the gallows. At best, he would have lost his career and all hope for honor and advancement.

Essex and his followers staged their disorganized uprising Saturday, February 7, 1600. It soon became clear that the citizens of London had no interest in joining them, and, disheartened, they retreated to Essex House, taking as hostages the lord keeper, the earl of Worcester, Lord Chief Justice Popham, and Sir William Knollys.[127] As the queen's forces surrounded the house, Essex's men barricaded themselves inside. Lord Admiral Nottingham cut off all access by land or water and stationed Lord Thomas Howard, Lord Gray, Lord Burghley, Lord Compton, Sir Walter Ralegh, and Sir Thomas Gerrard with a number of others on the landward side. He then chose Sidney, Effingham, Cobham, Stanhope, and Sir Fulke Greville to accompany him to the riverside face of the building. They assailed the garden and banquet house and successfully forced entrance to the grounds. Understanding that the Countess of Essex and Lady Rich were inside, they paused before they assaulted the house.[128]

Sidney was sent forth to negotiate with the rebels. He first spoke with Southampton, who said that to surrender to the queen would be to confess their guilt. If they were given hostages to guarantee their security, the earl said, they would appear before the queen; otherwise, he vowed, they would die fighting.

When Sidney reported this to Nottingham, the lord admiral said no conditions would be discussed, but they would allow Lady Essex, Lady Rich, and their women to leave. Southampton replied that his party would need an hour to remove the barricade and open the door and another hour to refortify it. This was granted, and the women came forth.[129]

"And yourself, my lord," Sidney asked Essex, "what do you mean to do? The house is to be blown up with gunpowder unless you yield."

"We would sooner fly up to heaven!" Essex returned.[130]

Sidney remonstrated. Finally, Essex agreed to speak with Nottingham, and with Southampton obtained the conditions under which they agreed to surrender. They were to be civilly used, to have an honorable trial, and Essex was to have his chaplain, Abdie Ashton, with him in prison. Although Nottingham said he could not promise Ashton, he agreed to ask the queen for it, and Essex and his men ceremoniously surrendered. So, around 10:00 P.M., after some twelve hours,[131] "that dismal tumult, like the fit of Ephemera, or one-day's ague, ceased. . . ."[132]

Essex was tried and condemned less than a fortnight later. He was executed on February 25.

Sidney cemented his alliance with Cecil. He continued to solicit the secretary's friendship, and in August, he arranged for Cecil to receive a quantity of a particular type of stone, available at Penshurst, for construction of his estate at Theobalds.[133] Their relations grew warmer, although Cecil did not obtain for him any of the offices Sidney hoped he might.[134] They continued on an amicable basis into James's reign, and by 1606 they were so friendly that Lady Sidney sent to Cranbourne one hundred apricots from her gardens, as "some token of her housewifery."[135]

As for Cobham, after Elizabeth's death he was doomed to failure. The Lords of the Council opposed him, and James suspected the Durham House group had conspired to discredit his claim to the throne. Removed from the lieutenancy of Kent, Cobham was ensnared with his brother in the Main Plot. In July 1603, he and Raleigh were committed to the Tower, and, despite his struggles to extricate himself, he was subjected to a show trial and a mock execution, after which he remained imprisoned in the Tower until he died in 1619.

Sidney's judicious shift of alliance was as much the result of good luck as foresight. His principal rival happened to put himself in opposition to Cecil, whose power remained intact. Although he successfully disassociated himself from Essex, he did not rise in prestige or position until after James's succession. He managed to spend most of the final three years of Elizabeth's reign out of Flushing, but, despite his petitions to Cecil for various vacant positions, his career stagnated until the queen was gone.

NOTES

1. Stone, *Crisis*, p. 459.
22. Windsor, 19 October 1593, *HMCD* 2:145.
3. Sidney to Lady Sidney, "This Fryday" [26 October 1593], ibid., 2:145.
4. Sidney to Burghley, Dover, 24 December 1593, SP 78/32, fols. 382–83.
5. Sidney to Lady Sidney, 17 December 1593, *HMCD* 2:146.
6. Sidney to Burghley, Dover, 27 December 1593, SP 78/32, fol. 384.
7. Sidney to Lady Sidney, Dover, 6 January 1593/94, *HMCD* 2:146.
8. Sidney to Lady Sidney, Dover, 29 December 1593, ibid., 2:146.
9. Diary of Events by Burghley, 1594, *HMC Salisbury* 13:506–7.
10. Sidney to Lady Sidney, Dover, 6 January 1593/94, *HMCD* 2:146.
11. Sidney to Burghley, Dover, 27 December 1593, SP 78/32, fol. 384.

12. Sidney to Burghley, Dover, 24 December 41593, SP 78/32, fols. 282–83.

13. Sidney to Burghley, "In the Tramontina," 9 January 1593/94, SP 78/33, fol. 16.

14. Two letters by Sidney, damaged by fire, MS Cotton Caligula E.ix. fol. 169, British Library, London, England. The first, dated Dieppe, 11 January [1593/94], appears to be to Burghley; the second, of 13 January (incorrectly dated 1598), cannot be to Burghley, for it expresses Sidney's desire to see his correspondent at Gisors. It was probably to Edmondes, with whom Sidney worked closely during his embassy.

15. Diary of Events by Burghley, 1594, *HMC Salisbury* 13:147.

16. Sidney to Lady Sidney, Dieppe, 14 January 1593/94, *HMCD* 2:147.

17. Sidney to Burghley, Nantes, 26 January 1593/94, SP 78/33, fols. 64–65.

18. Sidney to Burghley, Nantes, 27 January 1593/94, SP 78/33, fol. 70.

19. Sidney to Burghley, Chartres, 4 February 1593/94, SP 78/33, fols. 75–76.

20. Sidney to Burghley, Chartres, 8 February 1593/94, SP 78/33, fol. 83.

21. Sidney to Essex, Chartres, 8 February 1593/94, SP 78/33, fols. 75–76.

22. Sidney to Burghley, Chartres, February 1593/94, SP 78/33, fols. 90–93. Scribal copy; original (?) in British Library, Cotton MS Caligula E.ix, part I, fol. 168.

23. Ibid.

24. Sidney to Lady Sidney, Chartres, 20 February 1593/94, *HMCD* 2:147.

25. Queen Elizabeth to Sidney, 27 February 1593/94, SP 78/33, fols. 114–15.

26. Sidney to [Burghley], Chartres, 27 February 1593/94, SP 78/33, fols. 117–18.

27. Sidney to Burghley, Mante[*sic*.], 2 March 1593/94, SP 78/33, fols. 24–24.

28. Sidney to Burghley, St. Denis, 6 March 1593/94, SP 78/33, fols. 26–27.

29. Sidney to Lady Sidney, Paris, 22 March 1593/94, *HMCD* 2:147.

30. Sidney to Burghley, 12 March 1593/94, SP 78/33, fol. 136.

31. Sidney to Lady Sidney, Paris, 22 March 1593/94, *HMCD* 2:147.

32. Diary of Events by Burghley, 1594, *HMC Salisbury* 13:147–48.

33. Memorandum by Sir Robert Sidney during his embassy to France, [1594], *HMCD* 2:147–48.

34. Sidney to Thomas Philippes, 2 December 1596, *CSP Dom.* 4:321.

35. Motley, *UN* 3:369–72.

36. Additional MS 12066.

37. Chamberlain to Carleton, London, 20 October 1598, McClure 1:49.

38. Chamberlain to Carleton, London, 27 May 1601, ibid., 1:122.

39. Whyte to Sidney, London, 14 December 1595, *HMCD* 2:200.

40. Whyte to Sidney, Strand, 22 October 1595, ibid., 2:297.

41. Neale, *Elizabethan House of Commons*, p. 215.

42. Robert Lacey, *Robert, Earl of Essex* (New York: Atheneum, 1971), p. 175.

43. Whyte to Sidney, 21 February [1596/97], *HMCD* 2:236.

44. Whyte to Sidney, Strand, 27 February 1596/97, Collins, 2:20. *HMCD* prints this letter (2:238–39) without the comments by Essex.

45. Whyte to Sidney, 21 February 1596/97, *HMCD* 2:235.

48. Whyte to Sidney, 27 February 1596/97, ibid., 2:238.

49. Ibid.

50. Hilton Kelliher and Katherine Duncan-Jones, "A Manuscript of Poems by Robert Sidney: Some Early Impressions," *British Library Journal*, ser. 2, vol. 1 (November 1975): 107–44; Katherine Duncan-Jones, "'Rosis and Lysa': Selections from the Poems of Sir Robert Sidney," *English Literary Renaissance* 9, no. 2, (Spring 1979): 240–63.

51. Whyte to Sidney, 21 February 1599/[1600], *HMCD* 2:440.

52. Violet Wilson, *Queen Elizabeth's Maids of Honor*, 2nd ed. (New York: E. P. Dutton, [1922?]).

53. Whyte to Sidney, 12 September 1599, *HMCD* 2:390.

54. Whyte to Sidney, 23 November 1599, ibid., 2:417.

55. Whyte to Sidney, 21 February 1599/1600, ibid., 2:440.

56. Whyte to Sidney, 24 February 1599/1600, ibid., 2:441.

57. Whyte to Sidney, 2 March 1596/97, ibid., 2:242.

58. Essex to Sidney, 4 March 1596/97, ibid., 2:242.

59. Whyte to Sidney, Court, 6 March 1596/97 ibid., 2:245–46.

60. Whyte to Sidney, Strand, 16 March 1596/97, Collins, 2:29–31.

61. Whyte to Sidney, Strand, 7 March 1596/97, *HMCD* 2:246.

62. Whyte to Sidney, Strand, 12 March 1596/97, ibid., 2:248–50.

63. Sidney to Burghley, Flushing, 13 March 1596/97, SP 84/54, fol. 132.

64. Whyte to Sidney, Strand, 19 March 1596/97, *HMCD* 2:252–53.

65. Sidney to Lady Sidney, Flushing, 21 March [1597], ibid., 2:253.

66. Whyte to Sidney, 30 April 1597, ibid., 2:273.

67. Ibid., 2:257–58.

68. Whyte to Sidney, Strand, 12 March 1596/97, ibid., 2:246.

69. Whyte to Sidney, [19 May], ibid., 2:281.

70. Ibid., and Whyte to Sidney, Richmond, 4 October 1597, ibid., 2:293.

71. Whyte to Sidney, Strand, 12 March 1596/97, ibid., 248:250, et passim.

72. *Return of Every Member Returned to Serve in Each Parliament,* 2 vols., ("Ordered to be printed by the House of Commons," 1878), 1:431 (hereafter abbreviated "Official Returns").

73. Ibid., 1:433.

74. Whyte to Sidney, Richmond, 4 October 1597, *HMCD* 2:293.

75. Whyte to Sidney, Strand, 13 October 1597, ibid., 2:295.

76. Neale, *Elizabethan House of Commons,* p. 30.

77. Whyte to Sidney, Strand, 26 October 1597, *HMCD* 2:299.

78. Whyte to Sidney, Richmond, 9 October 1597, ibid., 2:294.

79. Whyte to Sidney, Strand, 23 October 1597, ibid., 2:298.

80. Whyte to Sidney, Strand, 22 October 1597, ibid., 2:297.

81. Sidney to Essex, 29 January 1597/[98], Additional MS 6177 (a copy), British Library, London, England.

82. Whyte to Sidney, Strand, 25 January 1597/[98], *HMCD* 2:313. It is also strange that Whyte should refer to a remark made in a letter written four days later; perhaps Sidney spoke of it to him earlier.

83. Sidney to Essex, 29 January 1597/[98], Additional MS 6167, British Library, London, England.

84. Sidney's statement to Essex as Earl Marshall of his claim to the title of Lord Lisle, *CSP Dom.* 12:269–70.

85. Whyte to Sidney, 1 February 1597/[98], *HMCD* 2:317.

86. Ibid.

87. Stone, *Crisis,* 99–100.

88. Whyte to Sidney, Strand, 22 October 1597, *HMCD* 2:297.

89. Whyte to Sidney, 11 February 1597/98, ibid., 2:320.

90. Whyte to Sidney, 30 January 1597/98, ibid., 2:316.

91. Whyte to Sidney, 12 February 1597/98, ibid., 2:321–22.

92. Whyte to Sidney, 4 March 1597/[98], ibid., 2:329.

93. Browne to Sidney, Flushing, 12 May 1598, ibid., 2:355.

94. Whyte to Sidney, Baynard's Castle, 19 April 1600, ibid., 2:455.

95. Ibid.

96. Whyte to Sidney, 4 April 1597, ibid., 2:262.

97. Whyte to Sidney, 13 October 1600, ibid., 2:487.

98. Browne to Sidney, 5 April 1601, ibid., 2:516.

99. Whyte to Sidney, 28 October 1597, ibid., 2:300.

100. Whyte to Sidney, 18 March 1597/98, ibid., 2:332.

101. Carleton to Chamberlain, London, 25 March, 1598, *CSP Dom.* 5:36.

102. Whyte to Sidney, Nonesuch, 12 September 1599, *HMCD* 2:389.

103. Ibid., 2:390.

104. Whyte to Sidney, Strand Bridge, 15 September 1599, ibid., 2:391.

105. Whyte to Sidney, Penshurst, 20 September 1599, ibid., 2:392.

106. Whyte to Sidney, Baynard's Castle, 29 November 1599, ibid., 2:418.

107. Ibid., 2:421, 422, 427, 435, passim.

108. Whyte to Sidney, Baynard's Castle, 19 April 1600, ibid., 2:456.

109. Whyte to Sidney, 3 May 1600, ibid., 2:458; Whyte to Sidney, 12 May 1600, ibid., 2:461.

110. Whyte to Sidney, Baynard's Castle, 4 June 1600, ibid., 2:468.

111. Whyte to Sidney, Nonesuch, 8 August 1600, ibid, 2:476.

112. Sir Thomas Bodley, *Life of Thomas Bodley, Written by Himself,* (1647; rept. Chicago: A. C. McClurg, 1906), pp. 49–52.

113. Sidney to Burghley, Flushing, 28 August 1590, SP 84/38, fol. 216.

114. Roger Seys to Sidney, Lincoln's Inn, 15 May 1591, *HMCD* 2:117.

115. Sidney to Lady Sidney, [Court], 20 September 1594, ibid., 2:156–57; Sidney to Lady Sidney, Richmond, 26 October 1594.

116. Whyte to Sidney, 13 November 1595, ibid., 2:185–86; Whyte to Sidney, London, 22 November 1595, ibid., 2:187.

117. Whyte to Sidney, 3 January 1595/96, ibid., 2:205.

118. Lacey, p. 127.

119. Whyte to Sidney, Whitehall, 19 December 1596, *HMCD* 2:202–3.

120. Sidney to Essex, 29 January 1597/[98], Additional MS. 6177, p. 83, British Library, London, England.

121. *DNB*, s.v. "Devereux, Robert, Earl of Essex."

122. Ibid.

123. Whyte to Sidney, 2 October 1595, *HMCD* 2:398.

124. Sidney to Cecil, Flushing, 19 November 1599, SP 84/59, fols. 152–53.

125. Sidney to Cecil, 26 December 1599, SP 84/59, fols. 208–10.

126. Sidney to Cecil, Flushing, 4 August 1600, SP 84/60, fols. 264–65.

127. *DNB*, s.v. "Devereux, Robert, Earl of Essex."

128. *The Works of Sir Francis Bacon*, ed. J. Spedding, 14 vols. (London: Longmans, Green 1868–74), 9:273.

129. G. B. Harrison, *The Life and Death of Robert Devereux, Earl of Essex* (London: Cassell, 1937), pp. 291–92.

130. Vincent Hussey to _____, 11 February 1600/01, *CSP Dom.* 5:550.

131. Spedding, 2, 9:273.

132. *CSP Dom.* 5:550.

133. Sidney to Cecil, 25 August 1601, SP 84/61, fol. 259.

134. See, e.g., Sidney to Cecil, Flushing, 5 February 1601/02, SP 84/61, fol. 27.

135. Lisle to Salisbury, Greenwich, 24 July 1601, *HMC Salisbury* 18:209.

[8]

Domestic Life and Personal Business

Barbara Gamage was born in Wales, daughter and heiress of an untitled but substantial family of Norman extraction. Her elaborate pedigree, drawn up in 1608 and neither more nor less trustworthy than other genealogies devised for King James's new aristocracy, describes her descent from one Paen Gamedge, a captain who came to England with William the Conqueror.[1] Barbara's learned and well-liked father, John, died in 1584,[2] leaving his daughter his fortune and his extensive land holdings in Wales. Her inheritance and her personal attractiveness made her a desirable object for marriage to one of Elizabeth's ambitious young courtiers. A sudden scramble took place, and within a fortnight, with the connivance of the earl of Pembroke and over the objections of Sir Walter Raleigh, the new heiress was married to young Robert Sidney.[3]

Robert and Barbara were married at St. Donat's in Glamorganshire, the home of her guardian, Sir Edward Stradling. The earl of Pembroke was among those present at the ceremony. Although it is possible, as Stone suggests, that the newlyweds had never met before their wedding day,[4] they could have become acquainted at Ludlow when Sidney was in Wales with his father. Dodging opposition from the queen and from Raleigh's supporters, the two young people married in haste, and, it developed, barely in time. Although bold enough to ignore Raleigh's warning to Stradling not to allow Barbara to marry without the queen's consent, they would hardly have dared disobey the queen's own command that no marriage take place. Fortunately, that order arrived too late: Elizabeth's special messenger galloped into St. Donat's a few hours after the wedding rite was over.[5]

Elizabeth probably entered a mark against Sidney on her private scorecard, and perhaps his marrying against her wishes was among the reasons she did little to advance his fortunes. Nevertheless, nothing more was said about it, and Elizabeth at least outwardly forgave the couple. Despite the haste and sense of collusion surrounding the wedding, Robert and Barbara built a long and happy marriage together.

Although the two were often separated, their affection for each other, their attention to their mutual concerns, and their desire to be together never wavered. When Sidney was not in Flushing, he had to spend much time at court; after James's accession, he was appointed the queen's chamberlain, and that position also took him away from Barbara, requiring him to follow Anne's court. Sidney's correspondence, however, is remarkable for his warm and affectionate letters to his wife, in which he reiterates his love for her and his longing to be with her. They contrived to be together as much as possible. Barbara joined him in Flushing sporadically, but their concern for the children's health in the plague-ridden Low Countries, as well as other circumstances, dictated that she pass most of the 1590s in England. While there, she devoted most of her time to attending to the children, to their estate at Penshurst, and to doing what she could to help further her husband's career.

Shortly after Sidney took over the governorship, Barbara joined him in Flushing. Their first son, William, was born there in 1590; his father had to arrange to have him naturalized an English citizen by parliamentary order.[6] The name they chose was Sidney's grandfather's as well as the Prince of Orange's; probably their choice of the Princess of Orange as William's godmother[7] was made as much for politics as for amity.

The Sidneys developed lasting friendships with members of the House of Orange, particularly with Count Maurice of Nassau and with the Princess Mary. Robert often went into the field with Maurice, and he sent news of their friends by letter to his wife. Late in September 1590, when Barbara was advanced in pregnancy, Sidney wrote from Maurice's camp at Breda that "I wil not live if I be not with you before you be brought to bed, for nothing in the work[sic] shall stay mee but God from being with you. . . ."[8]

From the Hague he reported that "the yong ladyes"—presumably of Maurice's family, for they resided in that city—wished Barbara to send her sidesaddle to them for two or three days, so their saddler could copy it.[9] They exchanged correspondence and gifts until after the turn of the century. The Sidneys sent perfumed skins to "the young Prince"[10] and monkeys to the princess.[11] The relationship seems to have been typical of the friendship that develops between families of men who work together, and the Sidneys' eagerness to send gifts and honors to Maurice and the princess no doubt reflected Sir Robert's feeling that something was to be gained politically from a bond with the houses of Nassau and Orange. Whether or not this was a motivation, some real affection must have developed, or they would not have continued to correspond into the late 1600s, by which time Sidney had returned to England, so everyone expected, permanently.

Lady Sidney stayed with Sir Robert in Flushing for about two years following the establishment of their household there. They made their home in the governor's mansion, directly next door to Count Maurice's house. Merchants and townspeople, sailors from trading and military ships on shore leave, English soldiers going about their duty or play, all passed by the wide street between the house and the New Haven. The Sidneys had a fine view of that harbor and must have spent some of their pensive moments watching the ships move in and out of the docks. Probably, too, they had a view of the rooftops of the Old Town, a scene more picturesque from the distance of the governor's house than from the streets within. On the side opposite the harbor and the Old Town, the Sidneys' home had a formal garden, smaller and perhaps less elaborate than Penshurst's, but, under Sidney's knowledgeable guidance, no doubt carefully trimmed and stocked with a variety of exotic fruit trees. A small section of parkland connected with the property was left less cultivated to give a charming illusion of wilderness beauty.[12]

By May 1592, Lady Barbara had begun to think of returning to England. Although Sidney feared if she left he would not see her again until Michaelmas (September 29), he regarded the final decision as hers: "You know," he assured her, "it is left to your own best liking."[13] She probably left with him when he took leave of Flushing in December, and by February 1593, they were certainly in England.[14] Sidney spent a couple of months at his house in Dougat.[15] Although there is no evidence that Barbara was with him, no letters to her dated from Dougat survive; since he never failed to write to her when they were separated, we may infer with some safety that she accompanied him.

While they were in England during the first part of the decade, the Sidneys made Penshurst their home base. Sir Robert frequently followed the court, writing to his wife from Windsor, Greenwich, and London. For the most part, she stayed in Kent while Sidney pursued his business. He forwarded necessities and small luxuries to her and reported his progress in his suits to the queen, along with bits of gossip. He sent her delicacies such as apricots, cherries, and Parmesan cheese, and on one occasion arranged for her to receive a small horse, called a hobby, which she thought might fit her saddle. Here he was acceding to her wishes against his own judgment, for he thought any hobby would be too weak and skittish to be fit for her.[16]

Despite his absence from her, Robert's affection for Barbara never flagged over the years. He sent her special treats he acquired at court, and remarked disparagingly about other courtiers' faithless behavior.[17] Over and over, year by year, he assured his "sweteheart" of his affection and his desire to be with her. He asked her to write often to him, insisting "nothing can be so welcome heare as the good news of your own and my little ons welbeing."[18]

By 1594, when Sidney expressed that wish, there were already several little ones. William had been born in Flushing, Mary and Catherine had already arrived, and Barbara was pregnant with their third daughter, Philippa, who was born in August of that year.[19]

In 1594, they began to consider ways they might be together more often. Shortly after he returned home from his mission to France, Sidney fell ill and was ordered by Dr. Gifford to take a lengthy "physic," which involved interminable sweatings. He wanted to be with his wife at Penshurst but was prevented from leaving Greenwich and London by the course of the treatment.[20] This miserable experience must have sharpened his desire for the comforts of his wife's company.

She proposed to join him in Greenwich toward the end of May, but he thought she would not be comfortable there as long as the queen and her court were present. He suggested she wait until after Elizabeth began a new progress, which was planned for a week later.[21] The spring and summer passed, apparently with no removal of Barbara from Penshurst. Perhaps the fact that she was again advanced in pregnancy deterred her more than anything else from making a move.

Sidney was detained at court into the summer of 1594, while he pressed suit for the revival of his horse company. There he remained until after Lady Sidney gave birth to their third girl, Philippa, born August 18, 1594. As he helped arrange the christening from the court, inviting Lady Essex and Lady Compton to be Philippa's godmothers and Lord Mountjoy to be her godfather, his impatience grew more intense. "I pray to be with you," he wrote to his wife, "for never man was more weary of a place then I of this."[22]

Late in September, they planned to meet at Barnelms. Sidney thought her visit there would be "kindly taken," and it would provide an opportunity for them to be together briefly. Meanwhile, he had conceived another idea: Barbara should move to their estate at Otford for the winter. There she would be only sixteen miles from London, with no bad roads between her residence and the city. The company, he thought, was better, she would not have to worry about Penshurst and the extensive construction project under way there, and she could help him decide on and manage the disposition of Otford Park. He proposed to discuss this plan when they met at Barnelms.[23]

The rendezvous at Barnelms was cancelled, however, when he heard the queen was about to move, so that great numbers of courtiers would be passing through the area. Additionally, a smallpox epidemic was raging, and Lady Walsingham was afraid to travel to Barnelms.[24] Lady Sidney apparently remained at Penshurst while Sidney continued to pursue his business at Richmond and in London.

The Otford idea also withered, whether because Barbara preferred not to live there or for some other reason. Within a month after Sidney made the suggestion, his correspondence with his wife indicates they had conceived the idea of moving her to London for the winter. Sidney planned to ask Pembroke for the use of part of Baynard's Castle, and he hoped to get it, for he could hear of no other adequate lodging in London.

Sidney was determined that he and his wife should spend the winter of 1594/95 together, but their plans were not easily accomplished. London was growing increasingly crowded as the custom of spending the "season" there developed. Stone notes that many businessmen, aristocrats, and their families, bored with life in the country and attracted by the city's metropolitan elegance, took to spending part of the year in London, a habit that developed with great speed between 1590 and 1620.[25] With this influx of people, it was not easy to find a place to stay. Evidently, the plan to use Baynard's Castle did not work out, for Lady Sidney remained in Penshurst past Christmas, 1594, and in February, Sidney wrote to her that he had found "a suitable house" in London.[26] This was perhaps Sir John Harrington's, into which Sidney expected to move his wife that March. It was fully furnished, so that she would have to move no household goods up from the country.[27] However, Sidney's cousin Hastings, who was occupying the house, fell ill with the measles, making it impossible for Lady Sidney to take over the building. Sidney hoped to get a Mr. Willoughby's house for her, or, failing that, Sir Edward Hoby's.[28] The whole idea seems to have gone awry, for there is no evidence that Lady Sidney moved to London that winter.

The following summer, Sidney had to return to Flushing. Abhorring the idea of being separated from him, Lady Sidney proposed to join him. Her distress over his departure upset Sir Robert: "Sweet Barbara," he wrote as he was about to set to sea from Margate, "as you love me do not discomfort yourself, you are one of the greatest joyes of my lyfe."[29] He was concerned for her safety during the proposed journey, for it was an exhausting trip and she was again five months pregnant. They argued: he opposed her making the passage, particularly alone and without him there to protect her. Nevertheless, he left the choice to her, for pleasing her, he said, "is the next way to have me contented."[30] Throughout August, she held firm in her resolve to join him; he planned to send Captain Goring, one of his most trusted subordinates, to accompany her, reminding her that should she change her mind and decide not to make the journey, nothing would be lost but the captain's pains. She began to waiver before his resistance.

At last, near the end of August, he hit upon a way to keep her in England. While Essex assured her that Sidney would have leave to return to England for the winter, Sir Robert observed that if she came over, she would have to stay there while he returned to England on business during the winter, "for you and your children must not pass and repass the seas so often. . . ." If he did not make the trip to England when he had the opportunity, he might not be able to return for another year and a half, and his business there was urgent. Observing that she would not be willing to remain in Flushing while he spent the season in London, he implied that her presence there would impede his career by preventing him from leaving the Low Countries when he might do so were she in England. He finished by reiterating the importance of his obtaining leave to return to England that winter.[31]

Within the fortnight he was congratulating her on her wise decision to stay in England. Perhaps in consolation, he sent her two hogsheads of claret and a quantity of sack, the latter to be aged for four or five years at Penshurst. And he revived the plan to set up a residence for her in London. "It wil be troublesome," he observed, "to goe up and down to Penshurst this winter": evidently he expected her to spend some time in

London, whether or not they had a semipermanent base in the city, and despite her gravid condition, and he hoped to spare her the trouble of traveling back and forth.[32]

Rowland Whyte was again sent about Sidney's business. He soon reported that he had arranged for them to rent a house belonging to Alderman [Richard] Catcher, a merchant with whom Sidney certainly dealt in the Low Countries. Catcher wanted £50 a half year, and the place was furnished with everything but bedding;[33] it was located next to Austin Frier's gate.[34] Arrangements were made, and Whyte obtained the house at a rent of £40. Even at the lower rate, Lady Sidney feared the cost would be too high, and she was reluctant to make the move. She procrastinated until the end of October. First Philippa, then Bess, and then Catherine caught the measles, but Whyte at last persuaded her to come away with Mary, William, and Philippa, leaving Catherine at Penshurst to recuperate. Bess was sent to "Mrs. Sidney"—probably Thomas Sidney's wife—in Otford to recover.

The arrangement with Catcher took a fortunate turn. Early in November, Catcher asked Sidney to help him recover £100 due him from an Amsterdam merchant, promising that if he got it, the Sidneys would have the house rent-free.[35] Sidney did attempt to accomodate him, for toward the end of the month Whyte remarked that the Alderman's friend had finished his business in Amsterdam and he thanked Sidney for his willingness to please him.[36] No evidence survives to show that the debt was recovered, but the positive tone of Whyte's reports suggests so. Although Sidney had difficulty supporting the London residence, it appears the hardship came not from the rent, but from the cost of paying and feeding the extra servants they needed.

Lady Sidney's fears that the London house would cost them more than they could afford were confirmed by Sidney's complaint, two weeks after she arrived, that the household was too large. He felt she could spare some of the sixty people she employed in the house. He thought eleven women were excessive. Though he did not know exactly what their services were, he was sure she could get by with four fewer: "some of your women," he remarked, "are kept onely to wayte upon the rest." The presence of two boys, named Robin and Frank, also seemed pointless; Sidney thought Will Sidney must have better playfellows available.[37]

This expensive venture certainly had other motivation than the city's cosmopolitan attractions. Since Lady Sidney did not move until after her husband arrived in Flushing, the couple's desire to be together could not have been their primary reason, although he evidently felt confident that he would return to England that winter. One reason Whyte advanced to persuade her to make the move when her children were passing the measles between each other was that her presence in London would free Sidney of much trouble traveling up and down to Penshurst.[38] Sidney wanted her to pass the winter among friends: Lady Huntingdon, Lady Rich, Lady Elizabeth Clinton, and Lady Cumberland, among others, were in London. In addition, he expected her to spend some time furthering his business affairs, although he of course employed Whyte to carry most of that load. Specifically, he wanted her to solicit their most influential friends to obtain his leave; to this end, he urged her to "visit often my Lady of Huntingdon and assure her how much I love and honor her. . . ."[39]

Lady Sidney might not, of her own volition, have chosen to reside in London for the social life there; her reluctance to leave Penshurst and the energy Whyte had to devote to dislodging her hint that she lacked enthusiasm for city life. She seems not to have reveled in the company of courtiers. Sidney observed, when he advised her not to join him in Greenwich during the spring of 1594, that she would be "ecceeding pestred" by the crowds of people with whom he dealt there. It is also significant that the passing of Elizabeth's progress by Barnelms was enough to dissuade Lady Sidney from meeting her husband there.

Once in London, Lady Sidney began to campaign for Sidney's return. He directed her to approach the Lord Admiral in that cause, saying it was extremely important for him to receive a three-month leave that winter.[40] At the same time, Sidney expected her to run the new household on a tight budget: "be as good a houswyfe as you may, for I assure you charges grow terribly upon me heer," Sidney wrote from Zealand.[41] All this was a heavy burden, for she was near the end of another pregnancy. When she arrived at the court to join the struggle to obtain Sidney's leave, the Lord Admiral and "all that tribe" expressed their pleasure at seeing her and pitied her having to make the journey so near her time. She took three of the children with her, to the delight of the Lord Admiral, who told young Mary she was already "a fitt mayd" for the queen. Whyte urged Sidney to write appreciatively to his wife for the pains she took to procure his return, for, he reported, she was exhausted by the time she got back to Baynard's Castle.[42]

The strain involved in the endeavor seems to have adversely affected Lady Sidney's health. Days before she was due to deliver, she came down with the measles. The disease was somewhat more dangerous in the sixteenth century than it is now; before the discovery of antibiotics, bacterial complications, such as meningitis, caused a fair number of fatalities. Although the doctor believed it would not prove dangerous to the baby because Lady Sidney was so near delivery, few of her friends would risk exposure, and Whyte feared the "great ones" Sidney hoped to have as the child's godparents would be unwilling to come to the christening. As her fever and cough progressed, Lady Barbara grew more depressed and agitated. She missed her husband, and at one point exclaimed despairingly that now, when she had most need for his presence and comfort, it was not God's will for her to have it. She was somewhat comforted by the arrival of some letters from Sidney; and it is to be hoped that Whyte kept to himself the news that Essex had failed to obtain Sir Robert's leave. At the height of her discomfort from the measles, she went into labor. Fortunately, the delivery was swift and the birth normal, and by nine o'clock on the night of December 1, they had "a goodly fatt boy . . . as full of measles in the face as he can be."[43] He suckled and cried vigorously, and within three days "the baby and the mother were free of any sign of the disease."[44] The father never knew his wife had been ill until she was safely brought to bed and was well again.[45]

Sidney wanted as the boy's godmother Penelope Lady Rich, the same Penelope Devereux who had been the object of his brother's admiration and the inspiration for Stella, the central figure of Philip's sonnet cycle, *Astrophel and Stella*. As godfather, he wanted Charles Blount, Lord Mount-joy, one of Elizabeth's greatest generals and, incidentally, Lady Rich's lover. Lady Rich, being warned about the measles in the Sidney household, declared there was no danger after eight days and resolved to accept the honor. When Lord Mountjoy heard Lady Rich was to be godmother, he was much pleased and assured Whyte he would join them on the appointed day. Sidney asked that William Lord Compton be invited as the other godfather; he also accepted.[46]

Penelope Lady Rich was, in addition to being a long-time friend of the Sidney family, Essex's sister. Mountjoy was allied with Essex, and, as Elizabeth's outstanding general, was as well able to help Sidney's military career as to speak positively of him to the queen and to Essex.

The choice of godparents delayed the cristening for a month. The two lovers, of course, each insisted on attending the ceremony in the finest form possible. So, when Mountjoy developed an ague, he wanted Lady Sidney to delay the christening until his health improved. She agreed and sent him word that he should appoint the day himself as soon as Lady Rich returned to London, whence she had briefly departed.[47] She returned by December 26, but the christening was again put off, this time until New Year's Eve. Lady Rich claimed it was at Compton's wish, but Whyte told Sidney he suspected "a tetter that suddenly broke out in her fayre white face . . . keapes your son from being christened."[48]

At last, on New Year's Eve, Sidney's son was christened Robert by Mountjoy, Compton, and Lady Rich. The ceremony took place even as Sidney was en route back to England, called back at the request of his suddenly widowed aunt, Lady Huntingdon. The godparents presented the baby with matching bowls, whose value Whyte estimated at £20 apiece. Many gentlemen and gentlewomen attended, including Lady Cumberland and her daughter, Lady Essex and her daughter and son, and Lady Dacres with her daughters.[49]

Sidney's stay in England following the death of his uncle was relatively brief. By the end of August 1596, he was safely back in Flushing.[50] Lady Barbara had returned to Penshurst and was pregnant again. Sidney wrote that he wanted Southampton, Lord Thomas Howard, and Lady Cumberland to be sponsors if the baby was a boy; if a girl, he wanted Lady Cumberland, Lady Thomas Howard, and Southampton or, if the latter was out of the country, Shrewsbury.[51] The child, he said, was to be named after one of the godparents.

The baby, a girl, was born in February. This time the christening plans were complicated by Lady Sidney's mistaken hope that Sidney would receive leave to come home in time for the ceremony. Southampton and Lady Sussex agreed to be godparents and the arrangements were set into motion.[52] Lady Bedford was asked to be the other godmother, and she agreed; however, at the last minute she sent word that she could not come, nor would she nominate a deputy.[53] Bess Sidney apparently took her place, and the little girl was christened Bridget, after Bridget Ratliffe, countess of Sussex. Lady Bedford sent a bowl, as from a third godmother, and again the guests made an illustrious group, including among others the countesses of Darby and Southampton, Lady Compton, Sir Thomas Garret, and Mr. Roger Manners.[54]

Bridget's godparents represented the most fervent of the earl of Essex's followers. The child was born at the time her father was engaged in his maneuvering for the wardenship of the Cinque Ports. Bedford, Sussex, and Southampton were reckless, profligate, and passionate supporters of Essex. Henry Wriothesly, earl of Southampton, was attainted following Essex's uprising, but he was restored by James I. Bridget Ratliffe's husband, Robert, earl of Sussex, was notoriously promiscuous and syphilitic.[55] Lucy Russell, much attached to the Sidney children,[56] was countess of Bedford and sister-in-law to Margaret Clifford, countess of Cumberland. Lady Cumberland was a sister of Sidney's influential aunt, Lady Warwick, a good enough reason alone to nominate her as Bridget's godmother. Lady Cumberland was an ally of Essex and of Gelly Myrick. Her father, the second earl of Bedford, had purchased George Clifford's guardianship through the Court of Wards for the purpose of marrying the young earl to Lady Margaret. The union was no less miserable than one might expect, as their daughter, Lady Anne Clifford, revealed in her diary. Lady Cumberland's brother, Edward Russell, third earl of Bedford, married Lucy Harington, another of Essex's circle. Bedford was a member of the "fast" London social set, and his contemporaries described him as a "fantastycall" figure.[57] Several of these unhappy people were distantly related to Sidney, and all were followers of Essex, whose patronage Sidney was currently cultivating.

Gilbert Talbot, earl of Shrewsbury, Sidney's second choice for Bridget's godfather, was a member of Cecil's faction; Elizabeth once sent him as ambassador to Henry IV. Perhaps Sidney intended to hedge his bets with this choice. Too, Shrewsbury's family was ultimately allied with Pembroke's when Talbot's daughter, Mary, was wed to Sidney's nephew, William, third earl of Pembroke.

If the Sidneys regularly socialized with the likes of Bedford and Cumberland, they ran with a fast crowd. Just how close their friendships were is difficult to know. The invitations to act as godparents for the Sidneys's daughter may indicate nothing more than a wish to build goodwill between themselves and Essex through the earl's friends. While a pious and sentimental occasion such as the christening of his daughter would seem a time for Sidney to gather his family and favorite friends, his use of his son's christening to arrange a romantic encounter of political interest to him suggests that he felt neither piety nor sentimentality toward the ceremony and its actors. There is danger in any attempt to assess Sidney's and Lady Sidney's characters in the light of the personalities of the men and women with whom they socialized. As long as he desired a career in Elizabethan government, Sidney had no choice in the men with whom he kept company. He was allied with the Essex family and faction, and his lot was cast with the Bedfords, the Cumberlands, and Sussexes. Whatever he thought of their private lives, he kept his opinion to himself. Lady Barbara seems to have been friendly with the ladies who were married to gallants such as Sussex, Southampton, and Shrewsbury, but there is little indication that she and Sir Robert were regularly involved in the high life of London society during Elizabeth's time.

Lady Sidney's most affectionate friends seem not to have been drawn exclusively from the Essex circle. While she was close to Frances, countess of Essex, Sir Francis Walsingham's daughter and Philip Sidney's widow, and to Lady Essex's mother, Lady Ursula Walsingham—friendships that continued even after Essex's fall[58]—at the same time she seems to have enjoyed the company of Sidney's rival, Sir Walter Raleigh, and his lady, Elizabeth. She also visited Lady Katherine Howard, who had been sworn of the Privy Chamber in 1599[59] and was the wife of the Lord Admiral. Robert's sister, Mary Herbert, countess of Pembroke, has been described as one of Barbara Sidney's closest friends,[60] although if this is true it is not reflected in the correspondence preserved in the Dudley and De L'Isle papers.

Sidney's most genuine, long-lasting friendship appears to have been with Rowland Whyte. Whyte's social position, several rungs below Sidney's, removed more barriers to this friendship than it erected, in that it took them out of competition with each other. Jealousy and conflicting ambition could not interfere with their comradeship in the way they must have stood between Sidney and other male members of his social class. Whyte, the son of Griffith Whyte (a.k.a. Wynne, Welsh for *White*) of Nigol in Caernarvonshire, seems to have come to the Sidney family through his own family's association with the earls of Pembroke; his grandfather, John Wynne, served William, earl of Pembroke, and was renamed "Whyte" by him to avoid confusion with another servant of the same name (Birch, *Progresses of James I*, 1:494n) Intelligent and loyal, Whyte possessed qualities of character that would have made him more desirable as a confidant and friend than those whose nobility was attested to only by their pedigrees. His letters make it clear that he was a welcome member of the Sidney household. Like a doting uncle, he watched the Sidney children grow. He helped Lady Sidney with day-to-day details and problems of finances, child care, and social planning. He ran interference for her when she went to court on her husband's behalf, and he took care of all Sidney's business while the governor was in the Low Countries. He had no fear of offering Sir Robert his sound, practical advice, freely suggesting he should cool his ambition and content himself with the comfortable lot to which he was born. He knew husband and wife well enough to suggest discreetly when Sidney should put in a word of appreciation and comfort to Lady Sidney, and he knew how to use Sir Robert's own arguments to move the reluctant wife out of Penshurst and up to London. Nevertheless, in September 1599, Whyte married secretly. It was two months before he informed Sidney. Yet nowhere is there any indication that Sidney was closer to any man than to Rowland Whyte.

Although attempts to deduce the Sidneys' personal predilictions from what is known of their friends and relatives are risky, an examination of the character of Sidney's younger brother, Thomas, is surely not out of order and might afford some insight into Sir Robert's character. Thomas was aligned by marriage with the Puritan element. Still a minor at Sir Henry Sidney's death, he had been placed under the earl of Huntingdon's guardianship and so went to live with his aunt and uncle.[61] In 1592, he married the widow of Walter Devereux, Margaret Dakin, a woman of strong Puritan tendencies. Lady Elizabeth Russell wanted to marry her son by an earlier marriage, Posthumus Hoby, to Lady Margaret, but was frustrated in her scheme in Huntingdon, who was also Devereux's guardian. Margaret fell in love with Thomas, and Huntingdon decided to favor their marriage, which took place in December 1591.[62]

Thomas died in 1595,[63] and Hoby began immediately to pay court to Lady Margaret again. He enlisted the aid of his uncle, Burghley, and attempted to gain the support of the Huntingdons and the Sidneys. Sir Robert promised to do what he could to further Hoby's suit. When Lord Huntingdon decided he was the real owner of Lady Margaret's property and threatened to take her to court, she married Hoby because he was Burghley's nephew and so represented a strong defense against the earl's designs. Like Margaret, Hoby was also a Puritan.[64]

No unequivocal evidence shows that Thomas Sidney was a Puritan. His background, like his brothers', disposed him to radical Protestantism, but Margaret's grief at his passing suggests no fundamental differences spoiled their married harmony. That Sidney was willing to back Hoby's suit suggests that any distaste he might have had for Puritanism was not strong enough to cause him to oppose Lord Burghley's nephew.

In 1597, the strain of Sidney's frustrated efforts to advance his fortunes combined with his financial difficulties to force him to give up the London household and bring Lady Sidney to Flushing. That spring, Sidney's circumstances were so straitened that he could not even scrape up the £10 for Lady Sidney's weekly allowance; he had to pawn some of their silver to meet their daily expenses.[65] He was discouraged over his failure to obtain any favor at court, and he wanted his wife at his side: "I will not hereafter have you so long from me if I have a choice," he vowed. He was disgusted with their fruitless attempts to curry favor through their influential acquaintances. "Wee must make the best of our own," he wrote to her, "and make much of one another, and care only for them that deserve wel of us. . . ."[66]

Lady Sidney's move to Flushing was complicated by the problem of what to do with the children. Sidney wanted to farm out the three oldest, Mary, Catherine, and William, to their relatives, but Lady Barbara was reluctant to leave them. Mary was frantic at the very idea, Whyte reported; she "doth fall a weeping and my Lady when she perceives it doth bere her company." The little girl appealed to Whyte to petition Sidney to let her go to Flushing, for she insisted she was too young to part from her mother. Sidney hoped to send William to Sir Charles Morison, where Lady Sidney least objected to having him raised. Meanwhile, she proceeded with her plan to cross the Channel with all her children.[67]

Collins prints a letter in which Sidney responds to these plans with the strongest objections. According to Collins, Sidney pointed out that Mary was almost ten and Kate almost eight, and he felt it was time, according to the custom of the period, that they were out of their father's house. "I know your Delight in them, makes you not Care; what is best for them," he remarked, and although he softened his criticism with assurances that she was an excellent mother, he thought her overfondness for them would spoil them. He also believed the air was dangerous in Flushing—waves of plague periodically passed over the Low Countries, and malaria was endemic—and he promised that if she did bring them over and anything happened to harm them, she would never again have her way in their upbringing.[68]

The Historical Manuscript Commission's version of this letter, dated two days after the diatribe Collins produces in his edition, is more moderate: in it, Sidney left the decision up to his wife concerning the two girls, but he expressed his preference that seven-year-old William be left at Sir Charles Morison's, where he would be well looked after and would lose no time in his education. In the HMC letter, Sidney remarks that he is afraid of the effect the air might have on the children, but makes no threats against his wife should they become ill in Flushing.[69]

However Sidney phrased his protest, Lady Sidney was troubled over the possibility that the children might fall ill in Flushing. She offered all three to Lady Huntingdon, but the countess felt herself too much in debt to take on the children. Apparently the plan to lodge Will with Morison was defeated, and Lady Sidney did not know where to leave them unless at Penshurst with a schoolmaster and some servants.[70] She finally went over to Flushing at the end of May; the specific provisions she made for the three older children remain unclear, but it is certain that she took Will Sidney, for Sidney remarked at the time on his arrangements for a schoolmaster for him in the Low Countries.[71] The warrant for her passage, dated May 30, includes an unspecified number of children and servants to accompany her.[72]

Barbara and Robert Sidney had eleven children, of whom five survived them. Henry, their second son, apparently was born and died in Flushing.[73] Bridget and Alice died in infancy, within three months of each other in 1599.[74] Their youngest daughter, Vere, died in July 1606, at about four years of age.[75] William and Philippa died after they reached adulthood. Collins, in his *Memoirs* (vol 1:120) mentions a son, Phillip, based on Rowland Whyte's letter dated September 25, 1595, saying "Mr. Phillip can go alone." This probably refers to Philippa, who was then about a year old and must have just been learning to walk.

Evidently the Sidneys were blessed with a particularly charming brood, for Whyte was not the only one to remark on Sidney's "sweet children;" "such a sight," he said, "can a man see nowhere else" than at Penshurst.[76] Lady Huntingdon reported that the queen often spoke of the three older children, Mary, Robert, and Catherine, and that she never saw a child with better or bolder grace than Mrs. Kat.[77] Little Robert also made a good impression when the time came to present him at the court. At St. George's feast in April 1600, Whyte brought in the boy when the assembled knights were at dinner, and he "played the wag so prettily that all took pleasure in him."[78] Lady Sidney, who toward the end of the decade took on the responsibility for her nephew, Philip Herbert, was careful in bringing up all the children, and saw to it that they were trained in the knowledge and social skills appropriate to their birth.[79] If she was profligate in anything, it was in her affection for her children: Whyte remarked, when she went to Greenwich in 1600 to solicit another leave for Sidney, that she did not have appropriate clothes, for she gave everything to her children.[80]

William was the eldest son, born in the Low Countries and naturalized an English citizen by Parliamentary decree. His father was determined to raise him to be a proper gentleman and worthy heir of the Sidney name. The Sidneys started their search for a tutor in 1596, when the boy was beginning to read. Sir Robert inclined toward a French tutor, for he felt "our Oxford yong men have seen nothing but the schooles, and need for most things themselves to be taught."[81] A Mr. Bird was retained, and he remained with the family until about 1605. When Lady Barbara took William to Flushing in 1597, however, Sidney provided a separate schoolmaster for him, a Dutch gentleman constrained by poverty to teach for a living. He spoke Dutch, German, French, Latin, Greek, and even some English, and Sidney thought he would be an appropriate mentor to send with Will on his tour of the Continent when the boy grew old enough.[82]

Sidney wanted Lady Barbara to dismiss Bird, but she did not do so; Whyte remarks that she liked Bird so well she did not know how to let him go, and in 1600 the tutor was either still with the family or had returned after an absence. By then, he had grown discontented with his position and offended Lady Sidney by "laying before her the want of education in herself, and therefore cold not judge of it in others."[83] It is possible that Barbara Sidney was barely literate, for her childlike signature suggests she was not a practiced writer.[84] Nevertheless, Bird's arrogance spurred Whyte to urge Sidney to tell the tutor either to do his job or to leave.

In 1605, while the freshly created Viscount Lisle was en route to Flushing, one of the Sidney sons was rumored to have stabbed his schoolmaster for threatening to whip him.[85] This certainly referred to Will; the gossips indicated the boy had been attending the Prince of Wales and was dismissed because the king was so displeased over the incident. Will had been attending the prince in the fall of 1604 and had been accompanied by Mr. Bird.

The tutor was recovering from his wound by August 1605, as Viscount Lisle's estate agent, Thomas Golding, reported, but his attitude was not improving. Bird was indiscreet enough to demand to return to Penshurst; Golding told him to stay someplace in London with his surgeon until he was fully healed.[86] Lisle was relieved to hear that Lady Lisle refused to take Bird back at Penshurst, and remarked that he cared no more about the man now that he was recovered.[87] Although Bird suffered a relapse,[88] he received no further sympathy from the Sidneys and his career at Penshurst was finished. When Will went abroad in 1610 for a projected three years of travel, he was accompanied by a new companion, one Benjamin Rudyard.[89]

Perhaps this episode was the reason William was not admitted to the Knights of the Bath at the time his younger brother Robert was. Sir William Browne remarked pointedly on the omission; Robert was listed among the twenty-four new knights admitted in honor of the creation of Prince Henry as Prince of Wales in 1610.[90]

Of course, the viscount expected his oldest son to follow in his footsteps, and, probably as much to begin to establish him in a position to succeed to the governorship of Flushing as to pick up the income involved, Lisle bestowed one of the garrison's companies on Will in November 1606.[91] Precocious as he might have been in having stabbed a man nearly to death the year before, the sixteen year old was not qualified to run a company, particularly since he resided in England at the time. Lieutenant-Governor Browne installed Ensign Watkins as de facto captain, ordered that the boy's colors should take precedence over his own, and promised to serve Will as faithfully as he served Lisle.[92] Will remained in England, where he matriculated at Christ Church, Oxford, on February 27, 1606/07.[93] In 1611, he was knighted, but at the end of 1612 he died of smallpox.[94] His passing was sudden; he had been thought to be almost well. Lord Lisle was left with only one son to carry on his name and fortune.

The boy born with the measles grew into a vigorous child, well able to withstand the vicissitudes of sixteenth-century life and health care. In an age when one could die of lockjaw or gangrene from a minor cut, "Robin" survived a serious accident that involved one wound described only as "dangerous," another on his head, and a third and painful one on his hip, as well as numerous scratches and bruises. The mishap occurred when he was twelve and took place at Oxford, where he had been studying for a year with his brother.[95] No evidence suggests that either boy was studious—indeed, Sidney had to order them to return to school from their vacations. However, Robert inherited his father's interest in history and added a number of entries to Lisle's commonplace book, which was devoted to the subject. He also developed a lifelong penchant for journalizing and left a loquacious diary that forms a large part of the Dudley and De L'Isle papers.

Early on, Lisle procured a company at Flushing for Robert. In 1610, Captain John Sidney died, leaving a company vacant in the garrison. Side-stepping a promise to the prince, who expected to be given the next vacant company, and bypassing Captain Sidney's brother Phillip, who expected to succeed to this company, Sidney placed his fourteen-year-old son in the position.[96] Robert took over no more responsibility than did William. In time, though, he did build a military career in the Low Countries, and after Flushing was returned to the Dutch, the young Sir Robert obtained a position as colonel of the English regiment that remained in Zealand in the pay of the States General.

As a young man, Robert was said to have resembled his deceased uncle, Sir Philip, with a long, pock-marked face "of high blood."[97] Married in 1616 to Dorothy Percy, daughter of Henry, earl of Northumberland, Robert succeeded his father as Viscount Lisle in 1618 and as earl of Leicester in 1626. Under Charles I, he was sent on embassies to Christian IV of Denmark, to the Duke of Holstein, and to France, and he was appointed a privy councillor. Although he was associated with a faction known to be Protestant without being Puritan and inclined to support the king against rebellion, his attitude toward French Protestantism earned him Laud's hostility and a reputation for Puritanism. In 1641, he was appointed Lord Lieutenant of Ireland, but the rebellion there combined with his own bookish, unassertive nature to keep him in England and make his brief tenure in office miserable. Out of favor for a period, he retired to Penshurst. When Charles I was executed, Northumberland recommended that his sister, Lady Leicester, take charge of the Princess Elizabeth and her brother, the duke of Gloucester. The royal children were brought to Penshurst, where they resided for over a year, until they fled to the continent. Pressed by his legal proceedings, Leicester half-heartedly pledged his faith to the Commonwealth, but when, in 1660, he returned to his seat in the House of Lords, he voted in favor of Restoration. Charles II reappointed him a privy councillor in 1660, but he soon retired to Penshurst, to take no further part in politics. He and Lady Dorothy had six sons and four daughters, including Philip, third earl of Leicester, Algernon, the renowned Republican, and Dorothy, made famous by Waller as his "Sacharissa."[98]

Mary, born in 1586 or 1587,[99] was the eldest of the Sidney daughters and a precocious and affectionate child. It was she who insisted on accompanying Lady Sidney to Flushing in 1597, and Whyte remarks upon her longing to receive letters from her father.[100] Mary was wed to Sir Robert Wroth in 1604. She led an active social life at James I's court, and, like her father, soon became known as a sympathetic supporter of the arts. She performed in Ben Jonson's *Masque of Blackness* (Twelfth Night, 1604/05), and he dedicated his play, *The Alchemist* (1610), to her as well as addressing to her a sonnet ("The Underwoods," No. 46) and two epigrams (103 and 105). Other writers paid tribute to her, among them Chapman, who included a sonnet addressed to her in the preface to his translation of Homer's *Iliad,* and George Wither, who described her as "Arts Sweet Lover" (*Abuses Stript,* epigram 10). Wroth died in 1614, followed, two years later, by their only child. Lady Mary managed her own affairs, but was so financially pressed that she had to obtain the king's protection against her creditors. In 1621, she published "The Countess of Montgomery's Urania," a romance in the style of Sir Philip Sidney's *Arcadia.* She closed the four-book volume with a collection of poems reminiscent of her father's verse. The work was perceived as satirical, and some of the amorous adventurers at court, seeing themselves reflected in it, expressed their resentment. She removed the book from circulation, and the controversy subsided.[101]

Philippa was the last of Lady Barbara and Sir Robert's children to predecease them. She was apparently one of Sidney's favorite children, although he writes rather little of her in his correspondence until after her death. Ben Jonson, who, after Lord Lisle became established at James I's court, was an intimate friend of the Sidney family, wrote a pretty epigram to Philippa.[102] She was married to Sir John Hobart, later earl of Buckinghamshire; for this occasion, her father produced the substantial portion of £4,000.[103] When she died in 1620, Lord Lisle wrote that "my hart is to full of grief to use many words. . . . Wee have lost as worthy and loving a daughter as ever father and mother had."[104]

The Sidney family seat was and is at Penshurst. Sir Robert took great pride in the manor and park there. Penshurst Park and the adjoining village of Penshurst are situated in the valley of the Medway River, which flows through the loveliest countryside in Kent. The manor was granted to Sir William Sidney in 1552 by Edward VI, an event recorded for posterity over the gateway to the grounds. At the time the Sidney family acquired it, the building already was graced by an impressive great hall built by the previous owner, Sir John de Pulteney; the sixty-foot-high room built of traceried local sandstone streaked with iron deposits has been called the finest surviving example of a fourteenth-century great hall.[105] Sir Henry Sidney added a range of brick buildings on the west side and the entire front of the courtyard, including a gatehouse dated 1585. Sir Robert's additions comprised a long gallery on the west side linking the southern side with the gabled buildings erected by his father, and a series of state rooms, including the Solar Room, Queen Elizabeth's Room, and the Tapestry Room. He also built new stables and a costly new fence around the deer park.

The building projects at Penshurst were one of Sidney's favorite avocations. He left the work for the most part in the care of his employee, Robert Kerwin, who, when Sidney was away, was supervised by Lady Sidney. He felt no discomfort about his wife's ability to take command of the projects and to handle the large expenses involved. "I need not send to know how my buidings goe forward," he wrote to her, "for I ame sure you are so good a housewyfe, you may be trusted with them."[106] Kerwin occasionally sent Sidney reports on their progress and estimates of costs; he was very proud of the new wainscotting on the gatehouse, which was worked in with the old only after great difficulty.[107]

Quality construction came no cheaper in the sixteenth century than it does in the twentieth, and Kerwin's progress reports invariably contained requests for money; £15 and £20 at a time to pay workmen; a £500 estimate on the stables and tower,[108] weekly charges of £15, continuing arrears of 20 marks here, £50 there.[109] At times, Sidney had difficulty carrying the endless expense. "I know not how to provyde for the present and especially for the paiment of my workmen,"[110] he confided to his wife in 1594. Time did not improve the Sidneys' financial status enough to make the costs any easier to bear. "I never was in that case in my lyfe as I ame now," he wrote in 1607. Besides £2,000 in debts incurred in London plus the interest accruing, the household debts, "many of them to poor and clamorsom persons," came to £1,000.[111]

The ruinous cost of the construction prompted Thomas Golding to reply to Lisle's 1610 scheme to enlarge the deer park with a bold remonstrance. The loss of rents, he observed, would deprive Lisle's posterity of a large part of his hereditary income, and the viscount had run up a series of consuming debts. Penshurst already had as large a park as any in that part of England, capable of maintaining four hundred deer. The countryside, he remarked, was not sufficiently "sportely" to call "such for whose sake" Lord Lisle would enlarge the park—probably he hoped to attract the king and his retinue to Penshurst with these new facilities. Golding thought the popularity of hunting for sport only a fashion that was not likely to continue for long. "How you will raise money to make the work good," protested the fearless Golding, "I cannot guess."[112] Common sense prevailed, at least to a limited extent, and Lisle was persuaded not to enlarge the park but only to build a new and expensive fence around it.

One may reasonably wonder why, when Lisle's debts were bringing his estate to a "ruinous" condition, he persisted in costly construction projects at Penshurst. No doubt, he could not bear to see the elaborate projects going on at the earl of Dorset's country house, Knoll, without answering in kind. Cobham Hall and Somerhill were also nearby, and Penshurst could not be permitted to suffer in comparison to those buildings. Too, he must have felt some need to continue what he had begun; a sudden cessation of his projects, which began as early as 1594, would have made his financial plight painfully obvious. "If my ill-willers should know in what state I were," he remarked in 1607, "it were subject enough for them to laugh at mee forever."[113]

Penshurst had a reputation for hospitality; royalty as well as humbler friends were often entertained there. Queen Elizabeth danced with Robert Dudley in the ballroom and, years later, she revisited Sidney's estate in her old age. "Her Highness hath done honor to my poor house by visiting me," he reported to Sir John Harrington in the summer of 1600. "At going up stairs she called for a staff, and was much wearied in walking about the house, and said she wished to come another day."[114] The next reign brought another royal visit, when James I dropped by unexpectedly with his son, Henry, Prince of Wales, while out hunting one day.[115]

Lady Anne Clifford's diary gives a suggestion of how the gatherings at Penshurst went. In August 1617, Lady Anne's husband, Richard Sackville, earl of Dorset, went over from Knole to Penshurst, where he hunted in the park and met Lord Montgomery, Lord Hay, and much other company. Several days later, Lady Anne rode over on horseback and spent the day with Lady Dorothy Sidney, Elizabeth Lady Manners, Francis, Lord Norris, and Lady Mary Wroth. She returned home late that evening, accompanied part of the way by her young cousin, Barbara Sidney.[116]

Lisle must have wanted to maintain his ancestral home in such a way that it would continue to attract the illustrious guests who were important to his family's fortunes. Probably his limited financial resources, rather than any innate simplicity of taste, were responsible for the characteristic restraint and sense of masculine, homely comfort that Ben Jonson admired in his poem, "To Penshurst."

Sidney took great pleasure in the care of his gardens at Penshurst, and Lady Sidney was famous for her gifts of fresh fruit from the orchards on the estate.[117] They were particularly fond of apricots, one of many varieties of fruit that flourished there. When Sidney was feeling ill at Hampton Court, Barbara comforted him by sending him more peaches than he knew what to do with, to his delight and amusement.[118] In 1611, they had an especially fine harvest, "as fair a show as ever was seen hereabouts": cherries, plums, melicotons, peaches, pears, and apples, as well as large quantities of apricots, thrived in the gardens.[119] In his letters, Sidney frequently inquired about the gardens, and he occasionally sent trees from the Low Countries to be planted at Penshurst.[120] When a late frost struck while he was at Greenwich, he worried about the apricots and peaches, and later he proposed to enhance the grounds by establishing a heronry at Lompit Grove.[121]

Only one other estate among Sidney's many holdings occupied much of his attention: the manor and park of Otford. Sir Henry Sidney had applied for the possession of Otford in 1573, but failed to obtain it.[122] In 1587, Sir Robert was granted the stewardship of Otford,[123] and from that position he received the small sums of 2 d. a day for the care of the house, 4 d. a day for the gardens, and £13 13 s. 14 d. a year for the great park. A survey taken in 1596 inspired him with a passion to own the place, and a lengthy suit to the queen ensued. Elizabeth refused to part with it for some years. Sidney enlisted Buckhurst and Sir John Fortescue in his cause, but to no avail. About 1599, Sidney's rival, Lord Cobham, entered the competition, prevailing upon Fortescue, Buckhurst, and Cecil to urge the queen to grant it to him. The machinations wound on for months. Cobham tried to buy from a Mr. Johns his interest in the park and was assailed by Lady

Warwick, Lady Huntingdon, and Rowland Whyte. Burghley supported Cobham; Buckhurst opposed him, and the queen declined to favor anyone.[124] Finally, in November 1601, Elizabeth sold Otford to Sidney to help finance the Irish venture. Upon payment of £2,000, the queen granted Sidney the mansion, all the buildings adjacent to it, the soil on which they stood, the great park and its herbage and pannage, three lodges, and the deer and wild animals to be held for a small annual fee.[125] In 1605, Lord Lisle leased the demesne lands of Otford to Rowland Whyte, in reversion, for forty years.[126] Between 1601 and 1625, Lisle conveyed his interest to Nicholas Crispe and his own son-in-law, Sir Thomas Smith, and to Smith's heirs forever.[127]

Otford was a place of some historical interest. It had been built in the fifteenth century by Archbishop Warham and may have been a factor in a quarrel between Thomas Beckett and Henry II. William Lambarde called Warham's palace there "gorgeous," but quoted Erasmus as saying Otford was a place "more meete for a religious mans meditation, then for a Prinses pleasure" until Warham built his house there.[128] By the time Sidney obtained the property, the buildings had deteriorated—he estimated the cost of repairing the park at £300[129] and guessed it would take £1,000 to make the manor a fit place for the queen to stay.[130]

Probably Sidney wanted the park and manor at Otford mostly for financial and political reasons. Otford represented an income of £400 a year.[131] Naturally, too, he wished to prevent his enemy Cobham from picking up any more land in Kent. Land meant influence in the county elections. The more manors one controlled, the more freeholders one could influence. Sidney was advised to retain as much property as possible, "for by it you shalbe ever able to have many freeholders at your command, which in a mans own cowntrey is specially to be regarded."[132]

The Sidney family landholdings were widespread. At Sir Philip's death, Sidney inherited, in addition to Penshurst, estates at Lamberhurst, Salehurst, Mathersum, Brightling, Woodruff, and Michelmarshe, plus lands in Lincolnshire and Sussex, worth a combined yearly total of £1,090 in rents. Lady Sidney brought substantial holdings in Wales when she married him. The sale of some of this Welsh land produced, about the turn of the century, some £2,800. By the time of James's accession, Sidney had been forced to sell the Lincolnshire property and the lands upon the Sussex downs, but he still retained some of the Welsh lands and had added Otford to his holdings, so that his combined rentals totaled £1,790 a year.[133] In addition, Sidney inherited the estates of Robertsbridge Abbey in Sussex, which had been acquired by Sir Henry Sidney in 1538 in exchange for lands in Yorkshire that had been rented to Robert Sidney's grandfather, Sir William Sidney, in 1514.[134] The weald of Kent was rich in iron ore deposits, and, in 1541, Sir Henry erected a furnace and a forge near the abbey. He imported German and Dutch experts, who established production of iron and steel armor at Robertsbridge.[135] Sir Robert continued to operate the furnaces and obtained a small income from them.

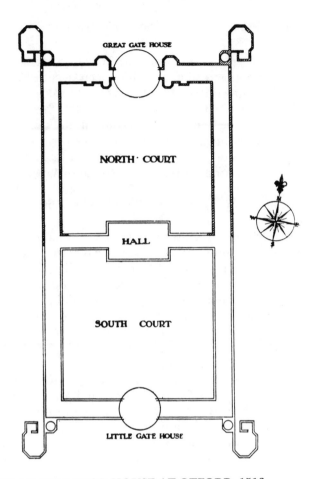

SKETCH PLAN OF MANOR HOUSE AT OTFORD, 1516
Source: Hesketh, facing page 5

This Plan is based partly upon the existing remains of the House, and partly upon information detailed in the Survey made in 1573.

(1) Existing remains are shewn locked in. The lower portion and foundations of the South end are, however, still partly *in situ*, but are omitted from plan as too fragmentary to enable a fair representation of this and of the building to be drawn.

(2) The portions hatched in are detailed in the Survey, but the length of the East and West galleries and the positions of the Gate Houses are pure conjecture.

(3) The portions not shaded are also pure conjecture, but are based upon an examination of the Site, and are supported by the Survey, and serve to indicate the general dimensions of the plan of the original building.

y Don Wayne

Sidney also inherited a complicated, long-drawn-out lawsuit between the Dudleys and Henry, Lord Berkeley that had begun in 1584. Berkeley lost properties worth about £390 a year to the Dudleys, which went to Sidney as their heir. After the accession of James I and the renewed influence of his allies, the Howards, Berkeley hoped to force Lord Lisle to come to terms over the lands. An agreement was reached in 1609, and the viscount surrendered the property in return for a cash payment of £7,320.[136] Lisle had already persuaded James to take back part of this property, Alton Woods, in exchange for his discharge of Lady Warwick's debts and a payment of £3,000.[137]

Review of the details of Sidney's domestic life suggests that, despite their unending financial difficulties and Sir Robert's frequent absence from home, the family was unusually close-knit. Sir Robert and Lady Barbara were as luckily matched a couple as any at Elizabeth's court: unlike many of their contemporaries, they appear to have loved each other despite their married state.

> Thy lady's noble, fruitful, chaste withall.
> His children thy great lord may call his own;
> A fortune, in this age, but rarely known. . . .
> Ben Jonson
> "To Penshurst," *The Forrest*

Lady Sidney was a warm and loving wife, a hard-working, successful mother, a gracious hostess. She was an efficient housewife at a time when the job entailed, for a woman in her position, supervision of a large staff of domestic servants, tutors, park stewards, gardeners, and farmhands; strict management of income due from a complicated variety of sources; the education and upbringing of nearly a dozen children; entertainment of houseguests who ranged from captains from Flushing to the queen of England; supervision of seemingly endless building projects; maintenance of houses in Kent, in London, and in Flushing. Her array of responsibilities would give pause to a highly paid business executive of our century. She handled this load with grace and skill, and in doing so provided Sir Robert with a home to which he was always eager to return.

NOTES

1. Pedigree of Lady Lisle, July 1608, KAO DeL'Isle, U 1500 F/13.
2. September 8, 1584, Stone, *Crisis,* p. 600. An elegy to Gamage survives as an example of the "new" Welsh free verse, rare before 1600. Printed in Thomas Parry, *A History of Welsh Literature,* trans. H. Idris Bell (Oxford: Clarendon Press, Oxford University Press, 1955), p. 177, it reveals little more about Gamage than that he was considered learned and that he was interred in London.
3. Dated 23 September 1584, F. B. Young, *Mary Sidney, Countess of Pembroke* (London: David Nutt, 1912), p. 50.
4. Stone, *Crisis,* p. 660.

5. Young, p. 51.

6. Sir Simonds D'Ewes, *A Compleat Journal of the Votes, Speeches, and Debates, both of the House of Lords and the House of Commons, Throughout the Whole Reign of Queen Elizabeth, of Glorious Memory* (London: Printed by J. S., 1708), p. 491, et passim.

7. Sidney to Lady Sidney, Hague, 22 May 1592, *HMCD* 2:127.

8. Sidney to Lady Sidney, 28 September 1590, ibid., 2:112–13.

9. Sidney to Lady Sidney, Hague, May 13, 1592, Additional Ms 15914, fol. 45, British Library, London, England.

10. Whyte to Sidney, London, 29 November 1595, *HMCD* 2: 191–92.

11. Gilpin to Sidney, 30 September 1596, ibid., 2:224–25.

12. MS. Cotton Augustus I. ii. fol. 105, British Library, London, England.

13. Sidney to Lady Sidney, Hague, 22 May 1592, KAO De D'Isle, U 1475 C81/17; also, incompletely transcribed, in *HMCD* 2:127.

14. Uvedall to Sidney, 27 February [1592/93], *HMCD* 2:131.

15. Uvedall to Sidney "at his hous at Dougat," February and March 1592/92, ibid., and ibid., 2:132–34.

16. Sidney to Lady Sidney, N.D. [? October 1, 1594], KAO De L'Isle U 1475 C81/27.

17. Sidney to Lady Sidney, [London], 3 June 1594, *HMCD* 2:153.

18. Sidney to Lady Sidney, [Greenwich], 21 May 1594, KAO De L'Isle, U 1475 C81/37.

19. Collins, 1:120.

20. Sidney to Lady Sidney, Greenwich, [1594], KAO De L'Isle, U 1475 C81/137; Sidney to Lady Sidney, [1 October 1594], ibid., C81/37.

21. Sidney to Lady Sidney, [London], 3 June 1594, *HMCD* 2:153.

22. Sidney to Lady Sidney, [23 August 1594], ibid., 2:154–55.

23. Sidney to Lady Sidney, [Court], 20 September 1594, ibid., 2:156.

24. Sidney to Lady Sidney, 22 September 1594, ibid., 2:157.

25. Stone, *Crisis*, pp. 387–88.

26. Sidney to Lady Sidney, Greenwich, 22 February 1594/95, KAO De L'Isle, U 1475 C81/56.

27. Sidney to Lady Sidney, Greenwich, 2 March 1594/95, *HMCD* 2:157.

28. Sidney to Lady Sidney, London, 4 March 1594/95, ibid., 2:158.

29. Sidney to Lady Sidney, Off Margate, 2 August 1595, KAO De L'Isle, U 1475 C81/61.

30. Sidney to Lady Sidney, Margate, 3 August 1595, *HMCD* 2:159.

31. Sidney to Lady Sidney, Flushing, 25 August 1595, ibid., 2:160.

32. Sidney to Lady Sidney, Flushing, 12 September 1595, ibid., 2:161.

33. Whyte to Sidney, London, 8 October 1595, ibid., 2:171.

34. Whyte to Sidney, London, 29 October 1595, ibid., 2:178.

35. Whyte to Sidney, 6 November 1595, ibid., 2:183.

36. Whyte to Sidney, London, 29 November 1595, ibid., 2:191–92.

37. Sidney to Lady Sidney, [Flushing], 13 November 1595, ibid., 2:191–92.

38. Whyte to Sidney, Penshurst, 23 October 1595, ibid., 2:176.

39. Sidney to Lady Sidney, Middleburgh, 27 October 1595, ibid., 2:177.

40. Sidney to Lady Sidney, Flushing, 25 August 1595, ibid., 2:160.

41. Sidney to Lady Sidney, Middleburgh, 27 October 1595, ibid. 2:177.

42. Whyte to Sidney, London, 29 November 1595, ibid., 2:191.

43. Whyte to Sidney, London, December 2, 1595, *HMCD* 2:193; Collins, 1:370–71.

44. Whyte to Sidney, London, 5 December 1595, *HMCD* 2:195.

45. Sidney to Lady Sidney, Flushing, 9 December 1595, ibid., 2:197.

46. Ibid.

47. Whyte to Sidney, Flushing, London, 14 December 1595, ibid., 2:197.

48. Whyte to Sidney, London, 26 December 1595, ibid., 2:204–5.

49. Whyte to Sidney, London, 3 January 1595/96, ibid., 2:205; Collins, 1:286.

50. Sidney to Lady Sidney, Flushing, 29 August 1596, *HMCD* 2:216.

51. Sidney to Lady Sidney, Flushing, January 1596/97. KAO De L'Isle, U 1475 C81/88.

52. Whyte to Sidney, 22 February 1596/97, *HMCD* 2:236–37.

53. Whyte to Sidney, Strand, 28 February 1596/97, ibid., 2:240–41.

54. Whyte to Sidney, 2 March 1596/97, ibid., 2:242.

55. Stone, *Crisis*, p. 662.

56. Whyte to Sidney, Baynard's Castle, 15 November 1599, *HMCD* 2:416.

57. Stone, *Crisis*, p. 662.

58. Whyte to Sidney, Baynard's Castle, 3 May 1600, *HMCD* 2:458.

Really a compilation
of inf in HMC letters

59. Whyte to Sidney, Nonesuch, 12 September 1599, ibid., 2:390; Whyte to Sidney, Baynard's Castle, 29 November 1599, ibid., 2:419.

60. Young, pp. 50–55, passim.

61. D. M. Meads, "Introduction," *The Diary of Lady Margaret Hoby* (London: George Rutledge, 1930), p. 9.

62. Ibid., p. 10.

63. Whyte to Sidney, London, 27 September 1595, *HMCD* 2:165–66.

64. Whyte to Sidney, London, 15 October 1595, ibid., 2:173.

65. Sidney to Lady Sidney, Flushing, 27 March [1597], ibid., 2:257.

66. Sidney to Lady Sidney, Flushing, 21 March [1597], ibid., 2:253–354.

67. Whyte to Sidney, April 4, 1597, ibid., 2:260–63.

68. Sidney to Lady Sidney, Flushing, 20 April 1597, Collins, 2:43–44.

69. Sidney to Lady Sidney, Flushing, April 22, 1597, *HMCD* 2:270.

70. Whyte to Sidney, Strand, May 13, 1597, ibid., 2:278–79.

71. Sidney to Lady Sidney, Flushing, 9 May 1597, ibid., 2:276–77.

72. *PC* 27:152.

73. Collins, 1:120.

74. Rubbings from the Brasses of the Sydney Family, Additional MS 393794, British Library, London, England.

75. Browne to Sidney, 16 August 1604, *HMCD* 3:304; John Chamberlain to Dudley Carleton, London, 23 December 1602, in N. E. McClure, ed. *The Letters of John Chamberlain*, 2 vols. (Philadelphia: American Philosophical Society, 1939), 1:178.

76. Whyte to Sidney, Penshurst, 28 September 1596, *HMCD* 2:246.

77. Whyte to Sidney, 21 February 1596/97, ibid., 2:235–36.

78. Whyte to Sidney, 26 April 1600, ibid., 2:457.

79. Whyte to Sidney, 22 December 1599, ibid., 2:424.

80. Whyte to Sidney, 12 April 1600, ibid., 2:455.

81. Sidney to Lady Sidney, Flushing, 24 November 1596, ibid., 2:227.

82. Sidney to Lady Sidney, Flushing, 9 May 1597, ibid., 2:276–77.

83. Whyte to Sidney, Baynard's Castle, 24 January 1599/1600, ibid., 2:434.

84. Sidney to Golding, N.P., N.D., KAO De L'Isle, U1500 C1/2.

85. G. B. Harrison, *A Jacobean Journal (1603–1606)* (New York: MacMillan, 1941), p. 219, 6 August 1605.

86. Golding to Lisle, Penshurst, 18 August 1605, *HMCD* 3:178.

87. Lisle to Lady Lisle, Flushing, 25 August 1605, ibid., 3:462.

88. Golding to Lisle, Penshurst, 25 August 2605, ibid., 3:192.

89. License to Sir William Sidney, son and heir of Viscount Lisle, and to Benjamin Rudyard, to travel for three years [Daguet], 15 January 1610, *CSP Dom.* 8:581.

90. Browne to William Trumbull, Flushing, 28 May 1610, in Great Britain, Historical Manuscripts Commission, *Report on the Manuscripts of the Marquess of Downshire*, series 80, 4 vols. (London: HMSO, 1924), 3:302.

91. Browne to Sidney, Flushing, 4 November 1606, *HMCD* 3:321.

92. Browne to Sidney, Flushing, 20 December 1606, ibid., 3:335.

93. Ibid., 4:279 n.

94. Chamberlain to Carleton, London, 17 December 1612, McClure, 1:397.

95. Thomas James to Lisle, [Penshurst], 31 August 1607, *HMCD* 3:399; Golding to Lisle, [Before 31 August 1607], ibid., 3:464.

96. Ibid., 4:235, 239, 241, passim.

97. Ben Jonson, "Conversations with Drummond (1619)," in *Ben Jonson*, ed. C. H. Herford and E. M. Simpson, 11 vols. (Oxford: Oxford University Press, 1925–52), 1:138–39.

98. *DNB*, s.v. "Sidney, Robert, Second Earl of Leicester."

99. Margaret A. Witten-Hannah, "Lady Mary Wroth's 'Urania': the Work and the Tradition," (Ph.D. thesis, University of Auckland, December 1978), p. 16.

100. Whyte to Sidney, Strand, 15 April 1597, *HMCD* 2:270.

101. *DNB*, s.v. "Wroth, Mary."

102. "Epigram to Mrs. Philip Sidney," in Herford, *Jonson*, 8:73.

103. Stone, *Crisis*, p. 507.

104. Leicester to Lady Leicester, Hampton Court, 30 September 1620, KAO De L'Isle, U 1500 C1/20.

105. Arthur Oswald, *Country Houses of Kent* (London: Country Life, 1933), p. 28.

106. Sidney to Lady Sidney, [May 1594], *HMCD* 2:153.

107. Robert Kyrwyn to Sidney, Penshurst, 1599/[1600], ibid., 2:426.

108. Kyrwyn to Sidney, Penshurst, 13 February 1599/[1600], ibid., 2:437–38.

109. Goldyng to Lisle, Penshurst, 10 April 1612, ibid., 5:45–47.

110. Sidney to Lady Sidney, Greenwich, 28 August 1594, ibid., 2:155.

111. Lisle to Lady Lisle, Court, 10 November 1611, ibid., 3:341.

112. Golding to Lisle, Penshurst, 6 May 1611, ibid., 4:265–67.

113. Ibid., 3:431–33.

114. Frederick Chamberlain, *The Private Character of Queen Elizabeth* (New York: Dodd, Mead, 1922).

115. Philip Sidney, "Penshurst Place," in *Memorials of Old Kent,* ed. Reverend P. H. Ditchfield (London: Benrose and Sons, 1907), pp. 215–27.

116. George C. Williamson, *Lady Anne Clifford, Countess of Dorset, Pembroke, and Montgomery, 1590–1696. Her Life, Letters, and Work* (1922; 2nd ed., Yorkshire: S. R. Publishers, 1967).

117. See, for example, Lisle to Lady Lisle, Hampton Court, 8 September 1608, *HMCD* 4:40.

118. Lisle to Lady Lisle, Hampton Court, 24 September 1609, ibid., 4:161.

119. Golding to Lisle, Penshurst, 6 May 1611, ibid., 4:266.

120. Sidney to Lady Sidney, Flushing, 2 October 1596, ibid., 2:226, et passim.

121. Sidney to Golding, Greenwich, 3 April 1605, ibid., 3:154–55.

122. Hesketh, p. 9.

123. Ibid.

124. *HMCD* 2:407–60, passim.

125. Hesketh, pp. 11–12.

126. *CSP Dom.* 8:222.

127. Ibid.

128. William Lambarde, *A Perambulation of Kent* (1576; rept. ed., London: Baldwin, Cradock, and Joy, 1826), p. 463.

129. Whyte to Sidney, 10 November 1599, *HMCD* 2:412.

130. Sidney to Cecil, Flushing, 6 February 1599/1600, SP 84/60, fols. 37–38; Whyte to Sidney, 2 February 1599/1600, *HMCD* 2:435–36.

131. Additional MS 12066.

132. Ibid.

133. Ibid.

134. KAO De L'Isle Catalogue, 1:25.

135. Ernest Straker, *Wealden Iron* (London: G. Belland Sons, Ltd., 1931), pp. 362, 178, 313.

136. Lawrence Stone, *Family and Fortune, Studies in Aristocratic Finance in the Sixteenth and Seventeenth Centuries* (Oxford: Clarendon Press, Oxford University Press, 1973), p. 249.

137. Sidney to King James I, [1604] *HMC Salisbury* 16:461; Warrant to Pay Robert Sidney £3,000, February 1611 [O.S.], Signet Office Docket Book, 503:5, Public Record Office, London, England.

[9]
Poet and Patron

Outdated
Croft etc

The identification of Robert Sidney as author of a ninety-page autograph manuscript notebook of poems was first announced in 1973 by P. J. Croft. Since the nineteenth century, perhaps because its green binding is lettered along the spine "Sonnets by the Earl of Leicester, M.S.," the work had been assumed to be Robert Dudley, Earl of Leicester's. A glance at the two men's handwriting reveals the disparity between their styles, and Croft demonstrates beyond any doubt, in his *Autograph Poetry in the English Language,* that the notebook was written by Sidney.[1]

The notebook, a sonnet cycle in many respects resembling Philip's *Astrophel and Stella,* is the longest autograph manuscript surviving from any poet of the Elizabethan period. That alone, the quality of the verses aside, makes it an extraordinary find. The manuscript contains thirty-five numbered sonnets and twenty-four other poems numbered separately, mostly titled "Songs," plus seven unnumbered poems that Sidney may not have intended to include in the final sequence. Taken together, the poems display a wide variety of prosodic form.

The papers seem to form a workbook. Sidney has heavily corrected the lines, irregularly numbered the pages, and in one place scribbled a note indicating a revision in the order of the sonnets. At the front of the volume a preliminary leaf is inscribed "For the Countess of Pembroke." The poems must be in draft form. Had Sidney regarded them as finished and ready for special presentation, he would have had them written up by his scribe, as did other writers of the time.

Katherine Duncan-Jones has suggested the manuscript is an "author's copy," and that Sidney, whose correspondents complained of his illegible handwriting, may have had a fair copy made and sent to Wilton, where it would have perished in the 1647 fire there. The present manuscript, then, would have been returned to Penshurst, whence it later emanated.[2]

When, on November 19, 1974, the manuscript was offered for sale at Sotheby's, its owner chose to remain anonymous. Because the manuscript contains two bookplates from Warwick Castle and because it had been last acquired for the Warwick Castle Library in 1842, unconfirmed speculation has suggested the owner was the present Lord Brooke, earl of Warwick.[3]

The notebook first appeared on record as lot 603, in Sotheby's sale catalogue of Sir Thomas Lloyd's library, dated February 22, 1833;[4] this catalogue correctly attributes the poems to Robert Sidney, first earl of Leicester. Noting the poetry's influence on the poems concluding the pastoral romance, *Urania*, written by Sidney's daughter, Lady Mary Wroth, Hilton Kelliher and Katherine Duncan-Jones have suggested the manuscript may have remained at Penshurst until it was acquired by Lloyd early in the nineteenth century.[5] The manuscript was purchased at the 1833 sale for £5 10s. by Thomas Thorpe. Later that year, he put it up for sale as lot 944, asking £10 10s. In his catalogue, Thorpe remarked that the poems must have been written by Sir Philip and transcribed by Sir Robert. Thorpe still possessed the manuscript the following year, when, in his sale catalogue, he numbered it as lot 601, and described it as the product of the first earl of Leicester.

The poems were purchased at this time by Edward King, Viscount Kingsborough, who had the manuscript rebound and the leaves gilt. It was then advertised in Kingsborough's 1842 sale catalogue of his Dublin library as lot 606 and acquired for 32s. by a bookseller, Thomas Rodd, who transferred it again to Thorpe. Perhaps deceived by the new binding, with its lettering identifying the poet only as "The Earl of Leicester," Thorpe ascribed the volume to Sidney's uncle, Dudley, in his catalogue issued between 1843 and 1848. This incorrect ascription was confirmed by William Blott, assistant president of the Inland, Foreign, and Ship Letter Office of the General Post Office, in a letter of January 24, 1848, which is attached to the front end paper. Blott's judgement seems to have been accepted until Croft's investigation proved its inaccuracy.[6]

From Thorpe, the manuscript was purchased in 1848 by Lord Brooke for the Warwick Castle Library, where it acquired two bookplates of that collection. Nothing more is recorded about its history until it appeared as lot 390 in the Sotheby's catalogue of Tuesday, November 19, 1974.[7]

Before Croft published his edition of Sidney's poems (*The Poems of Robert Sidney* edited from the poet's autograph notebook with introduction and commentary by P. J. Croft, Oxford: Clarendon Press, 1984), Katherine Duncan-Jones printed a modern-spelling text in 1981.[8] Its critical reception was poor. Duncan-Jones and Hilton Kelliher reproduced and discussed in detail sixteen of the poems in their *British Library Journal* article of autumn 1975,[9] and Duncan-Jones discussed twelve others in her article in *English Literary Renaissance*. Deborah Wright's study of the cycle produced a somewhat novel approach that has something to recommend it.[10]

Circumstances of Sidney's life during the 1590s plus internal and external evidence connected with the notebook and the poems suggest he wrote the verses around 1597. Themes of absence, bondage, rejection, unrewarded worth, and fruitless patience reveal that, while he wrote his cycle in the Petrarchan manner and worked within the genre's rigid conventions of subject matter, prosody, and imagery, he was preoccupied with the problems that beset him while he was maneuvering for advancement at court. At this time, he spent his longest single sojourn in Flushing, an enforced stay arranged by his rivals in England. Other themes suggest that the manner of his brother's death a decade earlier contined to haunt him. The literal matter of the love cycle, however, was probably fictional; that the poems celebrate a real amorous dalliance remains to be proven.

The most telling external evidence supporting a late 1590s date for the manuscript has been noted by Hilton Kelliher in the article he and Katherine Duncan-Jones published in 1975. The watermark of the paper, "a crowned shield of four quarters with an escutcheon superimposed on them," was first recorded in 1587, and it appears as late as 1614. Sidney wrote six letters on paper bearing this mark to his wife from Flushing between October 22 and December 25, 1596, and his lieutenant governor, Sir William Browne, used the paper to write five letters to Sidney between July 24, 1597 and April 23, 1598. Rowland Whyte entered in his account book on June 30, 1596 the purchase of "12 quire of gilt paper, xij s. ungilt paper v. s. hard wax ii x. vj d. for yr. Lo:" Thus a probable *terminus a quo* of 1596 can reasonably be accepted for the manuscript.

Song 6 ("Lady: Pilgrim") provides another clue in its formal resemblance to Sir Walter Raleigh's "Walsingham" ballad and to snatches of verse sung by Ophelia in Act IV of *Hamlet.* Shakespeare and Raleigh are thought to have based their lyrics on a popular song that may have been current late in the 1590s, and Croft suggests the same song inspired Sidney's ballad.[11] Kittredge, noting an allusion to the companies of child actors and the Wars of the Theatre (*Hamlet,* II. ii. 319–35), deduces a date between 1599 and 1601, when the children's companies began to present serious competition to adult companies, and concludes that the Stationer's Register entry of July 26, 1602 provides the latest date by which Shakespeare could have completed *Hamlet.*[12] The popular song, then, must have been current in the last years of the decade, certainly no later than 1602. Assuming Shakespeare, Raleigh, and Sidney would have lost interest in a light, insubstantial ditty once it grew dated, one may guess that Sidney probably wrote his ballad shortly before the turn of the century.

The verses' themes and imagery indicate that their author composed them during the darkest moments of his career, which came at this time. Sidney was discouraged over his failure to obtain favor at court after a decade of faithful service in the Low Countries. His alliance with Essex had culminated, in 1597, in his spectacular failure to gain the wardenship of the Cinque Ports, and it trailed off in a chain of repeated disappointments. The strain of Sir Robert's frustrated efforts combined with the Sidneys' financial difficulties to force them to give up their London household. In the spring, their circumstances were so straitened that Sidney could not even scrape up the £10 for his wife's weekly allowance, and he had to pawn some of their silver plate to meet their daily expenses.[13] Disgusted with their fruitless attempts to gain preferment through their influential friends, he called Lady Sidney to his side in Flushing, surprised Whyte by telling him to pursue a suit for a baronage instead of a concurrent one for the post of vice-chamberlain, and briefly retired from the struggle.

Sonnet Thirty-One evokes a mood consonant with the sense of defeat and discouragement Sidney's 1597 correspondence reflects.

> Gardens wch once in thowsand coulers drest
> shewed natures pryde: now in dead sticks abownd
> in whome prowd sumers treasure late was fowd
> now but the rags, of winters turncoate rest.

The image of a garden desolated by winter is one that he, who made a passion of the gardens at Penshurst, would have chosen as most expressive of a personal sense of loss. The line "I that fayre tymes lost, on tyme call in vaine" suggests he fears the best of his life is in the past and his decaying fortunes may never improve.

After eleven years in the Low Countries brought little recognition and no reward, Sidney understandably felt that time was no friend:

> Time cruel time how fast pass yow away
> and in my case from yowr own custome fly
> whyle I unknown in blackest shadowes ly.
>
> *Sonnet Thirty-Four*

The time he had patiently served in Flushing was not, as it turned out, an apprenticeship to a higher administrative post, but an exercise in frustration: "whoe to tyme trusts doth himself betray." In Song Eighteen, Sidney remarks that "delaies are death," and delay was exactly what he suffered as the queen's life eddied slowly to its end.

> . . . sense of present paines made not
> the feare appear of greater ill.
> But importunity hath gott
> Denials wch outright do kill.
>
> *Song Eighteen, 11. 5–8.*

Although the queen was led to believe that Sidney's income from the governorship and his companies at Flushing exceeded £2,000 a year in addition to much unreported graft, probably his total income in 1597 did not exceed £3,000, including the rents from his lands. Expenses in Flushing were extremely high, and he often had to use his own credit to obtain sufficient supplies and food for his men. The burden of maintaining three households was more than his finances could bear. Whyte's reports of the queen's exaggerated opinion of his wealth must have been galling.

> Alas why say yow I am ritch? when I
> doe begg, and begging scant a lyfe susteine.
>
> *Sonnet Twenty-One*

Too, "begging" exactly describes the tone of Sidney's and his lieutenant-governors' appeals to the government for ammunition, clothing, food, and fortification. The poverty of his troops must have reinforced Sidney's sense of his own shabby financial condition and exacerbated his resentment against the queen's continued refusal either to favor him or to supply the garrison adequately.

It is perhaps significant, too, that if Sidney wrote the poems in 1597, he did so in Flushing, where he had been informally rusticated as a result of the ill-fated endeavor to obtain the wardenship of the Cinque Ports. This circumstance would have resembled Philip's self-imposed exile at Wilton, where he composed the *Arcadia*.

The basic theme of the Petrarchan love cycle—endless, hopeless pursuit—serves admirably as a metaphor for Sidney's predicament. Like the lover, Sidney was engaged in a seemingly endless effort to obtain recognition from a thankless woman. He makes the narrator speak in terms laden with his own frustration, translating personal themes into abstract but familiar terms.

The overall argument can be summarized along these lines: the Poet loves a Lady, Charys (also called Lysa), with a pure and eternal love which he likens to religious devotion. To his despair, she breaks her vows to him when circumstances force him to leave her side. Her betrayal wounds him but does not kill his love. He pursues her; she rejects him. Obsessed with her, he suffers, but he revels in his agony. After a time, he grows bitter and says his love has gone to seed, transformed to hate. He tries to accept his fate and absent himself from her company, but ends finding absence more torment than presence. He returns to his pursuit of her, knowing the quest to be futile. Several poems seem not to be intended as part of the cycle, but they, too, echo Sidney's preoccupations of the 1597 period.

Playing repeatedly on the theme of absence, Sidney reminds the reader of the enforced absence from England he endured in 1597. In Song One, the lover compares himself to "An Anchorite, to living burial lead" (1. 21). He declares that his departure from the Lady, who is the delight of his life, causes him more grief than seeing "how some my fortunes cross" (stanza 3, 1. 15), a turn of phrase that brings to mind a 1597 letter to his wife in which he speaks of his plans being "crossed."[14] In the same letter, he expresses his feeling that the stagnation of his career is unfair and a fate unworthy of his talent, training, and birth; similarly, the poet in Song One describes his exile as his "unjust decay."

The special significance that the Petrarchan themes of absence and of departure enforced by duty had for Sidney exemplifies the appropriateness of the literary tradition to Sidney's personal dilemma. He personifies the absence theme three times, and allows the narrator to expand upon it repeatedly. Sonnet Thirty ("Absence I Cannot Say Thou Hyd'st My Light") suggests his frustration with the poor success of his campaign to put his career on a new track. Even while he was at court, he failed to persuade the queen to grant him any other sinecure than the one he held at Flushing. Time and again, like the rejected lover, he was rebuffed by his "lady," the queen, whether or not he managed to escape from Flushing to make his plea in person. "I present, absent ame; unseen in sight," he writes. The final two lines of Sonnet Thirty echo Sidney's distress over his fortunes:

> Present I see my cares avail me not
> Present not harckned, absent forgot.

In Sonnet Twenty-Three, another apostrophe to Absence, the lover complains of his captivity to a scornful mistress in terms that are rich with biographical implications:

> ... my lyfe, wch fetterd lyes
> and famisht, darck, in prison, cold doth rest,
> till when my lifes Queen present shines at last
> or medcin worse than greef it tries.

The cruel lady's repulses recall Queen Elizabeth's monotonous refusals of Sidney's suits.

> When I see her, I see scorns banner spred
> each word refuses, and each refuse gives death.

Two brief translations out of Seneca, which Katherine Duncan-Jones has identified as 11. 606–16 and 11. 398–403 of *Thyestes*, appear to speak directly to Sidney's concerns of the Cinque Ports period. Neither passage fits into the cycle. The first describes the turning of Fortune's wheel in terms that had become commonplace by the Renaissance. While those in high places may fall, those in humble circumstances may hope to rise:

> Let no man trust to much to seasons fayre
> Let none cast down of better tymes despayre.

The second makes a comment on Sidney's craving for fame and on the scant comfort allowed by the knowledge that, being neither powerful nor famous, he did not face the risks inherent to power and fame:

> ... a homely olde man I shal dy.
> on him a heavy death doth ly
> Whoe unto all men to much known
> unto himself doth dy unknown.

Another vein of peculiarly vivid language shows he was still haunted by his brother's unpleasant death, which had occurred a decade before. Robert was with Philip on the field before Zutphen and attended him as he lay dying of gangrene. At that time, Robert probably admired his older brother more than he did anyone else. By 1597, it must have been clear that much of Philip's fame as the perfect courtier and the gallant hero of the Protestant cause came from the circumstances of his death rather than from his accomplishments in life. Robert must have found it hard to reconcile himself to the gruesome manner of Philip's death, to its apparent futility, and to the irony of his posthumous fame.

The poems are permeated with images of wounds and slow suffering. Uniting all the pain is the idea that there is something inherently worthy in suffering that gives the sufferer solace or even cause to rejoice in his pain. The lover suffers in the cause of love and claims he is dying with its anguish. In Sonnet Twenty-Six, this convention is expressed in an image that brings to mind a picture of Philip's last days. The lover compares his love to a gangrenous limb, which must be cut off if he is to survive.

> Full of dead gangrenis doth the sick man lay
> whose death of part health of the rest must bee.

Elsewhere, the lover insists his anguish has a redeeming quality:

> The paines which I incessantly susteine,
> burning in hottest flames of love most pure,
> are ioies, not greefs, since each of them are sure
> witness, that faith, not will, in mee doth raine.
>
> Sonnet Two

Sometimes, he says, he clothes his wounds in glory:

> . . . on my ruins doe I builde my fame
> thus do my miseries appeer delights.

Anguish suffered in pursuit of a cause—love in the lover's case, the national religion in Philip's—is justified or even nullified by the worthy nature of the cause. The quasi-religious quality of the narrator's love, expressed in the divine nature that shines forth in the lady's features (Sonnets One, Three, and Sixteen) and in the devotion with which he serves love and the lady (Sonnets Four, Nine, and Thirty-Two; Song Eleven), suggests a metaphorical parallel between Philip's suffering and the lover's anguish. The nature of the lover's pain—traumatic, gangrenous, fevered— resembles the physical nature of Philip's. By his agony and death, Philip proved himself worthy of heaven and the queen's respect as the lover proves himself worthy of love's reward. Philip's redeeming devotion was vested in religion and in the developing phenomenon of nationalism; the lover is similarly devoted to love and the lady, expressed in neo-Platonic terms as a variety of religious experience.

> True vestale like wch wth most holy care
> preserve the several fyres [:] relligiously
> I doe mantein. . . .
>
> *Sonnet Three*

Robert found a way to come to terms with his brother's death, an end for which meaning could be established only in light of Philip's devotion to his faith and his queen, and he reveals that reconciliation in his individual-istic use of the Petrarchan conceit that suffering for love has an ennobling effect.

In her article, " 'Rosis and Lysa': Selections from the Poems of Sir Robert Sidney," Katherine Duncan-Jones reiterates the position she and Hilton Kelliher took in 1975. They suggested then that the lover's name, "Rosis," derived from Ro[bertus] Si[dneius] in much the same way "Philisides" was invented for the Arcadian character. The name "Lysa," they suggest, refers to a lady named Elizabeth, and the name "Charys," which occurs in four of the poems, derives from the family name "Carey." From this, they deduce that the sequence may be a celebration of a real or imaginary dalliance with Elizabeth Carey, daughter of Elizabeth Carey, Lady Hunsdon, patroness of Spenser and Nashe. In support of this propo-sition, they note that in Sonnet Twelve the lover says he was born on the lady's saint's day, and that Sidney was born on November 19, the day of St. Elizabeth of Hungary. They suggest, too, that the "toyes" to which Row-land Whyte alludes as a source of the queen's distrust involved some amor-ous behavior of his that took place at court in 1595 or 1596. Duncan-Jones also suggests that "Upon a Snufkin" might have been presented with the "perfumed skins" to which Whyte referred in October, 1595 (*HMCD* 2:171) as having been delivered to the still unidentified mistress of John Simmon. Whyte, Duncan-Jones suggests, may have been warning Sidney that his behavior was causing gossip at the court.

Some difficulties cling to this intriguing hypothesis. Literal identifica-tion of Sidney's lady with Elizabeth Carey is problematic. Born in 1576, Elizabeth was nineteen in 1595, when Duncan-Jones thinks the flirtation took place. That she was scarcely more than a child compared to the thirty-two-year-old Sidney might be allowed on the ground that liaisons between middle-aged men and teenaged girls are not uncommon. However, in 1595, Sidney was attempting to arrange a marriage between this particular girl and his nephew, William Herbert. The two young people were secretly meeting at Wilton in the fall of 1595,[15] because it was feared open talk of marriage would interfere with certain suits for land in which both Herbert and Elizabeth's mother, Lady Carey, were engaged. The marriage plans were broken off that winter by Herbert's father, the earl of Pembroke, to the annoyance of the earl of Essex and the girl's father, Sir George Carey.

Under these circumstances, the hypothesis that Sidney would have addressed a sonnet sequence celebrating his infatuation with Elizabeth Carey to her future mother-in-law is difficult to accept. The Countess of Pembroke may have been a friend of Lady Sidney, and it seems unlikely that Sidney would have been so indiscreet as to send her an admission of his faithlessness.

Elizabeth Carey married Sir Thomas Berkeley in February 1596, a year prior to the time Sidney probably wrote the poems. The Berkeley family was engaged in a suit with the Sidneys that dragged on for years and that was not conducive to affection between members of the two clans.

belabors obvious

The "two letters of [Sidney's] sealed with gold and the broad arrow-head, directed to two of the [queen's] maydes" that Kelliher and Duncan-Jones take as a clue to Sidney's amorous activities may indeed indicate some indiscretion. However, as we have seen in chapter 7, the slip was more likely political than romantic in nature. Kelliher and Duncan-Jones tie Whyte's later reference to the queen's remark about Sidney's "youthful toyes" to this incident, suggesting that here, too, Whyte alludes to some romantic liaison. The reference, in the same letter, to "the malice of the times" suggests the "youthful toyes" remark refers to the period of the Cinque Ports fiasco, when the atmosphere at court, at least for Sidney, was vicious. This was two years later than the time Kelliher and Duncan-Jones posit that Sidney was writing his poetry. Whyte alluded to the "toyes" in February 1599/1600. If, as Duncan-Jones hypothesizes, he was trying to warn Sidney to stop indulging in behavior that caused gossip in 1595, he was five years late in doing so. A veiled allusion was uncharacteristic of Whyte, who inclined to frankness where Sidney and his fortunes were concerned.

Sidney no doubt did write and speak to the women he knew in a manner that today might be regarded as flirtatious. "Ladies, you know, doe love protestacions and compliments," Whyte remarked, advising him to write in this vein to Lady Huntingdon.[16] In 1602, Sidney wrote gallantly to Mistress Anne Lovel, whom he addresses as his "cousin." In his letter, he thanks her for some unnamed favors and assures her of his affection, but on close reading his words say almost nothing. In the custom of his time, he might have addressed the same florid compliments to any lady, not intending them as anything more than ornate small talk. On the same day, he sent a brief letter, full of the current war news, to Sir Thomas Lovel, who might have been some relation to Mistress Anne.[17] He often sent gifts to ladies as gestures of friendship. In 1596, for example, he presented Louise de Coligny, Princess of Orange, with some monkeys,[18] which were accepted happily but not, one would expect, in a spirt of flirtation.

Sidney was unarguably happy with his wife. His correspondence reflects the consistency of their affection. Year by year, he assured his "sweteheart" of his love, insisting that "nothing can be so welcome heare as the good news of your own and my little ons welbeing."[19] He seems to have thought himself remarkable in this respect. "I would not for anything that the il husbands at the Court should know how fond I ame growne," he wrote, "to send you on this fashion the first dainties I can come by."[20] His exchanges with her continued in this vein until the end of her life. In 1620, writing to let her know "as now Your Ladyship is Countess of Leycester," the new earl ended his letter with this remark: "And sweethart, many yeares I pray God you may enjoy this name to my comfort, whoe will ever bee your most loving husband, Leycester."[21]

Song Six ("Lady: Pilgrim") has perhaps elicited as much comment as the rest of the poems taken together. The ballad appears at first reading to differ in content as well as in form from the other verses in the notebook.

Croft, Duncan-Jones, Kelliher, and I have taken it, in varying lights, as autobiographical and extrasequential. Deborah Wright, however, in a well-argued presentation, has suggested the poem has a function compatible with the sequence, and that its allusion to Raleigh's Walsingham ballad and to the contemporary "Gentle Heardsman," a poem in the same tradition, also serves a purpose within the cycle.

Wright points out that Song Six, without reference to the Walsingham allusion, shows that requited love is the *desideratum* of the sequence. It can be interpreted as urging the lady to recognize what she is forgoing. Since it is written from her point of view, it can also suggest to her the extent of her grief if she realizes the lover's worth too late. The allusion to the Walsingham ballad, Wright continues, implies that the lady has faults, and the allusion to "Gentle Heardsman" implies that grief and remorse await her if she fails him. The ballad is a tribute to her and an invitation to shared love, as well as an oblique reminder of her cruelty and the price she will pay if she fails to return the poet's love.[22]

In this view, the lady of the ballad is the sonneteer's beloved. It may be objected that the lady of Song Six, far from being a scornful mistress, seems to have loved her knight dearly; once she accepts that he is dead, she mourns

> Gone is ioy and pleasure:
> parfet love and care adieu
>   Farewel my lifes treasure. . . .
>
> Of my lyfe the summits were
>   the ioies his love did lend. . . .

However, she remarks—in keeping with Wright's hypothesis—"Faithles lyfe, true death, by thee/ our vowes in one shall live. . . ," and near the end of the ballad, she says that her lips had no power to bring him ease of mind, for he was "stung wth doubts wth longings mad." If indeed Song Six fits into the sequence as Wright has suggested, perhaps one may conclude that the poet's unhappiness is the result of his self-doubt or unfounded jealousy.

However one wishes to interpret Song Six, one cannot deny that the poem's lady and knight evoke Barbara and Robert Sidney. The unhappy knight turns his eyes "to the west . . . , where love fast holds his hart." The place of his exile, then, lay due east of the lady's home, as Flushing lies in relation to Penshurst. "Duty there the body ties," as duty consigned Sidney to Zealand, but "his sowle hence cannot part." The knight is as demoralized as Sidney was in 1597: "Spirits in him all spent bee/ all ioies in him end have." He is dying of a broken heart "neer unto the sea," where "absent ioies did him kill/ on a sandhil as he lay." The imagery suggests Flushing, a seaport in the sand on the Zealand coast. The knight tells the pilgrim his lady can be found "neer Medwayes sandy, bed," a reference to the Medway river, which flows through the village of Penshurst. This line has been revised from the less overtly literal "neer ritch tons sandy bed," another local allusion. The town of Tunbridge lies a short distance from Penshurst. The name *Tunbridge,* by analogy to *Cambridge* and *Oxford,* suggests a crossing over the river "Ton."[23]

The points of resemblance between the lady and Barbara Sidney are there. If Wright is correct in her surmise that Song Six fits into the sequence, it suggests that Sidney had a mental picture of Barbara as he visualized the characters in the sequence, which he intended to be fictional.

If Sidney did derive the name "Lysa" from "Elizabeth," it would not be surprising. It was one of the most common female names of the time. He was born on the saint's day of St. Elizabeth. It was also the name of the queen, the source of the real suffering (both his own and his brother's) that the lover's pain metaphorically recalls. Sidney could well have derived "Lysa" and "Charys" from Elizabeth Carey's name. He may have found the names euphonic; he may have chosen them for any number of reasons, ranging from a wholly different inspiration for the name "Charys" to the remote possibility that Elizabeth Carey was his lover.

The manuscript now in the collections of the British Library provides the only verse proven to have been written by Robert Sidney. An unconfirmed tradition holds that he wrote the lyrics to Robert Dowland's *Musicall Banquett* (1610).[24] No other poetry by Robert Sidney is known.

Sidney kept two lengthy commonplace books, one compiled around 1600, the other about twenty years later.[25] In them, Sidney reveals his passion for history; each is a collection of historical details concerning various ruling men or women. The first is organized under a series of specific, sometimes esoteric topics: lists of the kingdoms of the western and eastern empires, "principalities by election; principalities by succession of blood; princes which in theyr lifetime did appoint theyr successor," etc. Book I seems to be an attempt to cover all the many possibilities by which princes come into or go out of power, and the customs and circumstances of succession in the royal houses of Europe. Once having exhausted that subject, Sidney lists certain details about treaties and arbitration for treaties. Then he adds a few revealing topics that were of special interest to him: "examples of such as have bin raysed to great honor and happyness w[th]out contributing anything but very little of their own either industry or merritt as means to acquire the thing;" "that the Papall constitutions, and the Lawes of England are incompatible, and therefore it is impossible for an English papist to be a tru and faithfull subject to the Crowne of England." Many of the entries are annotated or enlarged in the hand of Sidney's son, Robert.

One of the most interesting entries, in light of the republican sympathies that cost the life of Sidney's grandson, Algernon, is made entirely in the second earl's hand, but annotated "partly out of a paper of my fathers." It is a brief discussion of royal prerogative, the gist of which suggests that Sidney believed the king's prerogative rested not in divine right, but rather depended on the "fundamentall Lawes" of the state he governed and varied from country to country. All princes, Sidney wrote, seek to extend their authority and free themselves from dependence on the will of the people, while the people attempt to obtain as much power as possible, "and hereupon growes the uncertainty of prerogative" (pp. 711ff).

The second commonplace book, dating from about 1620, traces the lineages of dozens of royal houses of Europe and the Middle East. It was perhaps of practical interest to one involved in diplomacy, for it provided a working knowledge of the background of most of the aristocracy a contemporary ambassador might encounter.

Another notebook survives, dating from 1604 or 1606.[26] It is partly devoted to twenty-two tables of money exchange copied out of a numismatic treatise by Juan de Mariana (1536–64), a liberal Spanish historian who taught in Rome, Flanders, and Paris during the 1560s. Sidney's interest in numismatics must have been on the order of a hobby, for the tables have little to do with contemporary money, except that two tables translate English coinage into sestertia. For the most part, they concern ancient Greek and Roman money. The remaining entries in the notebook concern metallurgy, a subject of interest to Sidney because of his ironworks at Robertsbridge, and further historical and genealogical topics similar to those of the two commonplace books.

These three manuscript notebooks confirm that the interest in history that Sidney expressed to his brother in 1580 stayed with him throughout his life. Because he painstakingly listed his sources, the notebooks reveal his wide range of reading, which covered an eclectic series of ancient and contemporary scholars. Many of these, such as Mariana and Jean Bodin (1530–96, author of *Six Livres de la République*), were among the avant-garde of their time. A few, such as Sir Henry Saville (1549–1622), were undoubtedly Sidney's acquaintances. They wrote in diverse languages. Most, contemporary scholars such as Georgius Agricola (1494–1555), wrote in Latin, but others wrote in English (Holinshed, Camden), Spanish (Mariana), and French (Du Bellay).

Following the custom of his brother and sister, Sir Robert expressed his interest in literature through his personal support of numerous writers. He began early, building friendships among the intellectuals whom Philip had met on the continent—Languet, Lobbet, Camerarius, Giphanius. The countess of Pembroke's circle included the most illustrious poets of Elizabeth's reign, and Robert doubtless had occasion to speak with Edmund Spenser, Michael Drayton, and Samuel Daniel. The latter was employed by the countess to tutor her son, William Herbert, and somewhat later, by Sidney's aunt, Lady Cumberland, to teach her daughter, Anne Clifford, whose diary is still an important source for students of the period. As early as 1590, Abraham Fraunce dedicated his *Symbolicae Philosophiae* to Sidney.[27] Thomas Powell, a Welsh poet, mentions Sir Robert in his dedication to *Loves Leprosie* (1598), and Thomas Moffet alludes to Sidney's "Sydneian Muse" in *The Silkewormes and Their Flies* (1599).[28] Sir John Davies, in his *Scourge of Folly*, mentions Sir Philip's poetic influence on Sir Robert.[29]

Robert Jones dedicated *The First Booke of Songs* (1606) to Sidney, by then
Lord Lisle, followed ten years later by Robert Dowland, who dedicated his
Musicall Banquett to Lisle and opened his collection with a piece called "Sir
Robert Sidney's Galliard." By 1616, Lisle's son was styled Sir Robert Sidney,
so the galliard may have been named for him. George Chapman dedicated
the 1609 edition of his *Iliads* to Lisle, "the most learned and Noble Con-
cluder of the Warres Art, and the Muses." George Wither dedicated *Prince
Henries Obsequies* (1612) to Lisle, wishing him "double comfort after his
twofold sorrow," an allusion to the loss of his son, Sir William. Evidently,
too, Lisle had something to do with Sir Thomas Wroth's translation of the
Aeneid, Book III (1620), for Wroth, a cousin of Sidney's son-in-law, Sir
Robert Wroth, speaks of "the eie of judgment" with which Sidney "graced
her lying in the docke."[30] Sidney donated £100 to the newly formed Bodleian Library, a contribution that was among the first and the largest of the
new century.[31]

One whom he did not patronize was Christopher Marlowe. In January
1591/92, Sidney arrested Marlowe, along with Gifford Gilbert, a goldsmith,
and Richard Baines, who accused the first two of counterfeiting. Sidney
thought Marlowe and Baines had deceived the goldsmith by claiming they
wanted him to demonstrate his skill and persuading him to coin an ersatz
Dutch shilling. He sent all three to Burghley for examination and trial.[32]
Nothing is known of the outcome, except that Marlowe was free in 1593,
when he was killed in a tavern brawl.

Evidently after James I's accession, Sidney became acquainted with
Ben Jonson, who praised Marlowe's "mighty line." Although it is believed
Jonson was a volunteer in Flanders during the 1590s,[33] he and Sidney
probably did not meet at this time. They were far apart in rank and social
position, and no occasion that would have brought them together is known.
Probably Sidney encountered Jonson in his official capacity as lord chamberlain. Anne was fond of the masque, and Jonson wrote a prolific number
of them for her entertainment. However they met, the playwright soon
endeared himself to the Sidney family. He seems to have been present on
the occasion of William's twenty-first birthday, and Professor J. C. A. Rathmell suggests that Jonson may have enjoyed a "quasi-tutorial relationship"
with Sir Robert's eldest son.[34]

He also developed a warm friendship with Sidney's daughter, Lady
Mary Wroth, and partook of the Wroths' hospitality at Durrants. Jonson's
gracious sonnet to her (*The Underwood*, No. 46) compliments her verse as
well as her personal graces, and his epistle to her husband, Sir Robert
Wroth (*The Forrest*, iii) seems to contradict his assertion in *Conversations with
Drummond* that Wroth was an unworthy, jealous husband. Jonson's editor,
Herford, thinks it unlikely that the poet could have written the compli-
ments to Wroth if he were the occasion for the jealousy, but he notes that
Fleay believes he was and argues that the poems to Celia (*Volpone,* ii, vii, and
in *The Forrest*) are addressed to Lady Wroth.[35]

Whatever the nature of Jonson's relationship with the Sidneys' daughter, he was on friendly terms with other members of the family. The countess of Rutland, Philip Sidney's daughter, entertained him, although her husband rebuked her for "keeping table with poets." She also wrote poetry, and Jonson thought her talent "nothing inferior to the Father."[36]

That Jonson's friendship with the Sidney family included Robert and Barbara Sidney is clear in his poem, "To Penshurst" (in *The Forrest*). Professor Rathmell has shown the veracity and intimacy of this poem in his article in *English Literary Renaissance;* little remains to be added to what he has said. In the poem, Jonson conveys a sense of the Sidneys' liberality, morality, and gracious hospitality, free from any trace of ostentation. He alludes to Sir Robert's love of gardening and to his orchard full of exotic fruits:

> The blushing apricot, and wooly peach
> Hang on thy walls, that every child may reach.

The humble as well as the proud are welcome at Penshurst. "All come in, the farmer and the clowne." When King James and Prince Henry, out hunting late, dropped by unexpectedly, they found Lady Sidney's "linnen, plate, and all things nigh/ . . . and not a roome, but drest,/ As if it had expected such a guest!" Jonson knew that none of Sidney's servants envied their well-fed guests, for the waiter, "knowes, below, he shall finde plentie of meate." He admires the lady of Penshurst's virtue, a quality he calls "rarely known" in that age. The children, he observes with satisfaction, have been taught religion.

> Each morne, and even, they are taught to pray
> With the whole household, may, every day
> Reade in their vertuous parents noble parts
> The mysteries of manners, armes, and arts.

Sidney's children imbibed those mysteries and passed them on to their own. Lady Mary Wroth was a minor poet of some note. Like her father and aunt, she entertained a circle of contemporary poets, whose efforts she encouraged and supported. William died before he could produce anything. Robert, although he seems not to have produced verse or fiction, was a prolific diarist. Robert's daughter and Sidney's granddaughter, Dorothy, became the model for Waller's "Sacharissa." The literary impulse that was born in Robert Sidney's time and flowered with such brilliance in Sir Philip thrived during several Sidney generations to enrich English literature for centuries to come.

NOTES

1. Peter J. Croft, 2 vols. (London: Cassell, 1973), vol. 1, item 22; see also pp. xii and xv.

2. "'Rosis and Lysa': Selections from the Poems of Sir Robert Sidney," *English Literary Renaissance* 9 no. 2 (Spring 1979):240–63.

3. G. F. Waller, "The 'Sad Pilgrim': The Poetry of Sir Robert Sidney," *Dalhousie Review* 56 (1975):691.

4. Hilton Kelliher and Katherine Duncan-Jones, "A Manuscript of Poems by Robert Sidney: Some Early Impressions," *British Library Journal* 1 no. 2 (1975):108.

5. Ibid., p. 109.

6. Ibid., p. 110.

7. Ibid., p. 113.

8. "The Poems of Sir Robert Sidney," *English* 30 no. 136 (Spring 1981):3–72.

9. Kelliher and Duncan-Jones, pp. 107–44.

10. Deborah K. Wright, *The Poetry of Robert Sidney: A Critical Study of His Autograph Manuscript* (Ann Arbor, Mich.: University Microfilms, 1980).

11. P. J. Croft, [Description of Notebook by Sir Robert Sidney], *Catalogue of Valuable Printed Books* (London: Sotheby November 1974), p. 98.

12. George Lyman Kittredge, "Introduction," *Hamlet*, by William Shakespeare (1939; rept. ed. Walton, Mass.; Toronto; London: Blaisdell, 1967), pp. x–xi.

13. Sidney to Lady Sidney, Flushing, 21 March [1597], *HMCD* 2:243–44.

14. Ibid.

15. Whyte to Sidney, London, 15 October 1595, *HMCD* 2:173.

16. Whyte to Sidney, 25 September 1595, ibid., 2:163.

17. W. Shrickx, "Letters in Belgian Archives of Two English Poets, Robert Sidney and Henry Wotton," *Revue des Langues Vivantes* 40, no. 5 (1974/75): 483–88.

18. George Gilpin to Sidney, 30 September 1596, *HMCD* 2:223.

19. Sidney to Lady Sidney, 21 May 1594, U 1475 C 81/37, KAO De L'Isle, Maidstone, England.

20. Sidney to Lady Sidney, 3 June 1594, *HMCD* 2:153.

21. Leicester to Lady Leicester, 30 September 1620, ibid., 5:421.

22. Wright, pp. 63–67.

23. Croft, *Catalogue*, p. 95.

24. Croft, *Catalogue*, p. 95.

25. KAO De L'Isle U 1475 Z 1/1 and Z 1/2.

26. Ibid., Z 1/3.

27. Ibid., Z 1/16. A scribal ms. signed and dedicated to Sidney in Fraunce's hand.

28. Kelliher and Duncan-Jones, p. 115.

29. I owe this observation to Katherine Duncan-Jones.

30. Kelliher and Duncan-Jones, p. 115.

31. William Dunn Macray, *Annals of the Bodleian Library* (Oxford: Oxford University Press, Clarendon Press, 1890), p. 20.

32. Sidney to Burghley, 26 January, 1591/92, SP 84/44, fol. 66. See also R. B. Wernham, "Christopher Marlowe at Flushing in 1592," *English Historical Review* 91 (April, 1976): 344–45.

33. Herford, *Jonson* 1:6.

34. J. C. A. Rathmell, "Jonson, Lord L'Isle and Penshurst," *English Literary Renaissance* 1 (1971): 251.

35. Herford, *Jonson* 1:35.

36. Ibid., p. 34.

Sidney at the Court of King James I

Sidney left a happy impression with King James VI when he ended his embassy to Scotland in 1588. James, an admirer of Philip Sidney, had more than one reason to expect to be charmed by Sir Robert that year: the crisis at hand made it imperative that Elizabeth send a persuasive ambassador, and the king had been secretly corresponding with Sidney's uncle, Leicester, in anticipation of the aging queen's demise. Sidney fulfilled the king's expectations and surpassed them, prompting James to congratulate Elizabeth on having sent "so rare a gentleman" to the Scottish court.

Other circumstances promised improved royal favor when the king took the throne. James knew that Sidney was a follower of Leicester, to whom the Scottish king had first attached his own ambitions for the English crown. Essex, too, had carried on a secret correspondence with James through his sister, Lady Penelope Rich. In weekly letters to the king, Lady Rich repeatedly assured James of Essex's support of his claim to the English throne. She also told him that Cecil, Nottingham, Raleigh, and Cobham opposed his claim, thereby undermining the faction that was set against Sidney's advancement.[1]

Fortune and the new king lost little time in smiling upon Sidney. The queen died March 23. On May 13, 1603, Sidney was created Baron Sidney of Penshurst.[2] James appointed him Queen Anne's Lord High Chamberlain and Surveyor, the second most exalted position in her council. The new Lord Cecil took the top position as her Lord High Steward. Her other officers included Sir George Carew, Sir Thomas Mounson, the earl of Southampton, Sir Thomas Somerset, and Mr. William Fowler.[3]

As soon as James was established, Cecil, dubbed Viscount Cranbourne, attacked Sidney's old enemy, Henry Brooke, Lord Cobham. Implicated in the Main Plot, Cobham was attainted and permanently put out of power. At the same time, James restored the title of earl of Essex to Robert Devereux, son of the deceased earl. For Sidney, these were happy developments. He and his family had maintained some of their ties with the Essex faction, so that with the rise of the new earl, the new Lord Sidney's old friends were part of the English set much in favor with the king.

The new Baron Sidney was at last in a position to reward Rowland Whyte. By June 8, 1603, Whyte received a grant, for life, of the Office of Constable of Caernarvon Castle.[4] Less than a year later, Whyte, by then Postmaster of the Court, obtained leases of certain lands in Leicester County and of a hamlet called Pengogo in Kemitmayne, County Caernarvon,[5] now County Gwynedd, Wales. The following spring, he was granted the lordship of Knoll, in County Kent.[6] Without doubt, Sidney's influence at court helped Whyte obtain these lucrative grants. In addition to assisting Whyte's cause at court, Sidney leased to him for forty years, in reversion, the demesne lands of Otford, the property for which they had struggled.[7]

Sidney's accountant records that the baron went to meet the king at Coombe Abbey, the home of Lord John Harrington, who had been chosen as Princess Elizabeth's guardian. Undoubtedly indulging his own taste as well as dressing for a sybaritic king, Sidney had his tailor make a suit of satin overlaid with silver lace, with a cloth-of-silver doublet and a velvet-lined gray cloak. He had a silver-laced saddle made to match: the cost of all this came to some £130. When the queen followed James into England a few weeks later, Sidney met her in an equally costly costume, this one of black satin overlaid with black silk and gold lace, a cloth-of-gold doublet, and a black cloak lined with plush; a "very ritch" saddle complemented that ensemble.[8]

Serving king and country under James I was a costly undertaking. The bills rolled in as the tides upon the shore, even before James began selling honors to the highest bidders. Creation as a baron cost Sidney nearly £100: the requisite robes came to £78 10s., and the fee for the gentleman porter at the ceremony was £8 6s. 8d.[9]

That Christmas (1603), Sidney attended a masque at Hampton Court, and again he had to dress in style. His suit consumed seventeen yards of cloth-of-gold; at £3 10s. a yard, the cost of the fabric alone came to £59 10s. But that was not the end of it; the panes of the hose and every seam on the doublet were embroidered, to the tune of £50. To this was added a cloak of uncut velvet decorated with gold lace and a hat embroidered in gold. For this astonishing costume and its accessories, the baron paid out "at least" £220. He also had a more modest suit made, of white satin laced with silver and tawny satin laced with gold, topped off with a black grosgrain cloak laced with silk and lined with unshorn velvet, which came to only £110.[10]

Baron Sidney joined the king's entourage when James passed through London for the first time, an occasion that called for the expenditure of another £461, this time for a satin suit in a shade of mulberry. The doublet and the panes of the hose were embroidered with pearls and further decorated with five yards of cloth-of-silver. A matching satin cloak, embroidered all over the outside with gold and lined with pearl-embroidered satin, together with a hat and footcloth of gold-embroidered mulberry velvet, completed the costume.[11] If it was true that James was taken with stylish dress, the queen's chamberlain could hardly have escaped his notice.

Sidney must have regarded the cost of clothing made for special occasions as extraordinary expense, although he had so many tailored that the charges soon became more ordinary than not. The daily expense of running his household also rose, for now he had to entertain royalty and keep his children properly attired to follow the court. Nevitt noted that, because of the many great feasts Sidney staged for the queen, the queen's brother, the States General of the Low Countries, and diverse noble guests, both at Baynard's Castle and at Penshurst, his weekly housekeeping costs averaged about £38. Sidney allowed his wife at least £100 a year for silks and spending money, plus another £50 for household linens. The combined costs, Nevitt estimated, came to over £2,900 a year.

Sidney's income undeniably improved under James, but not to such an extent that he could avoid running up a cumbersome debt. The king was profligate with his gifts to favorites and followers; Sidney benefited from James's generosity, but not until halfway through the reign. Before 1611, he had to rely on his existing income from his property and his offices at Flushing, his new offices at court, and presumably from whatever graft he could skim off the cash that passed through his hands as the queen's surveyor. His pay as governor of Flushing for twenty-eight days in 1603, for example, came to £95 4s.[12] and Nevitt listed Sidney's combined yearly income from the governorship and the company at Flushing as £1,600. With the rents from his property, his total annual income in 1603 seems to have been around £3,390.[13] In 1604, Sidney's aunt, the countess of Warwick, died and conveyed to him Alton Woods in Worcester. Unfortunately, she also left him £2,700 in debts to the king. Sidney made suit to James to be pardoned for the debt and to be granted the king's remaining right in the woods.[14] James so ordered it.[15] Several years later, Sidney profited by surrendering the woods to the Crown in exchange for £3,000,[16] a move probably prompted by his growing debt.

Following 1611, Sidney, now styled Viscount Lisle, began to benefit more directly and extensively from James's generosity. In April 1616, the king granted him the sum of £6,000.[17] In May, Lisle received a pension of £1,200 a year for the rest of his life, in recognition of his services as governor of Flushing.[18] In the same month, he was also granted another lifelong annuity, for £1,000.[19] Elizabeth, countess of Rutland, Philip's daughter, died in 1612, leaving most of her property and debts to Lisle and to her mother, the countess of Clanricard.[20] A few years later, James discharged all of Lisle's and Lady Clanricard's liabilities for debts still due the Crown from Sir Henry Sidney's estate.[21]

After James's accession, Sidney was able to avoid having to spend much time in Flushing. As a result, his correspondence with Whyte and his reports to the home government ceased. The administration of the garrison is recorded in the lieutenant-governors' reports, but the main source of information about Sidney's private and business affairs, Whyte's correspondence, was cut off. For this reason, the picture one may draw of Sidney's career under James's rule is necessarily less detailed than the rich image the earlier correspondence and the poems convey.

Baron Sidney maintained James's and the queen's favor through the first years of the reign, and, on May 4, 1605, he was at last awarded the title he had so long sought.[22] He received the title of Viscount Lisle on the same day the king created three earls and four barons. The new earls included Robert Cecil, now earl of Salisbury, and his brother, Thomas, who took the title of Exeter. The third was Lisle's nephew, Philip Herbert, who acquired, in addition to the title of earl of Montgomery, property worth 8,000 crowns a year.[23]

Sidney took the opportunities presented at James's accession to continue to build the alliance between himself and Cecil that he had established before Elizabeth's death. The arrangements Sidney made to transport a quantity of the much-admired Kentish limestone from Penshurst to Cecil's mansion at Theobalds were made out of no innocent sense of magnanimity. Lady Lisle sent apricots from the gardens at Pensurst to Theobalds when the king visited there,[24] and Lisle and his sister, the countess of Pembroke, took care to maintain a friendly relationship with Cecil.

Before long, Lisle had occasion to call on the new earl of Salisbury's favor, for he found himself by accident in an embarrassing predicament that put him in danger of permanent disgrace. Early in August 1605, Lisle asked for and received a leave of absence from the court to visit Flushing. As he was making the passage across the English Channel, a storm blew his ship off course. They were forced to land at Gravelines, a city in Flanders held by the Spanish governor in the Low Countries, Archduke Albert. Lisle continued his journey by land, passing through Spanish-held Flanders and Brabant on his way to Flushing.

When news of Lisle's detour reached England, his enemies, whom the Venetian ambassador called "many and great," suggested to the States General's agent, Noël Caron, that the governor had landed in Spanish territory not accidentally, but with the purpose of handing Flushing over to the enemy. Caron, alarmed, presented this preposterous charge to James, who convinced himself that it was so. The king commanded his council to send Lisle an order to return without a moment's delay, upon pain of death, confiscation of estates, and proclamation as a traitor.[25]

The Privy Council's letter to Lisle was somewhat more temperate,[26] but the order to return to London forthwith and explain his intentions must have struck him as ominous. Although he wrote reassuringly to Lady Sidney that the matter would be quickly and easily resolved,[27] his letters to Salisbury and the Privy Council reveal no such sense of safety. Matters were complicated by the fact that he had discussed with both Salisbury and Caron his plan to visit Antwerp while he was on the continent, taking advantage of what he regarded as the temporary amity between England and Spain to reconnoiter the place for future military intelligence. The viscount thought it strange that knowledge of that private plan was suddenly common among the French and Spanish factions at court.[28]

Rumors at court had it that he had visited the Spanish ambassador in England, had no doubt there concocted the betrayal, and had further developed the plan when he had gone to bid farewell to the visiting Spanish dignitary, Conde de Ville Mediana. Indignantly, he protested his innocence to Salisbury, reminding him of his years of proven loyalty, denying the truth of the rumors, and assuring him that, as he had said from the beginning, his purpose in the planned visit to Antwerp was strictly to gather information. The gist of Salisbury's reply can be guessed from the notes he scribbled on the back of Lisle's letter: that the king's suspicions were justified in light of Caron's agitation, the continuing hostilities between the Archduke and the States, and the diffidence of the French; that Lisle's proposal to visit Antwerp naturally bred suspicion, for it was a vain scheme, considering the enterprise of the Dutch.[29]

Lisle wrote to the Privy Council that he would return to London as soon as he could obtain shipping and adequate wind. He reiterated his innocence and noted that, because his legs were bad and he was under a surgeon's care, he might be slightly delayed.[30] Then he sent a private communication to Salisbury, complaining that he was ill-used in the affair, and that the Council was punishing him before hearing his case by ordering him to present himself upon his arrival, rather than allowing him to proceed directly to the court.[31] The Privy Council was somewhat mollified and replied that he had been called, not condemned; he could, if he desired, remain at Flushing until the return of his lieutenant governor, Sir William Browne, who had left for England the day before the Council's first letter reached Lisle.[32] Something in the viscount's letter irritated Salisbury, however, for he shot off a snappish *apologia* in which he remarked that if Lisle thought ill of him as a result of either his own imaginings or the hostile gossip of others, "I can only say I wish you to believe what might best serve your turn."[33]

Lisle did not wait for Browne. Placing the sergeant-major, Captain John Throckmorton, in command of the garrison, he sailed for England with the first favorable wind. He arrived at Canterbury on September 2, and wrote ahead to Salisbury that he was hurrying on his way, despite the discomfort of his bad legs.[34] Salisbury must have advised him not to injure himself in his rush, for when he arrived in London on September 5, he added to his note reporting his presence his thanks for the earl's favor in allowing him to make the journey in short stages, to spare his legs.[35]

Salisbury's angry letter apparently found Lisle in London. The day of his arrival, he wrote a second message to the earl, a submissive response praying him not to take his words personally. Cecil responded that Lisle had had no cause to react intemperately to the Council's order and to impute to them some scheme against him, but he added that the matter was forgotten and avowed his own impartiality.[36] How smoothly this rift in the two men's relationship was mended may never be clear.

Lisle did succeed in freeing himself from suspicion of complicity with Spain, and by the end of September the talk at the court was blaming Caron for taking alarm too easily. Popular opinion was especially persuaded, reported the Venetian ambassador, by the fact that everyone of the

Council and at the court had received presents from Spain except Sidney and three or four others, who were excluded because of their implacable hostility to the Spanish.[37] However, as the ambassador had noted at the beginning of the incident, Lisle had lost his chance of being named to the Privy Council, a position for which he was maneuvering; Lord John Stanhope was named in his place.[38]

Lisle's misfortune was greeted with glee by his enemies at court, even though he recovered himself fairly well. Sir John Chamberlain's remark to Ralph Winwood evokes the malicious, petty atmosphere of the Jacobean court. "I doubt not but you have heard how Viscount Lisle was called *coram* for his absurd journie by Flaunders to Flushing: and how he was faine to cry *peccavi* and confess his error. . . ."[39] Presumably, neither of those correspondents placed himself in Lisle's camp. One wonders, too, if Caron was guilty of more than credulity in repeating such a patently specious report to the king. Perhaps Lisle's opposition to the return of the cautionary towns to the Dutch, for which Caron had campaigned for years, had engendered some dislike for the viscount.

Lisle's "many and great" enemies comprised the larger part of the pro-Spanish, pro-Catholic faction at James's court. Henry Howard, earl of Northampton, the most powerful moving force within that faction, so detested Lisle that his dying wish was that none of his offices go the viscount.[40] When Northampton died in 1614, the wardenship of the Cinque Ports, which he had obtained after Cobham's attainder, again came open. Northampton had been using his position to aid in the smuggling of Roman Catholics in and out of the Cinque Ports.[41] Sidney maneuvered to obtain it, but Northampton's party prevailed; the king honored the earl's wish by settling it on his current favorite and Northampton's protégé, the earl of Somerset.[42]

Lisle could have had no more love for Somerset than he had for the dead Northampton. Somerset's dishonorable alliance with Frances Howard and the consequent humiliation of Lisle's friend, the earl of Essex, must have elicited the viscount's disgust, if his connection with the Spanish faction had not already done so. Lisle must have felt a dark delight at the scandalous revelations that led to Somerset's downfall, and we may be sure that, when he was summoned to the earl and countess's trial[43] for the murder of Sir Thomas Overbury, he did not go without preconceived opinion. He could not resist a cutting rejoinder to Somerset's claim that, if tarts were sent to Overbury in the Tower, the wholesome ones had been sent by himself and the poisoned ones by his wife: "If you had sent him good tarts," said Lisle, "you should have seen them convey'd by a trusty Messenger."[44]

No doubt Lisle was among the peers who promoted the rise of George Villiers, created Earl of Buckingham in 1617. With Somerset adjudged guilty of murder, the way was clear for a new man to supplant him, and Villiers, with his hostility to the Howards, would have struck Lisle as an improvement. The viscount was present at Villiers's creations to baron and to viscount. If he was disillusioned by Villiers's decision, in 1616, to support the Spanish Match, he must have felt nonetheless gratified by the earl's systematic destruction of the Howard clan's power.

Lisle's office as the queen's chamberlain seems to have been mostly ceremonial, and as he grew more advanced in years, he may have preferred it that way. He was forty at the time of James's accession, well past the midpoint of the Renaissance man's life expectancy. Politics in the Stuart court swiftly grew more dangerous than they were under the Tudors, as the destruction of a series of prominent men—Cobham, Suffolk, Buckhurst, Somerset, and Bacon, among others—attested. The decadent moral tone at court—Anne's court was described as "a continued maskarado"[45]—must have been repulsive to all but the most jaded. Probably as time passed, Lisle found neither strength nor taste to fight for the power and position he had desired under Elizabeth.

Exactly what his function as lord chamberlain was remains somewhat unclear. The 1771 edition of the *Encyclopaedia Britannica* describes the king's lord chamberlain as "an officer who has the oversight and direction of all officers belonging to the king's chambers, except the precinct of the king's bed-chamber. He has the oversight of the officers of the wardrobe at all his majesty's houses, and of the removing wardrobes, or of beds, tents, revels, music, comedians, hunting, messengers, &c. retained in the king's service."[46] The queen's chamberlain, a century and a half earlier, may or may not have had similar responsibilities. Nevitt's accounts suggest the office involved much costly social activity. Other sources indicate Sidney took charge of some administrative details, and it appears that, as governor of Flushing, he served as an advisor about affairs in the Low Countries. Some of his functions appear to have been almost secretarial: he relayed the queen's desires to Salisbury regarding such matters as her official correspondence.[47] He was involved, with the rest of the queen's council, in the collection of the revenues,[48] and, at least during the early part of the reign, he helped oversee the proceedings of Anne's courts of survey.[49] His new duties kept him away from home. He continued to report to Lady Sidney his frustration at not being with her, now that he was required to follow the queen and her court.

His responsibilities comprised, in addition to being present at Anne's court, a chain of costly public appearances, which often included his family as well. His daughter Philippa was among the throng nominated to be ladies-in-waiting to the queen, and young Barbara took part, at her father's cost, in an unsuccessful masque for the queen and king.[50] Master Robert Sidney was created Knight of the Bath in honor of the Prince of Wales's creation.[51] When the queen staged her famous Moorish masque at Whitehall, Lisle was in the audience and had another suit especially designed for the occasion; this one cost him £80.[52] He was present in the Parliament House at the creation of Henry as Prince of Wales.[53] He took part in the ceremony creating George Villiers baron of Whaddon and at

Villiers's creation to viscount.[54] He acted as judge in a tilting match at Hampton Court on King's Day, 1617/18.[55]

Some of his duties were somber: the queen commanded him to attend the autopsy of Princess Mary, who died in childhood (1607), so that she might be certain of the cause of her daughter's death.[56] Five years later, he marched in the funeral procession of Prince Henry, bearing the Prince's standard.[57] Another half decade brought the death of the queen, and again Lisle—by then earl of Leicester—took a prominent position in the procession to Westminster Abbey, accompanying the earl of Hertford (Anne's Lord Steward) before Prince Charles, who preceded the coffin.[58] Only a year before his own death, he served in another royal funeral procession, obtaining a position as one of the fourteen assistants to the king's chief mourner, Charles I.[59]

Once Sidney was created a baron, he gained the privilege of sitting in the House of Lords. He was present at each parliament between 1603/04 and his death in 1626.

Lisle also served occasionally as a diplomat. He was despatched to meet the French ambassador, Maximilien de Béthune, marquis de Rosny, when he arrived at Canterbury in June, 1603.[60] Remarks made by Sir William Browne suggest that Lisle took advantage of the occasion to urge the reinforcement of his garrison and that, perhaps with Rosny's support, he attained some success.[61] A month later, Rosny's brother-in-law, André de Cochefilet, baron de Vaucelas, passed through Flushing. Knowing he was acquainted with Lisle, Browne invited him to dinner and afterward reported their private conversation to the governor. Vaucelas revealed his concern that Queen Anne would influence the king in favor of peace with Spain, particularly by favoring marriages between her children and those of the Spanish royal family. Browne hoped that this was untrue and noted that perhaps the queen was allowing the French to think this so that the king's friendship would be "the more regarded by dear obtaining it."[62]

Such, of course, was not the case. We can be sure that Lisle opposed peace with Spain and the Spanish Match with all his energy. He supported the interests of the Low Countries before the Privy Council in matters of trade,[63] and, as his express motive for his planned visit to Antwerp indicated, he had neither hope nor desire that the hostility between the Protestants and the Catholics would be resolved in peace negotiations. Wary as he was of putting his political opinions in writing, the few traces of his stance that survive confirm his resolute anti-Spanish position. The entry he made in his commonplace book, showing that any Catholic was necessarily a potential traitor to England, certainly represented his prejudices. He was outraged when a Spanish woman gained entrance to the country and set up a "nunry" of English women. He thought the only consequence that would befall her was to be banishment, "so gently you see we proceed with such kind of people."[64] He may have actively campaigned for the marriage between the Princess Elizabeth and the Elector Palatine, and in 1612 Throckmorton repeated the governor's confident remark that the rumored wedding between the princess and the king of Spain would never take place, and that she would soon be settled in Germany.[65] Too, Throckmorton must have been echoing the governor's opinion when, in the same year, he expressed his hope to Lisle that the prince would never marry outside his own religion.[66]

No doubt Viscount Lisle's long-standing sympathy with the Protestant cause in Germany and the Low Countries led to his selection as one of the four royal commissioners appointed to attend the princess on her way to Germany following her marriage to the elector. Lisle and his colleagues, the duke of Lennox, the earl of Arundel, and Lord John Harrington, were given the title of ambassadors so that they could take precedence over the diplomatic agents stationed at the Hague and elsewhere.[67]

The journey to Bacharach and Heidelberg as part of that shimmering entourage must be counted among the highlights of Lisle's social and political careers. The cost must have been extraordinary. In addition to the £800 Nevitt lists as the sum total of the expenses for the trip, the accountant alludes to another £180 laid out for a suit of rich cloth tissue, a silk-embroidered tawny velvet cape, and appropriate accessories.[68] Lisle had to bear the expense of outfitting all his servants in England and at Flushing, his train of twenty-one attendants, his son, Sir Robert (who appeared in splendor at the princess's arrival at Flushing), plus numerous fine dinners and myriad other details in the undertaking.

Antonio Foscarini, the Venetian ambassador to England in 1613, described the plans for the princess's wedding voyage. On the way to Greenwich, the royal party, attended by an "incredible" crowd, would pass through Kent, where they expected to be met and accompanied by an infantry guard of two thousand. The king had ordered all the horsemen to be attired in an especially designed uniform replete with lace and plumes. Lisle and the other commissioners, who would proceed with the royal family, were to receive the counterdower, after which the princess, her new husband, and their attendants would embark aboard a fourteen-hundred-ton galleon, built for and named after the late Prince Henry. The ship, thought to be the most beautiful England ever had, carried six hundred arquebussiers and four hundred mariners. She carried no powder, but was accompanied by two pinnaces bearing ammunition. To further secure the royal party's safety, six royal galleons and sixteen other ships formed the Prince Royal's escort. Halfway across the Channel, they were to be met by the Dutch fleet, which would accompany them to the harbor at Flushing.[69]

The people of Flushing made elaborate preparations, beginning many weeks in advance, to receive the wedding party. Much had to be done: there was the harbor to be dredged, food to be ordered and prepared, lodging to be secured and made comfortable for royalty, ceremonies to be planned, companies of men to be outfitted and instructed in appropriate behavior, security arrangements to be made, detail after detail to be settled. Lisle sent a few specific orders to his lieutenant governor, Sir John Throckmorton, who was put in charge of preparing the festivities. His nervous letters to the viscount between early March and mid-April reveal the intense activity that took place at Flushing: plans, revised plans, alternate plans, twice-revised plans. Lisle decided to lodge Lord Admiral Nottingham and his train with Throckmorton, to the latter's astonishment. Throckmorton protested that he "dare not meddle with those great Lords, whom I knowe not;" he would prefer, he said, to play host to the viscount's son, Sir Robert. Lisle obliged him by accepting some other arrangement for Nottingham and placing Lord and Lady Harrington with him.[70] At last, after some delay because of bad weather and a pause off Sluys for a visit with the Prince of Orange, the party arrived at Flushing.

On April 29, they were met by the Flushing companies, dressed in their best uniforms, with Sir Robert Sidney's at their head. Sixty of "our handsomest musquetiers" formed a guard that saluted the newlyweds with volleys of musket fire, echoed by three volleys from the garrison's artillery. Local dignitaries and crowds of the common people were on hand. A shipload of provisions supplied the tables at Prince Maurice's house, where the party was entertained. The next day, Frederick left for the Hague. Elizabeth left on May 1 for Rotterdam, where her new husband joined her and accompanied her back to the Hague to be entertained by the States General.[71]

Lisle and the other commissioners had fulfilled their function when they arrived with the princess at Bacharach, but he, Lennox, and Arundel accepted the lady's invitation to accompany her to the end of her journey and visit Heidelberg.[72] The week-long passage up the Rhine was tedious, for all the towns on the river were infected with plague. The lords planned to stay in Heidelberg about six days and then go their separate ways, Lennox to Paris, the Harringtons to Spa, and Lisle directly to England.[73] They were well received along the way, although Throckmorton heard that the Princess was less than pleased with her entertainment at Amsterdam.[74] By the time they reached Goulshtyne in the Palatinate, Lisle had changed his mind about returning directly home, and decided instead to go via the Spa, accompanied by his son.[75] He even briefly considered traveling through Spain, but thought better of the idea.[76] When the royal party reached their destination in mid-June, they were greeted with three days of magnificent festivities, with massive feasts, jousts, duels, and other exercises.[77]

En route to the Spa, Lisle wrote from Cologne to Ralph Winwood, English agent at the Hague, and expressed his pleasure with the princess's reception on the continent. He thought she had been especially well received by the marquis of Ansbach, the duke of Wirtenberg, the administrator, the prince of Anhalt, and the electrice dowager.[78] Taking up lodging at the Golden Sheep, the viscount spent a leisurely three weeks taking the waters. Arundel and the others moved on, but Lord Darcy, Lady Elizabeth Lumley, and Lisle's old friends the Prince and Princess of Orange remained. While there, Lisle arranged, with the aid of Sir William Trumbull, the English agent at Brussels, for his son to attend an upcoming fête there, and to meet "the principal persons" of the city.[79]

Although he received word that the princess was doing well at Heidelberg, he was concerned about some "strange servants put about her in England." Confirmation of the likely war between Denmark and the States reached him, the first rumblings of the Thirty Years War.[80] Perhaps even at this time, Lisle had some premonition of the disaster that would befall the princess in Bohemia six years later.

The healing waters helped the viscount's aching legs, and he and Sir Robert decided to accompany the earl of Southampton homeward. They stopped at Aachen, where Lisle could soak his sore ankles in the hot water springs. From there he and his son proceeded to Flushing via Antwerp, where they stayed a day or two.[81] They reached Flushing by August 12, where, as usual, Lisle found nothing had been done about the repair of the fortifications. The States and the towns persisted in their reluctance to put any capital into the English-occupied property, blind, as Lisle believed, to the imminent danger from King Philip II.[82] Toward the middle of August, Lisle and Sir Robert set sail on a stormy sea.[83] Despite Throckmorton's concern, they reached England safely, and by August 15, Lisle had arrived at Bath, where he presumably continued to soothe his aching limbs and enjoy the stylish company.[84]

The remaining years of Lisle's governorship were peaceful, except for his involvement in the controversy over the Arminian professor, Conrad Vorstius. By 1610, Lisle's friend Maurice had fallen out with his old ally, Johan van Oldenbarneveldt. Barneveldt, who had arranged the Treaty of Truce with Spain in consort with Henri IV of France, was the chief of the French faction in the Low Countries and sympathetic to the Arminians. Maurice and the States of Zealand opposed Barneveldt, relying mainly on England for support against Spain. Barneveldt's intrigue with France stirred James's resentment, and the English king's hostility manifested itself in religious matters as well as in trade and in politics. As the struggle between Maurice and Barneveldt grew more pitched, James grew more hostile to the Arminianism that Barneveldt represented. So, when, following the death of Arminius in October 1609, Vorstius was nominated to succeed him at the University of Leyden over the opposition of Maurice's party, the Calvinist Gomarians (Contra-Remonstrants) turned for assistance to James. He obliged with an ill-considered attack on Vorstius, ordering his agent at the Hague, Winwood, to oppose the Arminian's establishment. Winwood followed his instructions and received a cool reception from the Dutch. After two "remonstrances" to the States General, he made a protestation that threatened the Dutch with a rupture between them and James. Meanwhile, under the tempering influence of Salisbury, the king's passion began to abate, and he moderated his attack, laying the blame for his indiscreet interference in Dutch internal affairs on Winwood. Vorstius, like Barneveldt, was ultimately defeated; he was exiled from Leyden and the Hague and spent most of his remaining days in Gouda.[85]

Lisle, of course, took an anti-Arminian position that was reflected in

Throckmorton's letters to him. Throckmorton was rabid on the subject of Vorstius, whose "atheisms and heresies" he believed were directed at poisoning the Dutch people against the English and designed to overthrow the States General. On his own, Throckmorton dealt with Sir James Maldere, the president of the States of Zealand, and received his assurance of Zealand's loyalty to James.

In August 1612, Lisle was ordered to Flushing, apparently to sound out the political situation in the Low Countries. He reported to James that Vorstius was at Tergau in Holland and marveled that his presence was tolerated. Resolutely opposed to the truce, Lisle perceived Arminian theology in political terms: he was convinced Vorstius's purpose was "to shake the resolutions of men's consciences by his own learning and incline them toward Popery as a first step in reducing the provinces to Spanish subiection." He reiterated to the king the importance of Flushing to the safety of England, despite the current affection between Zealand and James. He insisted that possession of the town was the key to control of the English Channel, the only route by which England could effectively be attacked, and urged James to remember that the place was worth as much care as could be bestowed on it.[86]

The exigencies of James's finances, however, took precedence over Lisle's reasoning. By 1616, the king's lavish spending, combined with the corrupt practices and maladministration of his officers, had virtually emptied the Exchequer. Supporting the cautionary towns cost money James no longer had; Lisle noted that the garrison of Flushing was in greater danger from mutiny by its unpaid soldiers than from any attempt by the Dutch to take the place by force.[87] James began to consider the expedient of returning the towns to the Dutch in return for an immediate cash payment. Lisle tried, in a tactfully worded communication, to dissuade the king and council from relinquishing the towns, but, forced to answer the question of whether the garrison could defend itself in its current condition, he had to admit that it could not, for the men were undersupplied and ill-equipped to do battle.[88]

The Dutch still owed some £600,000 to the English Crown under the treaty that had placed the towns in English hands as security for Elizabeth's loans, and only some rather tortured reasoning could justify returning them at a discount. Under a 1608 treaty, the Dutch were repaying the debt at the rate of £40,000 per annum. The Privy Council found that £26,000 of this went for the annual maintenance of the garrison; so the king was really only getting £14,000. Thus, at the end of fifteen years, by which time the whole debt would have been discharged, the king would have use of only £210,000. Caron offered the Council £215,000 for the towns, amortized over two and one-half years. The Lords thought it better to take the money in immediate payment; the king received £200,000, and another £15,000 was set aside to pension off the governors and those officers who would not be used in the English regiment that was to remain in the Low Countries in the pay of the Dutch.[89]

Lisle thought that the king had been forced to accept a bad bargain.

He remarked before the Privy Council that more regard should be given to the king's power than to his profit.[90] Nevertheless, he resigned himself to the inevitable. The restitution of the towns at this time proved more provident than any of the participants could have known. Had England maintained an armed force in the Low Countries when the Thirty Years' War began, she might have been pulled inescapably into ruinous conflict.

The task of reconciling Lisle to the loss of Flushing was no doubt eased by the £1,200 pension the king granted him, to continue for the rest of his life.[91] He was also dubbed Knight of the Garter, taking the place of Gilbert Talbot, earl of Shrewsbury, who had died May 6, 1616.[92] Chamberlain remarked that this honor was granted to Lisle "to grace him better now he is going over to render Flushing."[93] In addition, his son, Sir Robert, was to be colonel of the regiment of English soldiers that was to remain in the Low Countries in Dutch pay.[94]

Lisle and Sir Robert arrived in Flushing on May 30, 1616, and within a few days, the governor carried out the king and council's instructions to render his charge to the Dutch. The viscount thought the ceremony was well enough done, "since doon it must bee,"[95] although it did not pass without incident. Evidently the council's words for those who thought themselves dismissed without adequate recompense—that whatever they received from the king was out of his bounty and grace, for he had no duty to support them further[96]—did not suffice to quiet Lisle's men, who had grown accustomed to having to struggle for their pay. At both Flushing and the Brill, the soldiers rose up in near-mutiny and demanded to be paid for their clothing, the cost of which was still owed them. An angry dispute took place, during which Lisle was in some peril, but the men were finally satisfied when the States agreed to pay them six crowns apiece, an advance that was to be made good by the English government.[97] His duty discharged, the viscount accompanied his son to the Hague to see him installed as colonel of the new regiment,[98] and soon after returned to England.

Lisle's installation in the Order of the Garter corresponded with the fall of Somerset; the chapter following his dubbing-in on July 7, 1616[99] concerned the question of whether the discharged earl's arms should be removed. By the king's order, they were retained,[100] which must have been a matter of annoyance to the new knight battelier. In April 1618, the king appointed Lisle to a commission to examine the statutes of the order, with instructions to put into writing any corrections or additions the members judged might clarify the ancient statutes and articles.[101] Their recommendations covered a variety of administrative and customary details. For example, they proposed that the color of the ribbon worn by the knights, which formerly was left to each knight's discretion, be established as blue; that a specific place be appointed in Windsor Castle for the safekeeping of all acts concerning the Order; and that an annual report of the Order's proceedings be established.[102]

Lisle continued to rise in prominence and social status. At last, in 1618, he reached what for him must have been the symbolic pinnacle of his aspirations: on August 2, he was created earl of Leicester.[103]

The honor, which he had so long sought and undeniably deserved, was not conferred without shadow. James had been engaged in a lucrative trade in honors for some time. The income generated by the sale of knight-hoods had given rise to the creation of a new rank in the aristocracy, that of baronet, a title that could be purchased after 1611 for between £700 and £1,095.[104] The "project of baronets" proved so successful that, following 1615, the "mint of new dignities" went into wholesale production. Of the one hundred eleven peers James created during his reign, an unknown number among the three dukes, one marquess, thirty-two earls, nineteen viscounts, and fifty-six barons purchased their titles. The price varied ac-cording to the king's whim, but baronages went for £5,000 to £10,000, and Lord Cavendish and Lord Rich each paid £10,000 for their earldoms.[105] Naturally, this sordid trade bred resentment, especially among the older aristocracy. John Chamberlain reported their new dignities could not de-fend the freshly created earls from the "pens of malicious poets and libel-lers;" one rhyme in circulation following the 1618 creations labeled Leicester *vinosos,* William Compton, new earl of Northampton, "crazed," Robert Rich, earl of Warwick, *cornucopia,* and William Cavendish, earl of Devonshire, a usurer.[106]

Much confusion of a sort that implies under-the-table negotiation pre-ceded the new creations. Lisle was expected to be made earl of Warwick, and George Villiers to be Leicester. Instead, Villiers took the title of Buck-ingham, Rich obtained the more ancient title of Warwick, and Lisle had to settle for his uncle's title, a dignity to which he was entitled by right of descent.

No evidence that Sidney purchased either of his titles survives. Many of the honors James conferred on his followers were dispensed free of charge, and it is not impossible that he so graced the earl of Leicester. If Sidney had to buy the title of Leicester, the onus must fall on the king rather than on the new earl, for Sidney's claim to the title was valid. He had been the logical candidate since the death of Robert Dudley, the old earl's son by Lettice Devereux. Sidney was the sole uncontestably legitimate male survivor of the Dudley line, and as such, he could lay claim to both titles, Leicester and Warwick. If that were not enough, Sidney had spent a lifetime in honorable service to his country, as had his father and brothers.

Queen Anne may have had a hand in Leicester's creation; perhaps it was her influence rather than the new earl's cash that brought it about. Leicester wrote an exquisite letter to Lady Barbara to let her know "as now your Ladyship is Countess of Leycester." While two of the other new earls were content merely to receive their letters patents, Leicester thought he would have to receive an open creation, "to satisfy the Qn, whoe will have her worck made publick. . . ."[107]

Leicester's affection for his family was not diminished by his frequent

TABLE 7
SIDNEY-SMYTHE FAMILY CONNECTIONS

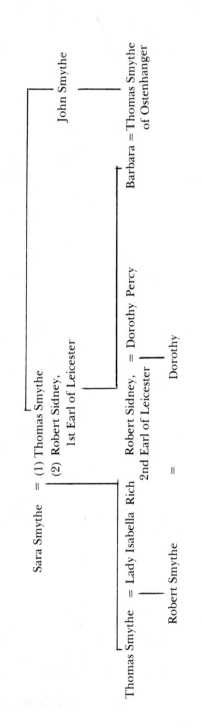

attendance at Anne's court. His concern for his daughters' happiness appears repeatedly in his letters to Lady Barbara, and he maintained a close fatherly relationship with each even after their marriages.

Seeing each girl married well was a costly responsibility. Mary was matched with Sir Robert Wroth in 1604; a dowery of £3,000 went with her. A like sum figured in the marriage of Katherine with Sir Lewis Mansell, a husband who, to Lisle's distress, proved unworthy. Mansell's treatment of Katherine was evidently abominable; deep in debt by 1607, Lisle worried that his own inability to make good the interest on the dowry would cause her father-in-law to "use my poor daughter the worse."[108] She grew ill and finally died in 1616.

Philippa was married to Sir John Hobart. Lisle had to borrow £4,000 to meet the dowry arrangements for that match. The Hobarts showed more appreciation for their new daughter and wife, and it appears that Philippa was as cherished by that family as by her own. Her father-in-law, Lord Chief Justice Sir Henry Hobart, wrote of his son's intense grief when she died in 1620, a sorrow that he understood and shared.[109]

Barbara, "a modest, sweet young lady," was married in 1619 to Thomas Smythe, the sole son of Sir John Smythe and nephew of Sir Thomas Smythe, Leicester's colleague in the administration of the Virginia Company. The match cost Leicester another £4,000, but young Smythe was said to have an annual income of £4,500, enough to support Barbara in comfort.[110]

This was the first of a series of marriages that intertwined the Sidney and Smythe families for several generations (see Table 7). After the death of Barbara's mother, Lady Leicester, the earl married the widow of Sir Thomas Smythe, his son-in-law's uncle. The elder Sir Thomas's son, Sir John Smythe, married Lady Isabella Rich, daughter of the earl of Warwick, and their son, Robert Smythe of Bounds and Sutton-at-Hone, married Leicester's granddaughter, Lady Dorothy Sidney.[111] This alliance between the two families had some political significance.

When Lisle's eldest son, William, died in 1612, Sir Robert was left as the viscount's only male heir. Negotiations for his marriage were more complicated than those for his sisters'. Two unsuccessful projects were undertaken in 1613, one to marry him to Sir Henry Savile's daughter and one to a daughter of Lord Burghley. Lisle invited himself and Sir Robert to dinner at Savile's one evening in March 1613, not knowing Lady Savile was sick in bed. They made an offer to Sir Henry for his daughter's hand, but Savile told the viscount he was already too far engaged in an arrangement with Sir William Sidley to reverse himself. Lisle was doubly disappointed at this news, for he had hoped to marry his own daughter, Philippa, to Sidley. Savile, too, was rather disappointed. He remarked that, had he been unencumbered, Lisle's offer might have broken his resolution not to match with nobility, for Sir Robert was considered "a very proper gentleman, exceedingly well given in every way."[112] In December, Sir Robert paid suit to Lord Burghley's daughter, Elizabeth, but she fell ill with the smallpox and, upon her recovery, married Sir Thomas Howard.[113] A suit for the daughter of one Master Watson was in progress when the young man conceived an inclination for Dorothy Percy, daughter of Henry, earl of Northumberland.[114] That match went forward, to the disgust of Watson, who threatened to sue.[115] In 1616, Sir Robert married Lady Dorothy, a match that was to make him brother-in-law to Lord James Hay, earl of Carlisle, a favorite of King James, but not, as it developed, of young Sidney. The two men soon quarreled and relations between them were never better than strained.

The match between Mrs. Barbara Sidney and Thomas Smythe of Ostenhanger was a manifestation of the financial and political alliance between Leicester and the faction represented by the elder Sir Thomas Smythe, young Smythe's uncle. Nowhere does their relationship appear more clear than in their dealings with the Virginia Company.

Along with Leicester, Walsingham, Sir Walter Raleigh, and many others of diverse political persuasion, the Sidneys had shown an interest in New World speculation since the 1580s. Sir Thomas Smythe, an old ally of the earl of Essex (he had been imprisoned following the earl's rebellion) devoted himself to the organization of companies to exploit the riches, real and supposed, to be gained abroad. He became governor of the East India Company after it received its charter in 1600 and continued in that position until 1621, when the company showed enormous profits.[116] He held the same position in the Bermuda Company after it was organized in 1615 by stockholders from the Virginia Company.[117] His prominence in the Virginia Company waxed and waned according to his party's success against the faction led by Sir Edwin Sandys.

In the complex pattern woven by the shifting factions within the Virginia Company, Sidney's allegiances traced the design of his personal sympathies and his public ambitions. The company was packed with old supporters of the earl of Essex—the names of Huntingdon, Pembroke, Smythe, Rich, Wroth, are listed in the company's charters.[118] Professor Alexander Brown, in his *English Politics in Early Virginia History,* sees significance in the radical Protestant element's interest in the New World, pointing out that all of the company of Sir Thomas Gates, the first governor of Virginia, had served under Prince Maurice of Nassau. He speculates that the Essex faction's letter inviting "his majesty's subjects in the Free States of the United Provinces" to join in the Virginia enterprise was addressed to the pilgrims.[119]

Between 1606 and its dissolution in 1624, the Virginia Company existed in two phases. During its first three years, it was controlled by the king through a council created by himself. During the second phase, the undertakers became proprietary, retaining their commercial functions and assuming the king's governmental functions.[120]

Sir Thomas Smythe took the office of treasurer of the Virginia Company from the beginning; the position corresponded to the governorship in the East India and Bermuda Companies. That Lisle was already a strong supporter of Smythe had been made evident by his opposition to Edward Jones in 1604, when the latter, suing for Smythe's place as ambassador to Muscovy, complained of Baron Sidney's hard dealings, which had been so extreme Jones was forced to leave the country.[121] The shifting factions within the company divided approximately into pro-court and anti-court parties, whose members' allegiances seem to have changed as circumstances altered. As of 1619, three quarreling factions, led respectively by Robert Rich, earl of Warwick (including most of the lords and gentlemen), Sir Thomas Smythe (the party of the merchants), and Sir Edwin Sandys ("the faction of the auditors"),[122] divided the company's members. Warwick's party joined temporarily with the Sandys faction, but in 1620, a year after the match between Barbara Sidney and Smythe's nephew, Warwick became friendly with Smythe and joined his cause. Southampton took over the old Warwick faction and united it permanently with Sandys' group. The Smythe-Warwick faction, in which Leicester was a prominent member, sided with the king against the interest of the Southampton party. Smythe was replaced by Sandys as treasurer in 1619, but, when the colony was almost wiped out by Indians in 1622, the court party used the disaster to gain the upper hand. In that year, Captain John Martin charged the company with denying him privileges granted to him by his patents, and Leicester, who was one of the two referees in the case,[123] seems to have sided with Martin. When, in 1623, Martin voted to surrender the Virginia Company's charter to the Crown, Leicester was among his supporters.[124]

The members of the two factions fell to savage quarreling. In April 1623, their representatives went before the king with various accusations and allegations, where Sir Edward Sackville, a Sandys partisan, behaved "so malapertly, and insolently, that the king was fain to take him down soundly and roundly."[125] With the collapse of the Spanish Match, James abandoned his purported plan to give Virginia to Spain, but he still desired complete control over it. Continuing controversy led to Southampton's house arrest by the Privy Council and the imprisonment of many of the other opposition members. Finally, on May 24, 1624, the Court of King's Bench vacated the company's charter and Virginia was acquired by the king as England's first colony.[126] After the dissolution, Leicester's ally Warwick, the son of Penelope Devereux, was made a member of the king's council for Virginia, the end result of the court faction's campaign to overthrow the company by "fair means or foul."[127] Leicester could not have involved himself intensely in the final struggle over the Virginia Company, for by 1623 he was old and his health was failing; he had been too ill even to venture downstairs most of that winter.[128]

That he lent his weight to the Warwick faction reveals where his sympathy lay after twenty years in King James's court. He still inclined away from religious and political tolerance, a penchant probably also reflected in his activities in the House of Lords. There he served on committees examining such questions as control of seditious books, witchcraft, control of recusants, Jesuits, and seminaries, the preservation of "the religion," abuse of the Sabbath day, etc.[129] In his mind, as in those of most of his contemporaries, religion was inextricably tangled with nationalism. His patriotism included the Protestant Low Countries, whose independence he considered vital to the king's security. Unremitting in his hostility to the Catholic countries, he expected to see England go to war with Spain, if not over ideology, then over survival. Considered a military expert on the Low Countries, Leicester was appointed to sit on an advisory Council of War in 1620/21, when James decided he ought to defend the Palatinate.[130]

Old age brought sorrow, poor health, and more debt to the earl. In 1621, he lost the two women who were dearest to him, his wife and his sister. Lady Leicester died suddenly late in May.[131] Her death must have been the more painful to the earl because it was unexpected. Only a few days before, Leicester had written that he was glad to hear she was well. He was attending Parliament and planned to return to Penshurst by Whitsunday Eve;[132] we do not know whether he was with her when she died. Four months later, the countess of Pembroke died of smallpox.[133]

He was deep in debt and could scarcely afford to aid his son, now styled Viscount Lisle, with a £200 annual allowance. Lisle complained that his father could not afford him sufficient means to live away from home, suspecting, in the manner of sons chafing to be free of their parents, that the earl would not, rather than could not, spare the money.[134] The intricate accounting of his expenditures prepared by Thomas Nevitt around 1622 seems to have been prompted by criticism of Nevitt's and the earl's mismanagement of the Sidney estate (see Nevitt's *apologia* at the end of the account book).[135] Following the earl's demise, his son was urged to administer the will in person, as swiftly as possible, to save what he could from the estate's creditors.[136]

Leicester so suffered from the gout that he was incapacitated for days on end. Miserable and lonely, he wrote to Prince Maurice praying him to spare his son's service in the Low Countries: "Hee is my onely son," he declared, "and since his mothers death my cheefest comfort."[137] The earl even wished Lisle would part with his regiment in the Low Countries, so unwilling was he to be without his son.[138] This desire was not granted, but Lisle did remain with his father, if reluctantly, during much of the last three years of his father's life.

Leicester's marriage to Sarah Smythe early in 1626[139] must have come out of his yearning for companionship. Sir Thomas Smythe died of the plague in September 1625, and Leicester must have been grieved at the loss of his friend and ally. The earl and the lady would have found much in common in their widowhood and their religious faith.

A glimpse of life at Penshurst under the aging earl's management can be seen in the orders "to be observed hereafter in his Honors house."[140] Every member of the household was required to attend chapel twice a day, where they were to "reverently behave themselves." There was to be no blasphemy, drunkenness, or fighting, and the porter was to shut the gates at 10 P.M., after which no one would be allowed to enter. Servants were permitted to visit the buttry between eight and nine in the morning and between three and four in the afternoon to refresh themselves with bread and beer, although the butler was to see that no one overimbibed. The earl's desire for orderliness and cleanliness are manifest in his orders to the groom of the chamber, the usher of the hall, and the master cook, each of whom was to maintain his place "as cleane and handsome as he can." Leicester's care for charity, too, made him provide that his usher see that all leftover food be put into a tub for the poor and not, he insisted, "otherwise purloyned."

Although he was often ill, Leicester kept current with the news of the court, maintaining a correspondence with Dudley Carleton and a number of observers on the continent. He found the strength to serve in the procession to King James's funeral in 1625, where he appeared as one of Charles I's fourteen assistants.[141]

He was returning by water from court to his lodging at Baynard's Castle when he was stricken by "an apoplexy." He survived a few days, long enough to be returned to Penshurst, but, shortly before noon on July 13, 1626, the earl of Leicester died.[142]

NOTES

1. M. Wilson, pp. 109–110.

2. Creation of Sir Robert Sidney to the Rank of Baron Sidney of Penshurst, 13 May 1603 [Grant Book, p. 3], *CSP Dom.* 8:8.

3. John Nichols, *Progresses, Processions, and Magnificent Festivities of King James I*, 4 vols. (1788–1821; rept. edition New York: B. Franklin, 1968), 1:268 n.

4. Dated 8 June 1603, *CSP Dom* 8:14.

5. Dated 8 March 1604, ibid., 8:87.

6. Dated 5 April 1605, ibid., 8:210.

7. Dated 8 June 1604, ibid., 8:222.

8. Additional MS 12066.

9. Ibid.

10. Ibid.

11. Ibid.

12. "Warrant to pay Sir Robert Sidney 95 li for 28 days entertainment as governor from the 6th of August to the 2nd of September," Additional MS 5753, fol. 280, British Library, London, England.

13. Additional MS 12066.

14. Sidney to James I (1604), *HMC Salisbury* 16:461.

15. July 1605, Signet Office Docquet Book, SO 3:5, Public Record Office, London, England.

16. February 1611 [O.S.], ibid.

17. Henry, Lord Danvers to Dudley Carleton, St. James', 27 April 1616, *CSP Dom.* 9:363.

18. May 1616, Signet Office Docquet Book, SO 3:6, Public Record Office, London, England.

19. Chamberlain to Carleton, 11 August 1612, *CSP Dom.* 9:143.

20. Dated 30 October 1612, ibid., 9:268.

21. Dated 17 July 1622, ibid., 10:426.

22. *DNB*, s.v. "Sidney, Robert, Earl of Leicester."

23. *CSP Dom.* 10:240.

24. Lisle to Salisbury, Greenwich, 24 July 1606, *HMC Salisbury* 18:209.

25. Nicolo Molin, Venetian ambassador in England, to the Doge and Senate, London, 14 September 1605, *CSP Venice* 10:271.

26. Privy Council to Lisle, Court at Grafton, 20 August 1605, *HMC Salisbury* 17:380.

27. Lisle to Lady Lisle, Flushing, 21 August 1605, *HMCD* 3:189.

28. Lisle to Salisbury, Flushing, 24 August 1605, *HMC Salisbury* 17:390–91.

29. Notes by Salisbury, ibid., 17:392.

30. Lisle to Privy Council, Flushing, 25 August 1605, ibid., 17:392.

31. Lisle to Salisbury, Flushing, 25 August 1605, ibid., 17:393–94.

32. Privy Council to Lisle, Court at Oxford, 30 August 1605, ibid., 17:403.

33. Salisbury to Lisle, [30 August 1605], ibid., 17:404.

34. Lisle to Salisbury, Canterbury, 2 September 1605, ibid., 17:411.

35. Lisle to Salisbury, London, 5 September 1605, ibid., 17:413–14.

36. Salisbury to Lisle, 7 September 1605, ibid., 17:416.

37. Molin to Doge and Senate, London, 28 September 1605, *CSP Dom.* 10:276.

38. Molin to Doge and Senate, 14 September 1605, ibid., 10:271.

39. Chamberlain to Ralph Winwood, 12 October 1605, in McClure, 1:209.

40. G. P. B. Akrigg, *Jacobean Pageant* (New York: Atheneum, 1967), p. 214.

41. *DNB*, s.v. "Howard, Henry, Earl of Northampton."

42. Reverend Thomas Lorkin to Sir Thomas Puckering, Bart., at Tours, in France, 12 July 1604, in Thomas Birch, *The Court and Times of James I*, 2 vols. (London: H. Colburn, 1849), 1:332.

43. "Names of Peers Summoned to the Trial of the Earl of Somerset," *A Complete Collection of State Trials and Proceedings for High Treason and Other Crimes and Misdemeanors from the Reign of King Richard II to the End of the Reign of King George I*, 6 vols. (London: Printed for J. Walthol Sen, et al., 1730), 1:331 (Hereafter abbreviated *State Trials*).

44. Ibid., 1:334.

45. M. Wilson, p. 183.

46. *Encyclopaedia Britannica*, 1771 ed. s.v. "Lord *Chamberlain* of the Household."

47. See, e.g., Sidney to Cecil, [1603], *HMC Salisbury* 15:390.

48. Privy Council to Sir Thomas Darnell, 3 July 1603, ibid., 16:163.

49. Sir Thomas Coningsby to Viscount Cranbourne and Lord Sydney, 4 October 1604, *CSP Dom.* 8:155.

50. Chamberlain to Carleton, 3 January 1617/18, Nichols, *Progresses of James I* 1:452.

51. Dated 3 June 1610, ibid., 3:344.

52. Additional MS 12066.

53. Dated 5 June 1610, Nichols, *Progresses of James I* 3:334.

54. Chamberlain to Carleton, London, 3 September 1616, McClure, 2:22; Chamberlain to Carleton, 24 August 1616, Nichols, *Progresses of James I* 3:187.

55. Nichols, *Progresses of James I*, 3:474.

56. Chamberlain to Carleton, London, 17 April 1619, McClure, 2:229–30.

57. Earl of Worcester to the Earl of Shrewsbury, 16 September 1607, Nichols, *Progresses of James I*, 2:153; Antonio Foscarini to the Doge and Senate, London, 29 December 1612, *CSP Venice* 12:407.

58. May 1619, Nichols, *Progresses of James I* 3:539.

59. Ibid., 3:1047–48.

60. Sidney to Cranbourne, Sittingburn, 6 June 1603, *HMC Salisbury* 15:125.

61. Browne to Sidney, Flushing, 30 June 1603, *HMCD* 3:39.

62. Browne to Sidney, Flushing, 17 July 1603, *HMCD* 3:41–42.

63. Sidney to Cranbourne, [1604, before August 20], *HMC Salisbury* 16:269.

64. Lisle to [William] Trumbull, London, 24 October 1613, *HMC Downshire* 4:235.

65. Throckmorton to Trumbull, 17 January 1611/12, ibid., 3:221; Throckmorton to Trumbull, 17 April 1612, ibid., 3:227.

66. Throckmorton to Lisle, Flushing, 29 April 1612, *HMCD* 5:47–48.

67. Virginia Wood, *Elizabeth, Electress Palatine and Queen of Bohemia*, rev. S. C. Lomas (London: Methuen, 1909), p. 161.

68. Additional MS 12066.

69. Foscarini to Doge and Senate, London, 18 April 1613, *CSP Venice* 12:253.

70. *HMCD* 5:90–106, passim.

71. Ibid., 5:104 n.

72. Wood, p. 73.

73. Winwood to Trumbull, Hague, 26 May 1613, *HMC Downshire* 4:115.

74. Throckmorton to Trumbull, Flushing, 27 May 1613, ibid., 4:117.

75. Throckmorton to Trumbull, 13 June 1613, ibid., 4:138.

76. Lisle to Winwood, Cologne, 18 June 1613, *HMC Buccleuch* 1:135.

77. Andre Paull to Trumbull, Durloch, 18/28 June 1613, *HMC Downshire* 4:145.

78. Lisle to Winwood, Cologne, 18 June 1613, *HMC Buccleuch* 1:135.

79. Lisle to Trumbull, Spa, 25 June 1613, *HMC Downshire* 4:154.

80. Winwood, Spa, 10 July 1613, *HMC Buccleuch* 1:138.

81. Lisle to Lady Lisle, Spa, 22 July 1613; Aachen, 29 July 1613; Flushing, 12 August 1613, *HMCD* 5:12.

82. Lisle to Trumbull, Flushing, 12 August 1613, *HMC Downshire* 4:179.

83. Throckmorton to Lisle, Flushing, August 1613, *HMCD* 5:115.

84. Throckmorton to Lisle, Flushing, 31 August 1613, ibid., 5:118.

85. Ibid., 5:xxxi–xxxvii; pp. 35–36 n.

86. Lisle to King James I, Flushing, 14 August 1612, SP 84/68, fols. 297–99.

87. Lisle to Privy Council, 1 April 1616, SP 84/68, fols. 46–47.

88. Ibid.

89. Memorandum re: the return of the cautionary towns, 1616, SP 84/75, fols. 206–8.

90. Chamberlain to Carleton, London, 6 April 1616, Birch, *Court and Times of James I* 1:397.

91. List of Officers of the Regiment, 27 April 1616, *PC* 34:515.

92. Installation of Lisle, 7 July 1616, *Armorial Register of the Sovereign and Knights of the Most Noble Order of the Garter* (London: John Camden Hotten, 1872), p. 31 (Hereafter designated *Order of the garter*).

93. Dated 27 April 1616, *PC* 34:514; see also Gregorio Barbarigo, Venetian Ambassador to England, to the Doge and Senate, London, 24 June 1616, *CSP Venice* 14:253.

94. *PC* 34:515.

95. Sidney to Carleton, Middleburgh, 6 May 1616 [*sic.;* probably June is correct], SP 84/72, fol. 190.

96. Privy Council's instructions to Lisle, 23 May 1616, *PC* 34:545–48.

97. Giovanni Battista Lionelle, Venetian Secretary in England, to the Doge and Senate, London, 24 June 1616, *CSP Venice* 14:253.

98. Sidney to Carleton, Middleburgh [*sic*] 6 May 1616, SP 84/72, fol. 190.

99. *Order of the Garter*, p. 31.

100. Chamberlain to Carleton, 20 July 1616, McClure, 1:121.

101. Copy of the King's Commission to my Lordes for the examining of the statutes of the garter, 26 April 1618, Additional MS 6297, p. 280, British Library, London, England.

102. Commission on the Garter at the Court of Whitehall on the 19th of May, 1622. . . ," MS Ashmole 1132, fol. 7, Bodleian Library, Oxford, England.

103. Creation of Robert Sidney, Viscount Lisle to the rank of Earl of Leicester, August 2, 1618. *CSP Dom.* 9:563. John Nichols, in *Progresses of James I*, 3:488–89, describes the ceremony celebrating Leicester's creation.

At Salisbury, on the 2d of August 1618, in the Bishop's Great Hall there, were created Robert Vicount Lisle, Erle of Lester, and William Lord Compton, Erle of Northampton, as followeth:

The Kinge not lying in the Bishop's Pallace, appointed the Great Hall within the said Bishop's Pallace to be prepared for the Creation aforesaid, which was hanged with arras, and a cloth of estate set up. The roome beinge furnished, the King's Majestie came privately from the howse of Mr. Sadler, where he lay, and about four of the clock in the afternoon placed himself in the said roome under the State. All things being thus in redines, the Vicount Lisle first was brought into the King's presence, in his surcot and hood only, bare-headed, accompanied by theis States and Officers as followeth: First, the Officers of Armes in their roabes; then Garter caryed the patent in his hand; next to him followed the Erle of Montgomery, who bare the mantell; the Erle of Arundell bare the sword; th'erle of Pembrok, Lord Chamberlain, bare the cap and coronet; the Vicount himself, supported on the right hand by the Marquis of Buckingham, and on the left hand by the Vicount Doncaster; and thus coming into the Presence doing their obeysances, brought the Vicount to the King, who [the viscount] kneeled downe. Garter delivered to patent to the Vice-chamberlein, the Vice-chamberlein to the King, who delivered it to Sir Robert Nanton, Principall Secretary, who on his knee read the said pattent with a loud voyce; and at the word 'Creamus' the King with the Lords put on his mantell, and at the words 'cincturum gladdi' they girded the Sword about his neck, and at the words 'cappe et curculi aurei' they put on his cap and coronet; the Erles who attend-ing being in the robes, and swords girt to them, put on their caps and coronets likewise. When the patent by Mr. Secretary was quite out, then the new-created Erle gave to the King great thanks upon his knee, and afterwards stood by on the right-hand of his Majestie in his robes and cap, untill theis Nobles who brought him went to fetch the ther Lord, who was brought in and created in the same manner as before. After all, the trumpets at the lower end of the Hall sounded, and so proceeded sounding before the Harolds and Nobles, and brought the Erles to their Chamber, where they were to rest till supper; who proceeded in this manner. The Vicount Doncaster formost; then the two new Erles together; the Erle of Montgomery and the Erle of Arundell; and the Lord Chamberlein and the Marquis of Buckingham. . . .

104. G. P. V. Akrigg, p. 234.

105. Ibid., pp. 235–36.

106. Chamberlain to Carleton, 8 August 1618, Birch, *Court and Times of James I* 2:84.

107. Leicester to Lady Leicester, London, 22 July 1618, *HMCD* 5:416–17.

108. Lisle to Lady Lisle, Court, 10 November 1607, ibid., 3:432.

109. Sir Henry Hobart to Leicester, 30 September 1620, ibid., 5:421.

110. Sir Gerard Herbert to Dudley Carleton, 14 April 1619, *CSP Dom.* 10:33.

111. William Berry, *County Genealogies: Pedigrees of the Families of Kent* (London: Sherwood, Gilbert and Piper, 1830), p. 251.

112. Chamberlain to Carleton, London, 11 March 1613, Mcclure, 1:436.

113. Carleton to Chamberlain, London, 23 December 1613, Birch, *Court and Times of James I* 1:283; Carleton to Chamberlain, 2 March 1613/14, ibid., 1:302.

114. Chamberlain to Carleton, 12 January 1615, McClure, 1:570–71.

115. Lisle to Lady Lisle, London, 2 July 1615, *HMCD* 5:300.

116. Louis B. Wright, "English Politics and Administration," in *The Reign of James VI and I,* ed. Alan G. R. Smith (New York: St. Martin's Press, 1973), p. 124.

117. Ibid., p. 126.

118. Alexander Brown, *The Genesis of the United States,* 2 vols. (Boston and New York: Houghton, Mifflin, 1891), 1:210; 2:542.

119. (1901; rept. edit., New York: Russell and Russell, 1968), pp. 6–9.

120. Susan M. Kingsbury, ed., *The Records of the Virginia Company in London,* 4 vols. (Washington: U.S. Government Printing Office, 1906–38), 1:11.

121. Edward Jones to Cranbourne, [1604], *HMC Salisbury* 16:444.

122. Kingsbury, 2:10–15.

123. "At a preparative court held for Virginia, the 20th of May, 1622, ibid., 2:10; "At a great and general quarter court. . . ," 22 May 1622, ibid., 2:27.

124. Ibid., 2:943–45.

125. Chamberlain to Carleton, 19 April 1623, MuClure, 2:126.

126. Wright, "English Politics," p. 125.

127. Kingsbury, 1:61–62.

128. Leicester to Carleton, 30 January 1623, *CSP Dom.* 1:485.

129. Great Britain, House of Lords, *Journals of the House of Lords, 1578–1714* (vols. 2–19) (n.p.: n.p., n.d.), vols. 2 and 3, passim.

130. Dated 13 January 1620/21, *CSP Dom.* 10:214.

131. Chamberlain to Carleton, London, 2 June 1621, McClure, 2:379.

132. Leicester to Lady Leicester, Whitehall, 12 May 1621, *HMCD* 5:424.

133. Sir Benjamin Rudyard to Sir Francis Nethersole, Whitehall, 11 October 1621, *CSP Dom.* 10:298.

134. Lisle to Carleton, 4 May 1622, SP Holland 184/106, fol. 167.

135. Additional MS 12066.

136. Nevitt to Leicester, London, 26 September 1626, *HMCD* 6:5.

137. Leicester to Carleton, London, 24 July 1622, SP 84/107, fol. 187.

138. Leicester to Carleton, 30 January 1623, *CSP Dom.* 1:485.

139. John J. Stocker, "Pedigree of Smythe of Bidborough and Sutton [1605–1684]," *Archaeologia Cantiana* 20 (1893):77; Berry, p. 251.

140. Orders appointed by the Rt. Hon. Robert Earle of Leycester to be observed hereafter in his Honors house, [1625–26], *HMCD* 6:1–2.

141. Dated 1 May [?] 1625, Nichols, *Progresses of James I* 3:1047–48.

142. In Thomas Birch, *The Court and Times of Charles I,* ed. Robert Folkestone Williams, 2 vols. (London: H. Colburn, 1848), 1:129; "To the Rev. Joseph Meade," London, 14 July 1626, Collins, 1:120.

Bibliography

I. Manuscripts

London. British Library. Additional MSS.
———. Cotton MSS.
———. Egerton MSS.
———. Harleian MSS.
———. Landsdowne MSS.
———. Stowe MSS.
London. Great Britain Public Record Office. Signet Office Docquet Books (SO 4).
———. State Papers, Foreign (SP 78): France.
———. State Papers, Foreign (SP 83): Holland, Flanders.
———. State Papers, Foreign (SP 84): Holland.
Maidstone, England. Kent Archives Office. De L'Isle MSS.
Oxford, England. Bodleian Library. Ashmolean Mss.
———. Rawlinson MSS.
———. St. Amand MSS.
Oxford, England. Christ Church College Library. Correspondence of Philip Sidney and Robert Dorsett. English translation commissioned by J. M. Osborn.
———. Battels (Daily, Michelmas 1577 to Michelmas 1579).
———. Chapter Book (1549–1619).
———. *Matricula Aedis Christi* (1546–1636).
———. Subdean's Book (1567–1616).

II. Printed Works

Acts of the Privy Council of England. 43 vols. (1542–1628). London: H.M. Stationery Office, 1890–1949.
Addleshaw, William Percy. *Sir Philip Sidney.* London: Methuen, 1909.
Akrigg, G. P. V. *Jacobean Pageant.* New York: Atheneum, 1967.
Armorial Register of the Sovereign and Knights of the Most Noble Order of the Garter. London: John Camden Hotten, [1872?].

The Arraignment, Tryal, and Condemnation of Robert, Earl of Essex, and Henry, Earl of Southampton, At Westminster, 19th February, 1600. London, 1671.

Bacon, Sir Francis. *The Works of Sir Francis Bacon.* 14 vols. Edited by J. Spedding. London: Longmans, Green, 1868–74.

Bain, Joseph. *Calendar of Letters and Papers Relating to the Affairs of the Borders of England and Scotland Preserved in Her Majesty's Public Record Office.* 2 vols. Edinburgh: H.M. General Register House, 1894.

Berry, William. *County Genealogies: Pedigrees of the Families of Kent.* London: Sherwood, Gilbert, and Piper, 1830.

Birch, Thomas. *Court and Times of Charles I.* Edited by Robert Folkestone Williams. London: H. Colburn, 1848.

———. *Court and Times of James I.* Edited by Robert Folkestone Williams. London: H. Colburn, 1848.

Blencow, R. W. *Sidney Papers.* London: John Murray, 1825.

Blok, P. J. *Correspondance Inédite de Robert Dudley.* Harlem: Archives du Musée Tyler, 1911.

Bodley, Sir Thomas. *The Life of Thomas Bodley, Written by Himself.* 1647. Reprint. Chicago: A. C. McClurg, 1906.

Bourne, Henry Richard Fox. *A Memoir of Philip Sidney.* London: Chapman and Hall, 1862.

A Brief Report of the Military Services Done in the Low Countries by the Earl of Leicester. London: Arnold Hatfield, 1587.

A Briefe and True Report of the Proceedings of the Earle of Leycester for the Reliefe of the Towne of Sluce. London: Thomas Orwin, for Andrew Mansell, 1590.

Brown, Alexander. *English Politics in Early Virginia History.* 1901. Reprint. New York: Russell and Russell, 1968.

———. *The Genesis of the United States.* 2 vols. Boston and New York: Houghton, Mifflin, 1891.

Bruce, John. *Correspondance of Robert Dudley, Earl of Leicester.* Camden Society, no. 27. London: J. B. Nichols and Sons, 1844.

———. *Letters and Papers of the Verney Family Down to the End of the Year 1639.* Camden Society, no. 54. London: J. B. Nichols and Sons, 1853.

Bruce, Philip Alexander. *Economic History of Virginia in the Seventeenth Century.* 2 vols. New York: Peter Smith, 1935.

Burke's Genealogic and Heraldic History of the Peerage, Baronetage, and Knightage. London: Burke's Peerage, 1938–67.

Butler, Nathanael. *Barnevelt Displayed, Or the Golden Legend of New St. John.* London: Printed by G. Eld, 1619.

Camden, William. *Annales: The True and Royall History of the Famous Empresse Elizabeth, Queene of England, France, and Ireland.* 3 vols. Translated by A. Darcie. London: H. Lownes, 1625–29.

Canny, Nicholas Patrick. "Glory and Gain: Sir Henry Sidney and the Government of Ireland, 1558–1578." Ph.D. dissertation, University of Pennsylvania, 1972.

Cave-Browne, Reverend J. "Knights of the Shire for Kent." *Archaeologia Cantiana* 21 (1895): 198–243.

Cecil, Algernon. *Life of Robert Cecil, First Earl of Salisbury.* London: John Murray, 1915.

Cecil, Robert, Earl of Salisbury. *Letters from Robert Cecil to Sir George Carew.* Edited by John Maclean. Camden Society, no. 88. London: J. B. Nichols and Sons, 1864.

Cecil, William, Lord Burghley. *Scrinia Ceciliana: Mysteries of State and Government: In Letters of the Late Famous Lord Burghley.* London: G. Bedel and T. Collins, 1663.

Chalkin, C. W. *Seventeenth-Century Kent.* London: Longmans, Green, 1965.

Chamberlain, John. *Letters of John Chamberlain.* 2 vols. Edited by N. E. McClure. Philadelphia: American Philosophical Society, 1939.

Chamberlin, Frederick. *The Private Character of Queen Elizabeth.* New York: Dodd, Mead, 1922.

Chapman, George. *Iliads.* London: Samuel Mecham, 1608.

Clark, Peter. *English Provincial Society from the Reformation to the Revolution.* Hassocks, England: Harvester Press, 1977.

Cobbett, William. *Parliamentary History of England.* 36 vols. London: R. Bagshaw, 1806–20.

C[ockayne], G. E. et al. *The Complete Peerage of England.* 13 vols. Rev. by Vicary Gibbs. London: St. Catherine's Press, 1910–59.

Collier, J. Payne, *The Egerton Papers.* Camden Society, no. 12. London: J. B. Nichols and Sons, 1860.

Collins, Arthur. *Letters and Memorials of State.* 2 vols. London: Printed for T. Osborne in Gray's Inn, 1746.

A Complete Collection of State-Trials and Proceedings from High Treason and Other Crimes and Misdemeanors from the Reign of King Richard II to the End of the Reign of King George I. 6 vols. London: Printed for J. Walthol Sen et al., 1730.

Croft, Peter J. *Autograph Poetry in the English Language.* 2 vols. London: Cassell, 1973.

——— . Description of the Autograph Notebook by Robert Sidney. *Catalogue of Valuable Printed Books,* pp. 95–101. London: Sotheby and Co., November 18 and 19, 1974.

Cruickshank, Charles G. *Elizabeth's Army.* Oxford: Clarendon Press, Oxford University Press, 1966.

A Declaration of the Causes Moving the Queenes Maiestie of England to Prepare and Send a navy to the Seas for the Defence of Her Realmes against the King of Spaines Forces. London: Christopher Barker, 1596.

Devereux, Robert, Earl of Essex. *An Apologie of the Earle of Essex against Those Which Falsely and Maliciously Accuse Him.* London: Richard Bradocke, 1603.

Devereux, Walter B. *Lives and Letters of the Devereux, Earls of Essex, in the Reigns of Elizabeth, James I, and Charles I, 1540–1646.* 2 vols. London: John Murray, 1853.

D'Ewes, Sir Simonds. *A Compleat Journal of the Votes, Speeches, and Debates, Both of the House of Lords and House of Commons, throughout the Whole Reign of Elizabeth of Glorious Memory.* London: Printed by J. S., 1708.

Dicey, Albert V. *The Privy Council.* Oxford: T. and G. Shrimpton, 1860.

Dictionary of National Biography. Edited by Sir Leslie Stephen and Sir Henry Lee. Reprint. London: Oxford University Press, 1921–22.

A *Discourse More at Large of the Late Overthrowe Given to the King of Spaines Armie at Turnhaut, in Januarie Last, by Count Morris of Nassawe, Assisted with the English Forces.* London: P. Short, 1597.

Dudley, Robert, Earl of Leicester. *The Correspondence of Robert Dudley, Earl of Leycester.* Edited by John Bruce. Camden Society, no. 27. J. B. Nichols and Sons, 1844.

—— *.Correspondentie van Robert Dudley, Graaf van Leycester.* 3 vols. Edited by H. Brugman. Utrecht: Kemink and Zoon, N.V., 1931.

Duncan-Jones, Katherine. "'Rosis and Lysa'" Selections from the Poems of Sir Robert Sidney." *English Literary Renaissance* 9 (Spring 1979): 240–63. See also Kelliher, Hilton.

Dwynn, Lewys. *Heraldic Visitations of Wales and Part of the Marches, 1586–1613.* Edited by Samuel L. Meyrick. Llandovery: N.P., 1846.

Edwards, Edward. *The Life of Sir Walter Raleigh.* 2 vols. London: MacMillan, 1868.

Elizabeth I, Queen of England. *Letters of Queen Elizabeth and King James VI of Scotland.* Edited by John Bruce. Camden Society, no. 46. London: J. B. Nichols and Sons, 1859.

Ellis, Henry. *Original Letters of Eminent Literary Men of the Sixteenth, Seventeenth, and Eighteenth Centuries.* Camden Society, no. 23. London: J. B. Nichols and Sons, 1843.

Esler, Anthony. *The Aspiring Mind of the Elizabethan Younger Generation.* Durham, N.C.: Duke University Press, 1966.

Espelin, Ross S. "The Emerging Legend of Sir Philip Sidney: 1586–1652." Ph.D. dissertation, University of Utah, 1970.

Finnett, John. *Finetti Philoxenis: Som Choice Observations of Sir J.F. Touchng the Reception and Precedence, the Treatment and Audience, the Punctillios and Contests of Forren Ambassadors in England.* Edited by J. Howell. London: T.R. for H. Tayford and G. Bedell, 1656.

Fogel, Ephrim Gregory. "The Personal References in the Fiction and Poetry of Sir Philip Sidney." Ph.D. dissertation, Ohio State University, 1958.

Foster, Joseph. *Alumni Oxoniensis (1500–1714).* Oxford: Parker, 1958.

Froude, James Anthony. *History of England from the Fall of Wolsey to the Death of Elizabeth.* 12 vols. New York: Charles Scribner's Sons, 1881.

Furley, Robert. *A History of the Weald of Kent.* 2 vols. London: Ashford, 1871–74.

Gachard, Louis P., ed. *Actes des Etats Généraux, 1576–1585.* Brussels: C. Marquardt, 1861–66.

Gardiner, Samuel R., ed. *The Fortescue Papers.* Camden Society, N.S. 6. London: J. B. Nichols and Sons, 1871.

——., ed. *Letters and Other Documents Illustrating the Relations Between England and Germany at the Commencement of the Thirty Years War.* Camden Society, no. 68. J. B. Nichols and Sons, 1868.

——., ed. *Notes of Debates in the House of Lords Offically Taken by Henry Elsing, Clerk of the Parliaments, 1621.* Camden Society, no. 103. London: J. B. Nichols and Sons, 1870.

——., ed. *Notes of Debates in the House of Lords Officially Taken by Henry*

Elsing, Clerk of the Parliaments, 1621. Camden Society, N.S. 24. J. B. Nichols and Sons, 1879.

—., ed. *Parliamentary Debates in 1610. Edited from Notes of a Member of the House of Commons.* Camden Society, no. 81. London: J. B. Nichols and Sons, 1861.

Gleason, J. H. *The Justices of the Peace in England, 1558–1640.* Oxford: Clarendon Press, Oxford University Press, 1969.

Great Britain, Historical Manuscripts Commission, *Calendar of the Manuscripts of the Most Honorable the Marquis of Salisbury, K.G., Preserved at Hatfield House, Hertfordshire.* 4 vols. London: H. M. Stationery Office, 1883.

—. *Calendar of Stuart Papers at Windsor Castle.* 7 vols. London: H. M. Stationery Office, 1902.

—. *Report on the Manuscripts of the Duke of Buccleuch and Queensbury Preserved at Montague House, Whitehall.* London: H. M. Stationery Office, 1899–1926.

—. *Report on the Manuscripts of the Earl of Cowper at Melbourne Hall.* London: H. M. Stationery Office, 1888–89.

—. *Report on the Manuscripts of Lord De L'Isle and Dudley Preserved at Penshurst Place.* 6 vols. London: H. M. Stationery Office, 1925–66.

—. *Report on the Manuscripts of the Marquess of Downshire.* 4 vols. London: H. M. Stationery Office, 1924.

—. *Manuscripts of the Earl of Essex.* 7 vols. London: H. M. Stationery Office, 1914.

Great Britain, House of Lords, *Journals of the House of Lords (1509 ff.).* N.P., N.D.

Great Britain, National Library of Scotland, *Catalogue of the Manuscripts Acquired Since 1925.* 3 vols. Edinburgh: H. M. Stationery Office, 1938.

Great Britain, Public Record Office. *Calendar of Patent Rolls Preserved in the Public Record Office.* Vol 4, *Elizabeth (1572–1575).* London: H. M. Stationery Office, 1973.

—. *Calendar of State Papers, Colonial Series.* 40 vols. Edited by W. N. Sainsbury. London: Longman, 1860.

—. *Calendar of State Papers, Domestic Series, of the Reigns of Edward VI, Mary, Elizabeth, and James I.* 12 vols. Edited by R. Lemon. London: Longman, 1856 ff.

—. *Calendar of State Papers, Domestic Series, of the Reign of Charles I, 1625–1649.* 23 vols. London: Longman, 1858–79.

—. *Calendar of State Papers and Manuscripts Existing in the Archives and Collections of Venice.* Edited by Horatio F. Brown. London: H. M. Stationery Office, 1900.

—. *Calendar of State Papers, Foreign Series of the Reign of Elizabeth, 1558–1582.* Edited by Wm. R. Turnbull. London: H. M. Stationery Office, 1863–1909.

—. *Calendar of State Papers Relating to Scotland and Mary, Queen of Scots, 1547–1603.* 13 vols. Edited by William K. Boyd. Glasgow, H. M. Stationery Office, 1915.

—. *Index of Inquisitions Preserved in the Public Record Office.* Vol. 4, *Charles I and Later.* Amended edition. New York: Kraus Reprints, 1963–.

———. *Index of Chancery Proceedings, Bridges' Division, Preserved in the Public Record Office*. New York: Kraus Reprints, 1963.

———. *List and Analysis of the Calendar of State Papers, Foreign Series*. 3 vols. London: H. M. Stationery Office, 1964–.

Greville, Sir Fulke. *Works in Prose Complete of the Right Honorable Fulke Greville, Lord Brooke*. 4 vols. Edited by Reverend Alexander B. Grosart. 1870. Reprint. New York: AMS Press, Inc., 1966.

Harrison, G. B. *The Life and Death of Robert Devereux, Earl of Essex*. London: Cassell, 1937.

———. *A Jacobean Journal (1603–1606)*. New York: MacMillan, 1941.

Haydon, Brigid. "Algernon Sidney, 1623–1683." *Archaeologia Cantiana* 76(1961):110–33.

Haynes, Samuel. *A Collection of State Papers Relating to Affairs in the Reigns of Henry VIII, Edward VI, Mary, and Elizabeth, from 1542–1570. Transcribed from Original Letters and Other Authentic Memorials Left by William Cecill, Lord Burghley, and Now Remaining at Hatfield House*. London: William Bowyers, 1740.

Hayward, Sir John. *Annals of the First Four Years of the Reign of Queen Elizabeth*. Edited by John Bruce. Camden Society, no. 7. London: J. B. Nichols and Sons, 1840.

Hearne, Thomas. *Reliquae Bodleianae*. London: John Hartley, 1703.

Hesketh, Captain C. "The Manor House and Great Park of the Archbishop of Canterbury at Otford." *Archaeologia Cantiana* 31 (1915): 1–24.

Holinshed, Raphael. *Chronicles of England, Scotland, and Ireland*. 1587. Reprint. London: Printed for J. Johnson, 1807–8.

Houlder, Robert. *Barnvels Apologie: Or Holland Mysterie*. London: Printed for Thomas Thorpe, 1618.

Howell, Roger. *Sir Philip Sidney: The Shepherd Knight*. London: Hutchinson, 1968.

Hull, Felix. "Catalogue of the De L'Isle Manuscripts." Kent Archives Office, Maidstone, England, 1969–1974. Typewritten manuscript.

Hurst, Quentin. *Henry of Navarre*. New York: Appleton-Century, 1938.

Jenkinson, Sir Hilary. *The Later Court Hands in England from the Fifteenth to the Seventeenth Centuries*. Cambridge: Cambridge University Press, 1927.

Jonson, Benjamin. *Ben Jonson*. Edited by C. H. Herford and E. J. Simpson. 11 vols. Oxford: Oxford University Press, 1925–52.

———. *Conversations with William Drummond of Hawthornden, 1619*. London: R. V. Patterson, 1923.

Judson, Alexander C. *Sidney's Appearance*. Bloomington: Indiana University Press, 1958.

Kelliher, Hilton, and Duncan-Jones, Katherine. "A Manuscript of Poems by Robert Sidney: Some Early Impressions." *British Library Journal*. Ser. 2, vol. 1 (November 1975): 107–44.

Kervyn de Lettenhove, Baron J. B. *Relations Politiques des Pays-Bas et de l'Angleterre*. 11 vols. Brussels: F. Hayez, 1882–1900.

Kingsbury, Susan M., ed. *The Records of the Virginia Company in London*. 4 vols. Washington: U.S. Government Printing Office, 1906–38.

Lacey, Robert. *Robert, Earl of Essex.* New York: Atheneum, 1971.

Lambarde, William. *A Perambulation of Kent.* 1570. Reprint. London: Baldwin, Dradock, and Joy, 1826.

Laslet, P. "The Gentry of Kent in 1640." *Cambridge Historical Journal* 9 (1948): 148–64.

Lee, Sidney. *Elizabethan Sonnets.* 2 vols. New York: E. P. Dutton, 1903.

L'Estoile, Pierre de. *The Paris of Henry of Navarre as Seen by Pierre de L'Estoile: Selections from L'Estoile's Memoires-Journaux.* Translated by Nancy Rolker. Cambridge, Mass.: Harvard University Press, 1958.

Lever, J. W. *The Elizabethan Love Sonnet.* London: Methuen, 1956.

Levy, Charles Samuel. "The Correspondence of Sir Philip Sidney and Hubert Languet." Ph.D. dissertation, Cornell University, 1962.

———. "The Sidney-Hanau Correspondence." *English Literary Renaissance* 2 (1972): 19–28.

Levy, Fred J. "Philip Sidney Reconsidered." *English Literary Renaissance* 2 (1972): 5–18.

———. *Tudor Historical Thought.* San Marino, Calif.: Huntington Library, 1967.

M., A. *A Relation of the Passages of Our English Companies from Time to Time, Since Their First Departure from England, to the Posts of Germanie and the United Provinces.* London: H. Gasson, 1621.

Macray, William Dunn. *Annals of the Bodleian Library.* Oxford: Clarendon Press, Oxford University Press, 1890.

———. *Catologi Codicum Manuscriptorum Bibliotecae Bodleianae.* Oxford: Clarendon Press, Oxford University Press, 1878.

Markham, Sir Clements R. *The Fighting Veres.* Boston and New York: Houghton, Mifflin, 1888.

Matthews, Hazel. "Personnel of Parliament, 1585–1588." Master's thesis, London University, 1948.

Mead, D. M. *The Diary of Lady Margaret Hoby.* London: George Rutledge, 1930.

Moir, Thomas L. *The Addled Parliament of 1614.* Oxford: Clarendon Press, Oxford University Press, 1958.

Motley, John L. *History of the United Netherlands from the Death of William the Silent to the Synod of Dort.* 2 vols. New York: Harper and Brothers, 1861.

Muir, Ramsay. *Muir's Historical Atlas, Medieval and Modern.* Edited by R. F. Traharne and Harold Fullard. 10th ed. New York: Barnes and Noble, 1964.

Nares, Edward. *Memoirs of the Life and Administration of the Rt. Hon. William Cecil, Lord Burghley.* London: Colburn and Bentley, 1831.

Neale, John Ernest. *The Elizabethan House of Commons.* New York: Yale University Press, 1950.

———. "The Elizabethan Political Scene." *Proceedings of the British Academy.* London (1948): pp. 96–117.

Newdigate, B. H. "Mourners at Philip Sidney's Funeral." *Notes and Queries,* 180 (June 7, 1941): 398–401.

Nichols, John. *The Progresses and Public Processions of Queen Elizabeth.* 3 vols. 1923. Reprint. New York: B. Franklin, [?1965].

————. *The Progresses, Processions, and Magnificent Festivities of King James I.* 4 vols. 1788–21. Reprint. New York: B. Franklin, 1968.

Orlers, Jan Janszen. *The Triumphs of Nassau, or, A Description of The Victories Granted by God to the Estates General of the United Provinces.* Translated by W. Shute. N. P.: N. P., 1610.

Osborn, James M. *Young Philip Sidney, 1572–1577.* New Haven: Yale University Press, 1972.

Parry, Thomas. *A History of Welsh Literature.* Translated by H. Idris Bell. Oxford: Clarendon Press, Oxford University Press, 1955.

Pearson, L. E. *Elizabethan Love Conventions.* Los Angeles and Berkeley: University of California Press, 1933.

Peterson, Douglas L. *The English Lyric from Wyatt to Donne.* Princeton, N.J.: Princeton University Press, 1967.

Philip II, King of Spain. *Correspondance de Philippe II sur les Affaires des Pays-Bas.* 5 vols. Edited by M. Gachard. Brussels: Librairie Ancienne et Moderne, 1848–79.

Philipott, John. *Visitation of Kent Taken in the Days 1619–1621.* Edited by Robert Hovendon. London: Harleian Society, 1898.

Prinsterer, G. Groen van. *Archives ou Correspondance Inedite de la Maison d'Orange-Nassau.* 10 vols. Leiden: Set. J. Luchmans, 1836.

Raleigh, Sir Walter. "As You Came from the Holy Land." In *The Renaissance in England.* Edited by Hyder E. Rollins and Herschel Baker. Boston: D. C. Heath, 1954.

Rathmell; J. C. A. "Jonson, Lord Lisle, and Penshurst." *English Literary Renaissance* 1 (1971): 250–60.

Read, Conyers. *Mr. Secretary Walsingham and the Policy of Queen Elizabeth.* 1925. Reprint. Hamden, Conn.: Archon Books, 1967.

Rebholz, Ronald A. *The Life of Fulke Greville, First Lord Brooke.* Oxford: Clarendon Press, Oxford University Press, 1971.

Relf, Frances H. *Notes of the Debates in the House of Lords, Officially Taken by Robert Bowyer and Henry Elsing, 1621, 1625, 1628.* Camden Society, no. 42. Offices of the Royal Historical Society, 1929.

Return of the Names of Every Member Returned to Serve in Each Parliament. 2 vols. "Ordered to be Printed by the House of Commons," 1878.

Schrickx, W. "Letters in Belgian Archives of Two English Poets: Robert Sidney and Henry Wotton." *Revue des Langues Vivantes* 40 (1974/75): 5, pp. 483–88.

Seward, Desmond. *The First Bourbon: Henry IV, King of France and Navarre.* Boston: Gambit, 1971.

[Shakespeare, William]. "The First Part of the True and Honorable History of the Life of Sir Iohn Old-Castle, the Good Lord Cobham." London: Printed by W. Jaggard for T. P., 1600 [i.e., 1619].

Sidney, Philip. *Memoirs of the Sidney Family.* London: T. Fisher Univen, 1899.

————. "Penshurst Place." *Memorials of Old Kent.* Edited by P. H. Ditchfield and George Clinch. London: Benrose and Sons, 1907.

Sidney, Sir Philip. *Works of Sir Philip Sidney.* Edited by Albert Feuillerat. 4 vols. 1912. Reprint. London: Cambridge University Press, 1962.

————. *The Correspondence of Philip Sidney and Hubert Languet.* Edited by William A. Bradley. Boston: Merrymount Press, 1912.

Sims, R. *An Index to the Pedigrees and Arms Contained in the Heralds' Visitations and Other Genealogical Manuscripts in the British Museum.* London: John Russell Smith, 1849.

Smith, Hallet. *Elizabethan Poetry.* Cambridge, Mass.: Harvard University Press, 1952.

Smith, Logan P. *The Life and Letters of Sir Henry Wotton.* 2 vols. Oxford: Clarendon Press, Oxford University Press, 1907.

Stocker, John H. "Pedigree of Smyth of Bidborough and Sutton (1604–1684)." *Archaeologia Cantiana* 20 (1893): 77 ff.

Stone, Lawrence. *The Crisis of the Aristocracy, 1558–1641.* Oxford: Clarendon Press, Oxford University Press, 1965.

————. *Family and Fortune: Studies in Aristocratic Finance in the Sixteenth and Seventeenth Centuries.* Oxford: Clarendon Press, Oxford University Press, 1973.

Stow, John. *The Annals of England from the Inhabitation until 1592. Continued unto 1631 (An Appendix, 1632) by Edmund Howes, Gent.* London: Richard Meighen, 1631.

————. *The Chronicles of England from Brute unto this Present Year 1580.* Newberrie: H. Bynneman, 1580.

Straker, Ernest. *Wealden Iron.* London: G. Bell and Sons, 1931.

Tannenbaum, Samuel A. *The Handwriting of the Renaissance.* New York: Columbia University Press, 1930.

Tenison, E. M. *Elizabethan England.* 13 vols. Royal Leamington Spa: Issued for the author, 1933–50.

Tex, Jan den. *Oldenbarneveldt.* 2 vols. Haarlem: Tjeink Willink, 1960–62.

Thompson, Edward M. *Correspondence of the Hatton Family, 1601–1704.* London: J. B. Nichols and Sons, 1878.

A True Discourse of the Overthrowe Given to the Common Enemy at Turnhaut, the Fourteenth of January Last 1597, by Count Maurice of Nassau. Sent from a Gentleman of Account, that was Present at the Service, to a Friend of His in England. London: Peter Short, 1597.

van Dorsten, Jan A., and Strong, Roy C. *Leicester's Triumph.* London: Oxford University Press, 1964.

Vere, Sir Francis. *The Commentaries of Sir Francis Vere.* In *English Books, 1641–1700.* Ann Arbor, Mich.: University Microfilms, 1961–.

Wallace, Malcolm. *The Life of Sir Philip Sidney.* London: Cambridge University Press, 1915.

Waller, G. E. " 'My Wants and Your Perfections': Elizabethan England's Newest Poet." *Ariel* 8 (1977): 3–14.

————. "The 'Sad Pilgrim': The Poetry of Sir Robert Sidney." *Dalhousie Review* 56 (1975): 690–705.

Walsingham, Sir Francis. *The Journal of Francis Walsingham from December 1570 to April 1583.* Edited by C. T. Martin. The Camden Miscellany, vol. 6. J. B. Nichols and Sons, 1847.

Warnicke, Retha M. *William Lambarde.* Chichester, Sussex, England: Phillimore, 1973.

Watson, George. *The English Petrarchans.* London: University of London, Warburg Institute, 1967.

Wedgwood, Dame Veronica. *Biography of William the Silent.* New Haven: Yale University Press, 1944.

Whetstone, George. *Sir Philip Sidney, His Honorable Life, His Valiant Death, and True Vertues.* London: Thomas Cadman, 1587.

Willet, Paul Ferdinand. *Henry of Navarre and the Huguenots in France.* 1893. Reprint. New York: AMS Press, 1971.

William, Prince of Orange. *Correspondance de Guillaume le Taciturne.* 8 vols. Edited by Louis P. Gachard. Brussels: C. Muquardt, 1850–66.

Williams, Sir Roger. *The Works of Sir Roger Williams.* Edited by John X. Evans. Oxford: Clarendon Press, Oxford University Press, 1972.

Wilson, George C. *Lady Anne Clifford, Countess of Dorset, Pembroke, and Montgomery.* 1922. Reprint. Yorkshire: SR Publishers, 1967.

Wilson, Mona. *Sir Philip Sidney.* London: Duckworth, 1931.

Wilson, Violet L. *Society Women of Shakespeare's Time.* London: John Lane, The Bodley Head, 1924.

———. *Queen Elizabeth's Maids of Honor and Ladies of the Privy Chamber.* New York: E. P. Dutton, [?1922].

Witten-Hannah, Margaret A. "Lady Mary Wroth's 'Urania': The Work and The Tradition," Ph.D. dissertation, University of Auckland, December 1978.

Winters, Ivor. "The Sixteenth-Century Lyric in England." *Poetry: A Magazine of Verse* 53–54 (February 1939): 258–72; (March 1939): 320–335; (April 1939): 35–51.

Wood, Mary Anne Everett. *Elizabeth, Electress Palatine and Queen of Bohemia.* Revised by S. C. Lomas. London: Methuen, 1909.

Wright, Deborah K. "Modern-Spelling Text of Robert Sidney's Poems Proves Disappointing." *Sidney Newsletter* 3 (1982): 12–16.

———. "The Poetry of Robert Sidney: A Critical Study of His Autograph Manuscript." Ph.D. dissertation, Miami University, 1980.

Wright, Louis B. "English Politics and Administration, 1603–29." In *The Reign of James VI and I,* pp. 140–59. Edited by Alan G. R. Smith. New York: St. Martin's Press, 1973.

———. *Religion and Empire: The Alliance between Piety and Commerce in English Expansion, 1558–1625.* Chapel Hill, N.C.: University of North Carolina Press, 1943.

Young, Frances B. *Mary Sidney, Countess of Pembroke.* London: Daniel Nutt, 1912.

Appendix
Genealogical Table for Robert Sidney, First Earl of Leicester, 1563–1626

Sidney's Descent through the House of Lisle

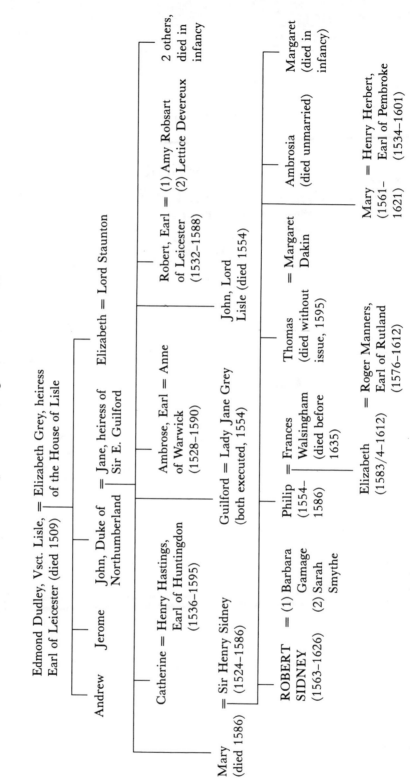

ROBERT SIDNEY = (1) Barbara Gamage (died 1621)
Vsct. Lisle, 1st Earl   Heiress of John Gamage of Coity, Glamorganshire
of Leicester (1563–1626)   (2) Sarah Smythe, widow of Thomas Smythe,
                              mother of Vsct. Strangford

William (ca. 1589–1612;
died without issue)

Catherine = Sir Lewis Mansell

Robert, Vsct. = Dorothy Percy
Lisle, 2nd Earl
of Leicester
(1595–1677)

Mary = Sir Robert Wroth
(1586–   (1540?–1606)
? after
1640)

Philippa = John Hobart
(1594–
1620)

Barbara = (1) Sir Thomas
              Smythe, Vsct.
              Strangford
          (2) Sir Thomas
              Colepepper

5 others, died in
infancy or childhood

Algernon
(1622–1683;
died unmarried)

Robert

Philip, 3rd = Katherine Cecil,
Earl of   daughter of
Leicester   William Cecil,
(1619–1698) Earl of Salisbury
              (died 1652)

Lucy = John Pelham
          of Laughton

Henry, Earl of Romney
(1641–1704; died unmarried)

Dorothy = (1) Henry Spencer,
(1614–1684)   Earl of Sunderland
              (2) Sir Robert Smythe

**Ancestors and Cousins of Robert Sidney
through His Father's Descent**

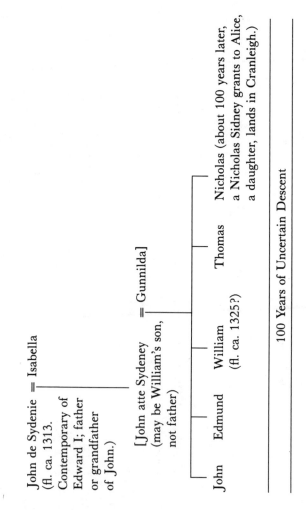

John de Sydenie = Isabella
(fl. ca. 1313.
Contemporary of
Edward I; father
or grandfather
of John.)

[John atte Sydeney = Gunnilda]
(may be William's son,
not father)

John   Edmund   William   Thomas   Nicholas (about 100 years later,
                   (fl. ca. 1325?)   a Nicholas Sidney grants to Alice,
                                                a daughter, lands in Cranleigh.)

100 Years of Uncertain Descent

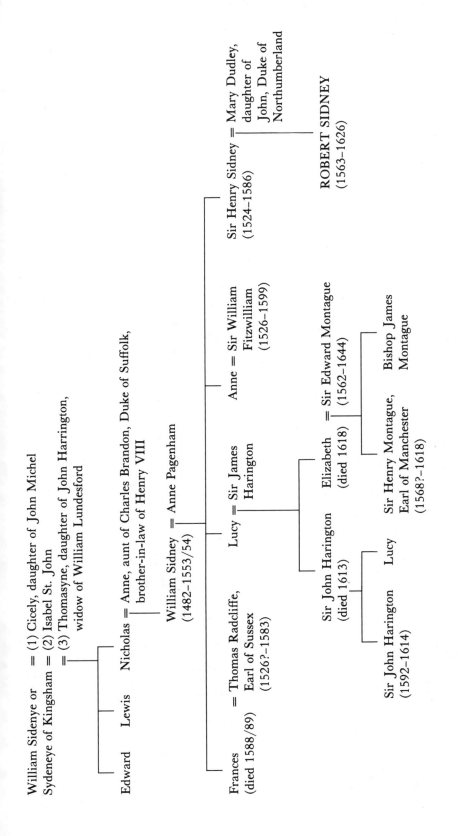

William Sidenye or Sydeneye of Kingsham = (1) Cicely, daughter of John Michel
= (2) Isabel St. John
= (3) Thomasyne, daughter of John Harrington, widow of William Lundesford

Edward   Lewis   Nicholas = Anne, aunt of Charles Brandon, Duke of Suffolk, brother-in-law of Henry VIII

William Sidney = Anne Pagenham
(1482–1553/54)

Sir Henry Sidney = Mary Dudley, daughter of John, Duke of Northumberland
(1524–1586)

Anne = Sir William Fitzwilliam
(1526–1599)

ROBERT SIDNEY
(1563–1626)

Frances = Thomas Radcliffe, Earl of Sussex
(died 1588/89)   (1526?–1583)

Lucy = Sir James Harington

Elizabeth = Sir Edward Montague
(died 1618)   (1562–1644)

Sir John Harington
(died 1613)

Sir Henry Montague, Earl of Manchester
(1568?–1618)

Bishop James Montague

Lucy

Sir John Harington
(1592–1614)

Index

Agricola, Georgius, 206
Albert, Archduke, 102, 213, 214
Alençon, Duke of Anjou, 38, 41, 43, 47
Allen, Cardinal, 125
Alva, Duchess of, 17
Alva, Duke of, 17, 75
Amelot (mentioned in correspondence), 35
Amsterdam, 219
Amyes, Captain Thomas, 134, 135
Anglicans, 27
Angus, Lord, 67
Anhalt, Prince of, 219
Anne (queen of England), 172, 210, 216, 217, 223
Ansbach, Marquis of, 219
Antwerp, 34, 41, 75, 124, 125; restored to Spain, 77, 88
Aristotle, 20
Arminians, 94, 220
Arminius, 220
Arnhem, 45
Arundel, earl and countess of. See Howard, Thomas
Ascham, Roger, 20, 24, 35
Ashby, 19
Asheby, William, 61–68 passim
Ashton, Adbie, 167
Ashton, Thomas, 24
Astrophel and Stella, 178
Audley, Lord, 44
Augsberg, 40
Aurelius, 40
Axel, 44, 45
Azeredo, Pedro Henriquez de, count of Fuentes of Toledo, 123

Babington, Uriah, 82
Bacharach, 218, 219
Bacon, Lady Anne, 19
Bacon brothers, 32, 46

Bacon, Sir Francis (Lord Verulam, Viscount St. Albans), 15, 17, 154, 164, 216
Bacx, Marcellus, 103
Bagnall, Samuel, 113
Baines, Richard, 207
Barbary, 128
Barnelms, 174, 175
Barneveldt. See Oldenbarneveldt, Johan van
Barras, Count of, 102–3
Barrington, John, 15
Baskerville, Nicholas, 113, 114, 115
Baskerville, Sir Thomas, 99, 113, 114
Bastille, 150
Bath, 220
Bath, Order of, Knights of, 184
Baynard's Castle, 175, 177, 212
Bayonne, 88
Beckett, Thomas, 189
Bedford, earls and countess of. See Russell, Edward; Russell, John; Russell, Lucy
Beecher, William, 84, 121, 122
Bergen-op-Zoom, 84
Berghen, 45, 97, 111
Berkeley, Henry Lord, 191
Berkeley, Sir Thomas, 202
Berkshire, earl of. See Norris
Bermuda Company, 226
Berwick, 61, 63, 68
Béthune, Maximilien, 145, 217
Bird (tutor), 183, 184
Biron, Marshall of, 148
Blocq, Nicholas, 133
Blott, William, 196
Blount, Charles (Lord Mountjoy), 161, 162, 163, 164, 174, 178
Bodin, Jean, 36, 206
Bodleian Library, 207
Bodley, Sir Thomas, 79, 86, 92, 97, 122, 163
Bohemia, 220
Bois-de-Luc, 101

Bolton, John, 83
Bolton, Thomas, 83
Borlas, Sir William, 81, 82, 84, 94, 111; as lieutenant-governor of Flushing, 77–78, 88, 130–31
Bosely, Reinold, 126
Bothwell, earl of. *See* Stewart
Boughton, 25
Boulogne, 151
Bourbon, Catherine de, 150
Bourbon, François de, duc de Montpensier, 147, 150
Bourne, Fox, 21, 44
Bowes, Sir Jerome, 26
Bowes, Robert, 68
Brabant, 58
Brandon, Charles, duke of Suffolk, 15, 161, 216
Brandon, Sir William, 15
Breda, 103, 172
Bredenay, 108
Brest, 146, 148, 149
Brill, the, 43, 77, 84, 126, 138, 222; governors of, 44, 94–95 n
Brisac, Duc de, 150, 151
Brittany, 112, 145, 146, 148, 149, 150
Broderode (soldier), 103
Bromley, Robert, 82
Brooke, Henry, eleventh Lord Cobham, 41, 165, 166, 216; implicated in Main Plot, 167, 210; opposes Sidney for Cinque Ports wardenship, 138, 139, 153–57 passim
Brooke, William, tenth Lord Cobham, 55, 107, 154, 157, 163
Brooke, Sir William, 157
Brown, Alexander, 206
Browne, Lady, 133, 134, 135
Browne, Sir William, lieutenant-governor of Flushing, 89, 94, 111, 117, 118, 120, 122, 129, 130, 131–32, 133, 136, 137, 184, 197, 214, 217
Bruges, 97, 99, 109
Bruno, Giordano, 37
Brunswick, Henry Jules, Duke of, 27
Brussels, 126
Buck, Captain (wounded at Steenwyck), 102
Burchgrave (Dutch leader), 59
Burchinshaw (embezzler), 120, 121, 122, 131, 160
Burghe, Thomas, Lord, 114, 120, 126, 138, 161
Burghley, Elizabeth, 225
Burghley, Lord, *See* Cecil, William
Burnham, Edward, 88
Buste, John, 23, 25, 34

Butler, Thomas, earl of Ormond, 38
Butrech, Peter, 39
Buys, Paul, 44

Caernarvonshire, 180
Caesar, 24
Calais, 114, 151, 152
Calvaert (Dutch agent), 150
Calvin, John, 20
Calvinism, 26, 27, 59
Calvinists, 39
Cambridge, 19, 205
Camden, William, 68, 206
Camerarius, Joseph, 41, 206
Canterbury, 214, 217
Cape Finistre, 123
Caracciolo, Pasqual, 37
Carew, Sir George, 163
Carey, Elizabeth, 202, 205
Carey, Elizabeth, Lady Hunsdon, 202
Carey, Fernando, 134, 135
Carey, George, second baron Hunsdon, 160, 202
Carey, Henry, first baron Hunsdon, 41, 63, 160
Carey, Sir Robert, 63
Carleill, Christopher, 42
Carleton, Dudley, 161, 229
Carmichael, John Lord, 63, 64, 66, 67, 68
Caron, Noel, 112, 213, 214, 215, 221
Casimir, Frederick, 26
Casimir, Duke John, 26, 27, 32, 36, 39, 40
Casimir, Lewis, 26, 27
Catcher, Richard, 83, 176
Catcher, Thomas, 83
Catholicism, 16, 27, 40, 215; attempts to reestablish, 19, 61; Sidney's suspicions toward, 59, 60, 217
Caudebec, 148
Cavendish, William, earl of Devonshire, 223
Cecil, Robert, Viscount Cranbourne, earl of Salisbury: 46, 55, 126, 152, 188, 210, 213; allies of, 154, 163, 179, 210; Devereux, Robert, relations with, 153, 161–62; oversees Robert Sidney's governance of Flushing, 89, 90, 111, 127; Sidney asks for patronage, 128, 129, 137, 157, 159; supports Sidney, 108, 112, 114, 164, 165, 166, 167
Cecil, Sir Thomas, earl of Exeter, 44, 213
Cecil, Sir William, Lord Burghley: 22, 75, 111, 114, 120, 153, 160, 162, 181, 189; comments on siege of Sluys, 97, 99; death of, 165; Dudley, Robert, relations with, 18, 158; negotiations with France, 146, 149,

151; oversees Sidney's governance of Flushing, 73, 80, 82, 86, 87, 92, 115, 116, 119; Sedgrave affair, 124, 126, 127; Sidney, Philip, relations with, 38, 58; Sidney, Robert, relations with, 60, 62, 85, 89, 101, 122, 123, 128, 130, 131, 157, 159, 207
Chamberlain, Sir John, 161, 215, 222, 223
Champagne, 146
Chapman, George, 186, 207
Chartres, 145, 147
Charles I (king of England), 185, 217, 219
Charles II (king of England), 185
Charles III of Loraine, duke of Maine, Guise, and Mercoeur, 150
Charles, archduke of Austria, 18, 19
Chiettes, de (governor of Dieppe), 146
China, 33
Christ Church, Oxford, 20, 21, 29, 184
Christian IV (king of Denmark), 185
Cicero, 20, 23
Cinque Ports: Sidney sues for wardenship of, 138–39, 153–57, 160, 165, 179, 197, 199, 200, 203, 215
Classis of Walcheren, 136
Clifford, Lady Anne, 18, 179, 188, 206
Clifford, George, earl of Cumberland, 179
Clifford, Margaret, countess of Cumberland, 179, 206
Clinton, Lady Elizabeth, 176
Cobham, Lord. See Brooke
Cochefilet, André de, 217
Colet, John, 24
Coligny, Gaspard II, Seigneur de Châtillon, 27, 145
Coligny, Louise (princess of Orange), 27, 28, 94, 172, 203, 219
Collins, Arthur, 182, 183
Cologne, 27
Compiège, 146
Compton, Lady Elizabeth, 174
Compton, William, earl of Northampton, 164, 166, 178, 223
Condé, Prince of, (Henri II de Bourbon), 145, 151
Conway, Sir Edward, 97
Copley (Sidney's kinsman), 129
Corte, Claudio, 37
Council of the North, 19
Council of Wales, 41
Court of King's Bench, 227
Court of Wards, 179
Cox (merchant's agent), 121
Cracow (Cracovia), 40, 41
Crispe, Nicholas, 189
Croft, P. J., 195, 196, 197, 204

Cruickshank, Charles G., 84, 120
Cuffe, Henry, 46
Cumberland, earl and countess of. See Clifford
Dacres, Lady Margaret, 164, 178
Dakin, Margaret, 181
D'Albert, Jeanne (queen of Navarre), 145
D'Angoulême, Mme (French courtier), 147
D'Anjou, Francis, duc, 145
Daniel (chaplain at Flushing), 136, 137
Daniel, Samuel, 206
Darby, earl of. See Stanley
Darcy, Lord, 219
Davies, Sir John, 206
Davison (English official), 86
Denmark, 41, 220
de Pulteney, Sir John, 186
Deputies of the Religion, 146
De Quadra (Spanish ambassador), 19
Derby, earl of. See Stanley, William
de Simier, Jehan, 38
de Valois, Margaret, 145
de Vargas, Juan, 75
Deventer (Dutch leader), 58, 59
Deventer, 102
Devereux, Frances, countess of Essex, 164, 174, 178, 180
Devereux, Lettice, countess of Essex, 18, 38, 223
Devereux, Robert, second earl of Essex, 44, 51, 83, 108, 112, 113, 137, 144, 175; allies of, 46, 163, 178, 179, 180, 226; and Elizabeth, 26, 97, 165; and Sidney,19, 46, 47, 60, 114, 163, 164, 197, 202, 210, 215; imprisoned, 165–66; opponents of, 19, 161–62; stages uprising, 60, 166–67; supports Sidney, 107, 138, 148, 152–57 passim, 159, 160, 177
Devereux, Robert, third earl of Essex, 210
Devereux, Walter, earl of Essex, 19, 26, 181
Devinis, Richard, 128
Devill (English soldier), 120
Devonshire, earl of. See Cavendish, William
de Walcher, Peter, 92
Digges (muster-master at Flushing), 86, 87
Dieppe, 146, 151
Doesberg, 45
Donne, John, 37
Dordrecht, 27
Dormer, Mary Sidney, 16
Dormer, Sir William, 16
Dorset, earls of. See Sackville
Dorsett, Robert, 20, 21, 24, 29, 34, 60; describes Sidney, 22, 23, 25

Dougat, 173
Dover, 145, 146
Dowland, Robert, 37, 205, 207
Drake, Sir Francis, 43, 44
Drayton, Michael, 206
Drury, Sir Robert, 107, 113
Du Bellay, Joachim, 206
Dublin, 17
Dudley, Ambrose, earl of Warwick, 17, 42, 51, 57, 83, 159
Dudley, Amy Robsart, 18
Dudley, Anne, countess of Warwick, 18, 19, 51, 114, 161, 179; as ally of Robert Devereux, 163; debts of, 191, 212; supports Sidney, 138, 154, 156, 189
Dudley, Edmond, earl of Warwick, viscount Lisle, 18
Dudley, Guildford, 16, 18, 28
Dudley, Henry, 17
Dudley, John, earl of Warwick, duke of Northumberland, 16, 18, 28, 161
Dudley, Robert, 72, 223
Dudley, Sir Robert, earl of Leicester, 15, 17, 19, 29, 41, 92, 94, 128, 196; allies of, 28, 196; death of, 67, 68; campaigns against Spain, 43, 44, 45, 58; Elizabeth, relations with, 18, 19, 38, 46, 162, 187; illegitimate son of, 72, 223; interferes in Dutch affairs, 44, 50, 86; profiteering by, 57; Protestantism, 19, 58, 60, 163; quarrels with Walsingham, 53, 60; Sidney's relations with, 55, 58, 59, 60, 159, 223
Dumblane, Bishop of, 62
Duncan-Jones, Katherine, 154, 195, 196, 197, 200, 202, 203, 204
Dunkirk, 99, 101
Dyer, Edward, 32, 41, 46, 51, 163
Dzinlinsky, Paulus, 122

Edict of Nantes, 145, 147, 149
Edinburgh, 61, 63, 64, 68
Edmondes, Thomas, 146, 147, 150
Education, 19–20, 23–24. See also Sidney, Sir Philip, education of; Sidney, Sir Robert, education of
Edward VI (king of England), 16, 186
Effingham. See Howard, William
Elizabeth (princess, daughter of James I), 185, 211, 217, 218, 220
Elizabeth I (queen of England): 15, 17, 35, 51, 154, 183; Alençon, relations with, 38, 41; cautionary towns, receives, 43, 77; death of, 137, 210; Devereux, Robert, relations with, 114, 155, 164, 165; Dudley, Robert, relations with, 18, 19, 38, 44, 46, 187; Dutch

suspicions toward, 92, 101–2, 116, 117, 118, 119; Henri IV, relations with, 146–52 passim; James I, negotiations with, 61, 62, 65, 67, 69; refuses to create new peers, 159, 161; Sedgrave affair, 124, 126, 127; Sidney, Philip, dealings with, 27, 28, 32, 36, 38, 44, 45, 46; Sidney, Robert, dealings with, 28, 36, 46, 128, 153, 155, 156, 160, 171, 188–89, 198, 199, 200. See also Tudor court.
Elyot, Sir Thomas, 20
Emmanuel, 19
Erasmus, 20, 24, 189
Esler, Anthony, 160
Essex, countess of. See Devereux, Frances; Devereux, Lettice
Essex, earls of. See Devereux, Robert (second earl); Devereux, Robert (third earl); Devereux, Walter
Everade, Michael, 134–35, 136, 137
Everett, John, 128
Exeter, earl of. See Cecil, Sir Thomas
Farnese, Alexander, duke of Parma, 43, 58, 61, 62, 99, 102, 122
Ferical, 17
"15" (unidentified friend), 155
Fitzwilliam, Anne Sidney, 16
Fitzwilliam, Thomas, 16
Fitzwilliam, William, earl of Southampton, 16, 17
Flanders, 33, 97, 99, 101, 106, 206
Fleming, Sir John, 94, 115, 134
Flodden, 16
Flushing, 32, 41, 93, 120, 182, 198, 218–19; abuses in supplying, 85, 115, 117, 121–22; conditions in, 135–36; contract regarding, 78–79, 81, 86; demands of governing, 72–75; 135–36; Dutch threat to, 79, 80, 102, 115, 118, 121, 134–36; English administration of, 29, 43–44, 50–60, 72, 77, 86, 119–20, 127–28, 129, 130–39, 178; fortifications of, 75, 77, 80, 117–118; in Sidney's poetry, 204; lack of supplies for, 81–82, 115–16, 221; made cautionary town, 43, 77; nepotism in English bureaucracy of, 129–30; overthrows Spanish rule, 75; payment of soldiers in, 44–45, 57–58, 70n; returned to Dutch, 117, 118, 137, 185, 221–22; Sidney assumes governorship of, 72–73, 77–79; Sidney's presences in and absences from, 137–39, 178; Spanish threat to, 106, 108, 119, 123, 126, 127, 132; strategic importance of, 75, 221. See also Sidney, Sir Robert, as governor of Flushing
Fontenay, 34
Fortescue, Sir John, 67, 137, 188

"40" (unidentified friend), 155
Foscarini, Antonio, 218
Foulckes, Captain, 145, 146
France, 113, 134, 161, 185, 220; Duke of
    Parma in, 99, 102; English presence in, 115,
    118, 120; reasons for visiting, 33; religious
    strife in, 43, 144; Sidney's embassies to, 55,
    138, 145–52
Frankfurt, 34
Fraunce, Abraham, 206
Frederick IV, elector Palatine, 219
Friesland, 102
Frobisher, Sir Martin, 87
Fuentes, Count. See Azevedo

Gamage family, 17
Gamage, John, 42, 129, 171
Gamedge, Paen, 171
Gardiner, Samuel, 116
Garret, Sir Thomas, 179
Garter, Order of the, 227
Gates, Sir Thomas, 226
Gelder (betrayed by Patton), 58
Gelley, Jacques, 92, 94
Germany, 27, 33, 134, 218
Gerrard, Sir Thomas, 166
Gertruydenberg, 27, 92, 103, 119
Ghent, 39
Gifford, William, 53, 173
Gilbert, Gifford, 207
Gilbert, Sir Humphrey, 20,42
Gilpin, Sir George, 79, 81, 90, 112, 117, 122
Giphanius (friend of Philip Sidney), 206
Giron, Don Fernando, 132
Gisors, 146
Glamorganshire, 171
Gloucester, Duke of. See Humphrey
Golding, Thomas, 184, 187
Gomarians, 220
Gonzague-Clèves, Charles de, duke of Nev-
    ers, 149
Goring, Captain, sergeant-major at Flushing,
    175
Gouda, 75, 220
Goulshtyne, 219
Gournay, 148
Grave, 44, 58, 109
Graveline, 132, 213
Gravesend, 44
Gray, Thomas Lord, 163, 166
Grayford, earl of, 63
Greenwich, 173, 174, 177, 183, 218
Grenville, Sir Richard, 42
Greville, Fulke, 18, 26, 32, 41, 51, 166; on
    Philip Sidney's death, 46, 50

Grey, Catherine. See Seymour, Lady Cath-
    erine
Grey, Elizabeth, countess of Kent, 18
Grey, Jane, Lady Grey of Wilton, 16, 28
Grisone, Frederico, 37
Groningen, 102
Gunpowder Plot, 123

Haddington, 64, 65
Hague, The, 44, 80, 102, 103, 111, 172; En-
    glish personnel at, 79, 219, 220
Hajek, Johannes, 22, 23, 25
Hamburg, 41
Hamilton, Lord Claud, 62, 64, 67
Hampshire, 16
Harington, Lucy. See Russell, Lucy
Harrington, Lucy Sidney, 16, 219
Harrington, Sir John, 175, 188, 211, 218, 219
Hart, Miles, 134
Harvey, George, 121, 122
Hastings (Sidney's cousin), 175
Hastings, Catherine, countess of Hunting-
    don, 19, 51, 176, 182, 183, 203; as ally of
    Essex, 163; supports Sidney, 18, 107, 154,
    189; widowed, 137, 164, 177
Hastings, Henry, earl of Huntingdon, 19, 51,
    62, 68, 181, 226; death of, 137, 164
Haultain (Hautain) sieur de, admiral of Zea-
    land, 135
Hawkins, Sir John, 87
Hay, Lord James, 188, 226
Heidelberg, 27, 218, 219, 220
Heneage, Sir Thomas, 51
Henri III (king of France), 145
Henri IV (king of France), 43, 146, 149, 179,
    220; accused of deceptiveness, 116, 117;
    converts to Catholicism, 144, 145; requests
    aid from England, 148, 150, 151
Henry II (king of England), 189
Henry VIII (king of England), 15, 28
Henry, Prince of Wales, 184, 188, 208, 216,
    217, 218
Heraugière, Governor (of Breda), 103
Herbert, Catherine Talbot, 28
Herbert, Henry, earl of Pembroke, 55, 164,
    174, 179, 202, 226; Lord President of
    Wales, 161–62; marries Mary Sidney, 28,
    29; Sidney, Robert, dealings with, 42, 43,
    157, 171
Herbert, Mary, countess of Pembroke, 15, 17,
    20, 32, 51, 213; death of, 228; marries
    Henry Herbert, 28, 29; Sidney, Barbara,
    friendship with, 180, 120; visits Elizabeth's
    court, 21, 22
Herbert, Philip, earl of Montgomery, 183, 213

Herbert, William, third earl of Pembroke, 162, 179, 180, 202, 206
Hertford, earl and countess of. *See* Seymour, Edward
Hesse, Landgrave of. *See* Maurice
High Commission in the North, 19
Hobart, Sir John, earl of Buckinghamshire, 186, 225
Hobson (Sidney servant), 25
Hoby, Sir Edward, 175
Hoby, Lady Margaret, 19
Hoby, Posthumus, 181
Hohenlo (Hollock), Philip, Count of, 45, 58, 103, 105; as Sidney's friend, 59, 60, 109
Holinshed, Raphael, 206
Holland, 84
Holst, 41
Holstein, Duke of, 185
Holy League, 145, 148
House of Commons, 157
House of Guise, 145
House of Lisle, 159
House of Lords, 185, 217, 227
House of Lorraine, 145, 151
House of Nassau, 172
House of Orange, 28, 38, 94, 172
Howard, Catherine, duchess of Sulffolk, 19
Howard, Charles, earl of Nottingham, 41, 87, 210, 219; and Cecil, 154, 161–62, 163; and Devereux uprising, 166, 167; and Sidney, 107, 137, 154, 157, 164
Howard, Frances, 215
Howard, Henry, earl of Northampton, 163, 215
Howard, Katherine, countess of Nottingham, 154
Howard, Thomas, earl of Arundel, 218, 219
Howard, Thomas, earl of Suffolk, 163, 166, 178, 226
Howard, William, lord of Effingham, 166
Hubner, Peter, 35
Huguenots, 60, 145
Hume, Sir James, 64
Humphrey, duke of Gloucester, 185
Humphrey, Lawrence, 20
Hungary, 40
Huntingdon, earl and countess of. *See* Hastings
Huntly, Lord, 61, 62, 64, 67

Ingolstadt, 40
Ireland, 15, 60, 125, 128
Isle of Wight, 123
Isocrates, 24
Italy, 24, 33–34, 40

James I and VI (king of England and Scotland), 63, 65, 68, 69, 77, 94, 117, 179, 210, 212; Elizabeth's offer to, retracted, 63–68 passim; funeral of, 217, 229; lavish spending of, 221; makes peace with Spain, 118, 132; opposition to claim to English throne, 167, 210; quarrels with Dutch, 134, 220; sells honors, 211, 223; Sidney, Robert, relations with, 63, 65, 68, 69, 210, 213; visits Penshurst, 188, 208. *See also* Stuart court
Jansson, Cornelius, 128
Jersey, 162
John of Austria, 26
Johns, Mr. (owns interest in Otford), 188
Jones, Edward, 227
Jones, Robert, 207
Jons, Griffin, 126, 128
Jonson, Ben, 185, 186, 188, 191, 207–8

Kelliher, Hilton, 154, 196, 197, 202, 203, 204
Kellsway, 25
Kermitmayne, 211
Kent, 16, 155, 173, 211, 218; Sidneys' prominence in, 55, 157, 165
Kerwin, Robert, 186, 187
King, Edward, Viscount Kingsborough, 196
Kingsford, C.L., 15
Kittredge, George Lyman, 197
Knights of Bath, 184
Knoll, 211
Knollys, Sir William, 166
Knowles, Sir Thomas, 97

Lake, Thomas, 115
Lambarde, William, 189
Lambart, Captain (wounded at Steenwyck), 102
Lanche (English soldier), 120
Lane, Ralph (governor of Rammekins), 130
Languet, Hubert, 22, 27, 32, 39–40, 60, 206; death of, 41; pedagogy of, 23–24, 33; Sidney, Robert described by, 34, 35, 36
La Noue, François de, 34, 60, 106
La Tour d'Auvergne, Henride, vicomte de Turenne, duc de Bouillon, 146, 148
Laud, William, 185
Lauterberg, 27
Lee, Sir Henry, 26
Leicester County, 211
Leicester, earls and countesses of. *See* Dudley, Robert; Sidney, Robert
Leicester, Lady, 51, 185
Leiden, 44
Leigh, Henry, 160
Leipzig, 39

Lennox, Duke of, 218, 219
Lester, George, 84, 85, 121, 122
Levy, F.J., 28, 46
Lewknor, Lewis, 127
Lincolnshire, 50, 152
Lisbon, 123
Lisle. See Dudley, Sidney
Livy, 24
Lloyd, Sir Thomas, 196
Lobbet ("Lobetius"), Jean, 23, 34, 35, 36, 39, 41, 206
London, 27, 55, 128, 173, 174, 175–76
Lorraine, 125
Lorraine, Catherine de, duchess of Montpensier, 151
Lovel, Mistress Anne, 203
Lovel, Sir Thomas, 203
Low Countries, 42, 57, 60, 75, 84, 126, 150, 220; and English negotiations with Spain, 77, 79, 80, 92, 118, 132, 136, 217; contract between England and, 88, 89, 90, 91, 115, 119; costs of war in, 116–17; disease in, 172, 182; Robert Dudley inteferes in, 44, 58–59; English forces in, 73, 77 (see also Flushing, as English garrison; Military); purchase cautionary towns, 221–22; relations between English and, 79, 92, 93, 101–2, 116–19, 136; trade between Spanish and, 87–91, 163; war between Spain and, 43, 108. See also Flushing; Zealand
Luca, 149
Ludlow, 171
Ludlow Castle, 25
Ludowick, Count, 75
Ludwig, Elector, 27
Lumley, John, baron, 163
Lumley, Lady Elizabeth, 219
Lundesford, William, 15
Lutherans, 26, 27, 35
Lyons, 147

Maddox, Griffin, 22, 25
Mainard (Burghley's secretary), 131
Main Plot, 167, 210
Maine, duc de. See Charles III
Maitland, Sir John, 63, 66
Maldere, Sir James, 221
Manners, Elizabeth, countess of Rutland, 188
Manners, Roger, earl of Rutland, 157, 163, 179
Mansell, Sir Lewis, 225
Mansfelt, Pierre Ernest, count of, 102
Mantell, Robert, 20
Margate, 137, 175
Mariana, Juan de, 206

Marlowe, Christopher, 207
Marrit, Abisag, 128
Martin, Captain John, 227
Mary (daughter of James I), 217
Mary, Queen of Scots, 16, 17, 18, 28
Maurice, Landgrave of Hesse, Count Nassau, Prince of Orange, 27, 34, 41, 58, 101, 112, 122, 219, 226. See also Nassau, Count Maurice of
Maximilian, Archduke, 26
Maxwell (imprisoned), 67
Meetekerk (wounded at Dunkirk), 101
Melanchthon, Philip, 36
Mendoza, Don Diego de, 17, 62, 75
Melvin, Sir Robert, 64
Meredith, William, 112
Meuse, 146
Michelmarsh, 16
Middleburgh, 87, 90, 111, 127
Mildmay, Grace, 19
Military, English: clothing supplied to, 82–83; desertion from, 119; Dutch mustering of, 120–21; food supplied to, 83–85; organization of, 74; pay of, 84, 85, 221, 222; profiteering in, 73, 79, 82, 83, 119, 120, 122; shortages affecting, 81–82, 115–16, 119, 198. See also Flushing, as English garrison; Sidney, Sir Robert, as governor of Flushing; Sidney, Sir Robert, military career of
"M.M." (English spy), 126
Mody (English spy), 126
Moffet, Thomas, 206
Montague, Edward, Lord Montague of Boughton, 22, 23, 25
Montgomery, earl of. See Herbert, Philip
More (Moor, Moore), Joyce (Joos) de, 134
Moravia, 41
Morgan, Sir Thomas, 75, 99
Morison, Sir Charles, 182
Morocco, 128
Motley, John Lothrop, 92, 116, 117
Mulcaster, 24
Munich, 40
Murray, Sir Alexander, 103
Muscovy, 227
Myrick, Gelly, 179

Nantes, 146, 147, 150
Naples, 123
Nashe, Thomas, 202
Nassau, Justinus de, admiral, 99
Nassau, Count Maurice of, Landgrave of Hesse, Prince of Orange: 27, 34, 41, 58, 101, 112, 116, 117, 122, 219, 226; Axel, 44,

45; Flushing, 75, 77; Nieuport, 106–7, 108; Sidney, Robert, friendship with, 28, 88, 92, 94, 209; Sluys, 97, 99; Steenwyck, 102; Turnhout, 103

Nassau, Philip William of, Prince of Orange, 26, 27, 39, 43, 75, 77, 172

Nassau, William of (The Silent), 38

Neale, John Ernest, 157

Netherlands. See Low Countries

Nevers, duc de. See Gonzague-Clèves, Charles de

Neville, Sir Henry, 161

Nevitt, Thomas, 51, 53; and Sidney's finances, 55, 64, 212, 216, 228

Newfoundland, 42

New World: English interest in 42, 226–27

Neiuport, 97, 106–8, 163

Nigol, 180

Nonesuch, 44

Norris, Sir Edward, 45, 92, 97

Norris, Francis, earl of Berkshire, 188

Norris, John, 43, 45, 97, 109, 139

North, Lord Dudley (?), 44

Northampton, earls of. See Compton, William; Howard, Henry

Northamptonshire, 25

Northumberland, earl and countess of. See Percy, Henry; Percy, Dorothy

Nottingham, earl and countess of. See Howard, Charles; Howard, Katherine

Nuestadt, 27, 34

Nuremberg, 40, 41

Nuys, 44, 58

O'Conor, Donough, 17

Oldenbarneveldt, Johan van, 44, 94, 103, 116, 117, 220

Oldenborow, 108

Oporto, 123

Orléans, 147

Osborn, J.M., 21, 22, 23, 37

Ostend, 45, 84, 92, 97, 106, 138

Otford, 174, 176, 188–89, 211

Overbury, Sir Thomas, 215

Oversell, 102

Owen, Hugh, 123, 126

Oxford, 19, 205

Oxford, earl of. See Vere, Edward de

Pacheco (Spanish governor), 75

Pagenham, Sir Hugh, 16

Palatinate, 228

Palatine, 26, 217

Palmer, Sir Henry, 89

Paris, 41, 62, 145, 150–51, 206

Parker, Sir Nicholas, 44, 112

Parma, Duke of. See Farnese

Parr, Catherine, 28

Patton, Aristotle, 58

Paulett, Sir Anthony, 162

Peckham, Sir George, 42

Pelham, Sir William, 45

Pembroke, earls and countess of. See Herbert

Pengogo (Wales), 211

Penshurst, 20, 42, 53, 172, 182, 183, 184, 185; acquired by Sidneys, 16, 186; construction at, 186–87; costs of maintaining, 54, 55, 212; daily routine at, 228–29; gardens at, 188, 198; royal visits to, 187–88, 208; Sidney family seat, 173, 174, 175, 176, 177, 181; stone supplied from, 167, 213

Percy, Dorothy, countess of Northumberland, 226

Percy, Henry, earl of Northumberland, 163, 185, 226

Philip II (king of Spain), 17, 26, 59, 60, 117, 145; and James I, 65, 69; and Netherlands, 43, 88, 89, 220; threatens England, 62, 65, 125

Philip the Good, duke of Burgundy, 75

Pigott, 45, 58

Plymouth, 44

Podway (Sussex lessee), 152

Poland, 134

Pomerland, 41

Pooley, Sir John, 112

Popham, Sir John (Lord Chief Justice of the King's Bench), 166

Pott, Thomas, 135, 136, 137

Powell, Thomas, 206

Prague, 27, 40

Primogeniture, rule of, 32, 40

Privy Chamber, 154, 180

Privy Council, 92, 112, 167, 217, 222, 227; and Dutch trade with Spain, 88, 89, 90; and Flushing garrison supplies, 82, 83, 84, 121, 122; orders from, to Sidney, 72, 80, 81, 120, 131; Sidney campaigns for position on, 156, 160; Sidney's correspondence with, 87, 154, 214; Sidney's entreaties to, 86, 114–15, 128

Protestantism, 26, 36, 39, 217; English radical faction, 19, 28, 38, 46, 50, 58, 60, 163, 226; European League of Protestants, 27–28, 38; in France, 144–51 passim, 185; Sidney's devotion to, 16, 46

Ptolemy, 37

Puritans, 19, 136. See also Protestantism; Protestants

Radcliffe, Frances Sidney, countess of Sussex, 16, 19

Radcliffe, Thomas, earl of Sussex, 16, 17

Raleigh, Elizabeth, 180

Raleigh, Sir Walter, 15, 41, 107, 108, 162, 166, 210; and Cecil, 163, 210; imprisoned, 167; and Lady Sidney, 180; and New World, 42, 226; opposes Sidney's marriage, 171; seeks vice-chamberlainship, 152, 160; Walsingham ballad by, 197, 204

Rammekins, Castle of, 75, 77, 80, 88, 89, 90; offered to Elizabeth, 43; Philip Sidney as governor of, 44; Thomas Sidney proposed as governor of, 130

Randolph, Arthur, 86, 94, 118

Rathmell, J.C.A., 207, 208

Ratliffe, Bridget, countess of Sussex, 153, 179

Ratliffe, Robert, earl of Sussex, 179, 180

Ravels, 103

Read, Conyers, 43, 51, 53, 63

Regensberg, 40

Reingould (Dutch leader), 59

Restoration, 185

Rhine, 219

Rich, Lady Isabella, 225

Rich, Lady Penelope Devereux, 26, 164, 176, 210, 227; as godmother of Robert Sidney, 166, 178; as Philip Sidney's "Stella," 163, 178; supports Sidney, 137, 155

Rich, Lord Robert, earl of Warwick, 223, 225, 226, 227

Richmond, 174

Ridolfi Plot, 159

Robertsbridge, 189, 206

Rochelle, 88

Rodd, Thomas, 196

Rome, 27, 149, 206

Rotterdam, 75, 219

Rouen, 148, 150

Rudyard, Benjamin, 184

Russell, Captain (commander of Flushing horse band), 111

Russell, Edward, earl of Bedford, 179

Russell, Lady Elizabeth, 19, 181

Russell, John, earl of Bedford, 16–17

Russell, Lucy, countess of Bedford, 179

Russell, Sir William, 60, 77, 111, 161, 162

Rutland, earl and countess of. See Manners, Elizabeth; Manners, Roger

Rye, 149

Sackville, Sir Edward, 227

Sackville, Sir Richard, earl of Dorset, 187, 188

Sackville, Sir Thomas, Lord Buckhurst, earl of Dorset, 137, 162, 163, 188, 216

St. Aldegonde, Philip Marnix van, 93

St. Anderas, 123

Saint Bartholomew Massacre, 145

Saint Denis, 149, 150

Saint Esprit, Order of the, 146

St. Lucan, 123

Saint Michel, Order of, 146

Salisbury, earl of. See Cecil, Robert

Sampson, Captain (Sidney's sergeant-major), 85–86, 97

Sandys, Sir Edwin, 226, 227

Savage, Arthur, 113, 114

Savile, Lady, 225

Savile, Sir Henry, 206, 225

Savill (Sidney's tutor), 37

Saville, Henry, 206

Saxony, 41

Sayaveldra, Antonio de, 125

Scheldt, 138

Schiedam, 75

Scotland, 18, 55, 60, 61, 62, 144

Scroope, Lord Thomas, 67

Sedgrave (Fitz James), Patrick, 123, 124, 125–26, 127, 137

Segrave, Christopher, 124

Segrave, Walter, 124

Senlis, 146, 147, 150

Seymour, Lady Catherine, countess of Hertford, 28

Seymour, Edward, earl of Hertford, 207, 217

Seys, Roger, 54, 164

Shakespeare, William, 15, 197

Shaw, William A., 116, 118

Sheldon, Sir John, 113, 114

Shirley, Sir Thomas, 44, 83, 87, 92, 112, 156; scandal involving, 57, 121, 122, 160; Sidney's friendship with, 57, 82

Shrewsbury, 20, 21, 24

Shrewsburg, earl and countess of. See Talbot, Gilert; Talbot, Mary

Shropshire, 17

Sidley, Sir William, 225

Sidney, Algernon, 185, 205

Sidney, Alice (daughter), 183

Sidney, Ambrosia, 15, 17, 20, 21

Sidney, Anne Pagenham, 15, 16

Sidney, Barbara (daughter), 188, 216, 225, 226, 227

Sidney, Lady Barbara (wife), 60–61, 123, 144, 149, 151, 156, 164, 216; character of, 191; death of, 225, 227; duties of, as household manager, 186–87, 191; expenditures of, on clothing, 55; friendships of, 181–82, 202; lacks money to maintain households, 54, 157; landholdings of, 189; marries, 42, 171;

moves to London, 176, 177, 181; pregnancies of, 172, 173, 174, 175, 177, 178; seeks support for Sidney, 137, 153, 154, 177, 183; in Sidney's poetry, 204, 205; weekly allowance of, 181, 197, 212

Sidney, Bridget (daughter), 153, 178, 179, 183

Sidney, Catherine (daughter), 173, 176, 182, 183

Sidney, Dorothy (granddaughter), 185, 188, 208, 225

Sidney, Elizabeth, Lady Rutland (daughter), 51, 176, 179, 208, 212

Sidney, Frances Walsingham, countess of Essex, 42, 51, 180

Sidney, Sir Harry, 129

Sidney, Sir Henry (father), 20, 25, 29, 36, 42, 43, 157, 189; applies for wardenship of Otford, 57, 188; Francis Bacon on, 18–19; claimed friendships with, 123, 124; death of, 50, 181, 186; debts of, 50, 212; expenses of, 28, 32, 54; as Lord Justice of Ireland, 15, 17, 22, 38; religious loyalties, 16, 19, 28; and sons, 20, 32–33, 40–41

Sidney, John, 129, 130, 133, 185

Sidney, Margaret, 15

Sidney, Lady Mary Dudley (mother), 16, 18, 21, 22, 38, 124; death of, 50

Sidney (Sydney), Nicholas, 15

Sidney, Sir Philip (brother), 17, 18, 29, 35, 41, 132, 145, 196; appearance of, 21, 185; bequest of, 50–51, 52–53; campaigns against Spain, 43, 44–45; death of, 45–56, 50, 108, 189, 197, 200–201; education of, 20, 23–24; Elizabeth I, dealings with, 28, 38, 44, 63; Flushing, governor of, 39, 43, 44, 50, 72, 77, 86; James I, dealings with, 63, 210; knighted, 42; literary works of 15, 163, 178, 186, 195, 206, 208; seeks advancement, 41; Sidney, Robert, relations with, 22–24, 26–28, 32, 33–34, 36–38, 40

Sidney, Philip, 130

Sidney, Philip, third earl of Leicester, 185

Sidney, Philippa (daughter), 173, 174, 176, 216; death of, 183, 186, 225

Sidney, Sir Robert, first Earl of Leicester, Viscount Lisle, Baron of Penshurst

—allies of, 210, 213, 215–16

—appearance of, 20–21, 29; 30n; 211

—appointed Queen Anne's Lord High Chamberlain, 210, 216, 217

—attitudes of: toward Low Countries, 101–2, 115, 116, 118–19, 121, 136, 228; toward Spain, 59, 125, 127, 136, 215, 217, 228

—birth of, 14

—character of, 22, 23, 34, 60–69, 101–2, 107–8, 109, 139, 154, 156, 173, 202–3, 229

—children of, 172, 173, 177–79, 182–86

—commonplace books of, 36, 37, 205–6

—created Baron Penshurst, 210

—created Earl of Leicester, 223, 231–32n

—created Viscount Lisle, 213

—death of, 229

—described, 34, 35, 36, 40

—diplomatic career of: 217; accompanies Princess Elizabeth to Germany, 218–20; ambassador to France, 55, 139, 144, 145–52, 173; ambassador to Scotland, 55, 61–69, 72, 144, 216; expenses incurred during embassies, 55, 144, 152

—distrusted by Elizabeth I, 28, 38–39, 47, 160

—dubbed Knight of the Garter, 222

—education of, 15, 20–26, 32, 33, 35, 37, 46

—efforts at advancement, 39, 41, 46, 49, 72, 137, 152, 161, 162, 181–82, 197, 213, 223

—expenditures by, 39, 40, 64, 111, 144, 152, 176, 187, 211–12, 216, 218

—extravagance of, 29, 41, 55

—finances of, 32, 51–57, 144, 152, 181, 187, 189, 190, 199, 211, 212, 222

—friendships of, 22–23, 172, 179–81, 206

—gardening, interest in, 167, 173, 188

—governor of Flushing: appointed, 39, 72, 77, 78; Anglo-Spanish peace proposals, 119, 217; authority of, 90–91, 102, 111, 113–15, 119; Dutch trade with Spain, 87–91, 115, 118, 160, 163; expenses, 156–57; gathers intelligence, 75, 123–27; governs *in absentia*, 118, 130, 137, 138, 139, 161; income, 138, 156, 160, 198, 212; lieutenant-governors under, 129–37 passim; obtains military companies, 111–12; opposes return of cautionary towns, 215, 221–22; profiteering, 57, 120, 121; relations with Dutch, 78–81, 85, 86–87, 91–94; requests leaves, 125, 137–39, 156, 160, 163, 165, 175; residence of, 172–73; responsibilities of, 72–73, 75, 111; seeks supplies for soldiers, 81–85, 115–16, 198. *See also* Flushing, as English garrison

—health of, 173–74, 214, 220, 227, 228, 229

—households maintained by, 55, 174, 189

—income of, 32, 54, 55, 57, 188, 189, 198, 212, 222

—indebtedness of, 228

—influence of Philip Sidney on, 19–25, 219

—James I's court, position at, 210, 211, 213–15, 216, 218–20

—languages spoken by, 23, 24, 36–37, 38, 39, 40, 206

—literary patronage, 206–8

—Maurice of Nassau, relationship with, 94, 97–99, 102, 103, 106, 219

—Military career of: 44–46, 99–109; captains company of footmen, 57, 58; discretion of, 108, 109; Dunkirk, 99, 101, 105; Elizabeth's disapproval, 99, 105–6, 107, 109; Nieuport, 106–8, 163; Turnhout, 102–3, 105; wounded, 102

—New World interests, 42, 227

—Parliamentary career: House of Commons, 42–43, 157; House of Lords, 217, 227–28

—pedigree of, 15, 18, 158, 159, 161

—Penshurst, interest in construction of, 186–88

—Poetry of: characteristics, 199, 202; Elizabeth I in, 205; excerpted, 198, 199, 200, 201, 204; identified as author of sonnet cycle, 195, 196; interpretations of, 202–4; Lady Sidney in 204, 205; themes in, 196, 197, 199–204

—political alliances: 210, 213, 215–16; with William Cecil, Lord Burghley, 163, 164, 167; with Robert Cecil, Earl of Salisbury, 214; with Robert Devereux, Earl of Essex, 155, 159, 163–4; with Robert Dudley, Earl of Leicester, 58–60

—relationship with Lady Barbara Sidney, 171–72, 173, 186–87, 191, 203

—religious allegiances of, 16, 19, 35, 56, 59, 60, 94, 136, 201, 217

—seeks Cinque Ports wardenship, 138–39, 153–56

—seeks house in London, 174–76

—seeks vice-chamberlainship, 152, 156, 157, 160

—sells land, 54, 152, 189, 191, 212

—Henry Sidney, relationship with, 21, 32–33

—Philip Sidney, relationship with, 22, 33–34, 36–38, 46, 197, 199, 200–201; Philip's debts, 50, 51, 53

—taste in clothing, 20, 211–12, 216, 218

—tours Europe, 32, 33–36, 40–41, 47 n, 48 n

—Vere, Sir Francis, relationship with, 104–8

Sidney, Sir Robert, Viscount Lisle, second Earl of Leicester (son), 21, 205, 219, 220, 297; birth of, 164, 177–78; diarist, 185, 208; serves in Flushing, 129–30, 133, 185, 222; created Knight of Bath, 184, 216; Sidney's expenses for, 218, 228

Sidney, Thomas (brother), 15, 20, 22, 51, 130, 176; death, of, 181

Sidney (Sydney), Thomasyne, 15

Sidney, Vere (daughter), 183

Sidney, William (son), 21, 94, 176, 182, 186,·

189; death of, 129, 183, 184, 207, 208, 225

Sidney (Sydney), Sir William, 17

Sidney Sussex College, 19

Simmon, John, 202

Sluys, 45, 123, 219; siege of, 92, 97, 99, 101, 109, 163

Smith, Sir Thomas, 189

Smythe, John, 225

Smythe, Robert, 225

Smythe, Sarah, 228

Smythe, Thomas, 225, 226

Smythe, Sir Thomas, 225, 226, 227, 228

Solms, George Everarde, count of, 101, 103

Somerset, Edward, earl of Worcester, 163, 166, 215, 216, 222

Southampton, 50. See also Fitzwilliam; Wriothesley

Spa, 219

Spain, 17, 27, 33, 55, 117, 125, 144, 213; Dutch war with, 43, 75; French war with, 145; hostility toward, 215; intelligence gathered regarding, 122, 123, 126; plans of, for Scotland, 60, 61, ·62; proposed league against, 150, 151; suspected English treaties with, 77, 79, 80, 92, 118, 132, 136, 217; trade between Dutch and, 87–91, 163; truce with, 220; war with, advocated, 58, 59

Spanish Armada, 43, 60, 62, 68, 116, 125

Spanish Match, 216, 217

Spenser, Edmund, 42, 202, 206

Spring, Captain (company recommended for), 128

Stanhope, Sir John, 129, 138, 155, 164, 166, 215; seeks vice-chamberlainship, 152, 160

Stanley, Elizabeth Vere, countess of Derby, 179

Stanley, Sir William, 58, 123, 126

Stapleware, 55

Star Chamber, 165

Steenwyck, 102

Stephen (Philip Sidney's servant), 51

Stewart, Francis, earl of Bothwell (plots to kill Maitland), 63–65

Stone, Lawrence, 19, 144, 157, 159, 171

Stradling, Sir Edward, 171

Strasbourg, 34, 35, 36, 39, 41

Stuart court, 185, 186, 214; decadence of, 216; factions within, 215

Sturm, Johann, 34, 35, 36, 41

Suffolk, Dutchess of. See Howard, Catherine

Suffolk, Duke of. See Brandon, Charles

Sussex, 16, 50, 152

Sussex, earls and countesses of. See Radcliffe, Frances Sidney; Radcliffe, Thomas; Ratliffe, Bridget; Ratliffe, Robert

Sweden, 41
Sydney. *See* Sidney

Talbot, Gilbert, earl of Shrewsbury, 28, 163, 178, 179, 180, 222
Talbot, Mary, countess of Shrewsbury, 179
Tarchognota, Giovanni, 36
Tassis, Jean Baptiste de, 58
Tergau, 221
Thames, River, 28
Theobalds, 167
Thirty Years War, 220, 222
Thornton, Thomas, 20
Thorpe, Thomas, 196
Throckmorton, Lady Dorothy, 135
Throckmorton, Sir John, 111, 118, 129, 130, 132, 137; as lieutenant-governor of Flushing, 133–36
Throckmorton, Robert, 136
Throgmorton, Arthur, 64
Trumbull, Sir William, 219
Tudor court: costs of advancing in, 55; and James' succession, 61, 63; factionalism within, 18, 161–63; mechanics of pressing suit in, 113–15
Tully, 24
Tunbridge, 205
Turks, 128
Turnhout, 102–3, 105
Tuscany, Princess of, 151

United Provinces. *See* Low Countries
University of Leyden, 134, 220
University of Padua, 34
Uvedale, John, 51
Uvedall, Sir Edmund, 111, 119–20, 121, 139; as lieutenant-governor of Flushing, 94, 131–32

Valck, Jacob van, 80, 86, 89, 90, 93, 117
Varrass, Count of, 105
Venice, 128
Venloo, 44, 58
Vere, Edward de, earl of Oxford, 38
Vere, Sir Francis, 112, 124, 127, 129, 138, 162; in battle of Nieuport, 106–7; and Sidney, 104, 107, 108, 109; in siege of Dunkirk, 99, 101; in siege of Sluys, 97; in siege of Turnhout, 103, 105; wounded, 101, 102
Vere, Sir Horace, Lord Vere of Tilbury, 102
Vernon, Elizabeth. *See* Wriothesley, Elizabeth
Vienna, 40
Ville Mediana, Conde de, 214
Villiers, George, earl of Buckingham, 215, 216–17, 223

Virginia, 226, 227
Virginia Company, 42, 226–27
Vorstius, Conrad, 134, 220, 221

Walcheren Island, 76, 102
Wacker, Johann Matthäus, von Wackenfels, 34
Wales, 171
Waller, Edmund, 185, 208
Walpole, Henry, 126
Walsingham, Sir Francis, 45, 46, 73, 116, 117, 127, 180, 226; and negotiations with James VI, 61–67 passim; and Philip Sidney, 27, 42, 50, 51, 53; and Sidney, 55, 57, 60
Walsingham, Lady Ursula, 51, 174, 180
Warham, Archbishop, 189
Waring, Joseph, 122
Warwick, earls and countesses of. *See* Dudley, John; Dudley Anne; Rich, Lord Robert; Rich, Lady Penelope
Watkins, Ensign (captain in Flushing), 184
Watson, Mr. (threatens to sue Robert Sidney), 226
Wechel, 39
Whipp, William, 126
Whitehall, 216
Whyte (Wynne), Griffith, 180
Whyte, Harry, 23
Whyte, Rowland, 22, 54, 84, 108, 112, 177; alludes to Sidney's "toyes," 154, 202, 203; education of, 22, 25; implicated in Shirley scandal, 160; land leased to, 189, 211; marriage of, 181; rewarded by Sidney, 127, 211; Sedgrave affair, 123, 124, 126; services performed by, 180–81; Sidney, Barbara, relations with, 176, 180, 181; Sidney children, relations with, 180, 182, 183; Sidney, Robert, relations with, 23, 25, 180–81, 211; Sidney's agent in court, 23, 55, 93, 113–14, 129, 137, 153–57 passim, 161, 162
Wilkins, Sir Thomas, 79, 80, 86, 92, 112, 122
Willemstadt, 105
William of Orange (The Silent). *See* Nassau, William of
William the Conqueror, 171
Williams, Sir Roger, 75, 109
Willoughby, Mr., 175
Willoughby, Lord George, 44, 60, 77, 82, 131
Wilson, Mona, 35–36
Wilton, 38, 42, 60
Wiltshire, 16, 28
Winchester, 16
Windsor, 173
Wingfield, Richard (captain in Flushing), 86, 118, 145

Winwood, Sir Ralph, 118, 215, 219, 220
Wirtenberg, Duke of, 219
Wither, George, 186, 207
Worcester, earl of. *See* Somerset, Edward
Wotton, Sir Edward, 159
Wright, Deborah, 204, 205
Wriothesley, Elizabeth, countess of South-
ampton, 153, 165, 179
Wriothesley, Henry, earl of Southampton,
163, 166, 167, 178, 180, 215, 216, 220, 222,
227; as ally of Robert Devereux, 163, 165,
166, 179
Wroth, Lady Mary Sidney (daughter), 134,
135, 173, 176, 177, 182; and Ben Jonson,
185–86, 207; marries, 225; as poet, 186,
196, 208
Wroth, Sir Robert, 185, 186, 207, 225, 226
Wroth, Sir Thomas, 207

Wynne (White), John, 180

Xenophon, 24

Yonge (receives letter from Sidney), 134
York House, 165
Yssel, 45

Zealand, 44, 84, 86, 93, 94, 131; and
fortification of Flushing, 80, 117–18; re-
volts against Spain, 75; and trade with
Spain, 87–91. *See also* Flushing; Low Coun-
tries
Zealand, Church of, 136
Zoete. *See* Haultain
Zutphen, 45, 46, 58, 60, 200
Zwin River, 97